T0158411

Tracking
King Tiger

LATINOS IN THE UNITED STATES SERIES

SERIES EDITOR

Rubén O. Martinez, *Michigan State University*

EDITORIAL BOARD

Adalberto Aguirre Jr., *University of California–Riverside*

Robert Aponte, *Indiana University–Purdue University Indianapolis*

Teresa Córdova, *University of Illinois at Chicago*

Julie Leininger Pycior, *Manhattan College*

Rogelio Sáenz, *University of Texas at San Antonio*

Tracking King Tiger

REIES LÓPEZ TIJERINA
AND THE FBI

José Angel Gutiérrez

Michigan State University Press • *East Lansing*

Copyright © 2019 by José Angel Gutiérrez

♻ The paper used in this publication meets the minimum requirements
of ANSI/NISO Z39.48–1992 (R 1997) (Permanence of Paper).

Michigan State University Press
East Lansing, Michigan 48823-5245

Printed and bound in the United States of America.

28 27 26 25 24 23 22 21 20 19   1 2 3 4 5 6 7 8 9 10

LIBRARY OF CONGRESS CATALOGING-IN-PUBLICATION DATA
Names: Gutiérrez, José Angel, author.
Title: Tracking King Tiger : Reies López Tijerina and the FBI / José Angel Gutiérrez.
Description: East Lansing : Michigan State University Press, [2019] |
Series: Latinos in the United States series | Includes bibliographical references and index.
Identifiers: LCCN 2018059368 | ISBN 9781611863352 (pbk. : alk. paper) | ISBN
9781609176129 (PDF) | ISBN 9781628953756 (ePub) | ISBN 9781628963762 (Mobi/prc)
Subjects: LCSH: Tijerina, Reies. | Mexican Americans—New Mexico—Biography. |
Civil rights workers—New Mexico—Biography. | Fugitives from justice—United States—
Biography. | Alianza Federal de las Mercedes. | Chicano movement—New Mexico—
History. | Land grants—New Mexico—History. | Mexican Americans—Land tenure—New
Mexico—History—20th century. | New Mexico—Ethnic relations—History—20th century. |
United States. Federal Bureau of Investigation—History—20th century.
Classification: LCC F805.M5 G88 2019 | DDC 978.9/0046872—dc23
LC record available at https://lccn.loc.gov/2018059368

Book and cover design by Charlie Sharp, Sharp Des!gns, East Lansing, MI
Cover photo: Reies López Tijerina speaking at an annual La Alianza
de Pueblos Libres Convention. Reies López Tijerina Collection,
Zimmerman Library, University of New Mexico.

Michigan State University Press is a member of the Green Press Initiative and is
committed to developing and encouraging ecologically responsible publishing
practices. For more information about the Green Press Initiative and the use of
recycled paper in book publishing, please visit *www.greenpressinitiative.org*.

Visit Michigan State University Press at *www.msupress.org*

DEDICATION

I DEDICATE THIS WORK TO THE CHILDREN REIES LÓPEZ TIJERINA HAD with Maria Escobar and Patricia Romero and to the memory of his brothers Margarito, Ramon, Cristobal, and Anselmo. I also dedicate this work to his grandchildren, who, like their parents, seldom saw their grandfather. Activists, like many politicians, do not make time for spouse or family; the cause is their main attraction, passion, love, and work. To be sure, Reies was not much of a father given his passion for his causes. First, it was the ministry; second, the Alianza, the land recovery movement. He did not provide economic support to his families as other fathers strive to do. His only income was membership dues from his organization, honoraria for presentations, and money donations. His book sales were paltry. He managed to own some property; the rents from that real estate barely paid the taxes and for travels to and from New Mexico. The violence directed at him was horrendous and plentiful; it did not discriminate. All those around him, especially his brothers, were also targets and subjected to being collateral damage. His first children, Hugh David, Rosa, Daniel, Raquel, Noe, Ira de Ala, and Maria, his first wife, and Patricia, the second wife and children, Isabel, Carlos, Harmonia, and Danitha, were specifically targeted by those who sought to hurt him by hurting them. And they did. His children and grandchildren did not enjoy much education, much less any inheritance. They are not skilled or trained or capable of dealing with the world he left them. Chronic poverty has been and will be their lot.

This book may not alleviate any of their individual and collective hurt and repression, but it will expose those who were behind the violence and oppression he endured, along with his family. To be a relative of Tijerina is to carry much baggage. In these pages, all will know how the politicians in government, from local to state to Washington, DC, conspired to harm and destroy the man and the land recovery movement he led. These interests did that so that all descendants and heirs of stolen land grants would continue living without their lands and its resources. Those who stole our homeland also stole our future. Those who imprisoned Reies and silenced him with the conditions of his parole extinguished much of what was the growing Chicano Movement. He was the only national figure during the era of the Chicano Movement to be imprisoned for a length of time for his political work, deemed crimes.

Finally, to his last wife, Esperanza, may you find ways to collect his papers, books, writings, and memorabilia to keep alive his legacy. Thank you for caring for him during his last years.

Contents

Foreword

Rubén O. Martinez

WHEN REIES LÓPEZ TIJERINA TOOK UP THE HISPANO LAND GRANT CAUSE in northern New Mexico, he stepped into the middle of a struggle that had been occurring for over a century. The Mexican American or Chicano land grant problem has existed since the American military conquest and take-over of northern Mexico in 1846 and 1847. The Treaty of Peace, Friendship, Limits, and Settlement, also known as the Treaty of Guadalupe Hidalgo, between the United States of America and the United Mexican States was signed on February 2, 1848. Proclaimed on July 4, 1848, the treaty, the result of a series of negotiations that followed the Mexican army's surrender in September 1847, officially ended the American Mexican War (1846–1848). Between September and February, the two nations struggled over the con-tents of the treaty, and between February and May, it wound its way through the ratification process. Specifically, the United States replaced Article 9 of the Treaty with Article 3 of the Treaty of Louisiana, removed Article 10 alto-gether, and suppressed the final paragraph of Article 12.

The treaty transferred 525,000 square miles of land to the United States, including all or parts of present-day Arizona, California, Colorado, New

Mexico, Nevada, Utah, and Wyoming, for a token $15 million paid over a period of five years. At the time, Texas already was part of the United States, having been made the twenty-eighth state of the Union in December 1845. As part of the treaty, Mexico agreed to give up all claims to Texas and recognized the Rio Grande as the boundary. In 1853, under the Gadsden Purchase, the United States acquired a portion of land in present-day southern Arizona and New Mexico from Mexico for $10 million and with it set the boundary for today's border between the two countries.

Negotiations over the contents of the treaty continued through late May 1848, with the Protocol of Querétaro, addressing issues that arose over Articles 9, 10, and 12, signed on May 26, 1848. In March, the U.S. Senate had amended the treaty, raising concerns on the part of Mexico. To allay concerns, the United States sent two new diplomats to exchange ratifications, with instructions to communicate that insistence on including Article 10 would end all prospects of peace. The meeting at Querétaro was held because Mexico's minister of relations wanted an explanation of the amendments prior to the exchange of ratifications. Signed by authorized representatives from each nation, the protocol affirmed the privileges and guarantees provided in the treaty signed in February. The congresses of each nation ratified the amended treaty in May before the protocol was signed on May 26. Mexico's president ratified the amended treaty with the protocol at the end of May; however, U.S. president James Polk withheld the protocol when he forwarded the amended treaty to the U.S. Congress requesting legislation to execute its provisions.

At the time of the treaty, an estimated two hundred thousand Spanish/Mexican and an unknown number of indigenous people resided in the lands acquired by the United States, and it is estimated that approximately one hundred thousand remained in their homeland, now the southwestern United States, as part of the conditions of the treaty. According to Article 8 of the treaty, Mexicans residing on the United States' newly acquired lands could decide to stay or move to Mexico, and if they decided to stay, according to the amended Article 9, they would

> be admitted at the proper time (to be judged of by the Congress of the
> United States) to the enjoyment of all the rights of citizens of the United

States, according to the principles of the Constitution; and in the mean-time, shall be maintained and protected in the free enjoyment of their liberty and property, and secured in the free exercise of their religion without restriction.

Clauses pertaining to the protection of "all ecclesiastics and religious corporations or communities" in Article 9 were suppressed.

Of critical importance is the fact that, during the negotiations over the proposed treaty, the United States rejected Article 10, which read as follows:

All grants of land made by the Mexican government or by the competent authorities, in territories previously appertaining to Mexico, and remaining for the future within the limits of the United States, shall be respected as valid, to the same extent that the same grant would be valid, to the said territories had [they] remained within the limits of Mexico. But the grantees of lands in Texas, put in possession thereof, who, by reason of the circumstances of the country since the beginning of the troubles between Texas and the Mexican Government, may have been prevented from fulfilling all the conditions of their grants, shall be under the obligation to fulfill the said conditions within the periods limited in the same respectively, such periods to be now counted from the date of the exchange of ratifications of this Treaty: in default of which the said grants shall not be obligatory upon the State of Texas, in virtue of the stipulation contained in this Article. The foregoing stipulation in regard to grantees of land in Texas, is extended to all grantees of land in the territories aforesaid, elsewhere than in Texas, put in possession under such grants: and, in default of the fulfillment of the conditions of any such grant, within the new period, which, as is above stipulated, begins with the day of the exchange of ratifications of this treaty, the same shall be null and void.

Secretary of State James Buchanan justified the elimination of Article 10 by holding that no power could separate an individual and his property without his consent, and that grantees of lands with valid titles could use the courts to maintain their claims.

So begins the dispossession of land from the country's newest citizens, who in the 1960s declared themselves Chicanos. No sooner had the signatures dried on the treaty documents than Americans began moving into the Southwest, especially into California with the discovery of gold in 1848. In 1850, California was made the thirty-first state in the Union, done so in record time. In California, the resolution of Spanish and Mexican land grant claims did not begin until 1851, when Congress established a commission to adjudicate titles to land claims. In New Mexico, where most of the land grants were located and where residents lived under martial law from 1846 to 1850, no mechanism existed by which to settle land grant claims until 1854, when Congress established the Office of the Surveyor General of New Mexico. The surveyor general was to survey public lands, report on land claims based on Spanish and Mexican grants, and ascertain the boundaries of pueblo lands. Despite the responsibilities of the surveyor general of New Mexico, few land grant claims were confirmed. By 1880, despite more than 1,000 claims filed, only 150 had been confirmed and reported to Congress, which had acted on only seventy-one of them. To address the growing backlog, the U.S. Court of Private Land Claims was established in 1891 and reviewed claims until 1904. Unable to complete its work, the court transferred unsettled claims to the General Land Office.

The ineffectiveness of U.S. offices to address the land grant claims of its new citizens was embedded in a broad context of the clash of cultures, fraudulent claims, American corruption, and federal government usurpation of communal lands. The clash of cultures centered on the systems of taxation, with Americans taxing the land and Mexicans taxing the harvest. Unfamiliarity with the American system put the new citizens in vulnerable positions, with language differences exacerbating their vulnerabilities. Fraudulent land claims complicated the confirmation process and contributed to the backlog. Corruption by foreign investors, lawyers, sheriffs, and judges further contributed to the separation of the new citizens from their lands. The most notorious of these cabals was the Santa Fe Ring, which included politicians and businessmen. They were instrumental in securing the Maxwell Land Grant, initially the Beaubien-Miranda Land Grant, in northeastern New Mexico, which at the time was the biggest private landholding in the world, with 1.7 million acres.

The overwhelming majority of Hispano lands in northern New Mexico were communal lands settled, managed, and used by the settlers and their descendants for over two centuries. Settlements were close to pueblos, indigenous farming communities. Disagreements over land between Hispanos, pueblos, and other indigenous peoples were mostly settled by the time of American entry. In some cases, disagreements were exacerbated by American involvement. Generally, the American legal system was hesitant to recognize communal lands, and controversies ensued until 1897, when the U.S. Supreme Court ruled in *U.S. v. Sandoval* that title to the commons lands under Spanish and Mexican law was held by the sovereign. Shortly after the turn of the century, the United States began establishing the national forests on what once were Hispano communal lands, but the controversies did not cease. It was Reies López Tijerina who took them to the national consciousness, if only for a brief period.

The land grant struggles continue today in New Mexico and, to some extent, in South Texas. This volume focuses on the U.S. government's surveillance of Tijerina and the activities used in undermining his work as he sought to recover the lands Hispanos continue to view as stolen from them. The author, José Angel Gutiérrez, knew and worked alongside Tijerina in promoting issues of the Chicano Movement. This volume is based on the examination of thousands of pages of documents from the Federal Bureau of Investigation, interview transcripts, newspaper stories, and other written accounts on Tijerina and the Alianza Federal de Pueblos Libres, as well as his personal relationship with Tijerina.

This volume by Gutiérrez is his second in the Latinos in the United States book series, the first being on César Chávez. It sheds light on the inner workings of the FBI and its activities in undermining the Chicano Movement and its multidimensional struggles for social justice. It is a pioneering study that sets the standard for what is sure to become a field of study as other scholars are inspired to examine how Latinos are maintained in a subjugated status by U.S. agencies of social control.

Acknowledgments

REIES HIMSELF IS FIRST ON THE LIST OF NAMES OF ACKNOWLEDGMENTS for sharing his FBI file with me and mentoring many of us in the Southwest with his teachings and political activism. There were many people who have helped in the production of this book. Former state senator Manny Aragon in New Mexico found the votes at every legislative session to fund the University of New Mexico, which in turn provided grants to scholars for research on the Southwest. I received such a grant once from Tobias Duran. I also had the help of a graduate student assigned to me during that summer of 2000, Eloy Garcia, now an attorney and PhD. He chronologically organized the FBI file, which became most useful as time came to write and find files. Rosa Tijerina helped me tremendously by finding persons, some family members, and others connected with the Alianza for me to interview, including herself, and shared her trauma of being Reies's oldest daughter. Those interviews and Tijerina's FBI file copies are archived at the Zimmerman Library at the University of New Mexico and also in my files at the libraries of Michigan State University (MSU) and the Nattie Lee Benson Latin American Collection at University of Texas at Austin.

Several others, Herman Baca, Rodolfo Acuña, Jesus Treviño, Rees Lloyd, Rosa Tijerina, and Reies himself, gave me photos to use in the publication. Thank you all.

Another major contributor to the making of this book is Dr. Rubén Martinez, the editor of the Latinos in the United States series at Michigan State University Press. He found funds to sponsor me during June 2016, 2017, and 2018 at MSU. Time and money are critical for writers, and he made it possible for me to have those June months. He also worked tirelessly with editing my drafts in addition to his regular work directing the Julian Samora Research Institute. Also critical to the publication of this book were Julie Loehr, Julie Reaume, and Kristine Blakeslee at the MSU Press. Their suggestions always made my writing better, clearer, and more marketable. Thank you again, Dr. Martinez and Press staff.

Lastly, my family suffered neglect while I left them behind when I traveled to New Mexico and East Lansing, Michigan, time and again. But they forgive and forget and are proud of my work as I am of them for being so tolerant and supportive. I love you each and all.

Onomasticon

WHAT FOLLOWS IS A LIST OF ABBREVIATIONS, TERMS, NAMES, CODES, NUM-
bers, locations, titles, and agencies that appear in this book.

AAG. Assistant attorney general of the United States, also sometimes referred to as the **AUSA**.

AD. Assistant director of the FBI.

ADEX. The Administrative Index initiated in 1971. When the Emergency
Detention Act was repealed, the FBI incorporated names from the
Agitator Index, Security Index, and Reserve Index. It was kept at FBI
headquarters and twenty-nine field offices of the time, computerized in
1972, and allegedly discontinued in January 1976.

ADIC. The assistant director in charge of a huge FBI field office such as Los
Angeles and New York. **SAC**s are under an **ADIC** in these offices.

Agent. A member of the investigative and administrative staff, not a clerk,
located in a field office. Also referred to as an **SA**, special agent.

Airtel. An internal FBI communication term for a message sent typically
from a field office to the director or Washington, DC, FBI office.

AG. U.S. attorney general.

Agitator Index or **ADEX** or **AI.** Formerly the Rabble Rouser Index; it changed names in March 1968.

AQ. The FBI Albuquerque field office.

ARA. The State Department designation for Inter-America.

Aztlan. The name for the Southwest in the Nahuatl language of the Meshicas/Aztecs, meaning "land in the north," referring to that part of present-day United States.

B. Informal language used by field agents and others to refer to the FBI.

BIA. U.S. Bureau of Indian Affairs.

BLM. U.S. Bureau of Land Management.

Block stamp. Found at the bottom right corner of the front page of most FBI documents, it indicates which FBI office the document is filed in and date of handling by clerks. The clerks will check off appropriate words: searched, serialized, filed or indexed.

BOP. Federal Bureau of Prisons.

BUDED. Bureau deadline.

BUFIL or **BUFILE.** The FBI's term for the bureau file located in Washington, DC, FBI headquarters, not the Washington, DC, field office, the WFO.

Bureau. The FBI headquarters, but often used in general for the FBI.

Caption. The subject matter title or name for an FBI file. All documents have a caption or a reference to a caption and are to be filed under that subject heading or caption.

Case file or **main file.** The name or caption or designation of a file where all relevant material is placed for that subject.

Case number or **classification number.** The assigned number in the classification scheme used by the FBI to distinguish and categorize files. In the late 1960s and into the 1970s, when the Alianza was most viable, the FBI had 210 classification numbers. From time to time new numbers are added or changes made to descriptions of categories.

Chicano. The ethnic self-descriptor of the activist generation among the U.S. population of Mexican ancestry that emerged after World War II.

Chicano Movement. The civil rights era roughly between the end of World War II and the Gulf War, the late 1940s to the early 1980s, propelled by the political generation of activists of Mexican ancestry who called themselves Chicanos.

Classified information. Material or information that is deemed to require protection from unauthorized disclosure. See Executive Order 12065. Before 1975, the FBI did not classify material not intended to be disseminated to other agencies; pre-1975 information now is designated exempt from disclosure under (b) (1), the national security exemption.

Clubs. FBI locations, not in or near FBI field offices, where electronic surveillance is monitored.

COINTELPRO. Counter intelligence FBI operations aimed at disruption, character assassination, neutralizing, destroying, immobilizing, and other dirty tricks against groups and individuals. Adapted from military operations for domestic use, COINTELPRO targeted groups and individuals beginning in 1956 and allegedly ceased in 1971. COINTELPRO-style tactics by the FBI have continued since then.

Communist. A term used by the FBI since the 1920s and defined broadly to mean persons that adhere to the principles of the Communist Party USA and other groups such as the Socialist Workers Party and the Progressive Labor Party. It also meant an occult force of influence that could infiltrate groups and the thinking of individuals.

Communist Index. The list of names of known Communists in the United States kept by the FBI since 1948. In 1956, the list was expanded to include persons associated with groups beyond communist or socialist political parties. In 1960, the name was changed to Reserve Index.

Confidential informant or **CI** or **CS.** A person who provides information to the FBI. Other names are snitch, informant, source, and PSI, for "person supplying information."

CPLC. U.S. Court of Private Land Claims.

DAS. The deputy assistant secretary in the Department of State.

DEA. The Drug Enforcement Administration, a branch of DOJ, established in July 1973.

Declassify. Remove security classification from a document, such as *top secret, confidential, secret*. Such a document has been *declassified*.

DETCOM. FBI code for detention of Communists. In 1969, this was replaced with PAP, for Priority Apprehension Program, to include all persons/ subjects on the Security Index whose apprehension is a high priority.

DID. The Domestic Intelligence Division of the FBI; during the Tijerina years of first surveillance, William Sullivan was the director of this division, then Mark Felt.

DOB. Date of birth.

DOJ. U.S. Department of Justice.

"Do Not File." Refers to files that are kept out of the Central Records System.

EP. The FBI office in El Paso, Texas.

FAFCS. Federal Alliance of Free City States (Alianza Federal de Pueblos Libres), the new name the Alianza took after DA Sanchez sought to compel Tijerina to turn over its membership lists.

FBI. The Federal Bureau of Investigation.

FBI HQ. The FBI's main headquarters.

FD. A designation used by the FBI for a documents to be used for a specific purpose. For example, **FD-4** is a routing slip; **FD-73** is an automobile record form; **FD-330** is an itinerary form; and **FD 340** is for a 1A envelope.

Field office. The main FBI office in a state or city. There are also resident agencies and liaison offices.

File number. A three-part series of numbers for an FBI file. The first group of numbers, say 100, before the first hyphen (-) is the classification number for domestic security, the type of case it is. The second set of numbers, between the hyphens (-), is the individual case number and is sequential, as in 922 being the 922nd investigation in that office. The last set of numbers is the serial or document number; 32, for example, would be the thirty-second document in that specific investigation. Hence, 100-922-32 means domestic security, the 922nd investigation out of that office, and document 32 in the file on that subject. Not all documents are serialized, and more than one file can exist on any given person or group or event. There were 210 classification numbers in 1968.

FOIA. The Freedom of Information Act. Also referred to as FOI/PA, for Freedom of Information and Privacy Act (1974).

Four Horsemen. The term made popular by historians Matt Meier and Feliciano Rivera, during the Chicano Movement for the four principal leaders by region: César Chávez in California, Rodolfo "Corky" Gonzales in Colorado, Reies López Tijerina in New Mexico, and this author in Texas.

GAO. Now the Government Accountability Office, it was named the General Accounting Office when Tijerina began his investigations into land claims.

GIP. The Ghetto Informant Program. It began in October 1967 to recruit informants for the FBI to monitor activity in ethnoracial groups such as Puerto Ricans, African Americans, Chicanos, and Native Americans. It allegedly ended in July 1973, but the FBI still recruits and maintains informants. In 1972 the FBI had seventy-five hundred such "ghetto informants."

GOM. A CIA term for the government of Mexico.

HUMINT. Human intelligence, referring to a source of information or the process of intelligence gathering and/or analysis that originates with a person.

Huston Plan. Drafted in 1970 by Tom Huston, aide to President Nixon, on the subject of renewed and expanded domestic surveillance activity after Hoover ended his COINTELPRO operations. The plan was partially disapproved by President Nixon; it continued until July 1973.

IES. The staff of the Intelligence Evaluation Committee, established January 1971. It prepared studies and evaluations issued by the IEC; it terminated July 1973.

INS. The Immigration and Naturalization Service. It was in existence from the late 1960s to post-9/11, when its name changed to Immigration Control and Enforcement Agency and it became part of the new Department of Homeland Security.

IRS. The Internal Revenue Service.

IS. Internal security. IS-1, IS-2, IS-3 are the sections within the Internal Security Branch of the FBI, for extremists, subversives, and research, respectively.

IS-C. Internal Security–Communist.

Legat. The FBI office attached to the U.S. embassy in another country. It assists domestic investigations by providing liaison in other countries.

These offices are also referred to as legal attachés, resident agencies, and liaison offices.

LHM. A letterhead memorandum sent from a field office to the director of the FBI or the Washington, DC, FBI office, comprising a cover letter and a detailed report covering a period of time and disseminated to other FBI offices and other agencies.

Liaison Program. The former, perhaps current, mandate to each FBI field office to contact, visit, and create goodwill with all airlines, banks, military and defense entities, hotels, schools and universities, stockbrokers, truck companies, news media, federal agencies, and civic organizations at least once every six months. Its purpose was to ensure the FBI would receive information from these sources when requested.

Limited investigation. A type of domestic security investigation to determine the need for a full investigation. It lasts only ninety days unless extended by FBI HQ.

MH/CHAOS or just **CHAOS.** The code name for a CIA program initiated during the late 1960s during the Johnson administration. It was exposed by the *New York Times* in 1974, which led to congressional investigations.

MPD. The Metropolitan Police Department, Washington, DC. It is not to be confused with the Capitol Police, with jurisdiction over federal buildings and properties.

NISO. The Naval Investigative Service Office.

NITEL. An internal FBI communication sent typically from a field office to the director or Washington, DC, FBI office after "normal" working hours, meaning in the evening into the night.

NSA. The National Security Agency; it is exempt by statute from FOIA requests.

OEO. The Office of Economic Opportunity. It was the administrative arm of the War on Poverty.

OO. The office of origin. Only in FBI HQ do each of the 210 classifications used in 1968 have an O or an OO placed in front of the file drawer. For example, 136 is the classification for the American Legion contact program. This program began in the 1940s and assumed Legionnaires were unpaid sources for the FBI on domestic security matters in their communities. "136-O," in this case, is used for complaints and miscellaneous nonspecific data relating to this classification. The OO is used to house policies and procedures that pertain to that classification.

POB. Place of birth.

POCAM. The FBI's code name for the Poor People's Campaign, held in Washington, DC, in the summer of 1968.

POTUS. President of the United States.

Rabble Rouser Index. Established in August 1967 by Hoover to identify and list individuals with a propensity to foment violence or racial discord. The name was changed to Agitator Index in March 1968. In 1970 the list contained 1,131 names.

RC. Resurrection City, the name given to the location of the Poor People's Campaign. It was also referred to as Tent City because the residents temporarily stayed in tents.

Reftel. A CIA term for reference to a prior teletype.

Relet [date]. Reference to a letter of [date].

RUP. La Raza Unida Party, a political party founded in the 1970s.

SA. (1) A special agent, a member of the regular staff in an FBI field office. (2) The San Antonio FBI office.

SAC. Special agent in charge, the person leading a local or field FBI office.

SCLC. Southern Christian Leadership Conference, the umbrella organization for Reverend Martin Luther King Jr.

SCOTUS. The Supreme Court of the United States.

SDS. Students for a Democratic Society, an organization of radical, counter-culture, white youth.

SNCC. Student Non-violent Coordinating Committee, an organization of black youth.

SOG. Seat of government, Hoover's self-description of his FBI HQ office.

SOG is also a CIA term for the Special Operations Group responsible for covert counter intelligence operations including MH/CHAOS.

Special agent. Any FBI agent.

Stat. U.S. statutes.

Subfile. A subdivision of a main file. It can be lettered or numbered and usually contains newspaper clippings, prosecution summaries, and handwritten notes.

Subj. The subject or the target.

T-[number]. A confidential informant or source, as in T-1 or T-5, who is temporary. The designation applies to that informant that one time only. The same number, therefore, can appear multiple times but may not be the same informant.

Teletype. An urgent communication typically from a field office to the director or Washington, DC, FBI office before the advent of the internet and reliance on telegraphing messages.

TGP. Theft of government property.

UACB. "Unless advised to the contrary by the Bureau."

US. United Slaves, an organization founded by Ron Karenga for black nationalists/activists. He was later a faculty member at California State University, Long Beach.

USA. A U.S. attorney or the U.S. attorney general's staff in a given area/city.

USC. (1) U.S. Code, federal laws. (2) U.S. court.

USDC. A U.S. district court, the lowest and local federal court in a jurisdiction.

USG. A CIA term for the U.S. government.

WDC. The FBI abbreviation for Washington, DC.

WFO. The FBI's Washington, DC, field office.

Chronology

September 21, 1926: Reies López Tijerina is born in Falls City, Texas, to Antonio and Herlinda López Tijerina. Brother Anselmo was born in 1919; Margarito on June 10, 1921; Ramon in 1922; and Cristobal on October 1, 1932. Mother Herlinda had ten children but only seven survived; the five boys and two girls, Maria born in 1924 and Josefina born in 1928.

June 12, 1927: Jerry Noll is born in Owatonna, Minnesota.

October 1, 1932: Cristobal Tijerina, Reies's youngest brother, is born in Marion, Texas. Wife is Felipa and they have five children, according to FBI report dated October 26, 1966.

1933: Reies López Tijerina's mother, Herlinda López Tijerina, dies when Reies is seven years of age and was pregnant with her eleventh child. The two surviving sisters are Maria and Josefa.

1946: Reies enters the Latin American Bible Institute as student.

July 30, 1947: Hugh David Tijerina, the eldest son of Reies and Maria is born in San Antonio, Texas.

February 2, 1949: Rosa Tijerina is born to Reies and Maria in Victoria, Texas.

1956: Tijerina buys 160 acres of land in Arizona for $1,400 to establish his commune, the Valley of Peace, between the cities of Eloy and Oro Grande, just north of the Papago Tohono O'odham Indian Reservation. Seventeen families join him; the men are called Los Bravos and Heralds of Peace.

April 18, 1956: Ira de Ala is born, delivered by Reies as the first child born in the Valley of Peace commune.

June 1956: Tijerina and some of his followers travel to Monero, New Mexico, where he learns from Zebedeo Martinez and Zebedeo Valdez about the theft of their land grants.

Fall 1956: Tijerina travels to Mexico to study documents at the Archivo Nacional de México and he discovers the Law of the Indies.

January 1957: Tijerina is threatened by the Arizona State Department of Education with jail time for not sending the children at Valley of Peace to the local schools.

March 18, 1957: Reies López Tijerina is charged with theft of six tires from a trailer.

April 5, 1957: Reies is charged with theft of federal property.

July 7, 1957: Reies is charged with aiding his brother Margarito escape from Pinal County jail. During this hearing, he walks out during the lunch break and becomes a fugitive for the next seven years.

August 1957: Tijerina and his family and others hide in an abandoned church in Gobernador, New Mexico. He meets Manuel Trujillo, who invites him to stay on his ranch property and live off the land.

1958: Noe, youngest son to Reies and Maria Tijerina, is born this year.

May 1958: While speaking to a group of land grant heirs, Tijerina is attacked and is defended by his brother Anselmo, who is arrested and jailed.

1959: Reies travels to Guadalajara, Jalisco, Mexico, in search of land grant archival records and Mexico City's General National Archive, where he first reads the Laws of the Indies.

December 12, 1959: Reies sends letter signed by eighty persons representing land grant families to President Eisenhower asking him to investigate and return land grants to the rightful owners.

1960: Reies goes to Mexico City to meet with President Adolfo López Mateos and present a five-hundred-signature petition. He is deported by López Mateos.

1961: Reies goes to Mexico City to meet with General Lázaro Cárdenas, former president.

February 2, 1963: The Alianza Federal de Mercedes is incorporated in New Mexico on the 115th anniversary of the Treaty of Guadalupe Hidalgo.

September 1963: Tijerina sends letter to President Kennedy about the land grant recovery movement.

Late 1963: Reies divorces Maria Escobar; they have six children: Hugh David (called Reies Jr.), Rosa, Daniel, Raquel, Noe, and Ira de Ala.

1964: The Alianza membership reaches six thousand members.

August 4, 1964: Tijerina is deported from Mexico to San Antonio, Texas, by Luis Echeverría Alvarez, later to become president.

January 12, 1965: Tijerina sends letter to President Johnson about the land grant recovery movement.

April 1, 1965: Reies began a radio talk show, *The Voice of Justice,* on KABQ-FM; a Spanish-language newspaper; and a weekly column in English in the *New Mexico Chieftain.* By August he is also broadcasting on television.

September 25, 1965: Reies marries Patricia Romero. Their children are Iris Isabel, Carlos Joaquin, Harmonia, and Danitha (called Donna).

December 20, 1965: The Alianza claims a membership of fourteen thousand.

1966: Alianza reports a membership of twenty thousand at its fall convention.

1966: Iris Isabel Tijerina is born to Reies and Patricia Tijerina. Shortly after, he travels to Spain to research land grant documents.

July 2–4, 1966: Tijerina and Alianza members begin a march from Albuquerque to Santa Fe to present a petition asking Governor Jack Campbell to investigate theft of land grants.

October 22, 1966: The Alianza Federal de Mercedes holds a convention at the Echo Amphitheater campground, claiming it is the property of the San Joaquin Del Rio de Chama land grant. The land grant descendants arrest two Forest Service agents, Phil Smith and Walter Taylor, during the occupation.

October 27, 1966: Reies, Cristobal, and three other Alianza members are arrested and charged with assault on the Forest Service agents and conversion of federal property. Bond of $5,000 is set for each of the five.

April 21, 1967: Tijerina meets with the new governor of New Mexico, Republican David F. Cargo.

May 19, 1967: A federal court order is issued to Tijerina for the membership list of the Alianza.

May 24, 1967: Tijerina resigns as president of the Alianza and does not comply with the court order.

June 3, 1967: DA Alfonso Sanchez orders state and local police to prevent the Alianza from meeting in Coyote, New Mexico. Eleven members are arrested and jailed.

June 5, 1967: Tijerina leads twenty men, daughter Rosa, and himself into the Tierra Amarilla Courthouse to execute a citizen's arrest warrant on DA Sanchez. He is not there. A jailer, Eulogio Salazar, and state police deputy, Nick Saiz, are shot. Reies, son Hugh David, Baltazar Martinez, a Vietnam veteran, and Jerry Noll flee to the mountains above Canjilon with two abductees, later freed.

June 6, 1967: Lieutenant Governor E. Lee Francis orders the National Guard to pursue Reies López Tijerina, those who fled to the mountains with him, and his brothers. Several types of police force join what is the biggest manhunt in U.S. history.

June 10, 1967: Tijerina travels to Santa Fe to surrender and is recognized by a store clerk. He is arrested in Bernalillo. He is charged with fifty-four criminal counts, including kidnapping and armed assault.

June 13, 1967: Tijerina begins serving thirty-five days until he is freed while his appeals are heard.

July 4, 1967: Baltazar Martinez surrenders.

August 3, 1967: Cristobal Tijerina surrenders.

November 6–11, 1967: Trial over Echo Amphitheater begins in Las Cruces.

December 15, 1967: Trial before federal judge Howard Bratton beings. Reies and Cristobal Tijerina, Jerry Noll, Ezequiel Dominguez, and Alfonso Chávez are found guilty of various charges stemming from the Echo Amphitheater arrests of Forest Service agents. Jerry Noll and Reies

Tijerina are sentenced to two years in prison, five years' probation, plus thirty days for contempt of court.

1968: Tijerina forms the People's Constitution Party of New Mexico and files to run for governor. He is disqualified based on criminal charges pending.

January 2, 1968: Eulogio Salazar is murdered.

April 4, 1968: Martin Luther King Jr. is assassinated.

April 25, 1968: The Tijerina family home is bombed in Albuquerque.

May 28, 1968: Tijerina and others arrive in busloads for the Poor People's Campaign in Washington, DC, see camp set up in Resurrection City, and move to Hawthorne School.

May 29, 1968: Tijerina sets up a picket line in front of the U.S. Supreme Court.

March 31–June 24, 1968: Reies is elected to be the Chicano leader during the Poor People's Campaign.

June 5, 1968: Robert F. Kennedy is assassinated. Tijerina is in Washington, DC, involved with the Poor People's Campaign.

June 1968: Reies meets with Secretary of State Dean Rusk to discuss return of land in the Southwest, the land grants held by the U.S. Forest Service as national parks.

November 6, 1968: Alfonso Sanchez loses his reelection bid as district attorney for Rio Arriba County, New Mexico.

November 12, 1968: Tijerina's trial on the Tierra Amarilla charges begins before Second Judicial District judge Paul Larrazolo in Albuquerque. Tijerina fires his attorneys and represents himself.

December 13, 1968: The jury acquits Tijerina on charges of kidnapping, false imprisonment, and assault.

1969: Synod of the United Presbyterian Church meeting in San Antonio, Texas, votes to return some land acquired in a land swap with the U.S. Forest Service west of Abiquiu known as Ghost Ranch. The land was formerly the Piedra Lumbre land grant.

1969: Robert De Pugh and Walter Peyson of the Minutemen of New Mexico are arrested and tried for violating the National Firearms Act. Prison officials place Peyson, a white supremacist, in the same cell as Tijerina in La Tuna Federal Prison with the hopes he will harm Tijerina.

March 15, 1969: Alianza headquarters on 1010 Third Street NW in Albuquerque is car-bombed, causing great damage and destroying the car belonging to Alianza vice president Santiago Anaya. Police detective Pat Gerber investigates the crime, no charges filed. The case remains unsolved.

May 6, 1969: Sander Vanocur narrates a NBC special documentary on "First Tuesday" about Reies López Tijerina titled "The Most Hated Man in New Mexico."

May 17, 1969: The Alianza sponsors a Spanish Language Parade walking from the University of New Mexico to the Old Town Plaza in Albuquerque. The parade coincides with Francisco Vasquez de Coronado's 1540 expedition through New Mexico.

June 1, 1969: Tijerina meets with the United Presbyterian Synod leaders to discuss transfer of land formerly the Piedra Lumbre Land Grant at the Ghost Ranch Conference Center.

June 7, 1969: At the Alianza's Fourth National Convention in Coyote near Abiquiu Dam, the delegates vote to have Tijerina arrest Governor David Cargo, who is in nearby Santa Rosa. Unable to find the governor, the delegates vote to arrest the scientists at Los Alamos Scientific Laboratory for crimes against humanity for their role in building the atomic bomb.

June 8-11, 1969: Patricia Tijerina tries several times to burn a National Forest Service sign near Gallina, New Mexico. She finally succeeds with a firebomb and barbed wire to hold burning debris to the sign. Reies is an observer. They drive to Coyote Ranger Station, site of another Forest Service sign she ignites. New Mexico State Police and plainclothes detectives Robert Gilliland and Jack Johnson arrive and arrest them. Tijerina points a .30-06 caliber rifle at James Evans, chief of Law Enforcement Branch, Forest Service, Southwest Region. Officer Jack Johnson points a rifle at Tijerina while surrendering to Manuel Martinez. Arrested are Patricia, Reies, Ramon, and Hugh David Tijerina and Carol Watson, Kerim Hamarat, Manuel Rudy, and Jose Aragon.

June 11, 1969: Reies seeks to citizen's arrest James Evans at his home and is jailed for violating terms of his bond release.

June 16–17, 1969: Bond revocation hearing is held by federal judge Howard Bratton. Tijerina's lawyer is William Kunstler.

June 23, 1969: Reies and Patricia attempt to serve a citizen's arrest warrant on Chief Justice Warren Burger. Tijerina files the arrest warrant with his clerk, John Davis, and obtains a receipt.

September 22, 1969: Tijerina is tried in federal court for aiding and abetting Patricia in burning the Forest Service signs and assault on a federal law enforcement officer.

September 28, 1969: Tijerina is found guilty on three counts.

November 18, 1969: Tijerina is retried by Judge Garnett Burks on the Tierra Amarilla Courthouse charges and found guilty of falsely imprisoning Deputy Sheriff Pete Jaramillo and assaulting Eulogio Salazar. Tijerina is sentenced to one to five years in prison. Governor Bruce King pardons Tijerina four days before he is to report to prison.

December 10, 1969: The Episcopal Church Executive Council votes to donate $40,000 to the Alianza.

January 5, 1970: Tijerina is found guilty and sentenced to two concurrent terms, one to five years and two to ten years in a federal prison. He is sent to La Tuna penitentiary in El Paso. He shares a cell with Joe Valachi, known Mafia killer.

April 4, 1971: The United States Court of Appeals, Tenth Circuit, upholds the federal district court conviction of Tijerina for the Tierra Amarilla Courthouse incident.

May 1970: Tijerina meets with Governor David F. Cargo in Santa Fe to discuss return of the land grants to rightful heirs.

July 26, 1971: Tijerina is released from federal custody, on parole for fifteen years. Parole prohibits any leadership position in the Alianza for three years and requires monthly reporting to probation officer Richard Martinez.

November 1971: Patricia Tijerina makes allegations against Albuquerque police officers for raping her while her husband is in prison.

1972: Tijerina's convictions from the Tierra Amarilla Courthouse takeover are affirmed by the New Mexico Supreme Court, 84 N.M. 432 and 504 P.2d 642.

April 8, 1972: Patricia Tijerina gives birth to daughter Harmonia; the First Conference on Fraternal Harmony is held.

August 31–September 3, 1972: The Raza Unida Party holds its national convention in Juarez / El Paso. Tijerina is a contender to lead the party as Chair but takes himself out of the election.

September 1972: Margarito Tijerina is released from prison after seven years.

October 21-22, 1972: National Congress on Land and Culture is held in Albuquerque by Tijerina.

April 7, 1973: The Second Annual Conference on Fraternal Harmony is held.

June 25, 1973: Patricia Tijerina gives birth to daughter Danitha.

1974: The New Mexico Court of Appeals affirms the judgment of the trial court from January 29, 1972, in support of the police who murdered Rito Canales and Antonio Cordova, 86 N.M. 697, 526 P 2d 1290 (Ct. App. 1974).

January 1, 1974: Tijerina begins writing a diary.

February 2, 1974: Tijerina attracts over two thousand persons to the eleventh anniversary of the Alianza, held at the building in Albuquerque. He buys six hours of radio time on KABQ to broadcast speeches and interviews with guests.

February 7, 1974: The New Mexico State Senate passes Joint House Resolution 15, which calls for the U.S. Congress to investigate Spanish and Mexican land claims in the state.

March 22, 1974: Tijerina moves his family to Madera, New Mexico.

April 6, 1974: The Third Annual Conference on Fraternal Harmony is held.

May 1, 1974: Tijerina's second-born son, Daniel, dies in an automobile accident at age twenty-one. He is survived by widow, Ivan Ramirez, and one son, Daniel II.

June 9, 1974: Tijerina's federal parole conditions end.

June 11, 1974: Governor Bruce King is asked to commute Tijerina's prison sentence.

June 29, 1974: Tijerina begins serving his second prison term in the New Mexico state prison.

December 18, 1974: Tijerina is released from state prison after serving only five months and eighteen days of a ten-year sentence.

April 5, 1975: The Fourth Annual Fraternal Harmony conference is held.

July 31, 1975: Tijerina, accompanied by daughters Rosa, Raquel, and Lita (Ira de Ala) travels to Juarez, Chihuahua, Mexico, to discuss proposed film on Tijerina to be titled *Chicano*.

October 4-10, 1975: The filming of *Chicano* is done partly in San Antonio, Texas. Jaime Casillas wrote the script and directed; Jaime Fernandez played Tijerina; Rosa played herself in the scenes dealing with Tierra Amarilla; and funding came from Rodolfo Echeverría, brother to the Mexican president Luis Alvarez Echeverría.

November 15, 1975: Tijerina and others, this author included, met with the next president of Mexico, José López Portillo, in Juarez, Chihuahua, Mexico.

January 1, 1976: Tijerina began writing his memoirs, *Mi lucha por la tierra*.

January 4, 1976: His father died at age eighty-four in Wichita Falls, Texas.

February 21, 1976: Tijerina moved his family out of the United States and relocates to San Juan del Rio, Queretaro.

May 8, 1976: The Fifth Annual Fraternal Harmony Conference is held and Tijerina announces a car caravan into Mexico on June 5, 1976.

June 12, 1976: President Luis Echeverría welcomed the eighty-six-person delegation that made the car caravan from Albuquerque to Mexico City.

November 2, 1976: Joseph Montoya lost his reelection bid for the U.S. Senate by fifty-eight thousand votes.

January 1978: Tijerina met with Texas land claimants to discuss their land claims, but by February the Texans decide to go it alone under the name Asociacion de Reclamantes de Texas.

January 28, 1978: *Mi lucha por la tierra*, Tijerina's 575-page autobiography, is published Mexico City's Fondo de Cultural Económica with an initial run of five thousand copies.

March 6, 1979: Tijerina filed a petition for pardon by the president after completion of his sentence.

March 20, 1979: Dr. Myra Ellen Jenkins publicized her discovery of an original Spanish document for the San Joaquin del Cañon del Rio de Chama land grant, proving the U.S. Private Land Claims Court wrongfully settled the claim in 1891 against the real heirs in favor of Anglos.

September 1982: Tijerina joined others at a rally in Taos, New Mexico, protesting the building of condominiums in Valdez, just north of Taos.

1984: Tijerina traveled to Israel to visit the Palestinian settlements.

December 1989: Chicano Activist Reunion is held at St. Anthony's Hotel, San Antonio. Tijerina leads the Chistes y Bironga session.

June 9, 1993: Tijerina married Esperanza Garcia Valladares by proxy in Albuquerque, New Mexico, because she was not a U.S. citizen and is unable to cross into the country. He married her in a formal ceremony in Uruapan, Michoacán, Mexico, on July 19, 1993.

1994: Tijerina's home near Coyote, New Mexico, is firebombed and destroyed along with many of his possessions, his library, and Alianza records.

1995: Tijerina returns to Uruapan.

1997: Tijerina moves a mobile home to the burned site of his home near Coyote, New Mexico, and continues to live there until he exiles himself again to Mexico.

October 19, 1999: Tijerina donates his papers to the University of New Mexico.

November 5, 1999: Tijerina meets with Governor George W. Bush to discuss the return of Texas land grants to their rightful owners.

November 11, 2000: Hugh David Tijerina, first son, died, survived by wife, JoAnn, along with two daughters, Bernadette and Justina.

2005: Tijerina leaves his home in Uruapan with third wife, Esperanza, and relocates to Juarez, Chihuahua, Mexico.

April 2006: Tijerina moves to El Paso, Texas.

August 3, 2007: Robert "Bob" E. Huber, died, one of two hostages taken during the Tierra Amarilla event by Tijerina's people. He was made to drive some of the Aliancistas away from the courthouse.

May 2007: Baltazar Martinez, participant in the Tierra Amarilla Courthouse citizen's arrest attempt, is shot to death by Tony Herrera. The trial on this manslaughter charge is held in the same courthouse. Herrera is acquitted at the first trial but found guilty of voluntary manslaughter in the second on November 11, 2008.

June 26, 2009: Tijerina receives the Ohtli Award from the Consul General of Mexico, Roberto Rodriguez Hernandez in El Paso, Texas.

2011: Tijerina receives the keys to the City of Las Vegas, New Mexico.

2011: Mike Scarborough completes the oral history of the Juan P. Valdez family, land grant heirs to the land near Cañones, New Mexico. Mike is the son of Judge J. M. Scarborough, who was in the Tierra Amarilla Courthouse the day Tijerina attempted the citizen's arrest. Later he was the judge who heard the case on the eviction notice claims posted by the Corporation of Abiquiu, land grant claimants. Mike Scarborough publishes *Trespassers on Our Own Land* from those oral histories.

August 25, 2012: Juan Valdez passed away at age seventy-four. He was born May 25, 1938 and was with Tijerina during the Tierra Amarilla Courthouse citizen's arrest attempt.

August 30–September 2, 2012: The Fortieth Anniversary Commemoration of the La Raza Unida Party National Convention was held in El Paso. Tijerina is a presenter on September 1, 2012.

September 2, 2012: Tijerina and his attorney, Rees Lloyd, in a conference call with José Angel Gutiérrez discuss Reies's will or living trust. Tijerina designates nephew Luis Tijerina as trustee, and makes that announcement at the Fortieth Anniversary Commemoration.[1]

April 12, 2014: Tijerina is enraged to learn that Cliven Bundy, his family and supporters, took possession of federal lands, refused to pay grazing fees and fines, and with weapons faced federal officials and Las Vegas, Nevada, metropolitan police seeking to remove them. There is no prosecution. Bundy seeks a second armed confrontation with federal officials in Harney County, Oregon. He is finally arrested twenty-two months later in Portland, Oregon.

Ammon Bundy and Robert "LaVoy" Finicum take armed possession of Malheur National Wildlife Refuge in Oregon and hold it for twenty-four days before the federal officials move in and arrest them. Finicum is killed by federal agents when he draws his weapon.

January 19, 2015: Blogger, photographer, and retired police officer M. G. Bralley posts his collection, exceeding 150 photographs, most of which had never been published, about Reies López Tijerina and members of the Alianza.

January 19, 2015: Tijerina dies in El Paso, Texas.

Introduction

Growing up in a segregated community that included segregated schools, I did not have much of an introduction to my own heritage except at home. The curriculum was all about the white folks and their greatness. We called the white people *Anglos* when we wanted to be nice and *gringos* when they acted badly or we disliked them. My father always referred them as *Los Americanos* but would add, "You know we were Americanos before they were"—meaning there was a Spanish America long before the thirteen colonies.[1] Both my father and mother knew their Mexican history and made me learn it as well. They also knew U.S. and Texas history but from the perspective of a Mexican. This perspective is based on the repeated takings of Spanish, then Mexican, then Chicano homelands without compensation in gross violation of the Takings Clause of the Fifth Amendment to the U.S. Constitution.

I learned that Rey José Primero was not really the Spanish king but a Frenchman put on that throne by his younger brother, Napoleon I. Orchestrated by Napoleon, the Louisiana Purchase was actually Spanish land prior to 1800 that was given to France. Napoleon sold the land to the United States when he needed money to fight England. He also sold Florida along with parts of Texas, Alabama, Georgia, Louisiana, and Mississippi. He also let the American colonists move their barges with goods on the Mississippi all the way to New Orleans. When the U.S. possession of these lands was complete, its citizens were the new neighbors to the Spanish Southwest, later to become Mexico. The second-to-the-last land grabs were Texas and the Southwest with the U.S. invasion of Mexico in 1846.[2] The last land grab was the taking of the remaining vestiges of the Spanish Empire in the Americas and Pacific during the Spanish American War of 1898. This U.S. invasion netted Cuba, Puerto Rico, the Dominican Republic, other Caribbean islands, and the patch of islands known as the Philippines, Guam, and Samoa.

From the day after the Treaty of Guadalupe Hidalgo was signed on February 2, 1848, into the next century, grabbing by gringos of Mexican lands continued. The U.S. Senate, before ratifying the treaty, excised Article 10, which guaranteed landownership by Spanish and Mexican land grantees would be held inviolate forever.[3] Subsequent claims by these grantees were denied by territorial governments whose decisions were approved by U.S. courts. The land between the Rio Grande and Nueces River in Texas was not covered by the 1848 treaty; those lands are still in dispute by grantees but in possession of gringos. The land grabbing continued unabated in the West. Later, President Lincoln, during his reign over Congress in the years of the Civil War, took millions of acres of land from Native Americans and Mexicans to build his Transcontinental Railroad. He claimed it was land in the "public domain."

To make sure these lands stayed in the possession of the United States, Congress passed the Homestead Act, which resulted in more millions of acres of land taken from Mexicans and Native Americans to settle over thirty-five million new immigrants from Europe. These were the people for white racial stock needed to create new states, slave or free. Adding insult to injury, Presidents Ulysses Grant and Theodore Roosevelt started the federal program that took more millions of acres to create the network of federal parks we now enjoy, for a nominal fee. The states followed suit.

Approximately two-thirds of all lands west of the Mississippi are in the hands of state or federal governments.

The resistance to these thefts were the organizing among the Spanish and Mexican communities of vigilante groups such as the Gorras Blancas and La Mano Negra.[4] To be sure, they did not succeed, but others that followed continued to try.[5] Reies López Tijerina was one of those. He was the only one of the Four Horsemen, as we were known—César Chávez in California, Rodolfo "Corky" Gonzales in Colorado, Tijerina in New Mexico, and the author in Texas—to fight land grant battles during the Chicano Movement. He also was the only one of the four to be imprisoned for his "crimes." None of the ones who committed crimes against him, his family, and members of his group, La Alianza de Pueblos Libres, were imprisoned. Yet the evildoers bombed his homes, shot at his cars, attempted assassinations, burglarized his offices, burned property, and had him under constant surveillance. Both the New Mexico State Police and the Federal Bureau of Investigation monitored his every move. When his wife and son were raped by law enforcement agents, neither agency investigated, much less prosecuted, the criminals. Tijerina never gave up his cause to the day he died. Fearful for his life and that of others close to him, he did leave the United States from time to time, but he always came back to finish the fight. Regrettably, the fight finished him. He died ill, old, and in poverty in El Paso. His legacy lives on in us.[6]

An entire generation, like me, learned our history of the loss of our homeland. Regardless of whether we were heirs or descendants, we lost title to and possession of the Southwest. This is the story of how I found out who Tijerina was, why he was important, and what consequences he suffered for the cause of land recovery.

Meeting Ramon Tijerina

On Sundays, usually after Mass, Willie Velasquez and I would pass out leaflets with information on why the Mexican American Youth Organization (MAYO) opposed the war in Vietnam. Our favorite places were the Alamo and San Fernando Cathedral.[7] We got a lot of attention at both places—and lots of arguments. A principal reason for MAYO's antiwar stance was that more than 20 percent of the casualties were Chicanos, while we were only a fraction of the U.S. population, about 6 percent at time.[8] The draft, as forced conscription was called then, enforced by the Selective Service System, drafted into military service more Chicanos than white kids.[9] The white kids got deferments based on hardship, such as the family owing a farm, being enrolled in college, being an only male child, medical reasons, and other exemptions, such as being a divinity student.

Tijerina availed himself of that exemption while in Bible school when he turned eighteen. He was so advised by the administration of the school. He was an exception to the experience of most Chicanos. Chicano kids were farmworkers, not owners, were pushed out of public school without high school diplomas, came from large families with lots of male children, and were healthy enough to pass the entrance physical examination for the military. Chicano kids did not wait to be drafted; they volunteered for military service, especially the marines.[10] If you were drafted, you were restricted to the army. If you chose the navy or air force, it was a longer term of duty.

One Sunday afternoon in February 1967, I was approached by a wiry, dark-skinned, slight man with small, rimless glasses who took my leaflet without comment. He was as tall as I and came close to me, almost nose to nose. He said his first name—"Soy Ramon"—by way of introduction. He then asked in a soft voice in Spanish if I knew about the Alianza Federal de Mercedes or of the Alianza de Pueblos Libres or of Reies López Tijerina.[11] *Ninguno,* I responded, "None." We had never heard of the Federal Land Grant Alliance, as it was referred to in English. He tried talking to me and Willie about the Alianza and Tijerina while we were passing out the leaflets. We tried to evade him and his conversation during this task. From past experience at leafleting, we knew some people would try to engage in adversarial conversation just to prevent us from leafleting others. They wanted argument to take time away from our task. We did engage with others, but only in small conversation as we thrust out the leaflet, such as greetings or "Please read this" and always, "Thank you for your support." We were trying to stay on task and ignore him.

Ramon Tijerina was undaunted. We both continued to hear him describe the purposes of the Alianza and the work of Tijerina about land grants in New Mexico. He recounted the taking of Echo Amphitheater and how they had arrested Forest Service guards for trespassing on their land, the Pueblo San Joaquin del Rio de Chama, the previous year, on October 22, 1966.[12] He was tenacious, and that brief introduction to the land recovery movement pricked our interest. It was enough for us to ask him to join us after we leafletted at our Sunday afternoon group teach-in at Woodlawn Lake, near St. Mary's University in San Antonio, Texas. Our teach-in was led by Professor Charles "Charlie" Cotrell, with whom I had taken classes while I was an undergraduate in Kingsville, Texas, and now was my teacher of graduate classes at St. Mary's University in San Antonio. The teach-in, a tactic we borrowed from the antiwar movement occurring concurrently with our efforts, consisted of readings, discussions, and analysis of current events among the cofounders of MAYO and other members. Usually, Charlie brought copies, or we made copies, of material we found interesting on others doing work similar to MAYO's. When some organization, program, person, event or happening was of great interest to us, we made plans to drive over and see firsthand what was going on. Ramon, we found out that late afternoon, was one of Reies López Tijerina's several brothers. He lived in south San Antonio and was working for the Alianza. He was doing the Alianza work in Texas among those who were land grantees. He knew of MAYO and wanted us to know he supported us. What he related about the Alianza, the Treaty of Guadalupe Hidalgo, and Reies's exploits, such as the taking of Echo Amphitheater, was mesmerizing. We wanted to know more.

At MAYO, those of us able to travel by car would do so in pursuit of information and contacts in these days before the internet, fax machines, smartphones, and cheap telephone communication. We traveled to Atlanta in the South in search of leaders of the Student Non-violent Coordinating Committee and the Southern Christian Leadership Conference. We traveled north to Austin and further north into Illinois, Wisconsin, and Michigan for talks with white radicals, members of the Students for a Democratic Society (SDS) and the Nation of Islam in Chicago. Some of the SDS members from Austin became part of the Weather Underground.

Prompted by Ramon, we traveled across the Southwest to learn about Tijerina in New Mexico; César Chávez in California, and Rodolfo "Corky" Gonzales and his group, the Crusade for Justice, in Colorado. We also made quick trips to El Paso and Glendale, Arizona, to help plan school walkouts in those places.

Ramon Tijerina's brief seminar that Sunday on the Alianza's land recovery movement opened our eyes to information never mentioned in school, college, or books; newspapers and news media never discussed this topic either. The five of us leading MAYO were college graduates, two of us in graduate school and the others with bachelor's or in pursuit of a bachelor's degree. We were totally unaware of this subject. This was our history and civil rights struggle, and we were woefully ignorant. Ramon convinced us that this was a struggle far greater than the school reform that MAYO was involved with in 1967. I began a fifty-year interest in the subject matter of land recovery and in Reies López Tijerina and the Alianza.

Later, when I viewed and read copies of FBI files in the 1980s, I knew that one day I would have to write a book about that surveillance. I published my first article on this subject in 1986.[13] Tijerina spent years as a fugitive, some of them unnecessarily because he neither was being pursued nor sought. A decade later, this aspect of his life with government surveillance prompted my first paper on Tijerina.[14] Few people believe our government would not only spy on us but seek to destroy our organizational leaders and efforts, protected activity under the First Amendment of the U.S. Constitution and federal and state laws.

In my prior book on César E. Chávez and his FBI file, I devote a chapter to the ultra vires acts that were made internal policy of the agency during the Hoover years and condoned, often directed, by presidents and U.S. attorney generals.[15] The FBI always investigated Chávez and his activities but never took a case against Chávez or the farmworker union to the U.S. attorney for prosecution. That same pattern developed with Reies López Tijerina and the land recovery movement; the FBI was ever present but never on the side of Tijerina or the Alianza members when their rights were violated or when harm was directed at him, his family, or members and their property.

A Brief Biography of Reies López Tijerina

Very little is known about the man. He was reluctant to provide details about his life to interviewers or in his writings; he wanted the focus to be on his doings, not familial roots. Most secondary sources have the same information, with few new details. In his book, *Mi lucha por la tierra,* he makes mention of some family members, births of some of his children, and his first two wives, and includes photographs of his family with Maria, the first wife. Santiago Tijerina, his paternal grandfather, was a fighter for his rights, particularly because he claimed to be an heir of a land grant in Laredo, Texas. According to Richard Gardner, Santiago and other men agreed on "the legendary 429 land grants of Texas, given to the people by the Spanish Crown."[16] Grandfather Santiago, born in 1850, told stories of lynching, beatings, murders, and burning of homes and barns by Anglo Texans and Texas Rangers trying to wrest possession of these land grants from the rightful owners. Once, he recounted, he was almost lynched by some whites.[17]

What we do know is that he was born in Falls City, Texas, to Antonio and Herlinda Tijerina on September 21, 1926.[18] His mother was Antonio's third wife. I have found no mention of the two other wives and possible children. Herlinda bore Antonio ten children, of whom seven survived: five sons and two daughters.[19] Herlinda, again pregnant with the eleventh child, died at age twenty-eight shortly after the birth of Cristobal in 1934.[20] His mother is buried in Poth, Texas.[21] Reies was sent to be raised by "an aged Indian, Nazario Vasquez," until he rejoined his brothers in 1956.[22] Josefa and Maria were the two sisters, and they also are absent in the literature, including the writings of Reies.[23] He offers one brief mention of a phone call from a sister, Josefa, in 1976.[24] This incident does indicate that she knew his phone number and that they probably communicated from time to time and knew their respective whereabouts.

Antonio took his boys, Anselmo, Margarito, Ramon, and Reies (and I assume the girls) on the migrant stream to West Texas, Colorado, Wyoming, Ohio, Indiana, and Michigan to eke out a living without Herlinda. J. Edgar Hoover, in a seventeen-page report dated February 16, 1968, to the Secret

Service, mentions that Antonio at age seventy-nine was residing in Wichita Falls, Texas ,"living with his third wife named VICTORIA." Perhaps Antonio married again after Herlinda passed away and took a fourth wife. Antonio lived to a ripe age of eighty-four years and died in Wichita Falls, Texas, on January 4, 1976.[25]

Reies at age four became another hand in the fields. In 1939, his family was in Michigan, where they stayed five years. It was in Michigan in 1942 that Tijerina met the preacher Samuel Galindo, who gave him a Bible and interested him in becoming a minister. By 1946, Reies and brother, Ramon, had left the family and enrolled in the Assembly of God Latin American Bible Institute in Isleta (Ysleta), Texas, a community later annexed by El Paso. He was a student there from 1943 to 1946, according to Hoover's report to the Secret Service (p. 2). His prior formal schooling and learning had been haphazard, involving many, many schools all over the country. Reies stopped attending school after the third grade (p. 2). He managed to learn English, but that was at age eleven, and to write and read much later.[26]

The older brothers, Anselmo and Margarito, had left the family long before, when they were in their late teen years. During World War II, Anselmo tried to enlist in the army and navy but was rejected for insufficient education. In Michigan, Anselmo got into trouble with the law and ended up in jail in 1959 and paroled in 1961 (p. 3). Margarito ended up in Indiana, where he killed a man and received a prison term; he was again convicted, this time for armed robbery, in New Mexico in July 1966 and sentenced to ten to fifty years (p. 3). Reies's land recovery movement brought the brothers back together in the late 1950s.[27] Upon graduation from the Assembly of God Latin American Bible Institute in Saspamco, Texas, Reies took a position as assistant preacher at a church in Victoria, Texas. He married on July 14, 1946, in Pontiac, Michigan, to a Bible-colleague and former migrant worker, Maria Escobar.[28] They began a family and later a traveling ministry, which is what brought the Tijerinas to Arizona and New Mexico for the first time.[29] He learned of the land grants firsthand from direct descendants of land claimants, which became his cause after he dropped religion. It was also in Arizona and New Mexico where his activities were first noted by local, state, and federal police authorities. The FBI was involved in investigating some crimes Tijerina was accused of in the 1950s, but no files from these years were released to Tijerina or to me in response to our requests.

Maria and Reies had six children, (Hugh) David, Rosa, Daniel, Ira de Ala, Noe, and Raquel. They divorced in 1963. In 1975, Daniel published a letter he prepared for the president of the United States. The opening reads this way:

> We have had it rough all of our lives and never had a home of our own. Ever since my father started this fight for justice here in New Mexico, it is very difficult for us to get a job. Our lives have been threatened. Our headquarters, where we also live now, has been bombed. The police and National Forest Service men have persecuted us and locked us up. I have also had to drop out of school twice because of my name. You see, the teachers don't like it very well.[30]

David and Daniel are both deceased, David from bad health and alcoholism at age fifty-three on November 11, 2000,[31] Daniel in an automobile accident at twenty-one years of age.[32] David and Daniel both left widows and families. Joanne Sandoval is David's widow, and Justina Tijerina is his only child, born in 1970.

Patricia Romero, New Wife

On August 8, 1965, Reies López Tijerina met seventeen-year-old Patricia Romero and married her a month later, on September 25. The couple made their home in the basement of the Alianza building in Albuquerque, shared by grown children from Reies's first wife. They had several children: Isabel Iris, Harmonia, Carlos Joaquin, and Danitha (called Donna later in life). This marriage endured the trials and incarcerations of Reies and much violence and ended in divorce.

Several years later, Reies relocated to Mexico and settled in Uruapan, Michoacán. There he met Esperanza Garcia Valladares. They agreed to marry. Without U.S. citizenship, the marriage by proxy took place in Albuquerque, New Mexico, on June 9, 1993; and, ten days later in a civil ceremony in Uruapan on June 19. When Reies became ill and needed medical treatments, he moved closer to the United States, into Juarez, Chihuahua, and would travel to El Paso's La Fe health center for medical attention. Esperanza could not accompany him across the border. Later, Reies obtained a visa for his wife to live in El Paso, and the couple settled into a low-income, subsidized housing unit near the La Fe clinic and health center. They ate complimentary meals there when possible, and he would get medical attention for his growing health issues. Their income was meagre and fixed. After Reies passed on January 19, 2015, at eighty-eight years of age, Esperanza continued to live in their apartment and obtained her U.S. citizenship on May 31, 2017, at age seventy-one. She still is befriended by the staff of La Fe, especially Estela Reyes and executive director Salvador Balcorta.[33]

Where Is the Literature?

The formal study of Mexican Americans did not begin until 1970, Arnoldo de Leon wrote in one of his many books.[34] The 1970s and beyond did begin to see books written on Chicano history and politics, such as the pioneering works by Rodolfo Acuña, Leonard Pitt, Armando Rendon, Luis Valdez and Stan Steiner, and Matt Meier and Feliciano Rivera.[35] In 1948 Carey McWilliams had produced *North from Mexico: The Spanish Speaking People of the United States*,[36] but few Mexican Americans were in college then, and even fewer professors utilized the book. The same holds true for George I. Sanchez's *Forgotten People: A Study of New Mexicans*.[37] And the important work by María Amparo Ruiz de Burton of 1885, *The Squatter and the Don*, had to wait until 1997 for editing by Rosaura Sánchez and Beatrice Pita.[38] This novel is the story of a participant observer of how the Anglo took over New Mexico land and richness from the natives and Hispanos.

Only in recent decades have the general public and Chicanos been introduced to the various precursors to Reies López Tijerina and the Alianza in fighting to get their lands back. *Mexicano Resistance in the Southwest*, by Robert J. Rosenbaum, documents those various struggles by individuals and groups. John R. Chavez squarely dealt with the question, What does the

Southwest represent to the Chicano? His work, *The Lost Land: The Chicano Image of the Southwest*,[39] was timely because the ethnic identifier *Chicano* was losing much ground to the federally sponsored label *Hispanic,* dating to 1977. The Office of Management and Budget, in Directive 15 in May 1977, mandated that the latter term be used on government forms to identify all Chicanos and Latinos, given that these latter persons could be of any race. In so doing, the U.S. government created only one ethnic group for the United States: Hispanics. Alternatively, people could label themselves non-Hispanic if they wanted to avoid a racial classification.

The following decade an analysis of the Treaty of Guadalupe Hidalgo, in the 1990 book by that title, was written by Richard Griswold del Castillo. This work for the first time exposed students to this treaty and the issue of land grants. Students generations removed from the U.S. invasion of Mexico in 1846 had never been taught in public schools or colleges about the treaty, much less ever read its contents and the history of fraud after the war by Congress in deleting previously negotiated terms. The year 1992 saw the publication of Richard L. Nostrand's *The Hispano Homeland*,[40] the first book documenting the Hispano experience in New Mexico and southern Colorado with census records, historical documents, and geographical maps. The historical record in English of the Southwest was being created among academics. Frederick Nolan followed suit with documents to produce *The Lincoln County War: A Documentary History* in 1992,[41] which traces how, when, and why Anglos were able to take more than three million acres of land in New Mexico. In more recent times, the land question has come under study again by contemporary authors and the U.S. government. In January 2001, the General Accounting Office (GAO) published a report listing and defining community land grants in New Mexico. The three tables that list grants identify 130 Spanish and Mexican grants and twenty-two community grants made by Spain to Indian pueblos. Appendix 1 offers data on the outcome and acreage patented of 295 land grants in New Mexico.[42]

A nongovernmental work by Roxanne Dunbar-Ortiz, *Roots of Resistance: A History of Land Tenure in New Mexico*,[43] studies pre-Columbian landholdings by tribal groups that were taken to award land grants, which became the inheritance of the United States post-1848. More recently, in 2013, David

Correia's *Properties of Violence: Law and Land Grant Struggle in Northern New Mexico* retraced some of Dunbar-Ortiz's earlier findings but also brings up to date the legacy of the Alianza and Tijerina. He utilizes FBI documents in chapter 5, "The New Mexico Land Grant War," to document efforts by the FBI, CIA, and state and county governments, and the local DA's personal vendetta, to destroy Tijerina and the land recovery movement.[44] In 2014, David L. Caffey, in *Chasing the Santa Fe Ring: Power and Privilege in Territorial New Mexico,* added to the historical record of the personalities in the Santa Fe Ring, including Thomas Benton Catron, Samuel Axtell, Thomas Burns, Amado Chavez, Stephen B. Elkins, James Proudfit, and Henry Atkinson.[45] This crew of thieves took almost all the communal land grants in New Mexico before it became a state.

An oral history interview in 2011 by Mike Scarborough of Juan P. Valdez, who was among those with Tijerina when he went to effect a citizen's arrest warrant on District Attorney Alfonso Sanchez at the Tierra Amarilla Courthouse on June 5, 1967, was made into a book-length memoir, *Trespassers on Our Own Land.*[46] Scarborough is the son of the judge who ruled against land grant claimants time and again, and was present inside his courtroom on the second floor during the so-called Tierra Amarilla Courthouse raid. Scarborough also wrote a paper that was submitted to the American Bar Association's Commission on Hispanic Legal Rights and Responsibilities on the negative attitude held by the U.S. government toward land claims under Indian, Spanish, and Mexican treaties and property rights.[47]

Scarborough's work is a first-person narrative of how the Valdez family went from being the first holders of a land grant in northern New Mexico in 1807, when Thomas Jefferson was president of the United States, to the great-great-great-grandsons barely making ends meet in the 1950s on the remaining fifteen hundred acres in four settlements consisting of 350 people, less than five acres a person. Juan Valdez's great-great-great-grandfather, Juan Bautista Baldez (sometime between 1807 and 1932, the surname changed or was changed by others), received the grant, along with ten other families, that became known as the Merced de Juan Bautista Baldez, 310,000 acres.[48] His father, Amarante, in 1932 had to leave the family home and moved to Canjilon because the land could not sustain the extended family.

Scarborough also provides the personal account of Juan Valdez as a core insider in the Alianza, privy to the most important decisions and actions taken by its members and Reies López Tijerina. His work is of extreme value for researchers interested in land grant and claims issues because Scarborough unearths new primary sources of information and passes them to our generations through the words of Juan Valdez. Scarborough, for example, found a 1903 *Denver Post* article quoting Justice William F. Stone, who sat on the Court of Private Land Claims (CPLC) for twelve years. In Stone's address to the New Mexico Bar Association in 1905 on the subject of title to land grant claims, he states:

> For more than a quarter of a century New Mexico and Arizona land titles were burdened with the incubus of uncertainty. The investment of capital, the development of mines and vast tracts of land, immigration and growth of cities, towns, and industries were all retarded.

And in the last sentence he stated:

> In addition to the benefits mentioned, the reversion to the public domain of the general government of more than 30,000,000 acres of land comes the [sic] like new cession of country to the United States—a region illimitable in the undeveloped wealth of its coal, metals, agriculture and health-giving climate.[49]

A bias toward new development and not preserving the land grants, which sustained a different culture and historic era, is clearly evident in this address.

According to Scarborough, the CPLC reviewed 301 claims totaling thirty-six million acres. They certified only 87 claims, which consisted of three million acres.[50] In other words, the CPLC took thirty-three million acres of land from legitimate owners and put them in the category of public domain, owned by the U.S. government. In the last sentence cited above, it is clear this justice, therefore all justices, knew and acted with malice to steal the land from claimants and their communal lands to impoverish them and their subsequent heirs forever. The result was of extreme economic benefit to the U.S. government and those like the Santa Fe Ring who also stole land. Missing in this accounting of theft of land is the value of the minerals and forestry, which could be converted into lumber. Again, Scarborough tells us that President Teddy Roosevelt in his presidential proclamation on October 12, 1905, took 1,271,732 acres of land to create the Jemez Forest Reserve, which included part of Canjilon, La Petaca, Vallecitos, El Rito, Ojo Caliente, and Tres Piedras, part of both the Chama and Juan Valdez land grants. Teddy Roosevelt stated:

> The entire stand of merchantable timber is estimated at 2,675,000,000 feet, B.M. [board measure] The non-merchantable timber is estimated at 145,000,000,000 feet, B.M. These figures are very conservative.[51]

So even this president knew he was stealing valuable timber from real people with real land titles to these forests, as other presidents had done and continued to do.

The University of New Mexico's Center for Land Grant Studies produces occasional papers on land grant topics. The first such publications were "The Tierra Amarilla Grant: A History of Chicanery," by Malcolm Ebright, in 1980, and "Spanish and Mexican Land Grants in New Mexico and Colorado," edited by John and Christine Van Ness, also in 1980. Robert Torrez's "La Mano Negra," Research Paper No. 46, appeared in 1994.

The Literature on Tijerina

César E. Chávez by far is the most studied, reported, analyzed, and discussed of the Four Horsemen—deservedly so for his championing the cause of Mexican-origin people in the United States, who overwhelmingly were seasonal farm laborers during the 1900s, until approximately the 1980s. Mechanization, pesticides, agricultural visas (a new bracero program), undocumented immigrants, and some educational attainment for Mexican Americans all contributed to changing the nationality of the people who were farmworkers in the United States by the late 1980s. Chávez was the first of the Four Horsemen to die, on April 23, 1993; the second was Rodolfo "Corky" Gonzales, April 12, 2005.[52] Tijerina ranks second behind Chávez in the number of secondary sources available on his persona and cause.

Tijerina's autobiography, *Mi lucha por la tierra,* covered his early childhood and family but mostly his years as a fugitive after his communal experience with the Valley of Peace in Arizona. His autobiography ends in 1976. Its last chapter, "La CIA," concludes with a commentary on the 1976 defeat of Senator Joseph Montoya of New Mexico, his nemesis for decades. The problem is that U.S. readers don't read Spanish; his story in his own words remained unknown until I edited and translated the work.[53]

The first books on Tijerina, much like the first books on Chávez, are mostly laudatory, vividly dramatized, focused mostly on what the press dubbed the "Courthouse Raid" in Tierra Amarilla; and often stop short of later years, when he was incarcerated. The first book was by Michael Jenkinson, *Tijerina,* published in 1968. It is a short but insightful 103-page monograph, most timely a year after the Tierra Amarilla Courthouse event. The photographs in this publication are rare, and some have not appeared in other publications, for example, the poster with "Elect Tijerina for Governor."[54]

Peter Nabokov in 1969 followed with *Tijerina and the Courthouse Raid.* It includes a "Chronology of Major Events" and a dramatis personae—names with titles of who is who in the narrative—that aid the reader in keeping up with the fast-moving account of the "raid" and the subsequent two trials and travels by Tijerina. Tijerina moved about the country frequently to raise funds and promote favorable publicity for his cause. This book also contains invaluable photographs, fifteen pages of them, which capture the arrests, personalities, and meetings of the Alianza. In 1971, Richard Gardner published *Grito! Reies Tijerina and the New Mexico Land Grant War of 1967.* There is nothing new in this work that Nabokov had not already covered. Gardner's contribution lies in the oral history interviews he conducted with participants and members of the Alianza.[55] Patricia Bell Blawis's *Tijerina and the Land Grants: Mexican Americans in Struggle for Their Heritage,* an unabashedly sympathetic treatment of Tijerina and his cause, also appeared in 1971.

Included in the Blawis book, and not elsewhere, are the three letters written in prison by Tijerina to his son Hugh "David" Tijerina. They are in Spanish but Blawis provides a translation in an appendix. Also included are the jury instructions on citizen's arrest given by the trial judge in *State of New Mexico vs. Reies Tijerina et al.*[56] Clark Knowlton wrote several articles and papers during this period, as well. See the bibliography for these references.

These sources add to both the biographical narrative of Reies López Tijerina and the land recovery movement. None of these works, however, provides a complete biography; there is some information, but not enough. None of these works goes past 1971, when Tijerina was released from prison and began, on April 8, 1972, organizing his Brotherhood Awareness, Peace and Harmony conferences. Conditions of his parole prohibited him from holding office in the Alianza, speaking on land grants, or organizing meetings of any kind regarding the land recovery movement. This is a topic waiting to be researched and written about. There is nothing available on his years in prison and countless court cases or his role in the Poor People's Campaign in 1968 in Washington, DC, except for one source. Gordon Mantler made limited mention of Tijerina's role in this event, as the Chicano representative within the ad hoc leadership hierarchy after Dr. King's assassination.[57] This work is among recent publications not specifically on Tijerina that include his contributions to the subject matter of the book. Most typically, a reference to Tijerina is found in history books dealing with the Chicano Movement, the Southwest, civil rights of Mexican Americans, and civil disobedience, as for example, in John R. Chavez's *The Lost Land*.[58] It was not until 2005 that a thoughtful work, by Rudy V. Busto, was published with a focus on the religious side of Tijerina. He analyzed the impact religion had on Tijerina's worldview and his activism. More importantly, he was researching and writing many years after the attempted citizen's arrest at the Tierra Amarilla Courthouse and Tijerina's prison years. Tijerina's autobiography had long been published as well. The secondary literature was history in and of itself; Busto brought a fresh perspective. His book took a unique look at Tijerina and his contributions to Chicano civil rights history. Busto in *King Tiger* tackled head-on the alleged anti-Semitism attributed to Tijerina and made comparative observations on topics covered by some

of the secondary sources. Little is added in terms of biographical information previously not made public. David Correia first used FBI documents to
produce an article on Tijerina. It focused on the patterns of state-sponsored
and state-tolerated violence directed at Tijerina, his family, and the Alianza
membership.[59]

The most recent example of new material on Tijerina and the Chicano
Movement is the work by Maceo Martinez, son of noted artist and Chicano
activist Malaquias Montoya, in *Chicano Movement for Beginners.*[60] Done in the
fashion of Mexican political cartoonist and illustrator Eduardo del Rio, aka
Rius, this book contains lots of illustrations by the author and mentions the
Four Horsemen, of course, including Tijerina. Ramón Gutiérrez has pub-
lished a chapter, "The Religious Origins of Reies López Tijerina's Land Grant
Activism in the Southwest," in *A New Insurgency: The Port Huron Statement in
Its Time,* edited by Howard Brick and Gregory Parker.[61]

In June 2017, a spate of newspapers ran articles to mark the fiftieth
anniversary of the Tierra Amarilla Courthouse incident. The *Santa Fe New
Mexican*'s story in 2017 included a photograph of Patsy Tijerina pregnant
and handcuffed while held in the sheep's pen immediately after the courthouse takeover.[62]

Need to Institutionalize the Study of Chicanos/as

Chicano studies as a discipline began to be programmed after hundreds
of Chicano student walkouts across the nation made that specific demand
part of their grievances against their schooling. They wanted to learn of
their history, culture, and contributions to U.S. society. They also demanded
bilingual education to learn, and in some cases, relearn Spanish so they
could speak with their grandparents. The irony was that all the southwestern states had Spanish as the dominant language following colonization by
the Spanish in the 1500s. Anglo expansionism brought the imposition of
English-only laws, first in the thirteen colonies, then in the west, including the Spanish-speaking lands. Protesting Chicano students in the late
1960s were successful with the passage of the Elementary and Secondary

Education Act of 1968. Title VII of that act became known as the Bilingual Education Act.[63] New Mexico, however, remained the only state with a dual-language constitutional environment; Spanish and English were both official languages.

In April 1969 the few Chicanos/as in academe met and drafted the *Plan de Santa Barbara,* which laid out an implementation plan for Chicano studies programs and departments.[64] California State University at Northridge, under the direction of Rodolfo Acuña, created the first, of what now is the nation's largest, such department.[65] A collective American ignorance should come as no surprise, that millions of Hispanics do not know the Spanish language, their culture, and their contributions made to U.S. history, much less the civil rights struggles of persons of Mexican ancestry. The history of civil rights in the United States historically has been limited to narratives based on the black struggle and more recently that of women and the LGBTQ communities. Chicano studies has moved away from the study of civil rights struggles, institutional racism, and income inequality, against anyone and anything connected to Mexican ancestry. Chicano studies has become in many universities a study of anything but Mexicans (the title to a book by Rodolfo Acuña).[66] The focus by Gen X and millennial scholars is not on ethnic or racial identity but on diversity, meaning sexual dissidence, the new LatinX. This type of diversity, however, is mere window dressing, without any substantive, quantitative incorporation and integration of persons of Mexican or other Latino ancestries at all levels of institutions in our country. Inclusiveness is not just documenting intermarriage rates between our children and those of other racial-ethnic groups, not when the U.S. government, as an example, continues to discriminate against and not hire those of Mexican ancestry, and other Hispanics, decade after decade, across the board in all departments and at all levels. This is true also at the state level. Inclusiveness or diversity is not equity when major foundations continue to discriminate against hiring those of Mexican ancestry, who know and have lived the experience, into top administrative positions. The Ford Foundation, for example, a couple of years ago hired an African American steeped in the civil rights struggles of that group to be its president. For vice president, the new president hired a fellow imported from Argentina to represent Latino interests within the institution. How can he even begin to understand this varied community? There are no significant numbers of program officers in any foundation who lived and know the experience of Mexican-ancestry people. The philanthropic dollars going to our community in the Southwest and major urban centers remain unchanged over the decades. Without voices within, no grant dollars flow out. Without numbers of voices within government, elected or appointed, at any level, no polices, personnel, or budget allocation will occur that protects and promotes our interests.

The subject matter of traditional Chicano studies, however, remains a contested pedagogy in the Southwest, as in Arizona, which banned the discipline and certain books.[67] Texas has repeatedly sought to rewrite the history books to exclude this history, and large numbers of places in the Southwest, where opponents believe it is not needed since this population is the majority, have done the same.[68] In other places around the country, say the Northeast and Midwest, there may be a Latino studies program or department, but, by and large, no such programs exist across the country's institutions of higher learning or community colleges, much less high schools. Ignorance about the struggles of people of Mexican ancestry continues unabated in higher education. And these research and teaching universities and colleges have the audacity to proclaim they are awarding degrees to those who have met the requirements for bachelor's and master's degrees, and even doctorates. These places annually graduate thousands of professionals ready to lead us in the coming decades. "Educated" people, ignorant of our struggles, are being produced in all fields, particularly people with education and humanities degrees.

The history book used in New Mexico public schools in 1986, *A History of New Mexico,* mentions the land grants once as a topic, in one paragraph consisting of eight lines.[69] The paragraph does mention the two types of land grants: to a person and to a group of persons to build a town (communal). A second mention in the book is on Tijerina and the Alianza under the subheading "Northern New Mexicans Have Problems." The authors list three major reasons for the problems: (1) Population loss; (2) "Second, the villagers of northern New Mexico lost land"; (3) "Third, the small farmers and ranchers had problems with the use of the forest land. This land was controlled by the United States Forest Service."[70] Reies López Tijerina is mentioned in the next two paragraphs in that chapter: "A newcomer to New Mexico, Tijerina was a preacher." The Echo Amphitheater takeover in the fall of 1966 is highlighted, as is the courthouse incident in June 1967 and "destroying government property" at a federal park. The conclusion reached by the second and third paragraphs is the following:

> This time the jury found him guilty. Tijerina spent more than two years in a federal prison in El Paso. Tijerina did not bring about the return of any land grants to the villagers of northern New Mexico. He also lost support after the raid on Tierra Amarilla. Still, Tijerina had caught the attention of young Hispanos. He and his followers had voiced the hopes of many New Mexicans.[71]

The review section of this last chapter does have three questions about the northern villagers, a geography review as to where Tierra Amarilla is located, and Tijerina's name to identify among those about whom it is asked, who are they and why are they important?[72]

Current Textbooks

There is an increase in productivity by scholars on topics germane to our history and heritage, but few survey texts, particularly in political science. I dare say the main one over time has been John A. Garcia's *Latino Politics in America: Community, Culture, and Interests*, now in its third edition.[73] The two others are Kim Geron's *Latino Political Power* and Lisa Garcia Bedolla's *Latino Politics*, now in its second edition.[74] In none of Garcia's editions does he mention the Alianza or Reies López Tijerina or the Chicano Movement. He did have several references to César Chávez and a note each for Corky Gonzalez and me in the first edition. Garcia avoids use of the term *Chicano* and opts for *Mexican community* if he makes reference to it at all. He goes to great lengths to explain the concept of pan-ethnicity and focuses on the growing Latinization of the United States, to favor *Latino* over *Hispanic,* as a more inclusive group term.[75] A perusal of the index in the second edition reveals that Gonzalez and I are not mentioned; Chávez is mentioned twice, as is Dolores Huerta.[76] The term *Chicano* is gone, as is *Hispanic,* in favor of *Latino.* Geron, on the other hand, discusses the Alianza and Reies López Tijerina, as well as those excluded by Garcia, in the context of the Chicano Movement.[77] Bedolla, like Geron, does make mention of the Chicano Movement and its male leaders at the forefront. She does explain the role of the Alianza and Reies López Tijerina within that context and credits him with the start of the Chicano Movement.[78] Bedolla also puts an end to the Chicano Movement by explaining that it was male-led, homophobic, and blind to feminism. In this work, gender has prevailed over Chicano cultural nationalism, heterosexism, and white middle-class feminism.[79]

The Unknown Four Horsemen of the Chicano Movement

My last stop as an academic, which ended in June 2015, was at the University of Texas at Arlington. I taught introductory and upper-division courses in Texas and American government, including graduate seminars, in political science for twenty-five years. Each semester I would ask students in all my classes to raise their hands if they knew something about Martin Luther King Jr., Malcolm X, Jesse Jackson, Stokely Carmichael, H. Rap Brown, Rosa Parks, Medgar Evers, and other black civil rights activists and leaders. About half of each class would raise their hands but in declining numbers as I kept mentioning names. If I asked about Native American leaders such Dennis Banks, Russell Means, or Leonard Peltier, rarely would I get a hand raised. The same would happen if I asked about Rodolfo "Corky" Gonzalez or Reies López Tijerina.[80] Nothing but blank stares. The only hands that would go up were in response to the name of César Chávez, and often they were thinking of the Mexican boxers, father and son, and not the leader of the United Farm Workers. They certainly did not know of my own activist history. By the end of the semester they did know something about the movement, because I infused Chicano studies content into every class. They also knew about

Reies López Tijerina, the Alianza, the Treaty of Guadalupe Hidalgo and the prior one in Texas, the Treaty of Velasco, and the land recovery movement.

Spanish Kings, Land Grants, and Treaties

Centuries ago, when monarchs ruled the lands in Europe and other regions, the king, queen, prince, or combinations of these titular heads of an area owned all property above and below the ground, including people, in some kingdoms. In Spain, kings gave land grants to people in exchange for establishing colonies in the New World, that is, Spanish America (which included all of North America as far north as Alaska, Central America and the Caribbean, South America, and into the Pacific, to include the Philippines). These kings awarding land grants were Ferdinand V in 1513, Charles V in 1523 and 1525, and Phillip II in 1596. Later the power to grant land titles shifted to overseers for the king closer to the actual location: "The royal *cedula* of 1684, which appointed Jironza Petris de Cruzate governor of New Mexico ... empowered the governor to make land grants."[81]

The public in the United States and Mexico does not know much, if anything, about land grants, the Treaty of Tordesillas, the Treaty of Velasco, the Treaty of Guadalupe Hidalgo, or the Gadsden Purchase. By the late 1950s and 1960s, they were historically far removed from present times. To be sure, Chicano students probably had not heard anything about these things in school because they, like Reies López Tijerina or César Chávez, probably had not finished the elementary grades. In the 1960s, when Reies López Tijerina made mention of the law of the land or specifically the Treaty of Guadalupe Hidalgo and the land grants, he was educating his audience. He almost memorized the entire six-volume set of the *Recopilación de las leyes de los reinos de las Indias,* first issued by Spanish king Don Felipe III on April 26, 1618 (hereafter *Las leyes de las Indias*). These Spanish laws were instructions on how to govern Spanish America (both continents as we know them today). There were two types of land grants: to persons for their livelihood and to groups of persons to form towns, *pueblos.* These communal lands were held in common by all inhabitants and their descendants in perpetuity without an owner other than the pueblo, the town or community. It could never be sold, traded, bartered, exchanged, or given to anyone. Moreover, in both the U.S. Constitution and New Mexico's, there are specific guarantees that those rights not addressed in these two documents remained inviolate in the hands of the people: Article 9 in the U.S. document and Article 2, Section 23 in New Mexico's. Both constitutions, as well as Supreme Court decisions prior to the Treaty of Guadalupe Hidalgo, also preserve the sanctity of private property: Amendments 5, 6, and later 14 in the U.S. document and in New Mexico's Article 2, Sections 4, 5, and 18, and Article 22, Section 4 (specifically applied to land grants in existence while New Mexico was a territory). The Alianza booklet *The Spanish Land Grant Question Examined* explained these constitutional articles, U.S. and New Mexico laws, and the *Leyes de las Indias*. In this booklet, there is also a quote, without citation, from the U.S. surveyor general dated July 15, 1859 (William Pelham at that time) clearly stating that he and all others knew someone other than the U.S. victors owned the land, individually and collectively, prior to February 2, 1848:

> The instructions of this office provide that the existence of a town when the United States took possession of the country being proven, is to be taken as prima facie evidence of a grant to said town; . . . and was recognized as a town by the Mexican Government, it is believed to be a good and valid grant, and the land claimed severed from the public domain.[82]

Officials knew of common land grants for building of towns, but acted otherwise, against the land claimants in their surveying and authentication procedures.

The *Leyes de las Indias*, Law 8, Title 8, Book 4, further mandated that towns or pueblos such as Albuquerque, Santa Fe, and Socorro could not be "incorporated as a town or city" by the territory or state of New Mexico, because they already existed. These already had their own local governments.[83] Tijerina when he confronted federal and state authorities quoted this legal fact, insisting that the heirs to land grants, Alianza members, were the government, not the ones elected by New Mexican voters. The land grant towns were free city-states according to the *Leyes de las Indias*.

Tijerina had learned these topics from self-teaching, by inspecting historical records in Spain and Mexico, and through oral histories recounted to him by elders in New Mexico. A Tijerina speech was captivating, not only in his dramatic and energetic delivery but also because the audiences liked what they heard; it was part of their history and legacy. It was about the laws that favored their claims to lost lands.

The Law of the Land

The U.S. Constitution, Article 6, Section 2, reads as follows:

> This Constitution, and the laws of the United States which shall be made in pursuance thereof; and all treaties made, or which shall be made, under the authority of the United States, shall be the supreme law of the land; and the judges in every state shall be bound thereby, anything in the Constitution or laws of any State to the contrary notwithstanding.

Section 3 states,

> The Senators and Representative before mentioned, and the members of the several state legislatures, and all executive and judicial officers, both of the United States and of the several states, shall be bound by oath or affirmation, to support this Constitution, but no religious test shall ever be required as a qualification to any office or public trust under the United States.

In my classes, particularly introductory courses on Texas and U.S. government and politics, after covering the topic by reading Article 6, I usually would follow up with a question or two in exams on what constituted the law of the land in the United States and the state of Texas. Too many of my students would not answer correctly; they remained locked in their mindset that the law of the land could only be those laws passed by Congress.

Never could it be "all treaties made, or which shall be made." In being wrong, they were correct, because the Treaty of Guadalupe Hidalgo has never been made the law of the land, particularly in regard to land grant rights. I was the one who was wrong, because I lived in the hypothetical academic world of theory as it should be.

What Treaty? What Law of the Land? What Land Grant?

Ignorance about people of Mexican ancestry is not limited to the United States. There are millions of ignorant people in Mexico as well. The United States as we know it today was Spanish America, from Valdez, Alaska, to San Miguel de Guadalupe (Jamestown), to San Agustin, Florida, to Santa Fe, New Mexico, and into California—all of it was once under the sovereignty of the Spanish Crown.[84] In fact, these Spanish explorers mapped most of the country and named hundreds of thousands of places: rivers, mountains, valleys, territories, settlements, harbors and bays, and cities. Beginning in 1820, after independence from Spain, several countries, including Mexico, deliberately eliminated the Spanish contributions in the Americas from Spanish-language books used in the public schools. Being Spanish was a bad identifier in Mexico for decades. Similar ignorance about Mexican history and political books is displayed regarding the huge land loss, on three occasions, to the United States—Texas (1835), and then the Southwest (1846), and then the final piece of land in La Mesilla (Gadsden Purchase, 1853). The land theft and subsequent loss of homeland was seldom mentioned, if at all, in Mexican schoolbooks, including the *Mexican Encyclopedia,* until 1976.[85] All land transfers from the Mexican sovereign to the Republic of Texas and, later, the United States sovereign, occurred based on treaties ending formal violence. The Treaty of Velasco covered Texas. The Treaty of Guadalupe Hidalgo covered the Southwest. Gadsden was a real estate deal for southern Arizona (Tucson). And, more importantly, the treaties entered into by the United States, together with the laws passed by Congress and the decisions of the Supreme Court, supposedly are the law of the land.

| The Treaty of Guadalupe Hidalgo

U.S. designs on Texas are documented as early as 1827, when President John Quincy Adams relayed via Ambassador Joel Poinsett a $1 million offer for the state, with the Rio Grande as the southern border. Refused but not undaunted, President Adams upped the price to $5 million and again was rebuffed. After Texans rebelled and established their nation, President Tyler offered Mexico $5 million for New Mexico. If Mexico ceded all lands to the Pacific, the United States would pay $25 million. A last alternative was to offer $20 million for all Mexican lands up to San Francisco Bay. The Rio Grande was a necessary acquisition for U.S. interests, as had been the acquisition of the Mississippi River as part of the Louisiana Purchase. The Mississippi connected the United States north to south; the Rio Grande allowed access from the Gulf of Mexico to El Paso, half way to what was to become part of the United States, California.

President Polk, successor to Tyler, then pushed for military occupation of "no man's land," the space between the Nueces River, which cuts across South Texas from Brackettville near Del Rio to empty into the Gulf at Corpus Christi, and the Rio Grande, from down by Brownsville to El Paso. The Rio Grande runs up from El Paso into New Mexico, almost into Colorado.[86]

The U.S.-provoked war with Mexico resulted, after two years of battles, from 1846 to 1848, in a huge land gain for the United States, the Southwest states we now call Utah, Nevada, California, Arizona, Colorado, New Mexico, and the "no man's land" in Texas. For Mexico, this loss of land doomed the nation forever to an asymmetrical relationship with the United States. Mexico not only abandoned people in the other Mexico but forfeited riches that could have enabled it to become an equal to the United States in modernization. Mexico gave up partial control of the Rio Grande and, north of that boundary, trillions of dollars in future wealth of land, new minerals, oil and gas deposits, timber, harbors and bays, and the gold, silver, lead, copper, and iron ore already being mined in the Southwest. As a result of this loss, Mexico remained an underdeveloped nation and the U.S. Southwest an underdeveloped region.

The treaty to end hostilities and official violence was negotiated from two adjacent towns, Guadalupe (the U.S. base) and Hidalgo (the Mexican base), hence the name: Treaty of Guadalupe-Hidalgo. It contained twenty-three articles in the original document signed by Nicholas Trist for the United States and the Mexican representatives. The U.S. Senate struck Article 10 in its entirety:

> All grants of land made by the Mexican Government or by the compe-tent authorities, in territories previously appertaining to Mexico, and remaining for the future within the limits of the United States, shall be respected as valid, to the same extent that the same grants would be valid if the said territories had remained within the limits of Mexico. But the grantees of lands in Texas, put in possession thereof, who, by reason of the circumstances of the country since the beginning of the troubles between Texas and the Mexican Government, may have been prevented from fulfilling all the conditions of their grants, shall be under the ob-ligation to fulfill the said conditions within the periods limited in the same respectively; such periods to be now counted from the date of the exchange of ratification of this treaty, in default of which the said grants shall not be obligatory upon the State of Texas in virtue of the stipula-tions contain in this Article.
>
> The foregoing stipulation in regard to grantees of land in Texas, is extended to all grantees of land in the territories aforesaid, elsewhere than in Texas, put in possession under such grants, and in default of the fulfill-ment of the conditions of any such grant, within the new period, which, as is above stipulated begins with the day of the exchange of ratifications of this treaty, the same shall be null and void.[87]

Article 10 clearly stated Mexican land grants were to be respected as valid. And Texas land grants would be reviewed to see if they had met the obligations imposed by Texas. The furor over this unilateral and arbitrary action by the United States in removing a negotiated and most vital Article 10 led to the signing of an additional document, the Protocol of Queretaro. This new agreement stipulated in its second article that the United States did not seek to annul the land grants. All grants with legitimate titles in

California and New Mexico up to May 13, 1846, and in Texas up to March 2, 1836, would be acknowledged.[88] But the protocol is not a treaty, nor a ratified amendment to the actual treaty. At best, it was a gentleman's agreement.

The modification of Article 9 in the original Treaty of Guadalupe Hidalgo consisted of substituting it with Article 3 from the Louisiana Purchase Agreement.[89]

The Gadsden Purchase

The boundaries delineated and set between the United States and Mexico while negotiating the Treaty of Guadalupe Hidalgo were found to be wrong by a few miles. The area from Gila Bend and Tucson to San Diego, California—*La Mesilla* to Mexicans—was omitted. Some communities south of El Paso—Isleta, Socorro, San Elizario, for example—were Mexican lands, but the United States had occupied them, given that the course of the Rio Grande had changed as it would again do with the Chamizal exchange of land from the United States back to Mexico in the late 1960s.[90]

Article 11 of the Guadalupe Hidalgo treaty obligated the United States to prevent Indian raids into Mexico from the U.S. side of the border. In 1848 more than 160,000 Indians lived in the border region; among them the fierce Comanches and Apaches, who had a history of raiding Mexican communities. From the signing of the treaty in 1848 until 1852, the military defense of the border cost the United States about $12 million. To be released from the obligations of Article 11, the United States offered Mexico $10 million for this piece of land, 29,142,000 acres. The U.S. argument was that the land was needed for a rail line from El Paso to Southern California. Earlier the United States had tried to buy rights of transit on land across southernmost Mexico, the Isthmus of Tehuantepec, for a rail line to connect the Gulf with the Pacific, without success. The United States not only stood to gain a rail line and reduced military costs if it exterminated the Indians in the area, which it ultimately did, but also the rich mineral deposits and mining already underway in that area. The deal was cut, the money paid, and the real estate deal consumed with a covenant running with the land, the *Tratado de Guadalupe Hidalgo* in Spanish with Article 10 and without any changes to Article 8.[91]

The following year, 1854, on July 22, Congress created the Office of the Surveyor General in New Mexico.[92]

Subsequent Interpretation by SCOTUS of the Treaty

Del Castillo wrote, "Since its ratification more than two hundred federal, state and district court decisions have interpreted the treaty, expanding and changing the meaning of the original treaty."[93] He found that in the two hundred or so cases decided by the Supreme Court of the United States, the Court tended to favor government, local and federal, over the land grant-ees. And he found similar favoritism for corporations. In *Botiller v. Dominguez*, 130 U.S. 238 (1889) the "Supreme Court held that the sovereign laws of the United States took precedence over international treaties."[94] Congress had to validate the claims, not the courts. This argument also was used to protect the owners of the Maxwell land grant who had bought parts of the grant dating to 1841. Spain first claimed this land in 1524. The original grant made by Mexico through the governor of New Mexico, Manuel Armijo, was to Narciso Beaubien and Stephen Luis Lee and covered 1,714,765 acres of lands occupied by Jicarilla Apaches and Ute Indians in Colfax County, New Mexico, with parts extending into Colorado.[95] This same creative interpretation was first used in denying claims in California. Christine A. Klein believes "approximately twenty-seven percent of land grant claims were rejected" by the California courts.[96] She also noted that SCOTUS and the California courts viewed the Treaty of Guadalupe Hidalgo as not "self-executing"; this is to say that property rights were not validated by the document—they had to be validated by Congress. Moreover, the Californio claimants only had until March 3, 1851, to file for judicial examination of their land grant or be forever barred. The legislation approving such claims would become the law of the land, not the Treaty of Guadalupe Hidalgo. The origin of this constitutional novelty stemmed from *Foster v. Neilson*, 27 U.S. (2 Pet.) 253 (1829), which had the effect of denying claims by Spanish land grantees in Florida after it was incorporated into the United States by the Adams-Onis Treaty in 1804. A subsequent case, *Tameling v. United States Freehold and Emigration Company,* 93 U.S. 644 (1877), involving the Sangre de Cristo land grant in the Territory of New Mexico, held two important rulings against land grant claimants. First, "Congress acted upon the claim 'as recommended for confirmation by the surveyor-general.'" Second, the two petitioners in the case only proved title

> to not more than eleven square leagues for each petitioner ... [As] the land within the boundaries in question is largely in excess of that quantity, the invalidity of the grant has been earnestly and elaborately pressed upon our attention. This was matter for the consideration of Congress; and we deem ourselves concluded by the action of that body.[97]

The Supreme Court knowingly failed to distinguish between private grants of land to individuals by the king of Spain and government of Mexico and community grants to groups of people, as in this case. Community grants were held in the names of individuals, one, two, or three persons, for example, but they held the grant for the group. It was not to be sold by them as if they held individual title. They were mere trustees of the communal land grant. By not distinguishing the types of grants being examined, the surveyor general and the courts could easily strip away from communal lands all the acreage they wanted if no document could be produced specifically naming these persons as trustees and the specific land described by metes and bounds as required by Anglo-Saxon law. In many instances, the only copy of a land grant would be given to the surveyor general or lawyers, never to be returned. In other instances, the land grant document had deteriorated beyond repair and recognition or had been lost, misplaced, destroyed, and damaged. These documents were written in ink on parchment, with a wax seal, in some cases three hundred years earlier.

Finally, after several decades of land theft and no legal recourse available to claimants in the forty-three years since the Treaty of Guadalupe Hidalgo was signed, Congress created the Court of Private Land Claims, on

March 3, 1891.[98] This court was given jurisdiction claims coming from the territories of New Mexico, Arizona, Utah, Colorado, and Wyoming.

Texas Cases and the Treaty of Guadalupe Hidalgo

The taking of Texas from Mexico was settled by the Treaty of Velasco in 1835, not Guadalupe Hidalgo in 1848. The Velasco Treaty did not set the boundaries for the Republic of Texas correctly. Of importance is that the area between the Nueces River and the Rio Grande became "no man's land" during this period. In two significant cases, Texas land grants were handled differently. In *McKinney v. Saviego*, 59 U.S. 365 (1856) SCOTUS ruled that the Treaty of Guadalupe Hidalgo did not apply to Texas. In *Texas Mexican Rail Road v. Locke*, 74 Tex. 340 (1889) the state supreme court ruled that Article 8 of Guadalupe Hidalgo did apply.[99]

The U.S. Court of Private Land Claims until 1982

Forty-three years after the signing of the Treaty of Guadalupe Hidalgo, the Court of Private Land Claims was established to hear claims against the U.S. government. Prior to this time, any persons seeking compensation from the United States had to file a petition in Congress. The court was comprised of three judges appointed for life. Money judgements issued by the court went to the Department of the Treasury for payment. These judgments were made part of the appropriations of the Treasury. In 1925 Congress added seven commissioners, to be appointed by the Court of Private Claims, to hear evidence and report on findings of fact. The CPLC judges then became a first board of review for claimants dissatisfied with the commissioners' findings; in 1955 the number of commissioners was raised to fifteen and two more judges were added to the court. In 1948, it was renamed the U.S. Court of Claims (67 Stat. 226); and combined in 1978 with the Indian Claims Commission, which was abolished; all pending cases were transferred to the renamed court. In 1982, the name was again changed to the U.S. Court of Federal Claims (96 Stat. 25).

Thomas B. Catron and the Santa Fe Ring

Thomas B. Catron arrived in Las Cruces, New Mexico, on July 27, 1866; his participation in the Confederate Army barred him from completing the study of law in his native Missouri. Nevertheless, by the following year Catron was admitted into the New Mexico bar, was learning Spanish, and was appointed district attorney for the Third Judicial District at La Mesilla, Dona Ana County. He was twenty-seven years of age and a Republican. At age twenty-nine, in 1869, he was appointed attorney general for the state. He moved to Santa Fe and became a member of the legislature.

A fellow lawyer, Stephen B. Elkins, was the ringleader of the Santa Fe Ring, with Catron the heir apparent. Together they founded the First National Bank of Santa Fe in 1871. In 1872, Catron was appointed U.S. attorney, and he married in 1877. About this time his friend and coconspirator in land theft, Elkins, moved back east. Catron was elected mayor of Santa Fe in 1906, holding that office until 1909, then was elected U.S. senator in 1912. By then he was the largest landowner in the United States, having taken interest in thirty-four land grants totaling over three million acres.[100] During the rise of Catron as political boss within the Republican Party, the territorial governor was Miguel A. Otero, from 1897 to 1906, another crony of Elkins and Governor William Pile. David Caffey in his work on the Santa Fe Ring identifies all the core, peripheral, and affiliated members of the criminal enterprise.[101]

Hispanos/Tejanos versus Mexican Labor in the United States

When Reies López Tijerina talked about the land grants in New Mexico, Texas, California, or anywhere for that matter, he was addressing himself to a select audience. Certainly, recent immigrants, resettled braceros, and non-land grant recipients did not identify with this Tijerina cause. They did not know the history of the other Mexico, now occupied by Anglos primarily. New Mexicans paid more attention than other audiences in the Southwest because of two simple facts: the native populations of the state were either Native Americans or descendants of the few Spanish/Mexican land grantees who remained on their lands as best they could after the Treaty of Guadalupe Hidalgo, in the case of the Southwest, and the Treaty of Velasco, in the case of Texas. This was Tijerina's audience. The second fact was that migration into New Mexico since the days of the first forays into these lands by Spanish conquistadors such as Cabeza de Vaca, Francisco Vásquez Coronado, and Juan Oñate, was very limited. Migrants from Mexico found it hard to traverse the great expanse of desert in central and northern Mexico to reach New Mexico. It is best to go to either Texas or California, then across to Arizona, New Mexico, or Colorado. The population of New Mexico remains the smallest of all southwestern states to this day.[102] These audiences for Tijerina were the Hispano people who received land grants; their descendent were the heirs. They still lived there, and many remembered the stories of their elders about how much land they used to own before the Americanos came and took it. They call themselves Spanish Americans, mostly ignoring any Mexican lineage whatsoever. In Spanish they refer to themselves as *Hispanos.* Their counterpart in Texas, with a similar history of their lands being taken, call themselves *Tejanos.* These people are not to be confused with those who follow a genre of music called Tejano. These are heirs to land grants, and in some cases these families, like Hispanos, have managed to hang on to parcels of their original landholdings.

Since before the Mexican Revolution of 1910, Mexican laborers have been crossing into the United States and returning to Mexico after earning a few dollars. The violence of the revolution lasted decades and pushed millions of Mexicans out of Mexico and into the United States; most of them did not return. Again, the bracero program, an alleged emergency war measure during World War II, lasted from 1947 to 1964 and introduced millions more Mexicans into the United States; most of them did not return unless they were caught in the deportation dragnets, launched during the Eisenhower administration, known as Operation Wetback.[103] These newly incorporated Mexicans became the foundation for the Mexican American generation that slowly began to assimilate into U.S. society as they fought against school and community segregation, labor exploitation, poor health and nutrition, little income, no electoral power, and violence.[104]

Remarkably, the Mexican American generation and their progeny, the Chicanos who did not seek assimilation into white society, became enamored with Tijerina and the land recovery movement. John Garcia explains it this way: "To Chicanos the Southwest is more than just their place of residence; it is their homeland, their lost homeland to be more precise, the conquered northern half of the Mexican nation."[105] The Garcia analysis continues into deeper levels of group consciousness both Anglo and Chicano. He states that Anglos are taught and understand the West to have been vacant land, a wasteland only made productive because of settlers who faced and defeated fierce Indians. The expansion of the railroads and accompanying commerce is attributed correctly to the vision of President Lincoln, a plan to connect the United States, much like President Eisenhower did with the interstate highway system: to connect all Anglos, east to west. To Chicanos this is occupied Mexico, or the Other Mexico. "Unlike Mexican nationals, Chicanos see the Southwest more readily than Mexico as their homeland, and consequently picture themselves more readily as a people of that region than Mexico."[106] Garcia closes his introduction to his book with this statement:

> The desire of Southwest Mexicans for recovery of the region has always been tied to their desire for cultural, political, and economic self-determination, a self-determination they believe can only be achieved through control of the space they occupy. The story of struggle for that environment is central to Chicano history.[107]

A Taking without Compensation or Apology

In 1944, Reies López Tijerina began to learn the art of public speaking. He was seventeen or eighteen years old and beginning study at a religious training institution, the Assembly of God Bible Institute in Isleta, near El Paso, under the tutelage of preachers there, the Masters of the Spoken Word. They would probably prefer to be called "Minister" or "Reverend," but that was their title then. Before there were degree programs in speech and communication, technical certificates in radio broadcasting or news reporting, and clubs like Toastmasters, where members practice public speaking presentations to each other, there was organized religion. In our time, the twentieth and twenty-first centuries, organized religious denominations in the United States and worldwide not only issue certificates and degrees in theology but incorporate the art of preaching biblical content. Law schools and doctoral programs today, ironically, do not teach students how to make a jury argument or summation or how to verbally present a lecture. The Assembly of God Bible Institute that Reies and his wife-to-be, Maria Escobar, and his brother Ramon attended did. Reies may have been ordained a Pentecostal minister in 1950, perhaps not. Brother Kensy Savage, superintendent of the Bible school, claimed that he did graduate because later they suspended him and revoked his credentials. One of the reasons for that banishment was that Reies began preaching against tithes to the church. He began to preach that the church was to help the poor, not take from them.[108]

Married by then, he and his wife traveled the United States as itinerant preachers; diplomas, certificates, pieces of paper did not matter. Women were not allowed to be ordained then but Maria Escobar, now Tijerina, was also a graduate of the Bible college. She was as able as he on biblical talking points. They made a formidable team, preaching in two languages. For years, they earned a living for their growing family, almost one child every year, from preaching at tent revival-type services across the United States, from New York to the Midwest across into Colorado, New Mexico, and California and back to Texas to see family. On one of those forays Reies spotted some land in Arizona he wished to own for his base. He acquired it in 1955 and founded his community, El Valle de la Paz (the Valley of Peace). In English, he referred to it as the Kingdom of God. This period is explained in chapter 1.

The Infamous Liberty Bell Can't Ring!

Over the years during which Reies led the land recovery movement he had to morph from Bible-based to land grant-based speeches. He learned to speak on many, many topics but all somehow related to the theft of the lands in the Southwest and his movement to recover those lands, the Alianza Federal de Pueblos Libres. One of my favorite speeches, which I heard several times, was on why the Liberty Bell can't ring.[109] Answer by Tijerina: "Because the United States is a thief and a murderer of peoples, not a protector of freedom, much less liberty."[110] The original cast of the bell had several inscriptions on it, including mention of the "Province of Pensylvania," with one *n,* as it was spelled then. Another was from the Bible: "Leviticus 25:10—Proclaim LIBERTY throughout all the land unto all the inhabitants thereof." This was Tijerina's starting point of his standard speech on the Liberty Bell. First, he would say something in Spanish, to shock the audience and capture their undivided attention, something like the following:

> Those Founding Fathers were liars. They mocked the words in the Bible. White people had slaves. They kept their African slaves. No liberty for slaves. White people killed all the Indians in the colonies and waged war on tribes across the Mississippi until late 1890s. No liberty for the Indians. In fact, the United States, defender of liberty and freedom, did not let Indians vote until 1924. Those Founding Fathers lied. And our homelands? They stole our lands, from Florida across through Texas and the Southwest by 1848. Those Founding Fathers lied. The Liberty Bell refused to honor the words of Leviticus. It was especially made in London for Pennsylvania. It would not ring when they first tried it in 1752. It would not be a party to these lies. They had to fix it time and again. But it will not ring!

Tijerina would continue with more history behind the other cracks that developed. He would start the litany:

> It did not ring for the Fourth of July in 1776.[111] It did not ring in 1824 when they began to take Spanish America; they took Florida and were starting to

steal Texas. It did not ring in 1835 when they tried to honor John Marshall at his funeral. Marshall was the main judge of the U.S. Supreme Court who made the concept of waste the law of the land.[112] Vacant land was wasted land; therefore, anyone who made it productive was the owner. He also used papal bulls to give them the right of discovery since the Indians were savages. It did not ring despite being fixed again in 1846 in honor of George Washington's birthday. Why? Because the United States was invading Mexico without a reason except to steal the Southwest, which they have done. The Liberty Bell will not ring because it knows it cannot stand for these lies.

This speech attacking an American iconic symbol always mesmerized the crowds; they never had heard such things about the Liberty Bell. But the crack, all two feet of it, is there for all to see in Philadelphia.

The Cricket and the Lion

Busto begins his book with another of Tijerina's favorite talks, about the cricket and the lion.[113] He used it as a metaphor to dramatize how the seemingly powerless and weak (the Alianza) could defeat a powerful and physically stronger foe (the government); it is another version of the David and Goliath Bible story. The cricket jumps into the lion's ear and begins its criketty-criketty noise. The lion begins doing himself great harm by clawing on his ear, trying to extricate the bug to no avail. Bloody and hurt, the defeated lion ultimately calls for a truce and acquiesces to the cricket's demands.

Tijerina's Obsession with Numerology

Tijerina was born on September 21, 1926. In numerology this date is converted as $9 + 2 + 1 + 1 + 9 + 2 + 6 = 30$. These digits are then added: $3 + 0 = 3$. He felt he was destined to be a "3," the third voice, as in the Holy Trinity;

a reminder of the three holy cities recognized by Islam—Mecca, Medina, and Jerusalem; a third factor between two warring factions, as in ying and yang; and a third party between heaven and earth, man. Three is a popular number in storytelling: counting to three before beginning a task or a race or a rhythm; Three Wise Men; and, three strikes and you are out![114] He also liked to apply numerology to the June 5, 1967, Tierra Amarilla Courthouse incident and to the Israeli Six-Day War, which began on that same date. Tijerina always mentioned this fact and inferred from it divine intervention and a celestial connection. He never explained to me or others what these connections, other than similar dates, meant. To repeat, he was a strong believer in numerology. Taking one number at a time, 6 + 5 = 11, or 2. Then 2 + 1 = 3 + 9 = 12, or 3. Then 3 + 6 = 9 + 7 =16, and 6 + 1 adds up to 7. In Judaism, Islam, and Buddhism, the number 7 is the most important number, as it is in the Bible's Genesis: creation in seven days; the seventh day is the Sabbath; seven deadly sins; seven virtues; "and the first sentence in Genesis, written in Hebrew ... comprises seven words and 28 letters ... four groups of seven."[115] Perhaps, since he was forever researching Judaism and the politics and relations of the governments of Israel and the United States, the Six-Day War fascinated him, while the outcome of Tierra Amarilla preoccupied his every waking moment while fleeing from capture by the National Guard. When he was not listening to shortwave transmissions between units of the National Guard and state police to avoid capture, he would ask his son David to get the latest on the Arab-Israeli war.

On June 8, 1967, Israeli airplanes and gunboats killed 34 and injured 171 Americans aboard the USS *Liberty*. Tijerina added the 6/8/1967 numbers to come up with 1. He interpreted this to mean that Israel was the number one ally of the United States. The casualty list of Americans killed and those hurt was made up mostly of National Security Agency operatives, not sailors. The *Liberty* was a NSA spy ship. It was in international waters some twenty-five miles north of the Egyptian coast, flying an eight-foot by five-foot U.S. flag, with its name in English brightly painted on the stern. The ship was monitoring electronic transmissions of both sides, Israeli and Arab, in this conflict and sending the intelligence back to CIA headquarters in Langley, which in turn passed it on to the president of the

United States. The CIA quickly exonerated the Israelis, who claimed the NSA ship had been mistaken for an Egyptian steamer, *El Quesir*.[116] After a symbolic protest by the United States to the Israeli government, the matter of Israelis killing Americans was dropped by politicians and media alike. The jubilation in the Western media and United States was centered on celebrating the Israeli defeat of three Arab nations in just six days— hence the Six-Day War. Tijerina was very vocal in opposition to this war because of two major outcomes. First, more U.S. aid to Israel would flow. He was not wrong on this point and often cited the work of Richard H. Curtiss, retired U.S. Foreign Service officer, quoting his *Washington Report on Middle East Affairs*. Curtiss estimated that between 1948, when Israel was carved out of Palestinian lands, to 1998, "the U.S. gave to Israel, with a self-declared population of 5.8 million people, more foreign aid than it gave to all of the countries of sub-Saharan Africa, all of the countries of Latin America, and all of the countries of the Caribbean combined—with a population of 1,054,000,000 people."[117] Charitable contributions flowing from U.S. sources to Israel add another $1 billion annually.[118] Second, the United States had the Israelis take possession of the West Bank of Palestine. Tijerina viewed the plight of the Palestinians as akin to that of Indohispano claimants in the Southwest. Both peoples had their lands taken with the help of the U.S. government. His critics utilized this position to brand him as anti-Semitic.

The FBI File and His Writings

Sometime in 1986 I returned from my own political exile in Oregon and stopped in New Mexico to visit Tijerina. We talked about translating his autobiography into English and the FBI files he had in his possession. I asked him for a copy which he readily agreed I should have to help me write "his story." We spent hours at a Kinko's in Albuquerque making copies and labeling folders. I am now just getting around to writing this story after carrying his file around the country during my relocations. I did edit and translate and got his autobiography published in 2000.

In 1994, Tijerina exiled himself to Uruapan, Michoacán, Mexico, and would return to New Mexico, particularly in June, to collect rents due on his lands. I would meet him in Albuquerque when I could and drive him around the state on these occasions. We would talk politics and current events, among other topics.[119] During one of these visits, on August 20, 1994, he gave me power of attorney to translate into English and publish his book, *Mi lucha por la tierra.* He also gave me a handful of sheets containing his ideas on Jews and Israel. He promised to send me copy of a typewritten manuscript in English when he finished it. He said the working title was *My Life, Judaism, and the Nuclear Age.*[120] After I had the manuscript in my possession, I did circulate that fact to some publishers I knew. I wrote a few letters of inquiry to other publishers. I was unable to get anyone interested in publishing his manuscript and, stopped trying by the time I finished work on his translation.

On *Mi Lucha* and Jewry

The draft pages Tijerina handed me on his views about Jews and the impending nuclear holocaust were thirteen typed pages in English, from his manuscript in the works. The thirteen pages were dated from December 20 to December 31, 1986.[121] His basic view was that the Jews were the first in developing the technology for the ultimate and only necessary weapon of mass destruction, the atomic bomb. Those countries, primarily Israel in the Middle East, with nuclear weaponry and delivery capability would ultimately use it against anyone else with nuclear weaponry in the world. If such a holocaust were to occur, it would be among industrialized nations located in the northern half of the globe. The gravitational pull would force the nuclear fallout toward the North Pole and away from the equatorial and southern cone nations. He urged those who would listen to consider moving further south. He was convinced that the Jews of Israel would be behind this nuclear confrontation given their belief in the Samson Option, destruction of all, even themselves. After 1991, Tijerina was more convinced of his theories by the Seymour M. Hersh publication *The Samson Option.*[122]

This book revealed how the United States allowed Israel to develop its nuclear capability while lecturing the world about nonproliferation of such weapons, and how the Israeli government captured and silenced the whistleblower Mordecai Vanunu with solitary confinement. Vanunu exposed the existence and extent of the nuclear program and arsenal in Israel that was and is helped along with foreign and military aid from the United States. The U.S. taxpayer contributes from $2 to $3 billion each year to Israel in various forms of assistance. From 2009 to 2011, U.S. taxpayers paid more for Israel's defense than did Israeli taxpayers.[123]

I deposited those pages on Jewry, along with the entire manuscript he gave to me later, at the Benson Latin American Collection at the University of Texas at Austin library. These resembled the pages of his autobiography in the latter chapters, especially. *Mi lucha por la tierra* is composed of nine parts; a *prologo* followed by seven *capitulos,* or chapters; each chapter was given a year as the title, except for chapter 2, "Mi vida de fugitivo," and the last one, "La CIA." The longest chapter in *Mi lucha* is the second, which runs for 207 pages, a book itself. Each subsequent chapter gets shorter in length; and in these Tijerina begins to make entries by date, as if he were keeping a diary. By chapter 7, "Año de 1976," his daily entries also begin to be fewer and scanty.

Effective Language

Reies, when he asked me to translate his autobiography, had finally reached the conclusion that communicating effectively with those he was trying to reach was best done in English. His book sales in Mexico were low, and practically nonexistent in the United States. Few of us in the United States knew in the 1980s how to read, write, or speak correct Spanish.[124] To this day, his book remains unreviewed by any journal, including those featuring Chicano content.[125] I have not heard from a single Chicano or Chicana that they have read Tijerina's book in Spanish. Few in Mexico are interested in Chicano history or civil rights or even the history of the other Mexico, the land and its peoples disjoined from Mexico proper after 1846. Tijerina found that out when he traveled into Mexico in pursuit of information on land grants and the Treaty of Guadalupe Hidalgo. The educated class and those among them holding public office did not know this history, nor were they interested. The working poor who held no power or position in government or institutions did not know it either, but they were interested in learning more about this era. These revelations are noted in his book.

He and I argued many times over his insistence on speaking to English-language audiences in Spanish and not English. He turned down movie offers because they were going to be in English. His forever argument was how badly he was portrayed in the documentary "The Most Hated Man in New Mexico"; why give his story to those who would not tell it as he wanted?[126] He also disapproved of the work done by those who wrote books about him because "they got it wrong, *no saben Español.*" I assume he meant the content was somewhat accurate but the nuance they gave the accounts in English was off. "Samuel Stewart from McGraw Hill" offered him a book contract. "I did not want to write my story in English. I wanted to write my memoirs in Spanish."[127] Doubleday offered to publish his memoirs in 1975, but he declined. "English is not the language of my heart, and I cannot express myself as spontaneously and sincerely as I can in Castilian."[128] He did write news columns in the early 1960s for a local Albuquerque newspaper in English, the *New Mexico Chieftain.* The point is that Reies López Tijerina did not help himself by speaking or writing primarily in Spanish to audiences for whom English would have been more effective at communicating and educating.

In 1970, we both attended the Hispanic Summit meeting called by members of the Congressional Hispanic Caucus. Tijerina had not been invited, only César Chávez and myself of the grassroots leaders. I offered to pay his way.[129] We flew into Washington, DC, and arrived at the conference together. I was introduced first and gave my talk in English. He spoke next and gave his talk in Spanish. The media types left the room within the first two to three minutes of his talk. A handful of them grabbed someone to translate for them because Tijerina was animated while giving his presentations; he was entertaining to watch. He not only was forceful in delivery but also engaging in his tone and inflection; non-Spanish speakers got that from him time and again within seconds of his first words, but they did not understand what he was saying. The message was lost in the delivery. And he did not change his mind on this point to the day he died. As Juan Valdez, a core Alianza member, would say, "He never liked anyone saying anything about what he was saying."[130]

New Mexico during Tijerina's Activism

It took decades after the Civil War for New Mexico's efforts to obtain statehood to bear fruit. Congress was not about to admit a state into the Union comprised of Indians and Hispanos. New Mexicans petitioned Congress for statehood several times. When the Anglo population reached 50 percent of the whole, Congress allowed it to become the forty-seventh state, on January 6, 1912. A year prior, on January 21, 1911, the state constitution was ratified by a three-to-one majority of voters; and approved by Congress after statehood. Article 5 of the New Mexico Constitution is important to this book because it states that the rights protected by the Treaty of Guadalupe Hidalgo will be preserved by the New Mexico government.[131] The state is divided into thirty-two counties governed by a Board of County Commissioners that exercise both administrative and legislative powers.[132] There is a sheriff elected in each county, but district attorneys are elected in thirteen judicial districts in which counties are grouped. District judges are elected from these same thirteen districts; however, during Tijerina's era New Mexico had thirty-nine district judges serving these districts.[133]

Military bases were established in New Mexico along with defense-related industries and the Los Alamos Laboratory to develop the atomic bomb between World Wars I and II. The population of New Mexico was about 681,187 in 1950 and grew to 1,016,000 by 1970. By 1980 the population was estimated to reach 1,220,000.[134] These were the decades of Tijerina's activism in the state. Jobs were plentiful. Bernalillo County, home to Albuquerque, the main city and only metropolitan area in the state, went from 35,000 people in 1940 to 400,000 by 1980; almost doubling its population every decade.

The southern and eastern parts of the state are like Texas—Protestant, rural, conservative, and Anglo. The northern part of the state is still predominantly Hispano, Catholic, rural, and Native American. Half of the land in the state is held by the federal government and the state, and New Mexico is the fifth largest in land area among the fifty states.[135] Another major demographic and economic development based on my personal observation is the migration of wealthy persons, many of whom are Jewish, from the eastern seaboard into Santa Fe and Taos. Their purchases of real estate have displaced Hispanos who cannot afford their ancestral homes dating several generations back, due to increased appraised values and therefore higher taxes. The Hispano working class is found in mobile home parks and makeshift housing outside the city limits of these two communities, from where they commute to work.

Organization of the Book and the FBI Files

In addition to this introduction, which frames the person targeted by the FBI, the first chapter describes his first run-ins with the law resulting in his becoming a fugitive. Chapter 2 is his view and interpretation of the Fifth Amendment's Takings Clause. There are eight more. Chapters 3 and 4, utilizing FBI documents, detail the extent of the federal surveillance, including events at the Echo Amphitheater and attempt at a citizen's arrest at Tierra Amarilla. Chapter 5 is about the Poor People's Campaign, while chapter 6 is devoted to the main source of information at Tijerina's trial, undercover agent Tim Chapa; it corroborates many of Tijerina's allegations of violence directed at him by local, state, and federal police. Chapter 7 traces the many courtroom dramas Tijerina and others faced and chapter 8, his prison years. The last chapter is about his exile to Mexico and his life out of the limelight, free of constant surveillance and harassment while in self-imposed exile; and his return to the United States, as he lived in squalor in El Paso, Texas, until his death.

Purposely left out is a chapter on the corruption of the FBI under J. Edgar Hoover and its illegal activities in stifling dissent and protest, disrupting and destroying leaders and organizations in the United States, particularly among minorities. I have omitted that material for two reasons: much literature exists on that subject, and I covered some of it in my previous book, on César Chávez.[136] Another effective way to stifle dissent by government is to hear the arguments made by the dissenters and do nothing about those issues afterward—just promise to do so. This was the case of the White House Cabinet Committee Hearings on Mexican American Affairs held in El Paso in October 1967. Vicente Ximenes, originally from Floresville, Texas, but a resident of New Mexico during his professional life, was appointed by President Johnson to head up a new Cabinet-level committee on Mexican American affairs and organize hearings to listen to problems of the Spanish-speaking. When Ximenes was being appointed, Tijerina was attempting his citizen arrest of DA Sanchez in Tierra Amarilla. When Ximenes sent out invitations to attend and present concerns and proposals at the hearings, Tijerina, among many others, felt excluded at not being invited. He promised to organize a caravan of protesters and disrupt the El Paso hearings. He never did. Ximenes's biographer, Michelle Hall Kells, writes that a purpose of her work is to address the fact that in the halls of academe no one knows of Reies López Tijerina, Vicente Ximenes, or the White House El Paso hearings.[137] Her work and mine may help document more of Chicano/a history and our struggle "for the land and our rights," as Tijerina phrased it in the title of his autobiography.

CHAPTER 1

The Years as a Fugitive

Reies López Tijerina's relationship with federal authorities, the U.S. Forest Service and the Federal Bureau of Investigation (FBI), began in 1956 at the Valley of Peace commune near Eloy and Casa Grande, Arizona, some fifty miles south of Phoenix.[1]

> One day a jet, a war plane, crashed on our property. The explosion scared us. We reported it, and they came to remove the remains of the airplane, but they did not ask about any damages or harm suffered by our inhabitants of the Valley of Peace.[2]

His next encounter with government officials was with the local school board and sheriff. Tijerina and his followers did not want their children to attend the local public schools in Eloy or Casa Grande. They wanted their own private, home-schooling program at their site. Some school board members and representatives persisted and came to the Valley of Peace to see who these odd people were. Tijerina and his male followers sported long

beards and sometimes robes instead of pants when not outside the commune working for wages.

At that time, an unfortunate event occurred for a victim and her family; a young girl was kidnapped by a local Anglo. On her way to school, she
had walked some three miles across deserted land to reach a bus stop and
waited for the bus by the roadside. She was kidnapped, beaten, and raped.
The ugly news was front-page material for weeks until the perpetrator was
found, charged, and jailed. Given this scenario, the school board allowed
Tijerina to set up a private school at the Valley of Peace.[3] The commune
members built a small, one-room school; later vandals burned it down.
The commune also erected a small church and storage facility.[4] Then the
inhabitants of the Valley of Peace had firsthand experience with juvenile
delinquents.

> One day, a group of young Anglos on horseback, between fifteen and six-
> teen years of age, came by. Without talking to us, they rode their horses
> over our subterranean homes. . . . They ran their horses over one house
> after another with pistols in their hands. . . . The first time they did this,
> we ignored them.

Ignoring them did not work; it seemed to encourage them. They came
back for more destruction, vandalism, and arson.

> One day we came from working, picking cotton, and we found two of our
> homes without roof tops. Some of our brave ones had made homes with
> wood and palm leaves. We had found two burned to the ground with all
> their belongings. Manuel [Mata], Rodolfo [Marez] and I went to report it to
> Sheriff Lawrence White. He listened to us and, at the beginning, indicated
> an interest in sending two of his agents out, but when we told him the
> markings on the horses that had been bothering us and told him from
> which ranch they came—we had followed them—Sheriff White changed
> his mind. He did not send anyone to investigate. We later related the same
> story to Don Pelkham, an FBI agent in Casa Grande, but he explained that
> that was not his jurisdiction. However, when the airplane, the jet plane

had landed, had crashed on our property, this same agent had visited out colony. But now, he ignored us completely.[5]

Those who visited the Valley of Peace, such as police officers, looked intently not only at the inhabitants and the odd physical appearance of the men with long beards and home-made, long dress styles, and at the subterranean homes in a desert village, but also at what was strewn about the land. The tires on a truck at the commune looked new. That seemed strange amid all the obvious poverty of the people and community. The local police authorities returned for another look at those tires on March 18, 1957. Six wheels and tires had been reported stolen off a trailer at a ranch near Toltec, New Mexico. Officers Kinard and Davis with the Pinal County Sheriff's Office at Casa Grande traced two of the tires to a truck registered to Reies López Tijerina. The police arrested Reies, his brother Margarito, and Sevedeo Martinez and charged them with grand theft. They also found five hats, a purchase order book, eleven canteens, three more tires, five axes, and three Coleman lanterns. The sheriff called in the FBI because these items had the inscription "U.S. Forest Service." Margarito was extradited to Indiana for violation of his parole, which restricted him to Texas. Reies and Sevedeo were released because the authorities could not prove they took the tires, though the items were found at the Valley of Peace.[6]

More than two weeks later, the police returned to arrest Reies again for grand theft. The police had searched the area surrounding the commune and found in a dry water well more items belonging to the Forest Service. Reies was not let out until April 5, when he posted a $1,000 bond.[7] During the time Margarito was waiting for extradition, Reies would visit him. Those jail visits put him in contact with many people in distress over the charges against them. One case that cost Reies his liberty and freedom was that of an Anglo jail inmate, his wife, Terry, and their little child. Maria and Reies visited her, taking her some milk and dresses, and brought her and the child into their home. Reies was able to make bail for Terry's husband and got him out of jail.[8] Two days later, on July 7, Reies, along with three others, was arrested again and charged with trying to help Margarito escape from jail. The police had found a map of the Pinal County Jail and hacksaw blades in their possession, and Terry was ready to testify against them. This time the bond for Reies was $5,000.

The next month, Reies presented himself for jury trial on all these charges.[9] His court-appointed attorney told him the local Anglo establishment wanted him out of the picture. The land his commune owned now was worth $1,500 an acre. They had burned his homes and even the schoolhouse so he would fear for their safety and leave. The attorney told him in no uncertain terms that he was going to be found guilty and given a long prison sentence. "Leave while you are still alive," his lawyer told him. Reies walked out the door into the street and hurriedly made it to the Valley of Peace. As best he could, he explained the court scenario and the lawyer's prediction. He quickly packed a few items and left the area. He promised Maria and their five children he would send for them.[10]

An FBI File

The FBI's eight-page report dated May 29, 1957, substantially corroborates the preceding story as related by both Richard Gardner in *Grito!* and Tijerina's autobiography.[11] The report states that Tijerina claimed to have no knowledge of how the items belonging to the Forest Service came to be in the Valley of Peace. As a man of God, he could not steal property from another. Moreover, he explained, he had just returned to the Valley of Peace within the last three days and there were people at the commune he did not even know. Anyone could have brought those items into it. He assured the local police while he was in custody that upon release, he would find out who brought those items there and what these items were. The report states that "Tijerina refused to answer any questions on his organization" (p. 4). He did tell them he was a minister ordained after study at the Assembly of God's Latin American Bible Institute in Ysleta, Texas.[12]

The FBI Albuquerque subsequently sent copies of their report, dated June 12, 1957, to Phoenix and, of course, the director of the FBI in Washington. It covers the activities of the month of May.[13] The gist of the report reads as follows:

On May 31, 1957, the facts of this case were discussed with Assistant U.S. Attorney JAMES A. BORLAND who declined prosecution in favor of local prosecution in Arizona. He authorized that the items recovered marked U.S. Forest Services be returned to that organization.

In my Freedom of Information and Privacy Act (FOI/PA) requests and those made by Reies, none of these referenced files were released. The entire FBI file has not yet been declassified for posting on the FBI website.

What Tijerina Did Not Mention and the Police and FBI Forgot to Ask

Tijerina believed his dreams were God's messages to him.[14] As a minister, he believed that God spoke to his earthly representatives; dreams were one method of communication. He had such a dream while in Visalia, California, where he, Manuel Mata, and Rodolfo Marez had gone a week after the birth of Ira de Ala on April 18, 1956, at the invitation of Cecilia Moreno and her husband, Luis. While there he got a telephone call from Guadalupe Jauregui, a Valley of Peace resident. The bad news was that the community had been flooded entirely; Reies's wife, Maria, and children, David (Hugh), Rosa (Rosita), Daniel, Raquel, and Ira were living under a tree. That night he had a vision. Three men came to take him to an ancient Realm. Once there he met an old man and seven others. The old man gave him a silver key and, gesturing, said, "You shall reign over all of this; and, over you, only me. Let's walk far over that way so you can see this majestic place and the great throne in the center."[15] Reies awoke from that dream or vision and ran to Manuel and Rodolfo, telling them, "Let's go to the Valley of Peace." Of that experience Reies wrote, "From that day on, I began to see things in a different way and to understand things that I did not understand before.... I believed in what I saw and planned on obeying, fulfilling the mission of those three persons who, I considered interplanetary messengers or angels."[16] Regardless of what he believed the mission to be and if the three men were angels or interplanetary messengers, Reies returned to the Valley of Peace. He excitedly explained his new mission to his wife and the wives of the men he was taking with him.

He rounded up Manuel, Rodolfo, Luis, Juan, and Simon in June 1956 and headed to Monero, New Mexico, in Luis Moreno's car.[17]

When they arrived in Monero they stayed with Zebedeo Martinez. When Reies was a newly ordained a minister, he and Maria began preaching in Colorado and New Mexico. Tierra Amarilla was one of the places they had stopped to preach. There they had met Martinez and learned about land grants. Tijerina asked Martinez to tell his group the story of the Tierra Amarilla land grant as he had told it to Tijerina once before. Zebedeo invited others to come relate their stories of land grants in Chama and Ensenada and how they had been stolen. Tijerina's group met again with Cristino Lovato at his home the next day. Lovato told a similar story. Reies was profoundly moved: "I felt in my heart a stab; these ancient humble people had a just and sacred cause. I felt in my body and my soul and my spirit that these people were worthy of justice."[18]

The New Mexico experience with these elders convinced Tijerina he had to find evidence of the validity of land grants in Mexico and learn about the Treaty of Guadalupe Hidalgo. The group returned to the Valley of Peace to gather their families and move to New Mexico in February 1957. Tijerina took his family to stay with brother Ramon in Texas. He visited with his older brothers, Anselmo and Margarito, also in Texas, and told them he would no longer preach religion from the Bible. He was now going to fight for the lands of his people. He then left for Mexico and was gone several months during 1957.

Upon return via Texas he recruited Margarito, newly released from prison, to join him in his new cause, and the three brothers arrived in the Valley of Peace. Margarito had left the family when he was about seventeen years of age and meandered to the Midwest. In an Indiana bar while drinking he beat to death another man flirting with his female companion. His court-appointed attorney recommended he plead guilty to involuntary manslaughter. While in the penitentiary for a decade, he learned how to read and write a little. When paroled, he was restricted to his native state, Texas.[19]

Tijerina may have been truthful in stating he did not know of any stolen items or who was living at Valley of Peace. He had been gone for months at a time almost all of 1955 into early 1956. Still the police or FBI did not ask of their recent whereabouts.

They all had been in New Mexico for some time before returning to the Valley of Peace. That winter season had been bitter and cold. The Tijerina group had to forage from the land, staying in abandoned buildings, and hunting animals for meat. Two of their group were arrested by Forest Rangers for eating deer meat and jailed. All the elders they met during these days related the same story of stolen land. Don Manuel Trujillo of Lumberton was his best teacher on the land grants. Additionally, he introduced Reies to the *Penitentes,* the Brotherhood of Jesus, a secret lay society dating to 1850, when Bishop Lamy, a Frenchman newly appointed by Pope Pius IX, was removing Mexican priests from their parishes.[20] One hundred years later, remnants of those groups in the late 1950s greeted Tijerina and were most eager to find another leader to redress these long trains of abuse by the Catholic Church, its politicos, and Anglo newcomer trespassers.

Life as a Fugitive

Tijerina immediately made plans to leave for New Mexico again with his family and hide at Don Manuel Trujillo's ranch. Don Manuel was not concerned when Reies told him he and his group were fugitives from Arizona and shared their story of abuse and injustice. Don Manuel offered them the use of his land. Don Manuel had a friend, though, a state police officer who, out of respect for Don Manuel, did not inform authorities about Tijerina's presence at the ranch. He told the fugitives that the FBI and local sheriff were on the lookout for them: "In December 1957, police surrounded Don Manuel's ranch. They arrested Manuel [Mata], Rodolfo [Marez], Zebedeo [Martinez], and Jorge Carrillo. None of them pled guilty to ... charges ... [of] having taken milk, sugar, lard, and beans from an abandoned camp."[21] Reies, however, was not captured.

Tijerina fled with his family to Texas and arrived in time to deliver his sixth child, a boy they named Noe. By May 1958, Reies was back in New Mexico, having left his family in Texas. He recruited another brother, Anselmo, to join his cause. At a meeting of the heirs to the Tierra Amarilla land grant had organized, Reies was invited to speak to the group. As Reies was beginning his talk, he was interrupted by the sergeant at arms, who asked him to sit down. Reies refused to heed his instruction, and he hit Reies over the head with his club. Anselmo jumped on the man and beat him with his own club. Hundreds of attendees joined in the melee. Police responded and jailed Anselmo at the Tierra Amarilla Courthouse; Reies managed to flee the scene. After eleven days in jail, Anselmo was allowed to escape by Eulogio Salazar, the jailer. Anselmo made it to the ranch of Pablo Zamora, who then took him to the Trujillo ranch.[22]

Police continued to visit the Trujillo ranch house over the next weeks. Manuel Trujillo, Don Manuel's son, and wife, Alicia, saved Reies once. When the sheriff's deputies entered the ranch home and arrested Manuel and his father, Reies and Efrain Escobar, his brother-in-law, hid in the couple's bedroom with Alicia somewhat undressed. Sheriff Crane did not enter the bedroom. Reies and Efrain sneaked out the back door and fled up the hill to the highest point so as to see roads and anyone approaching. Ultimately, Reies hid for weeks in a cave some two miles from the Trujillo ranch home; he spent his time reading. The police came six more times during his time at the hideout. By July 1958 Reies decided he should hide in Texas and left with Anselmo and Rodolfo. They reunited with Tijerina's family and quickly left San Antonio because he was informed that the FBI had been asking for information on Anselmo. They headed into west Texas, stopping in Plainview to work a bit and stay with a friend. On July 14, local police, a Texas Ranger, and Sheriff deputies surrounded the house where they were staying. David was playing outside, Maria and the other kids were in the back room with Rosita in the bathroom, and Reies and Anselmo were resting on cots in the main room. Hearing the first car arrive by the front door, Reies motioned Anselmo to crawl toward the bathroom. Another police car drove around the back of the house. Startled when her father and Uncle Anselmo opened the bathroom door with a hand motion to keep quiet, Rosita realized that, although she was naked as she bathed, her father and uncle needed to be inside the bathroom to hide.

Maria met the police at the door. She told them Rosita was taking a bath and that Reies and Anselmo had gone to the post office in town. Some police left in that direction, and the car in back was one of them. Reies cut the screen on the bathroom window, and he and Anselmo managed to wiggle out and run into the next-door lot. They encountered a pair of kids changing the oil in their car, who helped them escape by taking them to nearby Lubbock. Later that night Reies and Anselmo went back to Plainview to tell Maria they were going back to New Mexico. They slept between garbage cans behind a church in Plainview. The next day, Maria sent money with a minister's wife so Anselmo and Reies could pay for a bus ticket to Bloomington, New Mexico. They returned to the Trujillo ranch once again and hid in the cave. Later, Maria and the kids arrived. Reies decided to take them to Quanah, Texas, and pick cotton. Again the police came by the house looking for him. He now had a practice of sleeping outside the house they rented in bushes, weeds, or grass. He decided the only place to hide was in Mexico, and he took a train there in late August 1958.[23]

Archives, Documents, Books: Mana from Heaven

Upon arrival, Reies visited an acquaintance he made during his first visit to Mexico City, Santana Vergara and his family. Don Santana offered him a three-bedroom home for his family, encouraging Reies to bring them and leave the United States. Reies could not fathom that notion. He busied himself with acquiring books and searching for records on land grants at the National Archive. He found a treasure in a complete set of the *Recopilación de leyes de los reinos de las Indias,* the basic book on Spanish colonial policy toward the Americas containing 6,400 laws including the full details on the types of landownership being granted to settlers in the new Spanish lands of New Mexico. He learned of the 1,715 land grants made by Spain and Mexico in what now was the United States in Texas, Florida, Arizona, Colorado, Louisiana, Nevada, California, and New Mexico. In New Mexico alone the recorded grants covered a million acres: 12 grants of less than one thousand acres; 35 grants of from fifty to one hundred thousand acres; and, 19 grants of more than one hundred thousand acres. There were individual grants and there were community grants made for groups of people.[24] He also ran across information about another set of books he must find: *Las siete partidas,* four volumes of Spanish law to rule over daily life. He obtained a set almost a decade later during a 1966 trip to Madrid and Seville, Spain.[25]

Armed with these books, a new source of knowledge and power, together with the oral history lessons told him in New Mexico, he was ready to return the United States. But he had no money. His former *Valientes* from Valley of Peace had already agreed to sell the Arizona property, and he could use that money to fulfill his mission. They had bought it for $6 an acre in 1955, and now it was worth much more, but in desperate need he sold it for $35 an acre. Part of those proceeds went to pay the past-due property taxes on the land.[26] The Rockefellers were investing in the area just three miles from the commune.[27]

The historical irony of the location of the Valley of Peace. In the Spanish colonization era, most of the central part of what became the state of Arizona was the Peralta land grant. Shortly after the Civil War began, conflict erupted in Picacho Pass, located north of Tucson. Most residents fled the area. From 1880 to 1883, land-hungry James Addison Reavis took this opportunity to file fraudulent deeds to vast acreage from central Arizona to eastern New Mexico.[28]

Statute of Limitations Runs Out

Reies, while in Mexico City, visited the secretary of foreign relations to seek political asylum. He was denied on the grounds that he was not sought by any police agency in the United States or states of New Mexico or Arizona. Reies did not know then of the statute of limitations that tolled the time a person can be arrested for a crime. His time had run out within four years. His family arrived at Christmastime and brought money; they returned to the United States several months later for the cotton season. Anselmo arrived in Mexico in January, and he had some money. Meanwhile, Reies continued to seek information from lawyers, judges, politicians, academics, and journalists about the law of land grants and the Treaty of Guadalupe

Hidalgo. Anselmo decided to go back to the United States in May and was promptly arrested at the border crossing. He was sent to serve his sentence in New Mexico: two and one-half years for aggravated assault stemming from the *Penitentes* meeting. In September 1959, Reies was ready to go back and did so under a false name at the crossing in Laredo, Texas. Ramon told him where Maria was picking cotton. By mid-September Reies was picking cotton alongside his wife and family in Shamrock, Texas. When their big payday came, Reies packed up and left for Chicago, Illinois, to visit his sister Josefina and brother Margarito.

Elijah Muhammad and the Nation of Islam

By 1959 Margarito had been released from prison in Michigan City, Michigan, and made his way to Chicago to live with his sister Josefina until he could get on his feet again. Josefina called Reies and gave him the good news about Margarito's release from his parole violation sentence. At that moment, Reies decided to go see his siblings; but more importantly, he wanted to meet with Elijah Muhammad, head of the Nation of Islam. He knew of him from media accounts. He wrote, "I admired the strength of this man and his people.... I thought that maybe I could combine the trip to Chicago with an interview of Elijah Mohammad.... I was given an appointment."[29] Just three years prior the FBI had initiated their infamous COINTELPRO operations against black leaders, including Elijah Muhammad.[30]

A major character flaw of Reies López Tijerina, perhaps simply his lack of formal education and of reading informed sources, was how naive he was about U.S. government operations. Reies, to his dying day could not comprehend why the U.S. courts would not follow the Law of the Indies he "discovered" and the sections he pointed out to them that governed the land grants. Why would the courts and public officials not recognize his right to carry out a citizen's arrest? Why did the U.S. government not want to give the lands in their possession back to the rightful heirs? Why did the FBI not want to investigate his allegations of wrongdoing and criminal behavior against him, his family, and his property? He was so convinced of the righteousness of his cause that he was blind to political and economic interests that have made the United States what it is in the world. Because of his questions, the FBI targeted him as an enemy of the state.

Elijah Muhammad was in the same category of enemy of the state, but not in naiveté. For decades, the FBI had placed him and his group under surveillance. Surely Tijerina should have known that his visit to see Muhammad would be monitored by the FBI. He already knew he was under state and federal investigation from the recent experience in Arizona. Regardless, Tijerina sought out Muhammad in Chicago. Tijerina spent a week in dialogue with Muhammad, according to his own writings, at the Chicago headquarters of the Nation of Islam at 4748 Woodlawn. Elijah told him, "This . . . is only from my ear to yours." Having had to wait to see him, Reies was told:

> The reason I made you wait longer than necessary was because I wanted all my assistants to be present. I have asked Allah to guide me in creating unity between the Arabs and Africans and Latin peoples of the Americas. This is the day that we can begin that work. And, I know that if you could not speak for all the Mexicans, you would not be here.

Tijerina explained his efforts to regain the territories unlawfully taken from the land grantees:

> I told him briefly of my struggle for the land, and how the government had stolen our land. The U.S. Supreme Court had stolen the land from us with illegal findings and conclusions of law contrary to all the terms and stipulations of the Treaty of Guadalupe Hidalgo. The day ended very well for me.[31]

Back to New Mexico

Jubilant that he had made an alliance with the Nation of Islam and its leader, Reies returned to the Tierra Amarilla area and found a house in Ensenada. He dug two caves underneath the home to escape if he had to in an emergency. He met Eulogio Salazar, the jailer who had helped Anselmo escape. Reies began to trust Eulogio because he came in full uniform, gun in holster, badge, and often bearing gifts for Reies and his family. The Salazar family was also a land grant heir. Eulogio regularly reported to Reies which FBI agent had come around, who was looking for whom, and other intelligence information valuable to Tijerina. The information was always reliable. Eulogio obtained the information Reies wanted on Anselmo and the visiting days at the prison. Risking all, Reies thought he and Maria should visit him. Reies posed as Pablo de Anda, his brother-in-law, and his wife as Anselmo's sister. It worked. They got to visit for some time.[32]

The Eisenhower Letter

While in Mexico Reies drafted a lengthy memorandum on what rights the land grant claimants had under the Treaty of Guadalupe Hidalgo. When Milton Eisenhower visited Mexico on behalf of his brother, the U.S. president, Dr. Benjamin Laureano Luna did Tijerina the favor of personally delivering the memorandum. Another letter was posted to President Eisenhower on December 12, 1959. This letter contained more than eighty signatures of families, including that of Eulogio Salazar. A response was had in February 1960 from President Eisenhower. "The few lines were cold and without any flavor," according to Reies.[33]

Organizing the Alianza in New Mexico

The Alianza was incorporated in the state of New Mexico on October 8, 1963. The basic purposes stated were to organize all the heirs of land grants covered by the Treaty of Guadalupe Hidalgo. The organizing of the Alianza had begun in the late 1950s with Tijerina's first forays into New Mexico, when he thought of himself as a fugitive. He continued organizing in public during the early 1960s. By 1962 his work had drawn the attention of the district attorney, Alfonso Sanchez, and the state police. Tijerina was joined by his

brother Anselmo when he got out of prison in 1962, and by Cristobal in 1963.
The three of them lived together in an Albuquerque house.[34] Maria Escobar
had left him in 1962 and taken the six children. Their marriage was on the
verge of a divorce. Maria described some of the sources of their conflicts:

> He didn't care about luxuries. All he wanted to do was preach. Preaching,
> reading, fasting. When we were traveling, I had to wash clothes on the
> rocks sometimes, and when the car broke down, we would just leave it
> there. But when the kids were growing up I started to want to settle down,
> and that's when our arguments started. I like to laugh, he does not much.
> He's too fast and nervous. Maybe that is why we didn't make it together,
> because he's so fast, and I'm so slow to think. I married him because I
> believed he was chosen by God for a special purpose. I still do, but now I
> think he was chosen for this cause, for the poor of the earth.[35]

The brothers made their house the first office for the Alianza. The first
meeting of the Alianza was called for February 2, 1963, in Albuquerque and
attended by thirty-four people. Tijerina published the Spanish text of the
Treaty of Guadalupe Hidalgo via mimeographed copies. As Gardner notes,
"It was the first popularly available printing of the Treaty of Guadalupe
Hidalgo in the Southwest and probably in the United States in either Spanish or English. . . . The newspapers still took no notice."[36] By September 21,
1963, Tijerina was ready and called for the first constitutional convention of
the Alianza, held that day in a high school gym: "Representatives of some
50 land grants were there."[37] The Alianza was to hold annual conventions in
Albuquerque for the next eight years.

Alfonso Sanchez Takes Action

In a letter to J. Edgar Hoover dated July 22, 1964, Alfonso Sanchez wrote:

> Would you please forward an FBI kickback with references to the prior
> arrest and conviction record of the above referred to individual, which
> information will be used only for law enforcement purposes.

The above individual is allegedly involved in communist activities and inciting some of the Northern local residents on land grant matters.[38]

On the same day, Sanchez wrote to Sheriff Emilio Naranjo in Española, New Mexico, about Reyes Tijerina, aka King Tiger, aka Reyes Tijerina López:

I understand that the above referred to individual is the person responsible for the recent threatened acts of violence involving the Tierra Amarilla Land Grant. Would you please investigate this matter and other related matters and submit your report to this office, and if you need assistance, please let me know immediately.[39]

Three striking things should be gleaned from these letters. First is the huge seven-year gap in FBI files. Second, Sanchez knew which buttons to push by using the "communist" ploy with Hoover. Third, Sanchez was fishing for information on Tijerina. When did inciting residents on land grant matters become a state or federal crime? Regardless, July 22, 1964, is the beginning of formal, legal animosity between Tijerina and Sanchez.

No sooner had the Alianza been incorporated than Reies and the president of the Abiquiu Corporation, Amarante Serrano, traveled to Washington, DC, to meet with officials of the State, Interior, and Justice Departments to discuss the land grant issue. Richard Gardner captures some quotes from Reies about this discouraging trip in *Grito!* The Interior representative pointedly told them they "should be seeking a money settlement, and to shut up about the grants." At the State Department, "Representatives ... were even less sympathetic than those at Interior." "Tijerina's claims were 'so fantastic that it is difficult to form a defense in reasonable words.'" The only fruitful meeting took place with Attorney General Robert Kennedy. According to Gardner, quoting Tijerina, "Kennedy was apparently receptive and sympathetic during the short interview, but he made no concrete promises, and the meeting was never called to the attention of the Washington press."[40]

Following the DC trip, Tijerina headed to Mexico City, entering Juarez, Chihuahua, and driving to the national capital. His entourage consisted of his fifteen-year old daughter, Rosa, and four members of the Alianza. The purpose of the trip was to organize a car caravan from the United States to Mexico City to publicize the cause of the land grants and seeking to enlist help from the people of Mexico and its president. Tijerina had data on the sixty-six New Mexico land grants that were recognized by the U.S. Congress.[41]

However, he was arrested in a small town some 150 miles south of Juarez for speaking at the city plaza to protest the jailing of some local dissidents. He was released and admonished that foreigners could not interfere with Mexico's internal politics. Moreover, he was a guest on a visitor's permit which would expire thirty days from entry. Undaunted, he continued on the route and was promptly arrested on August 8. He was deported to Tucson and met by his brother Ramon.[42]

The FBI Kickback to DA Sanchez

The FBI responded quickly to DA Sanchez. The FBI Kickback consists of two pages on FBI letterhead and dated July 30, 1964, with the hand-stamped signature of J. Edgar Hoover. One page contains three listings on Tijerina, including March 19, 1957, for grand theft from the "Police Department Casa Grande Arizona." The next listing in the column reads, "Sheriff's Office Florence Arizona Reies Lopez Tijerina #5583-16706 April 5, 1957 grand theft." The final entry reads, "Sheriff's Office Florence Arizona Reis [sic] Lopez #5583 July 7, 1957 aiding a prisoner to escape." The second page has a stamp date of "5-28-59 M L" and "FBI record NUMBER 4 770 096." This is information on Anselmo Tijerina and lists his attempts to join the military: "Army Service Forces Army Anselmo Lopez Tijerina #106-DMM applicant May 28, 1943" and "Naval Recruiting Station San Antonio Texas Anselmo Lopez Tijerina #842-57-21 November 19, 1943." His criminal record has six entries: (1) "Sheriff's Office Port Huron Michigan Amselma Tijernia [sic] #13935-L December 1, 1946 unknown $35 fine or 20 days"; (2) "Police Department Port Huron Michigan Anselmo L. Tijerlina [sic] #4038 December 1, 1946 assault and battery $35 or 20 days"; (3) "Police Department San Antonio Texas Anselmo Tijerinja [sic] #91-D-18 November 14, 1953 drunk"; (4) "Sheriff's Office Tierra Amarilla New Mexico Anselmo Lopez #—May 26, 1958 assault with a deadly weapon." The next entry, number 5, is completely blurred or erased and is not legible. And lastly, (6) "PD Santa Fe NMex Anselmo Lopez Tijerina #12-121 5-5-53 ADW & escape 5-9-59 rel to Del Sheriff & trans to Tierra Amarillo [sic] Jail." Handwritten just below this entry are the words "convicted '54 Escape 2–5 yrs NM SM."

There are eight additional pages of supplementary material that follow in sequence. It is unknown whether they came from the FBI files or the New Mexico State Police files. To be sure, they originated with the arresting local offices. One page on a form used by Pinal County Jail in Arizona signed by Reies Tijerina is for his property in the amount of "$7.91, Vehicle registration, letter." Also listed in "Remarks" are the names of "Sevedeo Martinez, Margarito Tijerina, (Accomplices)." It lists the bond for Tijerina at "$2000.00."[43] The second page is the booking slip "No. 16708," and in handwriting next to these numbers is "5583" for Tijerina on his grand theft charge dated "4-5-57." The fields on the page for physical description have him as "Nat. M/M Age 30 Ht. 5'9" Wt. 145 Eyes BRW Hair BLK Comp. LIGHT Build. SLIM Education. 3rd Occp. MINISTRERY [sic] Date of Birth sept. 21, 1926 Place of Birth FALL CITY, TEXAS Married YES, MARRY [sic] ESCOBAR TIJE-RINA Arrested by KINARD-DAVIS Place CASA GRANDE Present Address 439 East Young Street, San Antonio, Texas Relative name and address Brother-Anselmo Lopez Tijerina, same as above. Scars and Marks Mustache."[44]

There are double-sided pages with copies of photographs taken at the booking of Reies López Tijerina, John Martinez Reina, Laverne Madeline Wasikowski, Norman Teo Wasikowski, Sevedeo Martinez, and Margarito López Tijerina with descriptive information on the back side.[45] And there are two more pages. One mostly in handwriting appears to be a "Visitors Name of Person Sending Letter" log for "Tijerina, Reies" when he was in jail in Florence, Arizona. Among the regular visitors and letters from July 24, 1957, to August 10, 1957, were his wife, "Mary, their California friends the Matas, Manuel, Adrian, and Alice, and Zebedas [sic] Valdez from Lumberton, N. Mex." This log also recorded the vehicle description the persons arrived in with license plate numbers and the addresses on letters.[46] The other is typewritten and is titled "Out of State Contact Men" and has five names typed across the top in columns. First is "Salvador Ramirez El Paso Texas";

handwritten above it is "has no connection," and the name is circled. Then comes "Anselmo Tijerina, San Antonio, Texas Mexico City John La Comb San Luis, Colorado Luis Aragon San Luis, Colorado Archuleta La Jara, Colorado" and just below these names are "?" for four locations, "Washington, D.C. Phoenix Los Angeles Denver."[47]

District Attorney Sanchez Digs In

District Attorney Alfonso Sanchez began a file on Tijerina, number 43-1. This file is extensive and contained court proceedings as well as police reports. There are police reports that corroborate the evidence gathered by the police in searching Valley of Peace for stolen government property.[48]

On August 3, 1964, in a letter with accompanying copies of the files I have described from Sanchez to "Chief of Police, Police Department, Casa Grande, Arizona and Sheriff's Office, Florence, Arizona," he continues his fishing expedition on Tijerina with bait in the second paragraph: "Said Individual is presently here in New Mexico, and I am contemplating filing criminal charges against him." Promptly, the sheriff of Pinal County, Coy K. DeArman, and his chief criminal investigator, Bill Ballard, responded to Sanchez in a letter dated August 10, 1964. They advise him that Tijerina was out on $1,000 bond "when court recessed for noon subject jumped bail and never returned." Then the killer paragraph for Sanchez and godsend for Tijerina: "The Statue of Limitations have [sic] run out so he is not wanted by our department at this time." A week later another killer message arrived, dated August 18, 1964, in Sanchez's office. James H. Green, chief of police for Casa Grande, Arizona, and detective Robert Myers were responding to Sanchez's letter. They reviewed the history of criminal charges against Tijerina dating to 1957. The grand theft charge, they stated, was "later dismissed in that Court for lack of evidence." The charge of aiding a prisoner to escape was pending, but Tijerina "jumped bond and failed to appear for Jury Trial. A Bench Warrant was issued for his arrest but has since been quashed and he is no longer wanted in this county."

A disappointed Sanchez called Chief Green to get more details, according to a letter from Detective Myers dated August 29, 1964, to Sanchez. They not only sent him "all available information on the above-named subject and the offences [*sic*] in which he was involved in this area" but also offered to have Bill Ballard "travel to Santa Fe to discuss it with you."

Knowing that there were no valid charges pending on Tijerina in Arizona or New Mexico, Sanchez began to hatch a plot to snare Tijerina in his conspiratorial web. With help from the state police, Sanchez began to identify the Alianza as a communist organization and Reies as a communist. Sanchez had access to state records and had a copy of both the articles of incorporation and bylaws of the Alianza, a nonprofit organization. In a document in the Sanchez file, 50-51, are both documents. The bylaws of the Alianza, Article 6, strictly prohibited from membership anyone with "communist affiliations." The following are selected words, some in italics for emphasis, from the Alianza's articles of incorporation:

I. The name of the Corporation shall be Alianza Federal de Mercedes (Federal Alliance of Spanish Land Grants)....

II. The objects and purposes are ... *to sustain Article Six in the Constitution of the United States* and Section Five of Article Two in the Constitution of the State of New Mexico....

VII. Number of directors constituting the first board of directors, also their addresses and tenure of office ... [There were nine persons listed with addresses, all with tenure of two years.]

VIII. In Witness Whereof, we have hereunto set our hands and seals at Albuquerque, New Mexico, on this, the 7th day of Oct. 1963. [Five incorporators signed: Reies, Jose A. Lucero, Santiago Anaya, Abenicio J. Sandoval, and Eunice L. Myrick.]

Witness my hand and notarial seal ... Thomas Padilla ... [Followed by his signature.]

In the bylaws of the Alianza Federal de Mercedes adopted a month later, on November 8, 1963, select words are as follows:

(Article I) *Any heir of any Grant,* (Spanish Land Grant) covered by the treaty of Guadalupe Hidalgo, can become a member....

(Article II) *Every adult member must pay dues.* ...One dollar per month on the 1st of each month.

(Article VI) Only the dues paying members are eligible to vote on any meeting or convention. ...All Heirs or members suspected of treason against the Alianza Federal de Mercedes, *or communist affiliation are prohibited to vote or to perform any activity for the Alianza Federal de Mercedes.*

(Article VII) (C) Annual Conventions shall be *held the first Saturday on the month of September;* and this shall be called Convention of the Royal Heirs.

The founding documents are very clear on the aims and purposes of the organization. The reference to Article 6 in the U.S. Constitution is to the supreme law of the land, which includes treaties that must be enforced, along with laws passed by Congress and the decisions of the Supreme Court. It prohibits communists from voting or performing any activity for the Alianza. It was not a communist organization. It was lawful in all respects and that is why it was chartered by the state. Sanchez knew this. Abuse of power as in the case of police is a terrible event. Abuse of knowledge and power by public officers is worse. Regardless, Sanchez pushed for vigilance and surveillance of Tijerina and the Alianza throughout the state by the state police.

The Infamous Eviction Notices, Summer 1964

Engineer Kenneth A. Heron from Chama, New Mexico wrote to the FBI office in Albuquerque on August 18, 1964, accusing the "Corporation of Abiquiu, Tierra Amarilla Land Grant [of attempting] to confiscate the properties of the Anglo land owners ...by terrorism." He cited as an example the dynamite bombing of an irrigation canal that had supplied water to three thousand acres of land for the past thirty years. The purpose was to destroy the canal and in so doing destroy crops dependent on this water supply. He simply reported the event and made the accusation; he offered no evidence linking anyone connected with the Abiquiu Corporation to the blast. He did not ask for an investigation.[49] And no response is found in the Sanchez file. Nevertheless, the Abiquiu Corporation leaders continued with their plans to serve notice on all trespassers of their intentions to evict them. The formal notices of eviction were posted as larges signs on fences and gates of Anglo landholdings in the county:

> No Hunting, Fishing or Trespassing. No Guns Allowed in the Tierra Ama-rilla Land Grant except from Border Patrol of the Said Grant. Anyone Caught Violating This Order Will Be Prosecuted By Order of The FEDI-COMISSARIOS of Tierra Amarilla Land Grant.

The eviction signs were accompanied with written notices to landowners by the Abiquiu Corporation. It stated that eviction from the lands granted to Manuel Martinez on July 20, 1832, would take place on October 20, 1964. The notice invoked the terms of the Treaty of Guadalupe Hidalgo as part of the supreme law of the land and therefore not subject to review by local judicial bodies, though "we perhaps would RECOGNIZE ... the International Court of Justice in The Hague, Holland." The notice also cited Article 2 of the state constitution "with special emphasis on Sections 3, 4, 5, 6 and 9, 16, 17, 20 and 23." It further informed the recipient that no intervention by local authorities should occur at the risk of "an armed clash" and requested police forces to stand down. The Anglo landowners sought legal refuge and protection from their local district judge, J. M. Scarborough in Santa Fe.

Undercover Agents

One of the principal undercover agents was Tim Chapa. Other agents were spread out in many cities, villages, and hamlets of the state as of September 1965: Tierra Amarilla, Ensenada, Questa, Lumberton, Chama, Arroyo, Chacon, Penasco, Las Trampas, Vallecitos, Ojo Caliente, and Truchas in the north and

Tecolote, Rowe, Pecos, Ribera, Tijeras, and San Antonio in the southern part of the state nearby or below Albuquerque.[50]

Sanchez had informants who submitted handwritten notes, which were typed into more legible copy. In these pages are forty-four names of the "Alianza Field Men Structure in the State of New Mexico" by location and the "Alianza Federal De Mercedes Formal Hierarchy" with an "Informal Hierarchy" listing only three of the Tijerina brothers; missing are Margarito and Ramon. The three-page handwritten report appears to be the source for some typewritten pages mentioned previously. These identify Tijerina's lawyers as "Joe L. Martinez?" and a "Manuel Garcia." An estimate of money in the bank account of the Alianza is "$144,000," and the report mentions "82 suits ready for filing to reclaim title to land (former Spanish grants) and to claim tax refunds." There is mention made of schisms within the Alianza; a group from Colonia Mexicana "says Tierra Amarrilla [sic] group is angry at Tijerina." In addition,

> Area of Rowe, Pecos to Villanueva reported theft ring operating—also said to be responsible for many thefts in Las Vegas—Pete Gallegos (Villanueva) reported sympathetic to Alianza—Two factions among heirs fighting Reies. Magdaleno Candelario—past pres. Atrisco heirs. Richard Griego—now from Atrisco called Tijerina a Communist & wetback. Reis [sic] broadcasts daily 6 am Sat & Sun 9 30 AM KABQ. (p. 3)

The anonymous writer admits that the information on "Reyes [sic] Lopez Tijarina [sic]" was obtained from State Police files, and Walter Kegel." Besides a review of past charges, now dropped or quashed in Arizona, the implied news was that reports, and some rumors, had been received from the field in northern New Mexico. The Communist plot rumor was that

> Tijerina and another man were in New Mexico at the instance [sic] of the Communist Party. Annoumous [sic] phone calls making threats, were being made according to "One A.B. Hollenbeck [who] likewise received telephone threats" as did one Truman Smith who reported that Mr.

Fulkerson's four mounted truck tires had been stolen and sugar put in
his gas tank and [that of] the secretary at Jim Fullers' Plumbing Company.

The town marshal also relayed to Fuller that his tractor would be burned
next. In another reported incident, "Mr. Heron was attacked recently by
someone who broke the screen door and came in, but she cannot identify
the assailants." Several of these reports also indicated that unsigned public
notices were being posted advising the property owners to leave everything
except for "personal belongings and one car."

The same source does mention that Mr. Heron had a reputation of selling nonexistent water rights and tracts of land to which he had no title.
"Two of the trustees of the [Alianza] Corporation" advised a foreman for
Mrs. Crane, Leo Smith, "that he best stop work on a fence as they were going
to take the land." A day or so later one of his cattle was shot. Another "steer
who strayed onto the road" was taken by one of the Alianza trustees and
impounded at a charge of "$7.00 a day."

Amarante Serrano, unidentified in the state police report, was on the
phone with the court reporter when talking to Judge Scarborough about
these goings-on. Apparently, the judge was going to hear the eviction notice
and conduct a hearing on the matter involving Tijerina and/or the Alianza.
Regardless, the judge explained that "this case was not to try the title to the
land." The reporter interpreted this to mean the judge was going to allow
testimony to get information on their "claims so as to avoid any appearance
of being unjust." Serrano was upset on the telephone and "insisted that justice was not being done; that he had sent copies of everything to Attorney
General Kennedy and President Johnson."

Serrano was the President of the Corporation of Abiquiu and was vocif-
erous in opposition to the hearing by this judge on the eviction notices. He
wrote a letter dated July 21, 1964, to the state attorney general, Earl Hartley,
with copy to Judge Scarborough informing both that they would not appear
at the hearing on their eviction notices and would proceed with their plans
for evictions as stipulated in the notices.[51]

In a subsequent two-page addendum to this report, "S.V. Noble" is the
handwritten signature at bottom right of the last page. Noble's source for

the information in the addendum was State Patrol Detective Lt. Freddy Martinez and a reporter for the *Albuquerque Tribune,* Gerald Moore. I assume Walter Kegel, Robert Romero, state police, and the U.S. attorney's office previously identified by him as those Noble called to prepare his report filled in more blanks in his investigation. Patrolman Martinez gave Noble new names of "other ring leaders . . . Marina Martinez, Juan Gomez, someone by the name of Manzanares and Walter Valdez, nearly all from Ensenada." The patrolman suggested "that an undercover agent might be able to locate and get evidence on Tijerina and that would stop the trouble." Moore, the newspaper man, told Noble that Tijerina was in Mexico "and is not behind this latest incident, he doesn't know who is." The newsman believed that "the people generally, in the area, are not involved in any violence but there are a few individuals, primarily the Mundays, [*sic*] the Harens, and their employees, and the member of their Board who might be." The first names—Mundy and Haren—are part of the cabal that stole the land. If reporter's statement was true, they were the ones doing the property damage, thefts, and making threats, with the intent to frame Tijerina.

Final Decree and Permanent Restraining Order

The directors of the Corporation of Abiquiu did not appear at the hearing as they had previously on the validity of their eviction notices. The plaintiffs, the State of New Mexico and the Chama Land and Cattle Company, had an easy time at the hearing of in the District Court for the County of Rio Arriba. They readily obtained their "justice." The court issued a lengthy final order against 158 defendants and "All Unknown Heirs to the Tierra Amarilla Land Grant." The permanent restraining order was signed by District Judge Paul Tackett, not Scarborough, and entered on October 20, 1964. The court determined it had jurisdiction over the parties and subject matter, heard evidence, examined the exhibits, and heard arguments all from only one side, then found

> that the Defendant, Corporation of Abiquiu, is not and cannot be the duly licensed land grant corporation . . . that the Corporation of Abiquiu

in Cause no. 1805 on file with the Clerk of the Federal District Court in Albuquerque, New Mexico, was adjudged an invalid corporation and permanently enjoined from existing as such.

The court in the final order invalidated every paragraph of the eviction notice and ordered all posted signs to be removed within five days from October 16, 1964. A certified true copy of the final decree and permanent restraining order was to be served on each of the 158 defendants.[52]

In a prior court case, *Mundy v. Martinez,* 61 N.M. 87 (1956), the land grant claimant lost his lands to Mundy because the state court found the description of the *higuelas* to be insufficient to establish the land as held in common. The judge ruled that the conveyance did not have the proper English description of the land. The case was appealed to the state supreme court, where Martinez lost again.[53] The heirs to these lands then organized themselves into the Abiquiu Corporation and continued to fight for the land without success.

And What about Water, Grass, Hunting, and Fishing?

Sometime in early to mid-1967 Governor David Cargo wrote to the secretary of agriculture "about the economic and social plight of Spanish-and-Mexican-American residents of New Mexico." The response from John C. Obert, assistant to the secretary, is dated June 28, 1967. It encloses pages titled "Grazing Association Data," which provide important information as to the anger and resentment on the part of Alianza membership against the federal government. These pages detail how permits to graze, cut wood, fish, hunt, and get water were reduced over time by the Forest Service and Bureau of Land Management. For example:

Alamosa Allotment ... Since 1947, allotments have been cut at a rate not less than 2% per year. In 1966, total allotments were cut 20%. 70 free milk-cow permits retracted in 1966. All free permits for bulls were retracted in 1966. 421 permits in 1947, 378 permits now. Total reduction since 1947: 40%.

And the entry for Tres Piedras Allotment:

> The Forest Service divided the allotment into 4 grazing units, and then determined the order in which they would be grazed. The units to be grazed first were dry, without water, and with very little grass. The men had to haul water, and finally many of them sold their animals rather than let them die.[54]

All of these reduced permits directly impacted the quality of life of those who once owned the lands and used them to feed their cattle, sheep, goats, and other livestock; feed themselves by hunting and fishing; harvest timber to make buildings and for heating and cooking; and obtain water to irrigate and to drink. As Jenkinson puts it,

> The subsistence rancher for whom bureaucracy was a thing to be avoided, now faced it at every turn. There were licenses to be bought for fishing and hunting. Permits were necessary to cut wood or graze cattle and sheep. And, the *Hispano* soon discovered that these regulations unlike many by earlier Spanish or Mexican edicts, could not be ignored with impunity. A man could be fined for killing a deer to feed his family, or fined if his cattle strayed onto National Forest land. . . . What did the number of sheep they grazed have to do with the future water supply for the city of Albuquerque? Why were Texans with polished boots and high-powered rifles hunting over the lands that were the birthright of the Hispano people? . . . Up to 1925, there roamed several substantial herds of wild horses . . . it was felt the grass cover was being too rapidly depleted. A massive round-up was held. As the animals nervously surged back and forth in the holding corrals, soft-spoken Hispanos leaned against the fence rails, pointing out the horses which belonged to them. If they had it, they then paid the fine to cover the trespass their mount had made upon National Forest land, and the horse was released to them. A man who could not come up with cash to pay for bunch grass his horse was charged with eating, as though it had been baled alfalfa. Most of the unclaimed horses were sold and shipped away. Four hundred and fifty horses were shot.[55]

The original owners continued to be forced off their meagre landholdings during the Tijerina era. They could no longer feed themselves, nor did
they know much else but farming and agriculture, making them virtually
unemployable except as manual labor in the lowest rungs of the market
economy of the 1960s and 1970s. With the election of David Cargo as governor in 1966, renewed hope swelled among the Hispanos who had voted
for him in the northern villages of New Mexico. Governor Cargo had called
on Washington to come out and see firsthand the dire need for the many
programs of the War on Poverty his state needed, especially the Office of
Economic Opportunity (OEO). The Forest Service (FS), OEO, the Catholic
Church, and the governor's office called a series of hearings on the poverty
of the northern part of the state and condition of New Mexico's twenty-
five thousand migrant worker families now unable to feed themselves on
their tiny landholdings. These hearings were to take place May 1-2, 1967,
and promised by Washington would be the presence of Assistant Secretary
of Agriculture John Baker. Not to be. John Baker was substituted with FS
regional representative William D. Hurst, who already knew firsthand the
complaints of the Hispanos—pasture use, grazing permits, water, firewood
rights, and fishing and hunting permits. Hurst cut the hearing to a one-day
affair. Most importantly, the only hearing day conflicted with the issuance
of cattle-grazing permits for the summer at the same time. Just fifteen
Hispano men found the hearing room in the state office complex, only to
discover that those listening to their testimony did not speak Spanish. They
were asked to present in English, a language they did not know.[56]

Renewed Violence and Destruction of Property

In desperation during the years of Alianza existence, some northern New
Mexico residents turned to destruction of property on Anglo landholdings
and other random acts of violence. The DA and FBI immediately suspected
Tijerina as being behind this renewed violence. Who else was talking about
taking the land back, and who else was calling non-Hispanos trespassers?
But the violence was widespread, even in areas like southern New Mexico

and the Little Texas area where Tijerina had little influence. Both Jenkinson and Nabokov describe incident after incident of such violence, and both corroborate the state and local authorities' efforts to arrest Tijerina for that destruction.[57] When the destruction involved federal property, the FBI reportedly investigated, but no arrests were ever made that involved Alianza members or any of the Tijerina brothers.[58]

The New Mexico State Police file contains copies of documents from the 1950s and updated to the day before the Tierra Amarilla Courthouse incident. These files are teletypes sent to Santa Fe, Albuquerque, and Espanola indicating that Tijerina was wanted under Rio Arriba County Warrant NBR 3935 for extortion.[59]

District Attorney Sanchez File 43-1

This file contains much correspondence already mentioned and copies of police records dating to the 1950s when Tijerina had his run-ins with law enforcement in Arizona. There is a seven-page report that is full of venomous accusations attacking the character of Tijerina.

The partial report begins with "The following information has been obtained by telephone, from State Police files, and from Walter Kegel." There was no information found in this research on either Walter Kegel or S. V. Noble, who has already been mentioned in connection with the report. Some of the most inflammatory and prejudicial material against Tijerina is these lines:

> Rumor has it that hewas [*sic*] born in Las Vegas, New Mexico and was educated in Mexico.
>
> The original rumor that I heard was that he and another man were up here at the instance [*sic*]of the Communist Party.
>
> The United States Attorney's Office, Walter Kegel, State Police Headquarters and others I have talked to over the telephone as well as Robert Romero's partial investigation indicate that he is a far left radical and they seem to think that there could be considerable truth to the rumor. (p. 1)

The report details various incidents of damage to property, about which the author concedes:

> Any connection to this incident would apparently be x to [*sic*] tenuous to be useable to the time of the hearing next Friday. Judge Scarborough talked to Amarante Serrano on the telephone and I was on the extension. The Judge assured him that this case was not to try the title to the land. Throughout the conversation Serrant [*sic*] insisted that justice was not being done; that he had sent copies of everything to Attorney General Kennedy and President Johnson and that their Civil Rights were being violated and that the rights were grants to them by the Guadalupe Hidalgo Treaty. I believe that Judge Scarborough will let them testify as [to] their claims so as to avoid any appearance of being unjust. (pp. 4-5)

Obviously, it did not occur to either Noble, the writer of this report, or the judge that they should not be engaged in conversations about a case pending before the judge without the parties having notice of such meetings and the opportunity to be present. Listening in on the conversation between the judge and a party certainly makes for an ex parte hearing, forbidden under the rules of civil procedure in any state. The judge certainly did not disclose someone else was on the telephone while he discussed the case with Serrano or disclose later in open court to Sanchez on the day of the hearing that Noble was on another line listening. Perhaps this was because Noble was an operative for the DA and in conspiracy with him to deny Serrano a fair and impartial trial.

In the last two pages of this report is the clear admission that Tijerina is innocent of vandalism. But the writer recommended that law enforcement officers continue to try to link him to the crimes of property destruction:

> Since dictating the above Iahave [*sic*] talked to patrolman Freddy Martinez [handwritten in "who"] investigated the earlier occurrences. He advised that blood shed [*sic*] would follow unless the matter is stopped at once, but that an undercover agent might be able to locate and get evidence on Tijerina and that this would stop the trouble. (p. 6)

Of vital importance is the legality of actions taken by these law enforcement personnel, from the local police, to the DA, state police, and state district judge. They were most interested in finding evidence on the part of Tijerina and "the Board," which refers to the land claimants of the Abiquiu Corporation, formerly the Manuel Martinez and the Tierra Amarilla land grants, for criminal charges. They were not interested in investigating the criminal behavior of Bill Mundy or of the Herons by their own admission and knowing who might be destroying their own property to frame Tijerina.

CHAPTER 2

No Apology, No Compensation

I n his speechmaking about the land grants, Tijerina frequently pointed out the inconsistent history behind apologizing for wrongdoing by the United States to other peoples and countries. He made references to instances in which the United States apologized for wrongdoing to other peoples; but it never apologized to the people of the Southwest for taking their lands. He mentioned President Gerald Ford's calling the internment of Japanese Americans during World War II a wrong; subsequently he revoked Roosevelt's executive order on that point.[1] Later, on August 10, 1988, Congress passed the Civil Liberties Act, which apologized for that internment and authorized reparations in the amount of $20,000 for each person held in those concentration camps during World War II, with a cap of $1.2 billion, and $50 million to establish a foundation to promote the cultural and historical concerns of Japanese Americans.

President Clinton, a decade later, reached a settlement between Latin American Japanese also interned in U.S. concentration camps during World War II and approved by a federal judge in June 1998. They received an official apology and reparations of $5,000 each.[2] As president, Clinton also began a national dialogue about race in this country and held a forum in Houston without a single person of Mexican ancestry on the panel, only whites and blacks.[3] Tijerina was surprised to learn that Congress by 2008 had apologized for the 246 years of slavery and the Jim Crow era. Another story Tijerina retold was that of Holy Roman Emperor Henry IV apologizing to Pope Gregory VII in 1077 for instigating church-state conflicts. Henry IV stood in the snow for three days to show his remorse.

More Examples from More Recent Times

After he returned from self-exile in Mexico in 2006, I visited Tijerina several times in his barrio hovel in El Paso. He was there because he could get free medical treatment at La Fe, the Chicano health center in the Segundo Barrio just blocks from his abode. He and his third wife, Esperanza, were destitute. Most of his bedridden day was spent on listening and watching the news. He often brought up current examples of apology without compensation by the United States for wrongdoings to others, but not those in the Southwest. I recall these: the United States offered an apology for the theft of the Kingdom of Hawaii—no compensation and no offer to return any of the 1.8 million acres of landholdings taken by U.S. interests and their Hawaiian accomplices, just an official, "We're sorry."[4] When Reagan was president he reluctantly turned the Panama Canal over to Panama after nearly a one-hundred-year lease by the United States. Tijerina would recall the right-wing slogan shouted by those who would "own" the canal forever, "We built it. We paid for it. We own it." Tijerina would bring up the history of the "U.S. Canal in Colombia," as he named it.

The story is almost a replica of how Hawaii was taken. The United States wanted a shorter route for travel by sea from the Atlantic to the Pacific, New York to Los Angeles, without going around South America between that southern point and Antarctica. The U.S. military fomented revolution in Colombia, the country with territorial rights to that stretch of land extending north into Central America dating to their independence from Spain in 1819. The United States created and then subsidized a rebel group to proclaim independence from Colombia for this area. They called their nation Panama. In return for U.S. recognition of the rebel forces and arms and naval protection, the United States obtained a long-term lease to cut a canal across Panama, which the United States built with its money and resources. Later, in 1921, the United States did pay another $21 million for that taking.[5]

Tuskegee Airmen

The wrongs done by the U.S. Public Health Service to 399 black men for forty years under the auspices of the Tuskegee experiment had started in 1939. Tijerina mentioned this atrocity of injecting nonconsenting and unawares black prison inmates with syphilis to observe reactions on other occasions. On May 16, 1997, he was surprised to learn that President Clinton at the White House faced and apologized to five of eight survivors of that horrible experiment on humans. Tijerina asked me if it was true that some of the men had gotten several million dollars in settlement of their claims. I explained that the survivors had been awarded a settlement of $10 million.[6]

Tulsa Riot

In February 2000 Tijerina was traveling to San Antonio from Albuquerque when an Oklahoma state commission, the Tulsa Race Riot Commission, recommended reparations for the survivors of the gross massacre of blacks in the Greenwood neighborhood of Tulsa during May 1921. He had stopped to visit my family and me on the outskirts of Dallas in Lancaster, Texas. He wanted to know how the blacks had gotten the state to pay reparations. He also wanted to know when Texas would investigate the many massacres of Mexicans committed by the Texas Rangers and others. In Spanish, he asked, "Why do they feign ignorance of these massacres when it is in their history books? They write it." He specifically asked me if I knew about the massacre by Rangers and U.S. Army troops in Porvenir, Texas, in 1918. I did not know at that time.[7] Among his many other questions was one about how my translation of his book from Spanish to English was coming.

The Hidden Apology to Native Americans, but No Land

A sound argument can be made that treaties entered by the United States and Native American tribes are worthless and have seldom been enforced. In fact, the 2.8 million acres recently awarded to several tribes in East Texas is yet to be enforced, much less paid in market value dollars.[8] In the 1980s several tribes were successful in obtaining judgments against the United States, such as the Passamaquoddy Tribe in the Northeast (Maine) which settled with Congress for $81 million. In *U.S. v. Sioux Nation of Indians, et al*, 448 U.S. 371 (1980) the Court affirmed the Indian Claims Court award of $88 million for the one-hundred-year taking and use of their lands in the Black Hills in South Dakota. The Sioux, however, have refused the money; they want the Black Hills. The money remains with the Bureau of Indian Affairs, in an account compounding interest; it amounted to more than $1 billion as of August 24, 2011.[9]

An appropriations bill, H.R. 3326, was submitted in the House of Representatives in 2010 titled Defense Appropriations Act. It was lengthy, as are all appropriation requests. But hidden in Section 8113, page 45, are these words:

> The United States, acting through Congress, apologizes on behalf of the people of the United States to all Native Peoples for the many instances of violence, maltreatment, and neglect inflicted on Native Peoples by citizens of the United States; and expresses its regret for the ramifications of former wrongs and its commitment to build on the positive relationships of the past and present to move toward a brighter future where all the people of this land live reconciled as brothers and sisters, and harmoniously steward and protect this land together.

Nothing in this section authorizes or supports any claim against the United States or serves as a settlement of any claim against the United States.

The president was urged to "acknowledge the wrongs of the United States against Indian tribes in the history of the United States in order to bring healing to [t]his land." In all the eight years in office, President Obama never referred to this apology.

The Takings Clause of the Fifth Amendment

Tijerina also would often switch his talk from these types of examples to the Fifth Amendment's "Takings Clause." He would utter pointed rhetorical questions:

> When is the United States going to return our lands? When is the United States going to give the Indians their tribal lands? When is the United States going to be tried by the United Nations for its crimes against our people? The United States never will. The United States will not compensate us for our stolen lands, and it will not apologize. These are takings prohibited in the U.S. Constitution.

The Fifth Amendment to most persons who are informed on the Bill of Rights means that an accused person does not have to answer pointed questions by the prosecutor. In the movies, many a gangster is often portrayed as stating from the witness stand, "I plead the Fifth." Sometime more eloquently, "I refuse to answer on the grounds that I may incriminate myself in contravention of my rights contained in the Fifth Amendment of the U.S. Constitution." The Fifth Amendment has more language covering other rights and protections, not just against self-incrimination. The Fifth Amendment's final sentence on point here is the Takings Clause. It reads as follows: "No person shall ... be deprived of life, liberty, or property without due process of law, *nor shall private property be taken for public use without just compensation*" (my emphasis).

There is no fundamental right to property in the United States of America.[10] There is only a fundamental right to "just compensation" and "due process" when such a taking by the government is for the public welfare or use. Due process simply means the government, local to federal, has to use the same procedural methods, including proper written notice, to take a person's property. There shall be no discrimination; everybody is to be treated the same. The "just compensation" means the fair market value of the property compared to other property similarly situated and used. Typically, the governmental entity or its representative, say a public utility or even private business providing, say, natural gas via pipeline for public use, will negotiate a price with landowners for the use of their land.

If the negotiations between property owner and those taking the land fails, then the government or its agent will sue the landowner to compel the sale for just compensation. Alternatively, the property owner can sue, raising the issue of a taking without just compensation. Experts are brought into the courtroom to testify on comparable sales, and either a settlement is reached, or the judge renders a judgment on value. The company gets access to the private property. The landowner will get money, whether pleased with the amount or not. The case is closed unless for error in the judicial proceeding, in which case an appeal can be filed to a higher court on the alleged error. The error must be egregious, not just the landowner's disliking the result.

No Apology, No Compensation!

Tijerina's point in this continuing dialogue with me and other audiences for decades about "no compensation and no apology" was that the land recovery movement should not die. There has been no relief offered, "no compensation, no apology," he would pontificate. He implored me on more than one occasion to drop my work with electoral politics and academic pursuits. "Just concentrate on getting the land back," he would pressure me. He offered me his private papers not donated to the Zimmerman Library at the University of New Mexico; his collection of rare books on the topic from Mexico and Spain that he had acquired since first beginning this quest; copies of original land grants made by various kings in Spain; copies of papal bulls; a collection of books that were the compilation of the *Leyes de los reinos de las Indias* (1680); and his many computations on pieces of paper to show how numerology was prophecy. He was as religious about numerology as he was about the land recovery movement.[11]

Tijerina's Case for Return of the Land Stolen

Toward the end of his life, Tijerina had framed several copies of papal bulls he considered the bedrock of his views on the lands in the Southwest. He placed them on the walls of his tiny apartment in El Paso. His favorite was the *Terra nullius* (empty land), issued by Pope Urban II in 1095, which gave kings and princes of Europe, Christendom, the right to discover and claim land in non-Christian areas. This is the origin of the Discovery Doctrine. The next, in 1452, was the authorization from Pope Nicholas V, who issued *Romanus pontifex,* in essence declaring war against all non-Christians throughout the world and authorizing conquest of savage peoples and their lands, who had no rights because they were uncivilized and subhuman. This is the claim that Christians have a God-given right to conquer, control, and take lands. Almost a century passed before two popes, Alexander VI in 1493 and Paul II in 1573, softened the treatment of native peoples in the Americas by authorizing conversion to Catholicism. Pope Urban VIII in 1635 declared excommunication for anyone holding Indians as slaves. Regardless, the colonization and subsequent founding of the thirteen colonies in the Americas by the Protestant British did not heed these papal bulls. They were not Catholics, but they used the doctrine for their purposes.

The taking of Indian lands and slavery of Africans was accepted practice because nonwhites were less than human. SCOTUS in 1823 inserted its notion of the Discovery Doctrine into the case of *Johnson v. McIntosh.* Thomas Jefferson in 1792 first declared that the Discovery Doctrine extended from Europe to the newly formed United States. Chief Justice John Marshall relied on papal bulls himself in reaching the decision, referring to *Romanus pontifex* and the 1493 *Inter caetera* papal bull, which applied to Spain's claim to conquer the New World. The case of *McIntosh* has never been overruled and remains a precedent in U.S. jurisprudence. In 1830, the first Indian Removal Act was passed by Congress to remove all Indians to lands west of the Mississippi. Spain had been exercising sovereignty and jurisdiction over those lands for three centuries. When the United States prepared to war with Mexico in 1845, the substance of the Discovery Doctrine was reformulated as Manifest Destiny:

> The right of our manifest destiny to spread over and to possess the whole of the continent which Providence has given us for the development of the great experiment of liberty ... is such that of the tree to the space of air and the earth suitable for the full expansion of its principle and destiny of growth.[12]

The final legal blow to property rights asserted by Native Americans, according to Scarborough, was given with the 1887 Dawes Act, in which the president was granted the power by Congress to remove lands from reservations that had been created for use by the Indians either by treaty, executive order, or act of Congress for the purpose of "securing homes to actual settlers ... disposed of by the United States to actual and bona fide settlers only."[13] Scarborough points out that President Harrison in his Farewell Address of 1892 made mention of how successful the Dawes Act had been in removing more Indians from their lands:

> The enormous cessions of Indian lands which have been opened to settlement, aggregating during this Administration [from 1889 through 1892] nearly 26,000,000 acres, and the agreements renegotiated and now pending in Congress for ratification by which about 10,000,000 additional acres will be opened to settlement, it will be seen how much has been accomplished.[14]

In Tijerina's mind, Indian lands were first taken by the Spanish kings during discovery, exploration, and subsequent colonization; then by the U.S. government under the same Doctrine of Discovery. The U.S. Congress for the next fourteen years went after the land held by grantees of Spanish and

Mexican land grants with the establishment of the Court of Private Land Claims in 1891, which took thirty million acres of these land grants, and through the first Forest Reserve Acts, which took an additional enormous number of acres, 145,000,000.[15] Mark David Spence provides a history of Indian removal from their lands viewed as the wilderness by whites. Regrettably, he only traces the history of land occupancy of areas today known as Yellowstone, Yosemite, and Glacier National Parks. He totally ignores the presence of Spanish land claimants in these same geographical areas.[16] And he ignores completely the fact that not all the "wilderness," as he termed it, was occupied by Indian tribes. The tribes were small in population numbers in the seventeenth century; and, dwindled to even less by the late nineteenth century.

From the 1950s forward, Tijerina's fight was not over this entire take-away, just over the land grants given by Spain, recognized by Mexico, and generally by the United States under the Treaty of Guadalupe Hidalgo. He wanted enforcement of those legal principles and the terms of the treaty.

Land Grants in New Mexico

In his research, Tijerina found evidence for the existence of 277 land grants issued in New Mexico by Spanish and Mexican authorities. Most of the land of these grants, or *mercedes,* was stolen by Thomas B. Catron with help from the surveyor general of the United States. Other land was made easier to steal because Governor William A. Pile in March 1870 ordered his librarian, Ira M. Bond, to destroy all the Spanish archives in New Mexico.[17] A subsequent governor, Bradford Prince, disposed of more official records by selling them to a businessman. These records have resurfaced and were subject to litigation in Kansas City, Missouri, at the time Tijerina was writing his book.[18] "Little by little, I reconstructed what had happened in New Mexico more than 110 years ago at the hands of the Anglos," he wrote in his autobiography.[19] Prior to this atrocity and blatant disregard for the rule of law, a soldier with the occupation army of General Kearney named governor of the newly acquired territory ordered the first burning of official Spanish records. He burned some in his chimney himself to heat his feet, according to Tijerina.[20] Tijerina found that in 1873, thirty-five land grants were approved by Congress based on the surveyor general's recommendation. The White House objected by questioning how these could be approved if the governor had burned the records years earlier. A new surveyor general was instructed to re-examine these claims. This man, George W. Julian, rejected twenty-three and approved only twelve; among them was the San Joaquin del Cañon de Chama, a community land grant.[21]

A new legal twist was added by Congress when it created the Court of Private Land Claims on March 3, 1891, due to the fact that the surveyor general's recommendations lacked executive power. All claimants had to present their documentary proof to this court to reestablish their legal rights to the land. By this time, few land claimants had original documents. Prior findings by other surveyors general notwithstanding, new filings had to be made; otherwise no proper claim for review was before the court. The state capital, Santa Fe, lost its communal land grant status because of this new legal twist. SCOTUS ruled against the claimants over Santa Fe on March 1, 1897. "Fifty years later Lansing Bloom ... found in the General Archive of the Indies, the document that contains the date and the order founding the city of Santa Fe (March 30, 1609)," Tijerina writes. He adds, "All the cases brought by Mexicans to the Supreme Court were lost. All the cases brought by the Anglos were won. Example: Thomas B. Catron sued for 1.5 million acres of land and won."[22]

Tijerina's allegations are corroborated by Malcolm Ebright in the first monograph published by the Center for Land Gant Studies, *The Tierra Amarilla Grant: A History of Chicanery*. He writes about claim No. 3 by Francisco Martinez, the Tierra Amarilla grant: "The grant was confirmed by Congress in 1860 ... and in 1881 the patent to the grant was issued by the Department of the Interior and picked up by Thomas B. Catron.... Since 1874, Catron had been buying the interests of the family of Manuel Martinez (Francisco's father), the successful petitioner for the grant. But the Martinez family did not own the grant. The grant was a community grant which under Spanish law could not be sold."[23] Ebright also supplied a footnote that states:

Of the nine men to hold the office of surveyor general before the Court of Private Land Claims was established ... three were land grant speculators: Dr. T. Rush Spencer, 1869-1972, owned a 1/5 interest in the Mora grant with Thomas B. Catron and Stephen B. Elkins in 1870 and at the same time served as an official of the Maxwell Land Grant and Railroad Company along with Governor William A. Pile. James K. Proudfit, 1872-1876, was one of the incorporators of new Mexico's first cattle corporation with Catron and Elkins among others. At the same time, he was openly propagandizing for the cattle industry in his official capacity and striving to secure increased appropriations to accommodate its need for surveys. He was finally asked to resign. Henry M. Atkinson, 1876-1884, continued to survey large areas of land usable only as cattle range, contrary to the homestead and pre-emption laws which required that surveyed land be agricultural and that it actually be cultivated. He was an incorporator of our cattle companies with a combined capitalization of $5,000,000, along with Catron and Deputy Surveyor William H. McBroom. The most notorious example of corruption in the Surveyor-General's office was the survey of the Maxwell Atkinson by John T. Elkins and R. T. Marmon. John Elkins was the brother of Stephen who was not only a bondsman for the surveyors, but also was promoter for the grant.[24]

Tijerina Obtains FBI Intelligence

Edwin Stanton, his mortgage holder and publisher of his weekly articles, called Tijerina one day to report that FBI agents were coming to talk to him about Tijerina and his plans to take a car caravan into Mexico to publicize his cause in September 1964. The FBI not only had taken out a subscription of his newspaper to read and clip his articles but also visited with Stanton regularly to inquire about the goings on at the Alianza building and Tijerina himself. Stanton suggested to Tijerina he come, sit unobserved, and listen to the conversation. "The name of the FBI agent that showed up was Gordon Jackson . . . he accused us of being a bad element and that the caravan would be a criminal act. The agent tried really hard to poison Ed's mind."[25] During this conversation Tijerina learned officially that he no longer was considered a fugitive from justice by the FBI. The agent accused Stanton of siding with the Alianza and Tijerina and informed him that Tijerina was a criminal and a fugitive from justice in Arizona and generally had a bad record. Stanton then asked, "Well, why don't you arrest him? 'Because the statute of limitations has run,' said the agent."[26]

That July, Tijerina made his last trip to Mexico seeking support from the government and was promptly arrested while speaking to students in Chihuahua City. Previously, he had personally delivered letters and memoranda on the land question in the Southwest to President López Mateos in 1959 and 1964. This time, after being released from jail in Chihuahua City, he went to see Luis Echeverría Álvarez, secretary of *Gobernación,* or attorney general, to deliver yet another letter asking for support for his car caravan and the Alianza in its goals. Within days, federal police agents took him early one morning for interrogation as to his purposes in Mexico. He was shirtless, having just roused himself from bed that morning when they came.

> While all this was happening, I thought again of Gordon Jackson and the interview he had had with Stanton. I became convinced that the Anglos were behind all of this, even in Mexico. . . . They took me to the airport. . . . The agents put me on a plane. . . . I felt embarrassed in front of all the tourists and other people who were well dressed. The pilot gave me a shirt, which I put on and thanked him for that. [He called Maria] "I was deported from Mexico because of the Anglos in the White House. I'm at Ramon's house here in San Antonio and am all right."[27]

Fast-Forward to New Mexico, 1967

The first face-off between District Attorney Alfonso Sanchez and Reies López Tijerina occurred on a stairwell at the Rio Arriba County Courthouse during the trial of Margarito Tijerina on July 16, 1966.[28] Sanchez himself was an heir to a land grant in the Albuquerque area and active member of the American G.I. Forum. He finished law school on the GI Bill because he had served in two wars, World War II and Korea. At one point, he was the lawyer for the Abiquiu Corporation. They were named defendants in the Payne Land and Livestock Company lawsuit of 1958 in which the company sought to quiet title on their possession of more than seven thousand acres of the Tierra Amarilla land grant. Sanchez prepared and filed a countersuit on behalf of the Abiquiu Corporation. Federal District Judge Waldo Rogers ruled on February 1, 1960, that title to the land belonged to the Payne Company and those contesting had no rights under the law since the *Tameling* case.[29]

During the course of his representation Sanchez had increasingly become a defender of the "rule of law." He was constantly admonishing his clients who wanted to oust the trespassers by any means necessary not to turn to violence. And constantly he was asking for more money for his work on the case, which he did after hours from his regular job at the district attorney's office. Finally, he withdrew from the case, disappointed with his clients and their financial straits and their increasing propensity to retake the land by force, according to Correia.[30] The Abiquiu Corporation lost the case. This history was unknown to Tijerina, as these events were occurring when he first arrived back in New Mexico in 1958. He just knew that Sanchez was now trying to stop him and the Alianza from the pursuit of their goals.

In the stairwell, Tijerina accused Sanchez of slander for calling him a communist and threatened to sue him. Sanchez countered with a careful denial, stating Tijerina was doing communistic things such as taking the land back, not recognizing the government, and setting up his own government: "That is communistic." And he accused Reies of lying about him to *Newsweek* magazine.[31] Tijerina did not know then that Sanchez had already alerted the FBI as to his activities in New Mexico. Sanchez had opened a file on Tijerina to track both federal and state activity because of engaging in "communistic activities" since 1962. Now Sanchez, unbeknownst to Tijerina, was also weaving a conspiratorial web to snare all the Tijerina brothers and Alianza members with criminal charges. Had Tijerina known all this, their argument may have escalated to a more serious confrontation.

Since 1962, Sanchez, working with the state police, had informants in every community that Tijerina had visited and organized a meeting. Tijerina had visited most of the towns in northern New Mexico. In conjunction with various local and state police agencies, the DA was trying to tie Tijerina and the members of the Alianza to every wanton act of destruction of property being suffered by landowners, the targets of the land grant claimants. Yet there was no direct evidence, only circumstantial tidbits. Sanchez and others set out to get that proof.

> Freddy Martinez, detective lieutenant of the State Police in charge of criminal investigation in Rio Arriba, began to put together what information he could on Reies and his brothers, consulting with his old friend, Emilio Naranjo, sheriff of Rio Arriba. Interest was expressed by numerous others, including Senator Joseph Montoya, who had always been able to count on a solid vote from the northern counties. The longtime *honchos* of the democratic establishment were coming awake to the possibility that there was something more dangerous in the wind than the usual aimless outbursts of anonymous violence and the floundering efforts of the Abiquiu Corporation.[32]

Sanchez, as a public official and chief prosecutor in the county, should have known about the New Mexico State Criminal Code's definition of a conspiracy: two or more persons contemplating a criminal or harmful act on another or their property.[33] And he should have known that as DA he could not use his office under the color of law to give the appearance of any deprivation of Tijerina's civil rights or those of anyone else. This is a federal law applicable to the DA and any other public official seeking to deprive others of their legal rights.[34]

But Tijerina, standing with the DA in the stairwell, was more preoccupied with his brothers' fate than with countering accusations. Both brothers, Anselmo and Margarito, had been charged with assault and battery back in the final days of November 1965. Anselmo was cleared given his alibi and possible mistaken identity by the key witness. Margarito and Anselmo did look very much alike; Sanchez proceeded to try Margarito.

He was found guilty and sentenced to ten to fifty years, plus the State of Indiana filed a hold after he served this time for a parole violation in that state. Margarito's trial outcome was not appealed in a timely fashion for lack of $1,500 to pay for the transcript. Reies's son Hugh, aka David, was also charged with perjury by DA Sanchez for testifying that Margarito was with him in Albuquerque the day of the assault.[35]

On October 9, 1965, Sanchez went after his own former clients of the Abiquiu Corporation. Instead of recusing himself for blatant conflict of interests in this continuing case he once represented, he filed a petition asking for a temporary injunction against them. He sought to prevent members of the organization from sending notices of eviction to those they considered trespassers on their lands and organizing armed patrols. Many members did not receive notices for the October 15 hearing during, which Sanchez had a field day given that no lawyers were on the other side. Judge Paul Tackett stopped the proceeding shortly after the noon hour and read his prepared statement, indicating his mind was already made up before the hearing. Judge Tackett not only granted the temporary injunction but also made it permanent. In order to avoid the permanent injunction, the Abiquiu Corporation changed its name to Colonia Mexicana effective January 1, 1966. Regrettably, it did not pursue federal civil rights violations against the DA and judge for not only preventing them from exercising their First Amendment rights of assembly and speech but also their rights to enforce the law with notices leading to citizen arrests for trespassing, and for ineffective due process by proceeding against them without giving proper and effective notice of the hearing. Those on the Abiquiu Corporation board also did not file a bar grievance against their former lawyer for prosecuting them.

Working the System or Outside the System?

Tijerina was tired of organizing marches and protests around public buildings. On July 2, 1966, just before Margarito's trial, Tijerina led a sixty-six-mile march from Albuquerque to Santa Fe to protest Governor Jack Campbell's refusal to meet with him on the land grant question. The governor refused to meet with the protesting marchers again on that July 4. Other Chicano leaders like César Chávez and Antonio Orendain had been rebuffed in similar fashion when they tried to address farmworker issues with their respective governors. Chávez was refused an audience after marching across half of California by Governor Edmund Brown, who preferred to be with Frank Sinatra in Palm Springs. And Orendain was stopped on the highway in New Braunfels, two-thirds of the way from the Rio Grande Valley to Austin, Texas, to be informed by Governor John Connally he would not be in Austin because he was going dove hunting.

In response, Tijerina and the protestors camped out on the capitol steps until the governor decided to stop Tijerina's media attacks on him by acquiescing to a meeting a week later.[36] He also asked the state historian, Myra Jenkins, to issue a report on Tijerina and the Alianza. The report made newspaper headlines across the state in that it accused Tijerina of running a con game by asking for membership dues and presenting fraudulent land grant documents, which she claimed were forgeries. She asserted that many Alianza members were not heirs to land grants, a prerequisite for membership.[37] Tijerina's lawyers were not enthusiastic over filing a suit for slander and defamation, but he persisted. The Alianza board of directors voted to sue her and the State of New Mexico, encouraged by Tijerina's rhetoric:

> To defend herself, she would have to produce proof from the state archives. She would have to prove that we were wrong, that there is no case for return of the land. It would have become a land grant case, you see. We would have taken it all the way to the Supreme Court![38]

The suit was filed, asking for $2 million in punitive damages, and promptly dismissed by the district judge for failure to state a claim, that having no legal case under the law. Again, Tijerina did not appeal this ruling in order to pursue his claims on the applicability of the Law of the Indies and citizen arrest rights. Tijerina was naive about the workings of the judiciary and the costs involved in litigation. Yet he set up the opposition by going into confrontations head first with limited resources, including no lawyers. And the issue of how much money he was taking in from the one-dollar-a-month membership dues, when he claimed to have one thousand, then three thousand, then five thousand, and even twenty thousand members, precluded his claims of indigency.[39]

Over the years, Tijerina had written letters signed by land grant family representatives on the issue to several presidents; none but Eisenhower responded. And that response was cold and curt in denying any relief.[40] U.S. Attorney General Robert Kennedy met with Tijerina the summer of 1964 but was non-committal and "refused to make any promises."[41] Governor David Cargo had been the only state official to meet with him in April 1967 to discuss the land grants in New Mexico for an hour. Governor Cargo asked for documentation on the matter so he could write to federal authorities about the issue. The Alianza had published a booklet outlining the causes of action and citing the applicable laws from the *Leyes de las Indias,* Treaty of Guadalupe Hidalgo, and both U.S. and New Mexico Constitutions. The governor admonished Tijerina and his followers not to take the law into their own hands. Tijerina made it clear to Governor Cargo that they had their own law and gave the governor a copy of their booklet, citing their sources and quoting their laws.[42] He told the governor they were tired of waiting for justice to be done and that their march to the capitol was the last human warning being given by land grant heirs to trespassers on their lands. The news media picked up the "Last Human Warning" line for their headlines.[43] Tijerina gave up on working within the system; they did not want to listen, much less agree that the Southwest belonged to land grant claimants and not the federal or state governments or the beneficiaries of the Santa Fe Ring land thieves. He was ready for more direct action based on the rights inherent to landowners. Tijerina announced, "This summer the people will take over San Joaquin del Rio [de] Chama once and for all."[44]

The Use of Citizen's Arrest Powers

The right of a person to conduct a citizen's arrest stems from powers found in the common law that was and is the foundation for most federal and state statutes in play during Tijerina's era.[45] In 2001, the citizen's arrest power was upheld by the U.S. Supreme Court in *Atwater v. Lago Vista,* 532 U.S. 318 (2001).[46] It is still controlling precedent in the United States as part of its law of the land and the Supremacy Clause of the U.S. Constitution.[47] The Supremacy Clause has been interpreted by SCOTUS to mean that federal law supersedes state law. Basically, the clause preempts any application of state statutes if there is a federal one that supersedes. Bilingual education in Texas is a good example. On the Texas lawbooks English is the only permitted language of instruction in the public schools. The law has been on the books since the 1920s, when the legislators wanted to stop the teaching in German in areas of Texas where German Americans lived, New Braunfels, for example. It is still Texas law, but no one applies that because bilingual education was made part of a federal statute. In New Mexico the state constitution incorporated bilingualism in Article 7, Section 2, to counter President Taft's Enabling Act of 1910, which demanded "as a condition of statehood that ability to read and speak English be a qualification for holding office."[48]

Specifically, private individuals have a right to make an arrest without a warrant. Citizen's arrests are subject to fewer constitutional requirements than arrest by law enforcement officers. A reasonable suspicion that someone has committed a felony permits a citizen to make a citizen's arrest. A citizen's arrest can be made for misdemeanors only if the misdemeanor involves a breach of the peace that was witnessed by the person making the arrest, that had just occurred, or that showed a strong likelihood of continuing. In making the citizen's arrest, the person can use only the amount of force that is reasonable and necessary. Deadly force can be used if the person making the citizen's arrest is faced with that threat of serious bodily injury or immediate use of deadly force. Deadly force can only be used as just described in order to prevent harm to oneself or others. Making a citizen's arrest inherently assumes risk of liability.[49]

Tijerina, after years of self-study, learned these concepts from countless lawbooks and treatises in both Spanish and English. He became an autodidactic lawyer, an expert on four main areas of the law: the U.S. Constitution; the New Mexico State Constitution; the Treaty of Guadalupe Hidalgo; and the Law of the Indies. He used these legal documents as the foundation for his cause. His worldview rested on these principal documents. From these documents, he would extrapolate pieces for his public pronouncements, speeches, writings, and arguments. His study of the Fourth Amendment on searches and searches led him to the power of citizen's arrest. He used that power most effectively to target an individual and crime. His bravado in making such an arrest empowered his followers and enriched his cause with notoriety. The resulting publicity was gold for his cause. He could not be stopped lawfully in making a citizen's arrest of Chief Justice Warren Burger or the scientists at Los Alamos for making a weapon of mass destruction, the atomic bomb. Tijerina argued that Burger had a duty to validate the Treaty of Guadalupe Hidalgo as part of the "supreme law of the land" clause in Article 2 of the U.S. Constitution and to overrule all prior precedents that had failed to do so. The scientists he accused of making weapons of mass destruction, a crime against all humanity. And had District Attorney Alfonso Sanchez been present in the Tierra Amarilla Courthouse and attempted citizen arrest on June 5, 1967, that probably would not have been a crime. But he was absent all day from that courthouse; perhaps he had been tipped off by an informant of the impending raid. If so, why were others there?

Boston Witt, New Mexico Attorney General

Boston Witt did not share the acute concern DA Sanchez had over Tijerina and his motives. Just months before the Echo Amphitheater takeover, he had this to say:

> We investigated his background with the assistance of the Mexican Government and the FBI. We could not satisfy ourselves that he is either a Communist or a Communist sympathizer. I do not at this time consider him an imminent threat in this state.[50]

Sanchez, however, was already working with federal district judge H. Vearle Payne to order Tijerina be made to tender the membership list of the

Alianza. Tijerina had ignored the first order from the judge. The service of the order was in question. Judge Payne issued a second order for the list to be in his courtroom by June 6, 1966. He sent U.S. Marshal Emilio Naranjo to personally deliver the second notice. He could not find Tijerina.

Sanchez gave up on the state AG and the "feds," as he called them, to curb Tijerina and the Alianza. Perhaps DA Sanchez refused to abide by federal law in affording the Alianza and its leaders their civil rights. It was not illegal to join and be part of the Alianza, a state-certified and federally chartered nonprofit organization. Sanchez organized his own task force to capture and control Tijerina once and for all. His team began drafting blank arrest warrants with blank charges, so they could be filled in once they had a suspect in custody. Sanchez was becoming the rule of law in his county. Nabokov wrote about this drafting process in this fashion:

> About half a dozen men had sat in the district attorney's book-strewn office. They included a Forest Service representative and the head of the state police narcotics division. State Police Captain T. J. Chavez outlined the various charges prepared for key Alianza leaders, ranging from unlawful assembly to driving without a license and public drunkenness. These offenses were to be ready reference for officers manning roadblocks that would we erected that evening and stay through Saturday. Blank complaints against the Alianza principals, authorized in advance by Sanchez, were also mentioned.[51]

This type of activity is a major conspiracy on the part of state and local officials to deprive Tijerina and the Alianza membership of their civil rights. Membership in the Communist Party is permitted in the United States, including New Mexico, let alone membership in the Alianza.[52]

Governor Cargo, on the other hand, was orchestrating an economic development plan for northern New Mexico. If jobs could be created and found, the people from these "land grant communities" could move from subsistence on the land to wage-and-hour lifestyles. He recruited consultants.

Taking Echo Amphitheater

Tijerina publicized the fact that his followers would camp out at the Echo Amphitheater and reclaim the land as theirs in the next month or so after the land grant heirs had elected their government. On October 15, 1966, some 350 heirs of the San Joaquin land grant had elected Jose Lorenzo Sanchez as mayor and a city council to govern the grant. Tijerina himself had bought land so he could be an heir and eligible for membership in the Alianza. Tijerina readied himself to use the citizen's arrest powers against the government police agents who would interfere with their plans.

Tijerina and Alianza members camped at the Echo Amphitheater, part of the 1.5 million acres of the Carson National Forest, on two consecutive weekends beginning on October 15, 1966. He called them "sit-ins." Both events were nonviolent. He returned with more than four hundred members traveling in a caravan of more than 150 cars and trucks on October 22. The caravan barreled into the park grounds, ignoring the fee payment required and stayed for four days. Sanchez, the FBI, undercover agents of the state police, and U.S. marshals busied themselves by writing down license plate numbers, photographing protestors and vehicles, and taking notes of behavior that might constitute destruction of federal property. The marshals served Tijerina and others with restraining orders preventing them from occupying the park. Utilizing the citizen's arrest power, the group held two Forest Service park rangers, Phil Smith and Walt Taylor in custody at Echo Amphitheater; and took control of a government truck.[53] These government agents had been arrested for trespassing and were awaiting trial by the Sons of San Joaquin, as the land grant ruling council called themselves. Jerry Noll presided over their four trials. When the Aliancistas had done their deeds, the FBI and state police moved in and arrested the Alianza leaders and removed the campers from the site.

The first substantial FBI reports, four, are dated October 24, 1966, from a redacted source and prepared October 22, 1966 in Espanola, New Mexico by Special Agent [name redacted] and dictated on October 24, 1966. The fifth report was done in Chama, New Mexico. The compilation of these reports amount to forty-two pages. Chama and Espanola are in opposite directions from Echo Amphitheater which implies that the FBI had advance notice of this takeover of Echo Park by the Alianza because the first reports were dated the same day but timed at 7:45 a.m. for Espanola (p. 19) and 7:15 a.m. for Chama (p. 30). Both the first and fifth reports placed Forest Service (FS) agents at the recreation area entrance to collect entrance fees and if refused to take down license plate numbers. For example, "[Name redacted], he took a FS employee from Taos, New Mexico, who was not in uniform, to the canyon entrance of Echo Park and assigned him to stay there and photograph anything that happened" (p. 19). The 11:00 a.m. report from Espanola stated a car caravan of about thirty cars had just passed by toward Echo Park and also reported that FS rangers could not hold back the cars crossing into the park area without paying the entrance fee (p. 22).

Later that same day two of the Alianza members staging the demonstration at Echo Park went to the Ghost Ranch Museum, where the FBI agents apparently were stationed, and identified themselves as Cirilio Garcia and Ezichiel [sic] Dominguez and showed identification cards indicating they were deputies of the Federal Alliance of Land Grants (p. 22). "They were driving a blue over white Chevrolet station wagon, bearing New Mexico License 29-472" (p. 28). The FBI agents and FS rangers both reported having taken photographs of people involved in the Echo Park takeover and seizing their trucks. Property inside the FS pickups, radio, and keys were returned to the rangers, and they were escorted out of the park area onto the highway (p. 23).

Another of the reports describes the role of the state police, which basically was to wait outside the Echo Park area off Highway 84 until called for assistance. Who was to call is not identified (p. 27). The state police reported that only forty cars were involved in the caravan that entered Echo Park (p. 29). When the state police heard over their radio that two forest rangers were being held by the crowd, they drove into the park area in time to witness the trial of the rangers by Judge Jerry Noll. The report from Chama estimated the crowd at "about 200" (p. 30).

The FBI agents from Albuquerque got busy sending three memorandums to their director in Washington, DC, dated October 25, 1966, with names, offense reports, and descriptions on each person arrested: Reies López Tijerina, Al Chavez, and Ezekial [sic] Dominguez; all three categorized as "Armed and Dangerous." The next day Albuquerque Special Agent [redacted with handwritten exemption "B7C" next to box for "Report Made By"] of the FBI sent to change the spelling of "Ezekial" to "Esequiel" and "Al Chavez" to "Alfonso Chaves" and Noll's first name from Jerry, an alias, to Gerry. Moreover, this one-page report also stated that "the execution of these warrants was held in abeyance upon Bureau instructions the afternoon of 10/22/66." Apparently, the U.S. commissioner in New Mexico, Owen J. Mowrey, had issued complaints and warrants for Noll and "four John Doe warrants" dated October 22, 1966, but the Bureau had advised the agents on the ground to hold off on execution.

On October 26, 1966, the full forty-page report was sent from the Albuquerque FBI special agent in charge (SAC) (his name redacted) to the U.S. attorney in Albuquerque with the FBI version of what transpired at Echo Amphitheater campgrounds. This version coincides with Tijerina's own account, that over one hundred persons arrived by car caravan at Echo Amphitheater and proceeded to arrest Walter E. Taylor and Philip Smith, the two FS employees, and impounded their FS pickup trucks. The report differs from Tijerina's account in that it calls the proceeding led by Judge Jerry Noll a "Kangaroo Court." It makes no mention of the court proceedings being based on citizen's arrests for trespassing on land grant land. The report did not mention that James Evans, another FS ranger, first pointed a rifle at Tijerina's head, at which point Tijerina got his own rifle, and pointed it at Evans. The SAC cited the federal statutes violated and the bond on each of the five persons charged be set at $3,500.

Tijerina and others were arrested on October 26, 1966, about 10:19 a.m. by a special agent whose name is redacted. Tijerina refused to be fingerprinted, but "he was told that his fingerprints would be taken, and they were taken over his objections" (p. 33). Tijerina had an attorney present, Melvin D. Rueckhaus, who advised him not to sign the waiver-of-rights form. He then was taken to the U.S. commissioner for search and arraignment (p. 34). At this time, Tijerina is described as being forty years old, 175 lbs., born September 21, 1926, in Falls City, Texas, of the white race with black hair and hazel eyes and standing seventy inches tall (p. 35). Cristobal Tijerina did not fare as well as Reies, who made bail and left the federal courthouse.

Cristobal "was arrested in the hallway near the U.S. Commissioner's Office, also fingerprinted, photographed, and arraigned and afforded bail but was jailed for an outstanding arrest warrant" (p. 36). The same happened to Ezequiel Dominguez for standing in the hallway of the U.S. Commissioner's Office knowing he had an outstanding arrest warrant. He also was booked and turned over to the U.S. marshal for detention (p. 40). Jerry Noll, who was with Cristobal and standing in the hallway of the U.S. Commissioner's Office, also was arrested and booked (p. 37). Later that day, Alfonso Chávez with his attorney Carlos B. Sedillo turned himself in to the U.S. Attorney's Office.

After these arraignments, the bond was set at $2,000 each and preliminary hearings set for October 28, 1966; however, Cristobal and Ezequiel were returned to custody for outstanding warrants. The FBI had recommended the bonds be set at $3,500 each in the SAC's Albuquerque report to the U.S. Attorney in Albuquerque dated October 26, 1966.

King of the Indies?

Jerry Noll, a fourteen-year-old Seattle teenager, was trouble. While in jail on three charges, he stabbed another inmate with a dinner fork, which lengthened his sentence. Doing the time, he read about Tijerina and the Alianza in the newspaper and promptly wrote to Reies asking to attend the upcoming convention and become a member of the Alianza. In this letter, he explained his connection to Tijerina's movement. According to his father, he explained, he was the "rightful 'King of the Indies'" because of the family lineage. His father tied them to the Hapsburg family of Germany and therefore to Queen Isabella de Castilla and some prophecy by Nostradamus. For some reason, Tijerina welcomed him into the fold and listed him as the "Historian of International Law" at the September 1966 Alianza Convention. According to Nabokov, Noll signed his official documents on behalf of the Alianza with the title "Don Barne Quinto Cesar, The King Emperor."[54]

Five days after the Echo Amphitheater events, Reies López Tijerina and four others were cited to appear before Federal District Judge Howard Bratton and face U.S. Attorney Victor Ortega. The charges were assault on a federal agent and confiscation of government property. After this hearing, the judge set bail of $5,000 on each one: Reies, Jerry Noll, Cristobal Tijerina, Ezequiel Dominguez, and Alfonso Chávez. The Alianza lawyer was Carlos Cedillo. But the trial was on the actions taken by Tijerina and the others against the federal agents, not the foundational allegation made by the Alianza that the FS rangers were trespassers on their land.

A few days later on November 10, a baby girl was born to Patricia and Reies Tijerina; they named her Isabel Iris after the Spanish queen Isabela de Castilla, who financed Cristoforo Colon's trips to the New World.[55]

The Alianza Membership Lists

In an underhanded move, DA Sanchez and the state police began planning on how to obtain the membership lists of the Alianza. If they knew who the members were and where they lived, human intelligence would be much more effective in stopping the Alianza by constant surveillance, personal interviews, and observation of their activities, which might lead to their arrests. The DA should have known of the U.S. Supreme Court case *NAACP v. Patterson* (or the other name also used *NAACP v. Alabama*), dating to 1958. In this case, the state sought to obtain the membership lists of the National Association for the Advancement of Colored People (NAACP). With that information, the state and local officials could find and thwart every move made by members of the organization. The NAACP countered the ex parte order restraining them from meeting and ordering production of the member lists. The NAACP complied with most of the court order except for the membership lists. They were held in contempt of court and fined $100,000 for failing to produce the lists. The state supreme court denied certiorari to review the contempt judgment but the U.S. Supreme Court granted certiorari. And SCOTUS held that the State of Alabama was not entitled to those membership lists, and that compelled disclosure would be a violation of the federal Constitution. The state case was reversed and remanded for proceedings and compliance not inconsistent with the SCOTUS opinion.[56] DA Sanchez, however, was arresting Alianza members and other family members for any violation under the law reported by his network of informants. He wanted the membership lists regardless of federal case law.

Lucky Break for the State

Sanchez heard the Alianza was to hold meetings in Coyote, New Mexico, around the middle of May and the first days of June. He alerted the state police to the information he had gathered from his informants and that he was going to arrest all the Aliancistas and the Tijerina brothers. The governor attempted to cool down the situation and met with some of the leaders from the Tierra Amarilla land grant. He promised to attend the Coyote meeting if they promised to stop their activity of posting notices, having armed patrols, and trying to arrest people for trespassing. They refused his conditions. Meanwhile, Sanchez went on with his plan and began mass arrests for unlawful assembly on May 14. He took to the radio the day before for a broadcast on local radio stations:

> As District Attorney, I wish to give notice to all Alianza Members who plan to be present and participate at the meeting in Coyote tomorrow, that said meeting is versus the laws since it is planned to take over private property. Criminal charges of unlawful assembly will be filed against all persons who attend. Penalty is six months in jail.... You are being misled by Reies Lopez Tijerina.... What he professes is Communism and is illegal.[57]

His first dragnet got him eighteen Alianza members, and he made plans to follow up with more arrests on June 3. When confronted with these bogus charges and false arrests, Sanchez shifted the blame to Judge James Scarborough, who had signed the arrest warrants and court order to produce the Alianza membership lists directed at Tijerina.[58] But Tijerina expected this to happen and resigned from the Alianza as a ploy to not comply since he was not the head anymore. The Alianza temporarily became a new organization with a different name, the Confederación de Pueblos Libres. Upon learning of this maneuver by Tijerina, Judge

Scarborough contemplated holding Tijerina in contempt of his court order. But it was not to be.

With roadblocks everywhere in northern New Mexico seeking to find Reies Tijerina to arrest him, State Police Captain Hoover Wimberly and other officers stopped two cars. Without search warrants but with blank arrest warrants instead, they took the occupants into custody and searched the cars. In one they found weapons and gas masks. In the other car, driven by Cristobal Tijerina, they found documents and the membership list of the Alianza, including ten account books indicating dues collection by each member's name. Adeliada Cargo, the governor's wife, was one, and she was in arrears for half of the 1966 dues, six dollars.[59]

While Governor Cargo was explaining to the press what was going on, he received a call from the state police chief, Joe Black, that they had arrested Cristobal Tijerina and found the membership lists, a treasure trove of evidence, including that of his wife.[60] Governor Cargo was furious with the DA and state police for their Gestapo tactics. He began making calls to see about releasing some of those being incarcerated and meeting with their relatives. Ramon Tijerina had also been arrested on the highway as he entered New Mexico from Texas, as was Anselmo Tijerina. In his case, the police charged him with a firearm violation.

Instead of heading up to Coyote, the governor made plans to fly to Michigan to visit his buddy, Governor George Romney, but not before he took to the radio waves to ask motorists not to go to Coyote or that part of the state and state that he would not be in attendance at the meeting as he earlier had indicated he might.

As relatives tried to make bail to get their loved ones released from jail in Tierra Amarilla, the DA and U.S. Marshal Emilio Naranjo added a new twist: they had to approve the bail bond in writing. Naranjo was not hard to find, and some did find him, but DA Sanchez was not to be found. He was as elusive as Reies López Tijerina. Cargo had left town, and arraignment on those charged was set for 9:30 a.m. on Monday, June 5, 1967, before Judge James Scarborough. Sanchez sent his assistant Norman Neel while he conferred with the FBI and others still seeking to find and arrest Tijerina. The proceedings were moved down to 1:30 p.m. and the first eight prisoners were released by midafternoon. Assistant DA Neel packed his files and left for Santa Fe. Judge Scarborough had retired to his chambers when shots rang out. Larry Calloway, UPI reporter calling in his story dropped to the floor of the telephone booth to avoid being shot by the Aliancistas running into the building. The infamous Tierra Amarilla Courthouse "raid" had begun. They came wanting to arrest DA Sanchez and release the remaining prisoners.[61]

CHAPTER 3

Citizen's Arrest

In April 1966, Cristobal and Reies Tijerina, having learned from elders in New Mexico about their loss of land, traveled to Madrid and Seville, Spain, to inspect documents with their own eyes. They searched for documents and laws to support the stories they had heard from the land claimants in New Mexico. Reies was convinced the federal and state governments had illegally used their police powers to help Anglo thieves usurp the rights of the land claimants and, therefore, those of their individual homesteads as well as the collective homeland of all Indohispanos. He had found as much in the University of New Mexico library archives, which he visited often in 1961.[1] Cristobal, with his eighth-grade education, was not much help with reading old Castilian Spanish, but Tijerina taught himself to read and understand these texts. He constantly asked archivists, legal scholars, and clergymen at the archives, bookstores, churches, law schools, and the street, anywhere he found someone willing to listen to his story of stolen lands in New Mexico, for help with definitions of words, phrases, symbols, and their meanings. He became an expert on these laws. He began to intellectually digest their application to the Treaty of

Guadalupe Hidalgo and, more importantly, to U.S. case law. These treatises became his new bible.

They found documents in Seville that housed the Archivo General de la Indias, which referenced time and again two sets of legal codification of applicable laws: *Las siete partidas* and *La recopilación de las leyes los reinos de las Indias*. He bought a four-volume set of *Las siete partidas* dating back to the thirteenth century and began to devour its content. He found the laws and regulations on governance of people, land, and communities insightful and applicable to the land grant cause of New Mexicans. In Madrid they found the multivolume *Recopilación* dating to 1680, which Reies also bought.[2]

As soon as they returned from Spain, Tijerina entrusted the translation of a booklet he had written on the most important laws and cases on the land question to Patricia Blawis, a volunteer with a Marxist viewpoint.[3] He also made plans to march on Santa Fe to present his demands that these Spanish codes should be respected in New Mexico according to tenets of international law.

The March on Santa Fe

On the July 2, 1966, Tijerina led Alianza members on a march to the state capitol in Santa Fe, much as César Chávez and Martin Luther King Jr. repeatedly were doing to press their case to the state and federal governments and the public. Letter writing and signed petitions sent to the governor and prior presidents had not produced meaningful results, sometimes not even an acknowledgment, much less a response. This time Tijerina was calling on Governor Jack Campbell to receive and listen to their claims and grievances.

New Mexicans, particularly the most Catholic of Hispanos, loved pilgrimages, and Tijerina tapped into that cultural soft spot; he recruited over three hundred pilgrims, women, men, and children, to march with him the sixty-six miles from Albuquerque to Santa Fe in the middle of a hot summer. At front of the marchers was an elder, Jose Luis Sanchez, on a donkey holding a flag representing the Tierra Amarilla land grant. They walked and camped alongside the road at dusk for three days. At times passing motorists would shout insults and obscenities, including gestures; at other times gunshots were fired into the air. When they finally arrived at the outskirts of Santa Fe, Tijerina was informed by Frank McGuire, director of the Office of Economic Opportunity, that the governor would not be receiving them; he was out of town. Realizing the power of the press, Tijerina decided to camp out and wait while he issued daily press releases and held impromptu press conferences. Once the governor returned, his aides met with Tijerina and the marchers on July 11, an effective tactic to get them out of town and out of the press. Tijerina presented him with another signed petition, this one addressed to President Lyndon Johnson, that Governor Campbell promised to ensure would be delivered. The meeting and petition was about investigating the land grant issue. Tijerina also gave the governor a copy of the Alianza's newly printed pamphlet on the land grant question.[4] One of those aides was the state archivist-historian Dr. Myra Ellen Jenkins, who was anathema to Tijerina. She had called him a charlatan, a thief, and a rabble-rouser in the press. The governor wanted her opinion on the land grant claims. According to Tijerina, she dismissed them summarily:

> In short, she said, "The land question has been settled many years back. This Alianza of Reies is seeking money and has no merit." Myra Jenkins' opinion simply promoted stereotypes and repeated the accusations that I had been falsely accused of in the past. In essence, what this lady, supposedly the expert on archives, was telling us was that we should accept the abuse, the theft that the Anglo has committed for the last hundred and twenty years. We shouldn't defend ourselves, much less join the Alianza. She said that the Alianza members were a group of racketeers.[5]

As chapter 2 mentions, Tijerina sued her for slander, claiming $2 million in damages, but the local district court dismissed his lawsuit. And President Johnson, despite assurances from the governor of delivery of the documents Tijerina gave him, did not respond to them.[6]

In 1979, several years later, Jenkins found in archives she was responsible for maintaining an original document for the San Joaquin del Cañon del Rio de Chama land grant. Tijerina was right about this claim and others. Nothing changed, however, because Tijerina was out of the land recovery movement as a condition of his parole; there was no Alianza, and no one brought a new legal action; and Tijerina was simply eking out an existence in Coyote, New Mexico, with Patsy and their four children.[7]

The Pamphlet on the Law over Land Grants

The Alianza published a twenty-page booklet with evidence of sources and cases of their rights to the lands in New Mexico.[8] This was an explanation in English of their position. The booklet organized the argument in an introduction, three succinct chapters, and a final commentary. It began, "The real issue in this instance, as set forth in this pamphlet, is the protection of property and of prior vested and paramount rights, which is a factor of importance to most everyone."[9] The central argument is explained this way in the pamphlet:

> Here on the Rio Grande, the Royal Laws of the Indies existed and still exist as the local law. For these royal laws have never been repealed or abrogated by any duly constituted authority. When the Empire of Mexico invaded and occupied New Mexico, the Royal Laws of the Indies remained in force. And when the United States of America invaded and occupied New Mexico, the Royal Laws of the Indies remained in force, except as changed by legislation; but such changes apply only to newly initiated rights and do not disturb prior vested rights, such as old royal grant rights. The Royal Laws of the Indies were continued in force, as the local laws and customs, and are the common-law, which is foreign to such old royal granted rights and concepts under the Laws of the Indies. And the old Royal Laws of the Indies is [sic] protected by the law of nations as the local law of New Mexico.[10]

The pamphlet continues with a quick denunciation of the English common law by contrasting its imposition over royal laws.

REIES LÓPEZ TIJERINA COLLECTION, ZIMMERMAN LIBRARY, UNIVERSITY OF NEW MEXICO

Reies López Tijerina at the Alianza building before Alianza's name was changed to Alianza de Pueblos Libres.

COURTESY ROSA TIJERINA

Hugh David and Reies López Tijerina, circa 1965.

Justice is His Creed

The Poor is h.. First Concern

ELECT
TIJERINA
for
GOVERNOR *Of New Mex.*

He will Champion the Constitution of New Mexico
He will Speak and Fight for the Poor
Like Robert Kennedy and Dr. King, He too will Die for the Poor. *Tijerina for Governor Commitee.*

Vote Nov. 5 '68 On The People's Constitutional Party

REIES LÓPEZ TIJERINA COLLECTION, ZIMMERMAN LIBRARY, UNIVERSITY OF NEW MEXICO

Flyer advertising Reies López Tijerina's election campaign for governor of New Mexico in 1968.

Reies López Tijerina in sombrero at center with unidentified supporters of Tijerina's bid for governor.

REIES LÓPEZ TIJERINA COLLECTION, ZIMMERMAN LIBRARY, UNIVERSITY OF NEW MEXICO

Anselmo Tijerina, brother, and Reies López Tijerina.

REIES LÓPEZ TIJERINA COLLECTION, ZIMMERMAN LIBRARY, UNIVERSITY OF NEW MEXICO

Rudolfo "Corky" Gonzales, three unidentified Native American leaders, and Reverend Ralph Abernathy.

Reies López Tijerina, three unidentified Native American leaders, and Reverend Ralph Abernathy.

REIES LÓPEZ TIJERINA COLLECTION, ZIMMERMAN LIBRARY, UNIVERSITY OF NEW MEXICO

REIES LÓPEZ TIJERINA COLLECTION, ZIMMERMAN LIBRARY, UNIVERSITY OF NEW MEXICO

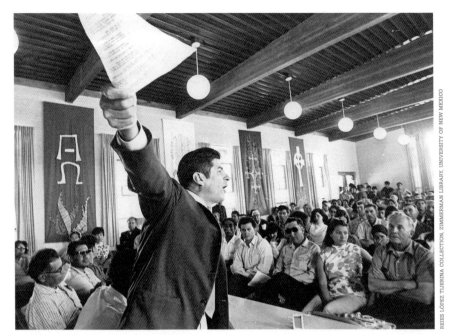

REIES LÓPEZ TIJERINA COLLECTION, ZIMMERMAN LIBRARY, UNIVERSITY OF NEW MEXICO

Reies López Tijerina speaking at an annual La Alianza de Pueblos Libres convention.

REIES LÓPEZ TIJERINA COLLECTION, ZIMMERMAN LIBRARY, UNIVERSITY OF NEW MEXICO

Reies López Tijerina, unidentified men, and Dennis Hopper, circa 1968.

REIES LÓPEZ TIJERINA COLLECTION, ZIMMERMAN LIBRARY, UNIVERSITY OF NEW MEXICO

REIES LÓPEZ TIJERINA COLLECTION, ZIMMERMAN LIBRARY, UNIVERSITY OF NEW MEXICO

Above: Reies López Tijerina at microphone with supporters including several members of the Brown Berets.

Left: Muhammad Ali and Reies López Tijerina.

COURTESY OF THE SECRETARY OF THE PRESIDENCY, MEXICO CITY, MEXICO

Jose "Little Joe" Hernandez, Ed Morga (LULAC), Frank Shafer-Corona, José Angel Gutiérrez, Reies López Tijerina, Harmonia Tijerina, President José Lopéz Portillo, Carlos Falcon, Eduardo Terrones (NCLR), Manuel Lopez (MAPA, California), and Antonio Morales (American G.I. Forum).

REIES LÓPEZ TIJERINA COLLECTION, ZIMMERMAN LIBRARY, UNIVERSITY OF NEW MEXICO

Left to right in front: Jaime Fernandez Reyes, the actor who played Reies López Tijerina, Jaime Casillas, the filmmaker, Tijerina, and Rosa Tijerina, oldest daughter of Tijerina and Maria Escobar. All others were crew members during filming of movie *Chicano.*

REIES LÓPEZ TIJERINA COLLECTION, ZIMMERMAN LIBRARY, UNIVERSITY OF NEW MEXICO

Reies López Tijerina and his wife, Patricia Romero Tijerina, with their three daughters, Isabel Iris, Harmonia, and Danitha

The new-comers to New Mexico, the Anglos, have been endeavoring to ignore prior vested and paramount rights in New Mexico, but such ignoring of such old rights do[es] not change the same. The Anglos, purporting to be the "conquerors" brought their own laws and doctrines (from English common-law sources) with them into this region, and, in the purported administration of the law, the Anglos have impinged upon rights and concepts of the inhabitants of New Mexico, and subject them more or less to the doctrines for the "new-comers" in the land, which are foreign here and shall always remain so. A great deal of confusion has been created in New Mexico by these Anglos who have no respect for international law or local law, and ... who have been and are endeavoring to foist upon the people of New Mexico English common-law, in order to terrorize the owners and heirs of these Land Grants into not exercising their rights under these grants.[11]

In the booklet are specific citations to cases decided by the U.S. Supreme Court upholding the supremacy of international accords, law, and treaties on land titles and property rights. There are no less than four such cases cited in chapter 1 in support of that supremacy and establishing SCOTUS precedent for upholding the land claims of Hispanos in the United States: *United States v. Percheman,* 7 Peters, 50, 86; *United States v. Moreno,* 1 Wall 400, 404; *Delassus v. United States,* 9 Peters, 117; and, *Soulard et al v. United States,* 4 Peters, 511 (no years provided by Tijerina).[12] However, in order by year, the *Percheman* case, 32 U.S. 51 (1832) was first, followed by *Peters,* 34 U.S. 117 (1835), *Soulard,* 35 U.S. 100 (1836), and *Moreno,* 68 U.S. 1 (1863).

The First Warning

Months before June 5, 1967, the day of the event known as the Tierra Amarilla Courthouse raid in the secondary literature, a legal notice was published in the *Albuquerque Journal.* The notice was a "Manifesto" signed by King Emperor of the Indies, Jerry Noll, aka Gerald Wayne Barnes, and aka Don Barne Quinto Cesar del Castillo.[13] It read:

Know Ye that. It is no longer feasible for the officers and agents of the Government of the United States of America to use words with doctrinal serenity and feign to be ignorant of the incontestable existence and real consequences of historical fact or of legal realities, as an excuse for their illegal activities beyond the territorial jurisdiction of the United States of America—*ignorantia legis et facto neminem excusat*—THEREFORE KNOW YE THAT, We, shall commence to liberate our kingdoms, realms and dominions.[14]

The attempts to "commence to liberate our kingdoms, realms and dominions" began by taking lands back at Echo Amphitheater Park, its current name in English.

The Claim

We chose October 15, 1966, as the day to take the land of San Joaquín. According to the original settlers and their descendants, the land grant consisted of six hundred thousand square acres, and we thought that the best site to provoke the confrontation with the federal government would be to take the area within the designated grant now called "Echo Amphitheater Park." We took that park by force and held it over the weekend. Their press immediately began their campaign against us, describing it as violent aggression.[15]

But not enough Aliancistas came to help or enough press to cover the "takeover" on the fifteenth, and Tijerina called for a second effort on the twenty-second.

The San Joaquin grant belonged to 350 families who had always stayed on the land, as did their heirs and descendants. King Charles IV of Spain had made that grant on August 1, 1806.[16] The Mexican governor of the time, Joaquin Alencaster, in turn designated Francisco Salazar the principal settler and impresario, along with thirty-one other families. Thomas Profit, the U.S. surveyor general, confirmed the rights to these lands and recommended the

U.S. House of Representatives committee approve the land title on February 14, 1873. Congress, however, approved a side deal with Thomas B. Catron of the Santa Fe Ring. The families, with Salazar, were dispossessed of their lands by this fraud and illegal action by Congress.

Eighteen years later, in 1891, Congress established the U.S. Court of Claims, but this land grant claim was not among those presented for validation. An English corporation bought interests in land from some of the original families, 472,000 acres, and it presented this claim to the Court of Claims. Oddly, the court refused the British corporation's claim on the grounds that Surveyor General Profit had validated the Salazar families and their heirs as true owners of these lands. Nothing happened.

On May 12, 1945, U.S. representative from New Mexico Antonio Fernandez presented the San Joaquin claim, requesting its true validation by the Seventy-Eighth Congress. Congressman Fernandez explained to his colleagues that the San Joaquin families had not had their day before Congress in 1871 or in court in 1891. He detailed to his colleagues the fraud of the Maxwell grant claim by Catron. He explained that in reality this land concession was the San Joaquin grant. Congress, however, did not take up the matter.[17] Over the subsequent years "a portion of the grant had eventually become part of the Presbyterian-owned and operated Ghost Ranch complex," and the remainder had been acquired by the government and made a part of the Santa Fe forest and a small national monument and park, Echo Amphitheater Park.[18]

Recovering Land: San Joaquin del Cañon del Rio de Chama

Jose Lorenzo Salazar, a direct descendent of the original settler, Francisco Salazar, had been elected mayor of Rio de Chama at a prior meeting of the descendants and heirs. Samuel Cordova was elected the marshal to enforce the law.[19] On October 22, the renewed effort by the elected officials to take over part of the San Joaquin land grant began. Tijerina brought more than 150 cars and vans to the park, including Juan Valdez. He had not made the Fourth of July weekend march or the first takeover of the Echo

Amphitheater. He recalled in his oral history that he brought a pair of boots rather than a weapon to the takeover for an express purpose. He told his grandson that he did something that at the time he was not real proud of but now was glad he did.

> After we made the citizen's arrest of Smith and Taylor and they were being held on the ground in front of a table, I went over to where Phil Smith was and kicked him in the butt.... He was the Ranger that was always giving my Father trouble about our cattle and sheep being on the forest. My Father had died the year before and I was still mad about how he'd been treated all his life—so I kicked Smith in the butt to get even for everything he'd done to make my Father's life so hard.... He grabbed my legs, but I broke loose and kicked him again. Then I thought if I could just talk to my Father, I would tell him that I was getting even for the way Smith had treated him all those years.[20]

The Consequences of the Echo Takeover

> First to arrive was a pickup bearing 72-year old Baltazar Apodaca of Canjilon and his friend Pablo Garcia. They parked near the entrance and passed time arguing with the ranger.... About 11 a.m. the convoy appeared, a long string of more than 50 vehicles, horns honking, flags flying. The lead cars swooped so close to the State Patrol cars that Captain Vigil had to throw himself out of their path.[21]

The Aliancistas took control of the entrance to the park by citizen's arrest of two Forest Service rangers, Walter Taylor and Phil Smith, who were trying to keep people from entering without paying for a permit.[22] "Two carloads of FBI agents stationed themselves to watch."[23] State Police Captain Martin Vigil and several state patrol cars "arranged themselves along the opposite side of the highway at a discreet distance from the entrance. Their radios informed them that Tijerina was four miles south, rallying his forces opposite the entrance to Ghost Ranch."[24]

The FBI Report on Echo Amphitheater Campgrounds

The FBI did not sit in their cars for long. They got out and intermingled with the crowd at the Echo campgrounds. A lengthy report was filed by the SAC, Albuquerque, to the director of the FBI, dated October 25, 1966, that was to augment the phone calls and teletypes to the Bureau from the twenty-second to the twenty-fifth. The subject heading of the memorandums—there were four memorandums in total—began with "Reies Lopez Tijerina-Fugitive, et al AFO, TGP."[25] The other two added the names of Al Chavez and Ezekial [sic] Dominguez; the last corrected aliases and spelling of names such as "Cris" to Cristobal, "Esequiel" as the correct first name, and "Gerry" for Jerry Noll. The content was to alert the director that the federal complaints and warrants issued by the U.S. commissioner on October 22, 1966, were being held in abeyance from execution until further Bureau instructions.

The forty-two-page report basically covers what the secondary sources, particularly Gardner and Blawis, had themselves written about the incident.

> About 150 people were present in the camp grounds ... four individuals ... wearing badges ... grab two employees of the United States Forest Service, Phillip Smith ... District Ranger of the Canjilon District, and Walter Taylor ... staff officer ... were taken ... where the judge of the group, Jerry Noll (phonetic) was holding court.... Two United States Forest Service pickup trucks, plus a Forest Service radio, all property of the United States Government, were impounded by Noll ... did not observe any weapons ... but he did see a gun on another individual who was a member of the group ... did not see the two Rangers beaten, abused, or struck by anyone ... they were handled roughly in being escorted before the judge. (p. 3)

The crowd had arrested more FS rangers, including Walter Taylor, again. He had broken loose from captors and made a run for his gun inside his vehicle. The .38 caliber revolver was confiscated and emptied of its bullets. Taylor had been a professional boxer, but he was no match for Cristobal Tijerina, who grabbed him as he reached the door of the pickup, spun him around to grab his tie and shirt, and said, "Shut up, you son of a bitch."[26]

The lengthy report indicates that "immediately following the receipt of the eye witness account from [name redacted], SA [(name redacted] contacted United States Attorney John Quinn" (p. 2). The FBI agent desired federal complaints to be filed against Noll and the others who had assaulted Smith and Taylor. He also wanted arrest warrants for these individuals. The "USA Quinn and SA [name redacted] filed a complaint before U.S. Commissioner Owen J. Mowrey charging them with violations of Sections III . . . and 641, Title 18, U.S. Code." Warrants were issued for Noll and the four John Doe subjects (p. 4). The FBI agents present at the Echo takeover took photographs. An FBI agent (name redacted) also began "to write down the license numbers of vehicles which had come into the area in a convoy" and was told to stop by Pablo Garcia (p. 7). Garcia identified himself to the FBI agent as "the boss." Bennie Ortega of Los Alamos in a Chevrolet Carryall "almost ran over [name of Martin Vigil redacted]." "Someone else took hold of [Walter Taylor redacted]'s arm . . . the person . . . was Al Chavez" (p. 8). The arrested rangers were allowed to gather their personal articles from the impounded vehicles, including "a pistol which[,] . . . hidden under a coat, fell to the ground . . . (p. 10). The FBI agents present saw "Moises Corrales of Canjilon cutting four trees in the Forest Service area with a power saw." Another watched as a man whom he could not identify "nailed a sign over a Forest Service sign in the recreation area. This sign had the words, '*Pueblo Republica de San Joaquin del Rio de Chama*, established 1806'" (p. 11). The report contains narratives from various other FBI agents and Forest Service personnel repeating their version of what happened to whom and identities of some of the Aliancistas (pp. 12–32). The report also identifies news media personnel by name who were present and taking video footage and sound recordings of the events as they unfolded. A two-way portable radio was taken from a FS pickup but was returned by Alfonso Chávez when requested.

Quinn recommended bond in the amount of $3,500 each. But Quinn also dismissed the October 22 John Doe complaints; instead the FBI filed complaints on October 24, 1966, which were issued. On October 26 all five subjects surrendered to Special Agents of the FBI . . ."following arrests, photographing, and fingerprinting, they were arraigned . . . with preliminary hearing set for 10:00 a.m., October 28, 1966, and bond was set in the amount of $2,000 each" (p. 33).

Jerry Noll did hold trials for those arrested, found them guilty, and passed sentence on them for trespassing, but suspended the sentence to show leniency.[27]

Remaining in the campgrounds, Aliancistas celebrated their victory over the U.S. government for a few days; then federal FBI agents and FS rangers swarmed the encampment armed with a restraining order issued by U.S. District Judge H. Vearle Payne.[28] They served only five of the perpetrators.[29] The five were Jerry Noll, Reies and Cristobal Tijerina, Ezequiel Dominguez, and Alfonso Chávez.[30] On their way out, the federal officers tore down the makeshift stenciled sign that read *Pueblo Republica de San Joaquin del Rio de Chama.*[31]

This first effort at using the strategy of a citizen's arrest did not fare well for Tijerina, Noll, and the other principal leaders of the takeover of Echo Amphitheater. Ultimately, they were the ones arrested, jailed, and made to post bond while their trials on these charges were set in motion. Two of them, Ezequiel Dominguez and Cristobal Tijerina, were imprisoned immediately for outstanding warrants, which they should have known would happen. Reies Tijerina, for some unknown reason, was not served with a restraining order at the campground, as were others. But according to the lengthy memo already above, he was arrested "on the 12th floor of the U.S. Court House" in the "hallway to the Office of the U.S. Marshall" (p. 34). His property was inventoried and returned to him: currency, comb, pen, keys, card case, expired and temporary driver's license, and "one metal container of prophylactics" (p. 34).

The Trial in Las Cruces

On his own motion, Judge Payne moved the trial from Albuquerque to Las Cruces, some 366 miles southeast, what is known about New Mexico as "Little Texas." Moreover, to shortcut the proceedings Judge Howard C.

Bratton, sitting for Judge Payne, conducted the voir dire of the venire (jury pool) persons himself, not letting the defense ask questions of prospective jurors. A third of the jurors selected worked for the U.S. government; three white women chosen worked at the air force base in Alamogordo. The townspeople of Las Cruces were papered with free copies of a John Birch Society pamphlet, *Reies Tijerina: The Communist Plan to Grab the Southwest;* and the local paper editorialized on the eve of trial that it was time to stop the "proponents of violence in our country." Bratton was a former chairman of the Public Lands Commission, and his wife was a property holder on a disputed land claim.[32]

The trial lasted a week and all defendants were found guilty. All but Reies and Jerry Noll received light sentences of two months in jail. They received two-year prison terms with bail set at $5,000 pending appeals.[33] Additionally, Judge Bratton added a probation condition to run for five years to top the usual conditions of probation. Should Tijerina "at any time . . . propose or advocate the use of violence in the pursuit of any objective it will be considered a violation of probation."[34] Within a year, Tijerina and Noll were held on charges for contempt of court for comments made about Judge Bratton at the 1967 Alianza convention. These speeches, as were all proceedings, were taped by state police, who had illegally tapped the sound system. Judge Ewing Kerr found both of them guilty and added thirty-day jail sentences and $500 fines on top of the time meted out for the Echo Amphitheater takeover.[35] They appealed the Echo case before Bratton but lost. The appeal was sent to the U.S. Supreme Court for review, and that writ of certiorari was denied.[36]

DA Sanchez's strategy shifted; he was now going to prevent them from meeting by arresting members of the Alianza as he had done at Coyote, New Mexico. The next gathering of Aliancistas was to be held June 2, specifically to discuss what to do about the DA. Sanchez had arrested eleven more persons going to that meeting and jailed them at the Tierra Amarilla Courthouse. A court hearing for these charges was set for June 5. Immediately, those present decided then and there to go after the DA at the courthouse in Tierra Amarilla (TA) and arrest him for violating their First Amendment rights to free speech, association, and petitioning of grievances to the government. Several persons were selected by Tijerina: Juan Valdez, Tony Valdez, Geronimo "Indio" Barunda, Ezequiel Martinez, Ray Morales, Tobias Leyba, Ventura Chavez, Baltazar Martinez, Baltazar Apodaca, Jose Madrid, Salomon Velasquez, Fabian Chavez, Alfonso Chávez, and David and Rosa, his eldest son and daughter. They got their weapons and headed for the courthouse in three vehicles.

The secondary sources all relate the basic same narrative of the attempt to arrest the DA and remove from jail the Alianza members being held on bogus charges of going to a meeting. Tijerina's account and that of Juan Valdez, a participant, are not much different than these versions. The "TA Raid," as it became known in coffee shops and local media, unfolded like this, according to the account of Juan Valdez:

> To begin with I want to make one thing clear—we did not go there to raid the courthouse ... we went there to make a citizen's arrest of Alfonso Sanchez, the district attorney. The story that "a group of revolutionaries raiding a courthouse in Northern New Mexico" got a lot of more attention than it would have had it been reported that we had gone there to arrest the District Attorney. We weren't a bunch of revolutionaries like Alfonso Sanchez wanted everyone to believe—we were just a group of land heirs trying to get the government's attention. All we wanted was a chance to explain how the government had mistreated our people and taken millions of acres from land grants our families had lived on for generations.
>
> On the morning of June 5, 1967 about 30 members of our group, the Alianza, and our families, got together for a picnic at Tobias Leyba's ranch here in Canjilon to discuss what we were going to do about Sanchez trying to keep us from having meetings and discussing our problems. We agreed ... that if we caught Sanchez at the courthouse, we'd put him under arrest, take him to Tobias' and have a trial.[37]

Juan Valdez said he was the first one to walk inside the courthouse, although Tijerina claimed he sent Rosa inside first to see who was present.[38] Regardless of who gave the signal to come inside and find DA Sanchez, a state patrolman, Nick Saiz, was standing to the left looking at a bulletin board in the lobby. Patrolman Saiz saw Juan Valdez with a .45 caliber pistol in his hand. Saiz reached for his. Valdez warned him not to go for his gun and to put up his hands. Valdez shot him as Saiz tried to unholster his weapon.

> I had put myself where I had no choice—unless I was ready to die—and I wasn't. It came down to I shoot him, or he was going to shoot me—so I pulled the trigger. The bullet hit him in the left arm and chest. . . . Benny Naranjo, his deputy, Pete Jaramillo and Tommy Cordova, the Justice of the Peace, came around the corner from the Sheriff's office. When they saw Saiz on the floor and saw me with the pistol they got down on the floor and Benny pushed his pistol toward me. Baltazar Martinez made Benny, Pete, and Tommy go to the back room where all the employees were and made to get down on the floor. The rest of us started up the stairs to the courtroom where we figured Alfonso Sanchez would be.

The courtroom was empty. The DA was nowhere to be found. Seeing the doors to the judge's chamber and jury room closed, someone slammed a third door shut. As the Aliancistas approached, someone inside fired three shots through the door, hitting no one: "Reies raised the machine gun he was carrying and fired a blast through the door." Inside was Dan Rivera, the undersheriff. As they pulled him outside, "Ventura hit him in the back of the head. . . . When we got back downstairs, I was glad to see that Saiz was still alive."

> Days after that . . . I heard that "Gorras" and Baltazar Apodaca had taken Larry Calloway and Pete Jaramillo as hostages and driven them to Canjilon in Pete's car. On the way to Canjilon Reies told me that Eulogio Salazar, the jailer, had been shot trying to jump out of a window in the Sheriff's office. After we started seeing flashing lights coming toward the ranch from near the church we knew we had to get out of there quick. . . . We ran to the fence, crossed it, and headed southeast into the forest. There were six of us. I was in front and Reies, his son Hugh, Indio, Moises, and Jerry Noll were all following. . . . When we left Canjilon we had two rifles, some pistols, a battery radio, and a pair of binoculars that Reies lost during the night. . . . It was raining so hard that when it started getting dark it was

almost impossible to see where we were going ... we were having to stop every 20 or 30 minutes for Jerry Noll to catch up ... three or four times I told him I was sorry but we had to keep moving and if he couldn't keep up maybe he should go back.

We got to Celestino Velasquez's cabin ... and we could stay in the cabin. Moises, Indio and I stayed at the cabin for three or four days after Reies left and one night we walked to a bar in Youngsville.... When we go to Espanola I found out that Luisa had been born two days after we'd been to the courthouse and that Saiz was alive and expected to live.

Valdez called a state patrolman, Romero, who had assured his wife he would not hurt Juan if he turned himself in. Valdez was arrested and taken to jail, then to the state penitentiary, where he stayed for several months awaiting trial.

Several months later, Valdez was arrested and jailed again when Eulogio Salazar was murdered. He was a suspect. In fact, all the TA raiders were jailed again at the state prison on mere suspicion. The crime remains unsolved to this writing.

Blaming Tijerina for the Murder of Eulogio Salazar

During the takeover of the TA courthouse, the jailer, Eulogio Salazar attempted to flee through a window. Tijerina wrote: "Our people yelled at Eulogio not to leave, that he was not going to get hurt." He left the courthouse in pursuit of Salazar, helped him by calling an ambulance, and then "ran back into the courthouse."[39]

The Muddy Sheep Pen

The plight of those at the picnic is not the narrative of interest for those secondary sources who wrote about the TA Raid, except for Blawis. She describes how the New Mexico Mounted Patrol, Forest Service rangers, state police, policemen from the Jicara Apache Reservation, and a battalion of the national guard converged on Canjilon. "They surrounded the wooded pasture of the Leyba's, where about 60 women, children and older men were camping on private property."[40] Included in this group was Rosa Tijerina, Reies's daughter, and Patricia, Reies's wife, with a seven-month-old child, Isabela. The group was marched at gunpoint away from the picnic area to a muddy sheep pen. They were held without water, toilet facilities, food, or shelter from the incessant rain, scorching sun, and cold night for twenty-six hours. Patricia Bell Blawis writes:

> It rained that night, and their barbecue, left unattended, had burned, so there was nothing to eat, and they were without clean water. Guards followed Rosa Tijerina and other young women to the outdoor toilet that had no door. When Patsy, Tijerina's young wife, asked a National Guard officer why they were being held, he said that it was in the hope of luring back their men. She sought permission to shelter her baby from the rain but was refused.[41]

Rosa and seven others were separated from the group and taken to jail in Tierra Amarilla, then the state penitentiary. Patricia, five months pregnant, was taken to the state jail in Santa Fe, the baby, Isabel taken by county welfare workers. She had "a miscarriage two days after being freed. The doctor confirmed that this was a direct result of what had happened to her while detained."[42] DA Sanchez told them without hesitation when Rosa asked why they were being detained that "he would not release Rose [sic] until her father surrendered."[43] One of the National Guardsmen answered that same question with "They're bait. The brass expects that that Mexican will come back in here tonight to try to free these people."[44]

The adjutant general of the national guard, John Pershing Jolly, on orders from the acting governor brought out the troops for the largest manhunt in the history of the United States: 350 soldiers, with 400 more on "standby," and two hundred vehicles, including buses, flatbed trailers, medical vans, jeeps, two-ton trucks, and two M-42 tanks. One tank was positioned so its cannon pointed down the road leading to the penned women, children, and old men. Jolly turned down an offer for a jet to do flyovers the mountains with hopes of sighting Tijerina and the others. Jolly had twenty thousand rounds of ammunition on hand and ordered twenty thousand more rounds from Ft. Bliss in El Paso. Bewildered at the questions by several detainees as to why they were being held as prisoners of war, Jolly responded, "That's a good question. I really don't have an answer."[45]

The homes of neighbors to the Lebya ranch were searched and the residents interrogated. Cars on all roads leading to Canjilon were stopped and searched, the occupants interrogated. The stop-and-search operation was expanded to all roads going north from Santa Fe. Three members of the Alianza driving north from Albuquerque, Victorino Chavez, Santiago Anaya, and Camilo Sanchez, were stopped. They were jailed on suspicion of driving north "to incite a riot."[46] Many other Alianza members who had nothing to do with the TA operation were confronted by armed police at their doors seeking to search rooms, closets, bathrooms, parked cars, and garages.

A sixteen-year-old girl, the daughter of Abelecio Moya who was charged in the raid, was then held on a warrant signed by Sanchez. It was learned that Sanchez had waited three weeks to arrest her on all twenty-eight charges connected with the raid and then took his time scheduling a hearing for her. When the girl was later released, all charges against her were dropped.[47]

No search warrants were ever produced; charges were never filed, nor was bail set on many of those arrested; they were all treated like prisoners of war. After several hearings to gather testimony and affidavits, the American Civil Liberties Union filed suit against State Police Chief Joe Black, Jolly, and DA Sanchez for these transgressions, asking for $39,000 in damages, but it was dismissed summarily by a judge in 1969. A jury did find that four state policemen had engaged in conduct that violated the civil rights of an Alianza member.[48]

The DA used the confiscated membership list of the Alianza to terrorize many while in pursuit of Tijerina and the others in the mountains. Tijerina writes, "No sooner had they taken this list than a campaign of police terror began against Alianza members, similar to what Hitler's Gestapo did to the Jews. The FBI and the state police began to visit the homes of each member of the Alianza."[49] The FBI corroborated much of this information in a May 16, 1969, which read in part, "Following the confiscation of membership lists in the summer of 1967 by state authorities numerous members have been harassed and bombings have occurred."[50]

The Alianza men who fled were hiding in the mountains and remained at large. While on the run from the army of police and soldiers, they stopped to rest at the places of several people they knew who lived or had cabins in the mountains. A blindfolded Peter Nabokov was taken to Tijerina's hideout and allowed to get his story.

> After Nabokov's story was published, DA Sanchez came to the newspaper office, fished the reporter's notes out of a garbage can in the alley, and threatened to arrest him and his editor, Walter Kerr, for refusing to reveal the source of their information. Sanchez then released a map he said was confiscated from the car of Cristobal Tijerina on June 2, to support his claim that the north was about to be taken over by "Castro-type Tijerina terrorists."[51]

The so-called terrorists turned themselves in, after taking precautions not to be shot in the process.

> One by one, they all returned voluntarily. . . . Moises Morales drove to the State Police office in Espanola, accompanied by his wife and father-in-law. While the FBI sought him in an extensive manhunt, Cristobal Tijerina, with his lawyer and bondsman, walked into Judge Angel's courtroom in Santa Rosa. Governor Cargo posted a $500 reward for Baltazar Martinez, who was reported by police to be wearing a girdle of dynamite[,] . . . turned himself in to his mother, she arranged surrender and collected the reward . . . to obtain a marriage license for Baltazar to marry his sweetheart.[52]

Reies López Tijerina, Hugh "David" Tijerina, and Uvaldo Velasquez drove to Albuquerque to surrender. According to Reies's account, they and left Coyote about eleven at night to arrive in Albuquerque the first hours the following Sunday morning. In San Isidro, about thirty-five miles from Albuquerque, Uvaldo stopped to gas up. He was about to leave when I told him, "Wait. Let me get a drink of some water. I'm very thirsty." I got off, drank water, and a young man saw me. I knew he would call to turn us in.[53]

And that the young man did.

A few minutes past midnight on Saturday June 10, an unmarked police car trailed a brown '60 Ford into the outskirts of Bernalillo, just north of Albuquerque. Coming from the opposite direction, a patrol car swerved in front of the Ford, and officers from both pursuing cars tumbled out. The two men in the front seat of the Ford offered no resistance. The man lying on the back seat was Reies Tijerina. He made no attempt to pull the .38 automatic from his back pocket. He knew that he had been recognized by a service station attendant 10 minutes before when he had left the car to get a drink of water.[54]

The FBI Files on the Manhunt and Arrests

At 2:27 p.m. of June 6, the day after the TA courthouse affair appeared in the national news, FBI Albuquerque urgently teletyped the director of the FBI with news: "Gerry Noll arrested approximately noon this date by New Mexico State Police in Navajo Canyon near Canjilon, New Mexico. Arrest made without incident and Noll incarcerated Santa Fe jail on local charges. Copies sent to New York, Los Angeles, and Seattle." In the report that followed from FBI Santa Fe dated June 7, the details of an interview with Noll in the Santa Fe jail were provided. "He was appraised [*sic*] of the identities of Special Agents [names redacted] and was furnished a copy of his rights. ... He executed a waiver of same." Noll apparently explained that he used the name Noll in New Mexico, but his real name was Gerald Wayne Barnes. Then, he went back to lying:

He related that on Monday, June 5, 1967, he had heard of the incident which had taken place at Tierra Amarilla, New Mexico, and related that he felt a search would be made of all residences in the county and, accordingly at that time he fled into the mountains. He stated he had been alone when he fled and had not been joined by any member of the Alianza Federal de Mercedes and that on Tuesday, June 6, 1967, he had been taken into custody by officers of the New Mexico State Police approximately 150 yards from a road which he had just crossed and apparently had been observed doing so. He stated he had no information as to the present whereabouts of either the officers or prominent members of the Alianza Federal de Mercedes as he had had no contact with them.

Gardner has a more dramatic and somewhat contradictory account of the Noll arrest.

Around noon, State Police received an anonymous tip that Reies Tijerina had gone to Hernandez, 30 miles to the south, to pick up a cache of arms. Anselmo Tijerina's empty house was entered and searched again. Police then went from house to house. Nothing was found. There were no arrests. However, a prize catch was made by two men on their way to assist in the Hernandez search. State Policeman Carlos Jaramillo and cattle inspector Julian Archuleta spotted a tubby figure scrambling along the lower cliffs of Chama Canyon and gave chase. After firing three warning shots, they were able to prod Jerry Noll out of a hole. He was unarmed. "They made me lean against the car and searched me and found my bag of tortillas," Jerry says. "Then they started banging my head on the fender and asking who I was. I told them, Gerald Wayne Barnes, but they wouldn't believe that and just kept on banging, so I said, Jerry Noll, but they said, 'Oh no, we know who you are, you're that nut, the king.' And then they put me in the car and banged my head on the dashboard all the way to jail."[55]

There are no released FBI files that indicate any communications between field offices and the Washington FBI office during the important events of late 1966 and 1967, such as the October 1966 takeover at San

Joaquin; DA Sanchez's dragnet of Alianza members and meetings; the Echo Amphitheater citizen's arrests; or the TA courthouse affair or subsequent manhunt. Yet, the FBI is mentioned by secondary sources and by Tijerina as being present and investigating his allegations of injustices suffered by land grant claimants. Tijerina writes,

> Several FBI agents—Ed Martin from Los Alamos, John Bass from Santa Fe and Wirt Jones from Albuquerque—met with Martin Vigil, state police commander from District 11 in New Mexico. The FBI agents had received instructions from Washington to investigate our claims. According to *The New Mexican,* the White House was asking for this investigation to learn firsthand the issues and their options.[56]

The FBI records on hand do show agents investigated much of what Tijerina said or wrote for violations of federal statutes. Undoubtedly, he was under constant surveillance by the FBI. For example, the June 8, 1967, letterhead memorandum (LHM) from FBI Albuquerque to the director titled "REIES LOPEZ TIJERINA, aka ETAL [*sic*] ASSAULTING A FEDERAL OFFICER; THEFT OF GOVERNMENT PROPERTY; CONSPIRACY; EXTORTION" is most self-serving. First, while the first two characterizations of his criminal history are correct from Arizona nearly twenty years past, there was no past or current record of any conspiracy on Tijerina's part. There was no charge of extortion, ever, unless one considers Myra Jenkins's libelous allegations that the Alianza dues were extortion. The Internal Revenue Service (IRS), while notified of these collections, is not found in the FBI documentation to have initiated any investigation of Tijerina or the Alianza, as an organization. It is possible the Alianza was a state corporation in New Mexico and not a federally designated nonprofit organization by the IRS, which hence had no jurisdiction to investigate anything.

Nevertheless, the June 8 LHM mentioned a news release allegedly sent by Tijerina to the United Press International (UPI) by mail postmarked from Espanola with an illegible date but received on June 8 that was being analyzed by the FBI, "since the content might possibly be regarded as threats." The LHM does contain the opinion of Jack L. Love, the assistant

U.S. attorney in Albuquerque. He is quoted as stating that "the veiled threats contained in the communication from Tijerina did not come within the purview of the Federal Extortion Statute." There is no copy of the press release with the "extortion" language among the released FBI files.

On June 13 an internal FBI headquarters memo "from A. B. Eddy to Mr. Gale on the subject of REIS [sic] LOPEZ TIJERINA; CRISTOBAL LOPEZ TIJERINA, also known as-FUGITIVE AND OTHERS ASSAULTING A FEDERAL OFFICER; THEFT OF GOVERNMENT PROPERTY-CONSPIRACY" simply informs Gale that Cristobal failed to appear for a hearing and is now subject to a manhunt. Cristobal had posted a $2,000 bond after he turned himself in and disappeared. FBI correspondence on the search for his whereabouts is in the released files. On July 14, according to an airtel from SAC, Albuquerque to the FBI director, a hearing to forfeit the bond was rescheduled until August 7, 1967, because the bonding company was not present for the hearing.

The June 13 memo also reported that "on June 5, 1967, this group attempted to take over a small New Mexico town and two policemen were shot, and it was necessary for the Governor of New Mexico to call out the National Guard to quell the violence" (p. 2). Apparently, this dramatic sentence got attention in Washington, because the next released FBI file is from the director of the FBI to SAC, Albuquerque and dated June 20. Hoover wanted the SAC to "insure that all pertinent observations of SA [name redacted] relating to this matter are incorporated in your forthcoming report." The important part of this one-page document is at the bottom:

NOTE: This relates to investigation requested by the Department in response to allegations that approximately 40 persons, including families of followers of group of Spanish-Americans who attempted to take over town of Tierra Amarilla, New Mexico, were held without charges in cattle pens by National Guard and New Mexico State Patrolmen on 6/6/67. Albuquerque by airtel 6/16/67. Furnished news clippings indicating that Colonel Black, Director, New Mexico State Police, had indicated SA Martin was in area following shooting incidents where various persons were taken into "protective custody."

Not only did the Washington FBI office reveal one of their special agents in the field in Los Alamos, "SA Martin," in this memo; it also confirmed that Tijerina's intelligence about the FBI agents in his midst were accurate.

A lengthy twenty-five-page report from FBI Santa Fe, dated June 20, 1967, begins with numbered page 8 at the bottom and continues to page 25, was compiled on June 16 and transcribed the seventeenth. It reported on what happened at the Tierra Amarilla Courthouse, with focus on the people held in the sheep pen. It reported that "Colonel JOSEPH A. BLACK, Director, New Mexico State Police was interviewed by SAs [names redacted] to give his account of what happened at Tierra Amarilla and Canjilon, New Mexico." Summarizing the report, Black said he was told by one of his officers that armed men with guns, automatic weapons, and dynamite had taken over the courthouse, shot two people, one of them his officer. He drove over and met with Officers Robert Romero and Freddie Martinez in Canjilon. The men were staked out at the home of Baltazar Martinez and Tobias Leyba, looking for Reies Tijerina, Tobias Leyba, and Jerry Noll. Black used his bullhorn to call out the occupants, and a young girl came out with a white flag on a stick (p. 8). She told them no men were inside, just women and children. Tobias Leyba was inside, however, and he came out. On his person, when searched was a six-inch butcher knife; he was instructed concerning his constitutional rights. The women and children were lined up against the wall of the Leyba house and photographed and their names taken.

Patricia Tijerina was present and arrested with her baby in her arms. The youngest son of the Tijerinas was also present and asked Black for their search warrant. Black supposedly responded they weren't searching, just looking for things which belonged to Reies Tijerina. DA Sanchez then told everyone, except Mrs. Tobias Leyba, they could go home. Allegedly she said she was afraid of Reies Tijerina and that he might come back and do her harm. Mrs. Baltazar Martinez was allowed to go to her home. The rest of the people "went to where they had been camped about 250 to 300 yards below the hill from the Leyba residence in a sort of pasture area" (p. 9). Black stated that all the people were told they were permitted to move about as they pleased but to inform the police, who were there to protect them, what they were doing and where they were going. They could get water at the

Martinez place (p. 10). The location of the Martinez home in relation to the Leyba residence was attached to the report; a crudely sketched drawing of building locations identified by name of owners. Black further stated that FBI SA Edgar L. Martin, the DA, press photographers, and newspaper reporters were all present during these activities. Black surveyed the people held and found that they were comfortable in their bedrolls, tents, campers and that "nobody wanted for anything." DA Sanchez left, and Black called him to ask if these persons were arrested and what to do with them. He was given the discretion to release or hold them. Black decided on holding them for "protective custody." Black further stated he "found Reies's 14-year old son among the people held and he was identified as being involved in the courthouse incident" (p. 10). He was not placed under arrest, however.

Black's statements contradict all secondary sources on the treatment of the people being held. His assertions border on the side of ludicrous. According to the report, he said to the FBI that "he informed the people they should go home" (p. 11). He noted that on Tuesday, June 6, the people in the encampment were playing games and all appeared to be very happy. When he learned they were running out of food, he instructed General Jolly to bring C-rations. When they did not open them, he told them to take them for the drive home. Supposedly, the people loaded these rations into their cars. Black allegedly told the people that the reason for the presence of soldiers with weapons who were surrounding them and watching them was their protection "from the members of the alliance who they thought might attempt to take some sort of vengeance on these people by shooting them" (p. 11). As far as sanitary facilities, Colonel Black stated that "these people picked the site themselves and the State Police had not control over that aspect of the matter" (p. 11).

Then, came the most amazing lies from Colonel Black:

> He added that these people were given the utmost care by the police in the area and he again stated that he saw several people in the area who were armed who said they were so armed for their own self-protection (p. 11). He also commented that he saw BALTAZAR MARTINEZ with sticks of dynamite placed around his waist under his belt and he added that MARTINEZ

took a shot at him and some of the other State Policemen in the area but fortunately MARTINEZ did not hit anyone. He emphasized the extreme danger presented by MARTINEZ pointing out that if MARTINEZ were hit by gunfire that he would explode and kill a great many people and destroy a lot of property. (p. 12)

BLACK stated that at the onset of the matter he instructed his officers not to shoot under any circumstances until he gave an order permitting them to shoot and that during the entire incident no State Patrolman fired a shot from his weapon. BLACK stated that his officers were also instructed not to violate the rights of any of the persons there in Canjilon or Tierra Amarilla area and not to engage in any form of police brutality in connection with the handling of the persons there. He stated that he does not believe that these orders were disobeyed by any of his men or by the National Guard.... this information which he is now furnishing would be substantiated by the reports of his officers ... Captain T .J. Chavez, Captain Martin Vigil, Major Hoover Wimberly, Officer Bob Gilliland, and Freddie Martinez, as well as Special Agent JOHN G. BASS JR. of the FBI. (p. 12)

He also named newsmen present during the holding of persons in the sheep pen.

In an accompanying report addendum sequenced in page numbers beginning with page 14 and dated June 21, 1967, another state police officer (his name redacted) refused to sign his waiver-of-rights form but told the FBI

he saw the people, the area, the soldiers and police when he arrived; some people told him they had been there since the "previous Friday and some on the previous Saturday, June 2 and 3, 1967." He then left to search for wanted men and returned "about 9:00 or 10:00 PM on June 5, 1967." He did not go look at the people in the area where they were when he left but volunteered that "they were not held in any form of pen and as far as he knew he stated these people were free to move around as they chose" (p. 14). "He emphasized the fact that there was no fence around the area where the people on the LEYBA property were encamped." (p. 15)

Another witness was Captain T. J. Chavez (but his name is redacted on this FBI document), who, according to Black's earlier statement, accompanied him to Canjilon. Captain Chavez also declined to sign the waiver-of-rights form or to have a lawyer present before making his declarations. The date of his statement was June 21, 1967, but it was dictated on June 19 and 20 to two SAs (their names redacted) in Santa Fe. His declaration is in total contradiction to the allegation by Black that Baltazar Martinez had dynamite. Chavez states that shortly after they arrived in that area, Baltazar Martinez and Baltazar Apodaca stopped near the police car in which he and Colonel Black were riding. "The latter two individuals according to [name redacted] were the persons who had just kidnapped newspaper reporter LARRY CALLOWAY and Deputy Sheriff PETE JARAMILLO" (p. 16). Yet Captain Chavez and Colonel Black did not arrest them, much less engage in a shoot-out, as Black declared in his earlier testimony on page 12. The declaration on this topic stops there.

The FBI interrogators continue with another subject, the daughter of Leyba, whose first name Captain Chavez could not recall. He did remember that on June 5 she came to him and said she did not want to stay there and "left the area" (p. 16). He also stated that

> no occupied residences were searched, that only abandoned houses were searched for wanted persons and he emphasized that Colonel BLACK had issued instructions to all of the State Police Officers to obtain warrants for any other occupied residences that they desired to search prior to doing so ... the articles which had appeared in Eastern newspapers and commented that these articles were completely inaccurate and untrue as the people being held in an enclosure at the LEYBA farm and as to the statements that promiscuous searches were made of residences in the areas without search warrants. (p. 17)

The jury that heard the ACLU lawsuit over this entire matter awarded damages to a plaintiff who complained of that very illegal search.

State Patrolman Freddie Martinez, DA Sanchez's favorite informant in northern New Mexico about Tijerina's activities, was the last to give testimony on what he saw at the Leyba ranch. According to the report, he was riding in the car with Robert Romero but did not observe anyone being held in a pen and under guard. Everyone was free to go at will, he stated. Interestingly, he notes that Colonel Black and at least twenty officers arrived altogether, but he makes no mention that Baltazar Martinez showed up as Black mentioned in his declaration. He clearly stated that "it was raining at the time" (p. 19). He is the first to mention the weather conditions, the major complaint of all being held in the sheep's pen without cover. He also claims to have been the first to identify Reies's younger son in the camp as being Daniel Tijerina. Officer Martinez "had received information that DANNY TIJERINA had assaulted Deputy Sheriff Salazar during the raid, but that DANNY TIJERINA was not arrested since he claimed that he had to help his mother and sister who were in the camp" (p. 19). Not to arrest a person, regardless that he was a juvenile, involved in the "crimes" they alleged the others had committed is absurd. However, FBI records on hand do not indicate to the contrary; maybe they did not arrest him or hand him to juvenile authorities for detention. There is no record either on David (Hugh) Tijerina, the oldest son, in the FBI files. Perhaps there are none, but then the FOIA requests made by Tijerina and myself did not cover these two sons, Rosa, Patricia, Maria Escobar Tijerina, or the other Tijerina brothers.

Daniel Tijerina's mother is Maria Escobar Tijerina, and she was not at the camp. Maria and Reies had divorced in 1962.[57] Patricia Romero Tijerina, the new wife, was at the camp and had been arrested. She was taken to jail in Santa Fe rather quickly. Freddie Martinez claims she and the seven-month-old baby were taken to the hospital in Santa Fe. Daniel's sister Rosa was also at the camp and involved in the attempted courthouse citizen's arrest of DA Sanchez. She was also arrested and taken to the state penitentiary within a couple of days. State Patrolman Martinez claimed that the photos of people in a fenced area were staged by a news photographer who posed them standing next to barbed wire. On page 21 is the crude sketch with an identifying description consisting of numbers of the structures and locations of the sites mentioned in the declarations made to the FBI, such as the Baltazar Martinez home, Leyba house, sheep pen, fence, campsite, and where the "campers" were allowed to find shelter when it rained. An aerial photograph of the penned hostages was taken by a state police officer (whose name is redacted) of these structures and locations; it is on page 22.

The FBI sent a special agent to serve as liaison with the state police in and around Canjilon. His declaration was taken, dictated, and dated on June 21, 1967, to one SA (his name is redacted) in Albuquerque. He saw persons, about twenty-five, up on a ridge behind the Leyba home. State police took photographs, and an undercover agent in plain clothes went to talk to them and wrote in a "stenographer's notebook." He could not see the guarded area where the individuals stayed, nor did he check the campground. Page 24 is titled "PERSONS IN CAMPING AREA."

Mysteriously, page 25, dated June 21, 1967, was dictated on June 20 before two SAs in Santa Fe. It contains no opening paragraph about constitutional rights, the right to have a lawyer present, or mention of any waiver form to sign. Yet it is another declaration from someone "interviewed in the Women's quarters at the Penitentiary of New Mexico in the presence of her mother at Santa Fe, New Mexico." More intriguing is that this page, the last of those released, ends with an incomplete sentence: "a guard went with them as far . . ." This abrupt and incomplete ending suggests the initial report was more than twenty-five pages long and that the released report is missing pages 1–11 and those after page 25.

This female declarant could be Rosa Tijerina, because her mother, Maria Escobar, did come to her aid when she heard the news of events at Tierra Amarilla. This female declarant states that while under guard they drank dirty water that accumulated from the rain and were not allowed to leave. Only one person, Todosio Garcia, asked to leave and was denied. "The entire group of people who had been encamped there were placed by the police officers in a police van which was locked by the police . . . [and] were released from this vehicle and told that the National Guard unit there would guard them" (p. 25). Their photographs were taken by Officer Freddie Martinez along with their names and their addresses

Colonel Black, bothered by the news stories covering the Tierra Amarilla incident and subsequent manhunt, sent a two-page letter dated June

23, 1967, to the congressional delegation from New Mexico. He asked in closing that his comments be inserted in the record of Congressman Resnick's subcommittee looking into complaints about police misconduct. The Black letter is a total denial of wrongdoing and so self-serving that it is shameless in its re-creation of some actions taken. First, he totally discredits the "eastern media" coverage about the part played by his police force in the matter as "deplorable, grossly distorted and totally unfair." Yet photographs of this event are featured in both the Gardner and Nabokov books confirming accounts by the detainees.[58] Second, he exaggerates to the point of fabrication: "Every officer assigned to this operation was hand-picked for his ability to act with discretion and particularly with forebearance [*sic*]" (p. 1). Black called out his entire force of 235 men to help capture Reies López Tijerina and the others, recruited more police from the Jicara Apache tribe, and, also called on the Forest Service rangers to assist. Lastly, he had some persons being held at the sheep pen arrested but not others. Rosa and Patricia were arrested, but not Daniel Tijerina. Tobias Leyba was arrested, but not Baltazar Martinez, who, Black claimed, shot at him. Officer Freddie Martinez claims Baltazar drove up to the car where Black and Captain Chavez were sitting, talked to them, and left without incident. Several of the declarants, all his officers, distorted and manipulated their testimony to the FBI to cover up the holding of women, children, and elderly men in a sheep's pen for days while it rained. They were held without food or water. Access to an outdoor privy without a front door up the hill and away from the holding pen was made available, but only under National Guard approval; and, then under supervision by a soldier.

No person that provided these declarations to the FBI was ever charged with giving a false statement or with obstruction of justice. The federal statute on this crime basically states that any person who by threat or communication tries to influence, intimidate, impede or otherwise derail federal officers of any U.S. court in their investigations is engaged in obstruction of justice.[59]

Illegal Strip Searches and Solitary Confinement

Most importantly, the documents, those prepared by Captain Black and those by the FBI as well, completely ignored the objections and protests made by Rosa, Patricia, and Reies of strip searches and solitary confinement. Perhaps "ignored" is not the correct assumption; "erased" or "covered up" may be better word choices. Rosa in her oral history interview with me stated that on June 5 and the following days she was undergoing her monthly menstrual flow. She was not provided with any sanitary napkins and had none, had to submit to strip searches, and was under observation at all times during visits to the sheep pen outhouse, and while in prison, by male soldiers and guards. When in solitary confinement she was also under observation when taken to shower, clean herself, and change prison garb, which she soiled due to her menstrual cycle.[60] Patricia was five months pregnant and nineteen years old when she was held at the sheep pen, yet she was handcuffed with hands behind her back and taken to prison. Her seven-month-old baby was taken from her and kept from her for two days. She was placed in solitary confinement without blankets. I assume she was strip-searched before being placed in her cell.[61] Patricia, as did Rosa, reported that male guards had taken physical liberties during these searches and movements in and out of police cars, in and out of cells, and while in solitary confinement.[62] Patricia miscarried two days after being released from prison.[63]

Reies also complained of being in solitary confinement on various occasions while jailed and imprisoned in New Mexico and for two weeks while at the federal prison in La Tuna, Texas.[64] The United States is the "only modern civilized society that sanctions solitary confinement … many states have abolished the use with juveniles and the mentally ill. There are many lawsuits pending regarding solitary confinement of pregnant women."[65]

White House Interest

This collection of declarations from the New Mexico State Police apparently was the extent of the FBI investigation on violations of civil rights of those held at Canjilon, as requested by the White House. The FBI files do not reveal any investigation or interrogation of any of the TA courthouse raiders. The interest by the White House could have been in response to calls and letters sent to President Lyndon Johnson about the harassment and violence directed at Reies López Tijerina and the Alianza membership, or it could have been that the White House had information that Tijerina was to attend the El Paso White House Hearings being planned for October 26 and 27, 1967, at which the Mexican president Gustavo Díaz Ordaz would also be present.

Copies of FBI communications on Tijerina and the El Paso hearings were included in released files and are included chronologically by dates coinciding with the TA affair and Canjilon prisoners being held by state police and national guardsmen. Moreover, copies of these communications were forwarded to the Secret Service and various FBI field offices. The FBI also appended to these sources a page from the June 16, 1967, airtel that contained information taken from the FBI's "Guide to Subversive Organizations and Publications," dating to 1961. A paragraph in the airtel on the *National Guardian* identified it as an official propaganda tool of Soviet Russia. The information on the *National Guardian* dated to 1947 and the work of the Committee on Un-American Activities. This referenced publication was "proof" of the Eastern media bias the New Mexico State Police complained about.

The FBI culture maintained by the director, J. Edgar Hoover, during his last years under President Nixon still loved any tidbit of information that smacked of communism, or as he pronounced the term, "Commonists." Hoover just need the slightest inference about suspected subversion or communist leanings to unleash his formidable resources in the field to destroy individuals and organizations. Anything sounding like a threat against a federal official would do to get his FBI involved. He got notice on or about June 23 that an anonymous telephone call had been made to the U.S. Attorney's Office in Albuquerque somewhat threatening the U.S. attorney, namely John Quinn. The alleged words used were "Please give him this message, 'if anything happens to Reies Tijerina, his ass is mud,' and then the caller hung up."[66]

Hoover wasted no time in writing to the director of the U.S. Secret Service to alert them of this threat and of Tijerina's past history of writing to presidents with complaints about the land grants in the Southwest.[67] Thereafter, the correspondence between SAC in the field and Hoover contained the stamped or typed words "ARMED AND DANGEROUS" on any document related to Reies and the Tijerina brothers, namely Anselmo and Cristobal. These words are tantamount to instructing the FBI agents in the field and any other federal official who received these communications from then on to be ready to face these armed and dangerous individuals and to meet deadly force with deadly force.

Tijerina's Release and the Harboring Statute

Tijerina, according to the FBI's informants, was to lodge at the Paso del Norte Hotel in El Paso during the White House hearings and attend the address by Vice President Hubert H. Humphrey at 11:00 a.m. on Friday, October 27, 1967. Tijerina was not among those being officially invited to present testimony at the El Paso hearings, adding fuel to the fire of discontent felt by many grassroots leaders across the country. They felt this was to be a whitewash of all ills and problems historically being voiced by the Spanish-speaking communities of Mexican ancestry in the United States. These grassroots advocates and activists took offense in that this was to be the first and only White House conference on Mexican Americans ever held. There had been many held on the status or problems of African Americans, but none on Mexican Americans.[68] But this notice of possible attendance at the El Paso hearings was not the real thrust of the message; Tijerina was free on bond with a condition that he meet with the U.S. marshal weekly and to obtain U.S. district court permission to travel beyond Bernalillo County, New Mexico. Failure to do so would result in his rearrest and new charges of violating parole conditions. Tijerina had been making comments that he was not invited to the hearings, but protestors were organizing a boycott of the conference. He was hinting to the public that he might join the protestors. Another important meeting that year, the National Conference for

New Politics, was to take place in downtown Chicago at the Palmer House hotel over Labor Day weekend, beginning on August 29. Tijerina was saying to his membership that he needed to go and explain their cause. Again, the FBI was in a quandary as to letting him go to Chicago or arrest him for not asking permission if he did not report to his assigned U.S. marshal. By airtel dated August 7 to the director, FBI, the SAC, Albuquerque reported that Tijerina was going to Chicago.

Meanwhile, Tijerina made bail set by Judge Joe Angel and was released from the state penitentiary on or about July 24, 1967. The airtel from SAC, Albuquerque to Director, FBI dated July 26 had this information. The airtel also reported that he was questioned on the whereabouts of his brother still at large, Cristobal Tijerina. The FBI also had interrogated every Tijerina family member, key Alianza members, and twenty-three others still begin held, according to this airtel, and threatened them with prosecution under the harboring statute, which made it a crime not to be forthcoming with any information about a criminal or fugitive when requested by a federal officer or U.S. court. Everyone, including Reies, declined having any knowledge or information on Cristobal's whereabouts; rumor had it he was somewhere in Mexico.

By teletype dated August 3, 1967 sent from the FBI in Albuquerque, Hoover was informed that Cristobal had been found: "407PM URGENT 8-3-67 RON FUGITIVE CRISTOBAL LOPEZ TIJERINA APPREHENDED THIS DATE BY BUAGENTS AT EMERGENCY ENTRANCE OF BCI HOSPITAL AND IMMEDIATELY TURNED OVER TO USM THERE. PHOENIX, EL PASO, DALLAS, SAN ANTONIO, AND DENVER DISCONTINUE. AUXILIARY OFFICES ADVISED AM ARMED AND DANGEROUS."

The additional FBI files on this arrest or surrender, as the case may have been, are convoluted. First, the airtel dated August 3 is not entirely correct in the wording if we are to believe the content of various other documents directly related to the "arrest" of Cristobal Tijerina, which are all dated August 8, supposedly five days after his arrest at the Bernalillo hospital. There is an FBI form titled "Memorandum for Identification Division" stamped "Aug 7 1968" with the handwritten date of August 4 pertaining to Cristobal López Tijerina among these documents. The form has entries, all handwritten, confirming "Date of Fug Card" as "6-19-67" and the blank under "Prosecution dismissed," the entry for City is "Albuquerque, N.M. Buagents." The date is "8-3-67 TOT USM" and under action to be taken on blank lines is written "per AQ tel 8-3-67." The FBI documents with the agency letterhead I refer to as being convoluted are dated August 8 from the FBI office in Albuquerque by the SA and could amount to six pages total. The first page with the handwritten number at bottom left is "226," scratched out, with "236" inserted. This page under "ADMINISTRA-TIVE DATA" has an opening sentence admitting failure in finding Cristobal Tijerina after looking in six cities in New Mexico "and other small places." Then in the last line it reads: "Results of this investigation are maintained in this file and since this investigation was all negative, it is not being reported herein." The next page has no heading but at bottom left has the handwritten and scratched page number "236" then "237" and centered at bottom "-B-" and below that "COVER PAGE"[69] The narrative on this page states Cristobal Tijerina surrendered to State Judge Joe Angel in Santa Rosa, New Mexico, on August 2. He had attorney Albert Gonzales with him. A new bond apparently was set by the judge, and he was released. Apparently, the FBI began a new manhunt for him immediately upon learning of this development. The SA (his name is redacted) in Albuquerque prepared a four-page report in which he states again the first information on the "arrest," except this time it reads: "Subject CRISTOBAL LOPEZ TIJERINA surrendered himself to FBI Agents through his attorney 8/3/67 at the BCI Hospital, Albuquerque, NM. Immediately turned over to USM. On 8/8/67 bond ... was declared forfeited in USDC, Albuquerque." The report continues with more interesting information, still convoluted in my estimation, that an informant (the name is redacted) on the evening of August 2, 1967 telephoned "SAC LEONARD BLAYLOCK" (another outed FBI agent by these very documents, which redact some names and not others) and advised him who had presented himself before Judge Angel and made a new bond and left. The narrative then states: "He [either the informant or Blaylock] indicated that he was most disturbed that the Judge did a thing like this without notifying State or Federal authorities but had no details" (p. 1). Apparently, the FBI, the informant, Judge Angel's court staff, or the judge himself were the source of leaked information to the Associated Press, which "telephonically inquired of SAC BLAYLOCK as to whether or not CRISTOBAL LOPEZ TIJERINA was still a Federal fugitive." Page 2 repeats this scenario of the telephone calls between the informant, the SAC in Albuquerque making the report, Judge Angel, and SAC Blaylock. Pages 3 and 4 of this report verify that Cristobal Tijerina did surrender himself to the FBI's SA (name redacted) "in the presence of United States Marshal [name redacted] and Deputy United States Marshal [name redacted] at the emergency entrance to the Bernalillo County Indian Hospital." But a new character emerged: "Immediately following his arrest, TIJERINA's attorney LORENZO E. TAPIA appeared at the hospital." The last page states that trial before Judge Howard C. Bratton on this case "was set for September 5, 1967" and that "CARLOS SEDILLO was attorney for CRISTOBAL LOPEZ TIJERINA." Later, an airtel from SAC, Albuquerque to Hoover dated August 28 informed him that the trial date on all defendants involved in the TA affair would be changed from September 5 to sometime between October 1 and October 15. "A definite date will be set later. The Bureau will be advised."

New Politics in Chicago

Deputy U.S. Marshal Benny Martinez met with Tijerina and Cristobal and their lawyer, Larry (Lorenzo) Tapia, who presented the case as to why travel to the Chicago gathering was important for the defense of both Tijerinas in their upcoming trials. Apparently, they met with success and permission was given by Deputy U.S. Marshal Martinez, because all three made it to Chicago.[70] The prime reason for going was to meet Dr. Martin Luther King, according to Tijerina, in order to "establish a solid alliance between the Spanish-Americans and the moderate Negroes." There is little information on what Tijerina accomplished while in Chicago for this conference. It can be inferred that he was intrigued by the diversity of participants, predominantly white and black, he witnessed coming together in alliance and coalition on some items, such as forming a national third political party with King as the presidential candidate and Dr. Benjamin Spock his vice president. This did not materialize, however, but Tijerina later did seek out alliance and coalitions with blacks beyond the Nation of Islam and Native Americans. And he did form another political party in New Mexico, the People's Constitutional Party. "We invited leaders from the Native American and Black communities. The Anglos had oppressed us all," he wrote in his autobiography.[71] While in Chicago, he must have had time to speak with Dr. King in Chicago and impressed King. Later, Tijerina reported as having received a telegram from Reverend King in March 1968 asking him to attend a meeting in Atlanta to plan the Poor People's Campaign later that summer.

Tijerina must have also obtained the U.S. marshal's permission to travel to El Paso for the White House hearings. He was there as a protestor, not an invitee of President Johnson. According to Tijerina, Johnson's ancestors were also land grant thieves like Catron. The Pedernales ranch, the Texas White House when LBJ was president, was on land taken from the family of Cecilia Saenz Montes.[72]

Alianza Conventions in Albuquerque

The first Alianza convention occurred on September 21, 1963, at the Rio Grande school "because our membership did not fit into the Alianza building anymore. Approximately 385 persons registered for this convention." Rosita, Reies's fourteen-year old daughter, worked as the file clerk and secretary, and son David did building maintenance and chores. Reies and his brother Cristobal lived in the back of the building. Every September, the Alianza would hold its annual convention.

The Alianza's fifth convention took place in Albuquerque on October 21-22, 1967. For this gathering, Tijerina had invited leaders of organization he met at the New Politics convention in Chicago, and they came.[73] Also in attendance were FBI agents, as at the first convention. Tijerina was already under FBI scrutiny from the day he rented home and office space on 1010 Third Street NE in Albuquerque. He explained the historical development of the Alianza it this way:

On August 3, 1962, I wrote the first plan to create the Alianza Federal de Mercedes. . . . It was a two-page letter. On October 22, 1962, my wife and I made plans to move further north. I circulated a second letter to create the Alianza de Pueblos y Pobladores. This second was not dated. I moved my family again to 600 S. Broadway. The Alianza Federal de Mercedes was already functioning but not incorporated. . . . During the month of January, we notified people that on February 2, 1963, we would come together to incorporate officially the Alianza Federal de Mercedes. I chose this date because that was the same day the Treaty of Guadalupe Hidalgo was signed. It was also the birthday of my daughter, Rosita.[74]

He had bought the building on Third Street with money from the sale of Valley of Peace as down payment and a note of $25,000 to Edwin Stanton, publisher of the *News Chieftain* newspaper. "As part of the purchase deal ... I also got to publish regular weekly articles in his newspaper. . . . The building had more than 10,000 square feet."[75] Tijerina moved there having divorced Maria Escobar in 1963, with custody of the six children awarded to the mother.[76]

CHAPTER 4

The War against Tijerina

The attempt to citizen's arrest DA Sanchez was to impact Tijerina and the Alianza in several important ways. First, it was an impromptu plan not well thought out, much less executed properly. They should have ensured themselves that DA Sanchez was in the courthouse on that day and time, not guess he would be. They were going to free the Aliancistas being held in jail. Yet they were already released: "Cristobal Tijerina had been released by Judge Scarborough minutes before the courthouse was struck."[1] Second, they had no backup plan in case they failed. Consequently, some of them, including Tijerina, fled into the mountains without food, water, proper clothing, and means of communications. Others went back to Leyba's ranch only to be arrested and placed in a sheep pen for days. Third, they shot police officers while in the search for the DA and took hostages with them as they fled the scene; kidnapping is a major crime. The persons taken hostage had nothing to do with the impromptu plan for the citizen's arrest of DA Sanchez. These hostages did nothing to impede them from the plan to arrest the DA; they served no purpose. Fourth, they were arrested and jailed for days after the event without communication with other family members, each other, and their lawyers. Lastly, Tijerina continued in the legal cases that followed as he had done on other occasions, the most recent being the Echo Amphitheater takeover, to go at it alone, without the advice of legal counsel. He had not prepared for this major component of his plan either, the arrests and court proceedings to follow. Not only was he trying to assert legal rights under laws from Spain and the terms of the Treaty of Guadalupe Hidalgo, but he was also ignoring the New Mexico and federal laws that applied to his actions. He thought and believed he was acting under the law, his version of what applied. Those thwarting him at every turn were acting under the color of law as police agents entrusted with enforcement and prosecution of the laws they knew about, not *Las leyes de las Indias* or *Las siete partidas* or the terms of the Treaty of Guadalupe Hidalgo. Tijerina never had translated into English those very laws he articulated at every opportunity. But for the booklet *The Spanish Land Grant Question Examined,* which contained brief, translated mentions of select portions of these ancient laws, no one knew what they said, only he; certainly not his lawyers, whom he changed too often and at the most critical of times, such as during trials. He was never prepared to fight legal fire with legal fire in the courtroom. Unfortunately, when he resorted to being his own attorney and prevailed on one occasion, that convinced him that he knew best what legal strategy to implement in each case; he did not.

The local and national press created the name of "King Tiger," a pseudo translation of "Tijerina"; tagged his citizen's arrest as a "Courthouse Raid," and perpetrators as violent men. They also made him "the most hated man in New Mexico," the title of the first documentary on the event, by Tom Pettit. In other parts of the country, he became a Chicano hero, a term he despised, but accepted the laudatory praise for his courage and audacity. Unlike his contemporary, César E. Chávez, who also traveled the speech-making circuit on campuses to raise funds and recruit volunteers, Tijerina did not recruit any volunteers to help further his cause. Chávez relied most heavily on Anglo volunteers to implement his boycott strategy, nationally and internationally. He relied heavily on Anglo and Jewish volunteers to staff his components of the union such as legal, finance, day care, health care, housing, and, more importantly, picketing activities. The secondary literature on Chávez is replete with this information on the role of volunteers in building the United Farm Workers.[2]

Tijerina did make some effort at working with Chicano groups such as the Crusade for Justice from Denver and the Mexican American Youth Organization from Texas. And he did make some effort at coalition building with Native Americans and blacks. However, the only significant alliance, which was temporary, was with the Southern Christian Leadership Conference during the Poor People's Campaign. The contact and relations with Ron Karenga's United Slaves (US), the Student Non-violent Coordinating Committee, and the Black Panthers were temporary and more symbolic than substantive. The white radicals in the Students for a Democratic Society (SDS) might have been willing to work with him, but he made no effort to contact them or take them into his fold when some SDS members attended his events, namely the annual Alianza conferences. Native Americans relations were more substantive but not sustained, and they were limited to the local leadership of local tribes in New Mexico, mainly those who could also claim ownership of the same lands covered by land grants. This was evident during the second Alianza convention, which featured speakers from the Taos Pueblo and Hopi tribal groups.[3]

Armed and Dangerous

The FBI LHM from El Paso of October 26, 1967, headlined "CONFIDENTIAL" is a two-page mini-biography of Reies López Tijerina. A redacted informant provided information on the physical characteristics of Reies, which were very accurate. Then began the amazingly prejudicial and continuous narrative:

> He is known to be a very violent man and has a very charismatic quality about him. Tijerina has no means of actual support and he has no regular job. He holds himself to be a minister of the Pentecostal Church. Presently, he is living off of the donations and memberships of the Alianza.

Extreme care should be taken with Reies Tijerina especially if he can assemble a crowd of Mexican-Americans of lower economic and scholastic achievement. He can very easily turn a crowd like this into a violent riotous crowd. He has the ability to make wild and unfounded statements and get crowds who don't know any better to go along with him. He has an uncanny ability to express himself verbally in Spanish. There is not a great deal of depth to what he says but nevertheless he can get crowds to listen to him. He speaks with evangelical fervor and is also able to feel out his crowd very well. [Redacted] this man warrants being watched very closely. (p. 1)

On the second page is the admonishment: "SUBJECT SHOULD BE CONSIDERED ARMED AND DANGEROUS BECAUSE HE PARTICIPATED IN ACTS OF VIOLENCE AND WAS ARMED."

Following this LHM is another page indicating that "5 pages are being withheld entirely" and these "document(s) originated with the following government agency(cies)." The handwritten acronym "CIA" is inserted. The following day, October 27, El Paso SAC by airtel to the director of the FBI adds more names to his prior transmission emphasizes how dangerous Tijerina is. The names are Baltazar Apodaca, Baltazar Martinez, Jerry Noll, Anselmo Lopez Tijerina, Cristobal Tijerina, and Reies's son Reies [*sic*] Hugh Lopez Tijerina Jr. This LHM also closes with the admonishment: "THE SUBJECTS OF THE ENCLOSED LETTERHEAD MEMORANDA SHOULD BE CONSIDERED ARMED AND DANGEROUS BECAUSE OF THEIR RELATIONSHIP WITH REIES LOPEZ TIJERINA AND HIS MOVEMENT."

The "armed and dangerous" closing was placed on almost every document that followed in the years to come. He was tagged forever with such labels as "messianic," "violent," "fiery," "Communist," and "un-American." Then came the big tag on the eve of his trial for the TA "raid."

Eulogio Salazar, Reies López Tijerina's Friend and Loyalist

Eulogio Salazar was no stranger to Reies López Tijerina. They met as early as September 1959 when Tijerina traveled to New Mexico. Eulogio was a jailer at the Tierra Amarilla Courthouse. Reies planned to stay at Tierra Amarilla at least the winter while he fixed a home in nearby Ensenada, New Mexico.

> While there, I met Eulogio Salazar. . . . He was the one that had freed Anselmo. Anselmo told me that before Eulogio released him, he had mentioned that we had many charges against us and that they would surely charge him also. Eulogio Salazar came to my house Christmas night. He brought "Christmas" or presents for my children. I shall never forget this act of charity toward my children, my wife, and me. He became most loyal toward our work. It he hadn't done these deeds, I would never have trusted him. He came in uniform with his pistol in his holster. Eulogio became our best contact. Thanks to him, we knew of the FBI inquiries made by other state agents who followed us. He would send word with our loyal ones.[4]

Reies writes this version of what happened on June 5, 1967, at the Tierra Amarilla Courthouse, and of his relationship with Eulogio Salazar:

> When we entered the courthouse, we wanted to keep everybody there so that no one would leave and go talk about the goings-on. Many of our people yelled at Eulogio Salazar not to leave, that he was not going to get hurt. Eulogio attempted to jump out a window, and shots were fired trying to make sure everybody stayed put. A bullet hit him. I saw his blood and recognized the consequences that would result from that. It upset me. My spirit burned because Eulogio was a loyal friend. The Anglo ranchers and police knew that also. Baltazar, others, and I ran after him. As soon as he had hit the ground, he started running towards his car, which was about thirty meters down the road. I wanted to tell him what we were trying to do, explained to him what was going on and that an ambulance would arrive shortly, if he would just wait. He would be treated better by the ambulance personnel than at home. I also asked him, 'Why did you run?

Didn't you hear us yelling at you?' And, he did not respond. I took him to
another car and told Baltazar and David to call the ambulance. As soon as
I took care of Eulogio, I ran back into the courthouse.[5]

He adds that other people eating in a restaurant nearby heard the
shooting and saw Eulogio running. These people, Oralia M. Olivas, Rose
Mary Mercure, and her husband, Placido, came to his aid and took him to
their home. They asked him who had shot him and he replied "the Tijerinas." Salazar was taken for medical treatment to St. Vincent's Hospital.[6]
The other state police officer, Saiz, was taken to Bataan Memorial Methodist Hospital with a compound fracture of the left arm and a punctured
lung.[7] On June 21, Salazar was questioned by Robert Gilliland and Thomas
Richardson of the New Mexico State Police as to what happened and who
had shot him. Tijerina writes, "Eulogio repeated what he had told Oralia,
his sister-in-law, Rose, and Placido Mercure, that the Tijerinas had shot
him. Robert Gilliland, after interrogating Eulogio and having him sign the
declaration, changed Eulogio's testimony from 'the Tijerinas' to 'Tijerina
had shot him.'"[8]

The first state trial on the TA affair began November 12, 1968, with
Judge Paul Larrazolo presiding and Tijerina acting as his own attorney.
In court, the testimony from Salazar was changed to "Tijerina shot me"
but not allowed to be introduced as evidence since Salazar was dead by
this time. The jury returned a verdict of not guilty on all three charges
on December 13, 1968. They did not believe the testimony of the state witnesses and believed Tijerina's version of what he was trying to do with the
citizen's arrest power.

The Murder of Eulogio Salazar

On January 2, 1968, around 8:15 p.m., Casilda Salazar stood at the window
of the small Salazar home and saw her husband's car drive up to the front
gate, only 120 feet away across the frozen yard. Eulogio got out of the car
and stood in the headlights to open the gate; she recognized him. She went

into the bedroom to get ready to attend the rosary services for [a] deceased friend. But her daughter called to her from the front window that the car was backing away from the gate.[9]

Thinking that her husband was probably going to check the cattle or was turning the car around to face the highway, Mrs. Salazar returned to the window in time to see the car back all the way down the highway toward the village. She presumed that her husband had gone back to the courthouse. When he had still not returned after several hours, she decided that he was spending the night with his brother Tito, whose bar in Tierra Amarilla had been burglarized the night before. She went to bed.[10]

Eulogio Salazar was murdered by unknown assailants when he showed up at his home after work. He was fifty-five years old. Casilda Salazar told Deputy Sheriff Dan Rivera what she found the next morning.

The next morning around 7:30, she started down the road to her babysitting job at a nearby trailer park and, at the front gate, discovered a large bloodstain in the snow and her husband's white cowboy hat lying nearby. She ran to the house and called Deputy Sheriff Dan Rivera and told him, "I'm afraid something has happened to Eulogio, there is blood all over."[11]

Patricia Blawis has a similar version of what transpired the night of the murder. From what she was able to glean from other media accounts, Mrs. Salazar and Eulogio had had supper at the home but he had returned to the courthouse. He promised to come back and take her to the wake of a friend: "Shortly after eight she looked out a window and saw her husband arrive at their front driveway, but in a few minutes the car lights backed away."[12] Blawis and Nabokov both differ from Gardner's accounts as to who discovered the bloodspot and white hat in the snow. Peter Nabokov's account states the discovery in this manner:

About 8 o'clock she telephoned his working partner, Undersheriff Daniel Rivera, who drove over. Pulling up to the gate, Rivera spotted Salazar's white hat in the middle of the lane. Then he noticed a stain in the road that looked like blood and hair. . . . A broken piece of plastic gun butt was discovered near the fallen cowboy hat.[13]

Experts said there must have been at least three killers, and rewards for information leading to their discovery were offered by TV Station KOB and by private sources.[14]

Cattle inspector Larry Turner is credited by Gardner and Nabokov, who identifies him only as "a rancher," with spotting the Salazar vehicle fifty feet down the roadside slope by a fence in the snow with what seemed to be a body inside. He flagged down a state trooper who investigated the car and body. "It proved to be the jailer's corpse. Twenty-four wounds were later counted. Salazar's face was beaten beyond recognition."[15] Gardner's version is that a terrible struggle must have ensued inside the car. "Ceiling fabric had been clawed away . . . dome light was broken . . . upholstery was saturated with blood; the face of the body was literally unrecognizable."[16]

According to police investigators, the first blow to Eulogio's head occurred when he started to climb back into his car after opening the front gate. Police found no other footprints near the Salazar front gate; they theorized that a second car with lights out had come up behind him, but no one, including the widow or daughter who had seen him drive up, reported a second car. If it was white in color, then with snow everywhere and no lights on, they could not have seen it. This became the ghost car theory. They did find a footprint of a crippled or one-legged man in the snow near the Salazar home. It was similar to one found near Bill Mundy's home when that was burned; so, the police picked up Lee Woods, a local resident who was a cripple, for questioning.[17]

The FBI's Domestic Intelligence Division posted an informative note dated January 4, 1968 in the Tijerina file, stating the body had been found on January 3. The New Mexico State Police submitted a five-page letter with three attachments in handwriting to Director Hoover ("ATTENTION: FBI Laboratory") dated January 17, asking for assistance with the case. "The results of your examination will be used for official purposes only, related to the investigation, or a subsequent criminal prosecution" (p. 1). The time of death, according to the person who performed the autopsy at Los Alamos Medical Center "was approximately 8:30 PM, Tuesday, January 2, 1968."

The state police letter previously mentioned had several components, among them a statement of facts:

> Mr. Eulogio Salazar, was a Deputy Sheriff/Jailer of Rio Arriba County, in Tierra Amarilla, New Mexico. His body was found in his car, a brown 1963 Chevrolet Impala 4-door sedan, 1967 New Mexico license 17-1846, Vin 2 1869 K 123 276, on Wednesday morning, January 3, 1968. The car and body were located about 5 miles southwest of Tierra Amarilla, New Mexico, on State Road #112 (This road leads to the El Vado State Park.)
>
> The car, when found, contained large concentrated areas of apparent blood in the left front seat and floorboard and the left rear seat and floor board. Apparent bloodstains were also apparent on the inside roof (ceiling or "headliner,") left and inside the four doors. The victim's body was in the front floorboard, with the head towards the steering wheel. The car had been run off the left side of SR # 112, down a slight embankment, in snow, and came to rest under a barbed-wire fence. Apparent bloodstains were apparent on the paved portion of SR #112, as well as apparent bloody foot-prints on the paved portion of the road, just north of where the car left the roadway.
>
> The victim's hat was found in the dirt (snow-packed) by a gate in the entrance to the victims's [sic] home in Tierra Amarilla. A heavy, concentrated, apparent blood spot was also found at the gate to the victim's home. (p. 1)

The remaining paragraph in the statement of evidence recited the distances in miles from the victim's home to the Tierra Amarilla Courthouse and to the roads leading to the point on SR 112 "where the car and body were found" (p. 1). The other four pages of the letter list the types of evidence being submitted for FBI testing, such as blood samples taken from his body during autopsy, the inside and outside of the car, and the ground mixed with snow. His clothes, ten items, were sent along with six items found on the victim's body; and nine items removed from Salazar's car on January

5, 1968 (pp. 2 and 3). "Items 30 through 32 are <u>not</u> submitted at this time, per your suggestion" (p. 4). This line suggests there was telephonic or some other form of communication between the state police and the FBI about what to submit for testing. Then the letter on page 4 asks specifically what examination should be done on the blood, hair, wood splinters, envelope, scalp washings, and other fibers. Three handwritten pages attached to the letter are notes titled "Dictation" and related to the paint chips taken from the Salazar car. "Our file number in this case is State Bureau # 50275. If important information is developed, we request notification by telegram or telephone collect" (p. 5). Copies of this letter with attachments were sent to DA Sanchez, SAC FBI in Albuquerque, Leo Conroy, FBI Identification Division assistant director C. Lester Trotter, and one person, whose name is redacted, at the state police headquarters in Santa Fe.

18 U.S. Code 2384, 2385, and 2386

The U.S. attorney general, on the day after the Tierra Amarilla citizen's arrest attempt by members of the Alianza Federal de Mercedes (AFDM) was made, requested the FBI investigate the matter with intent to initiate prosecution. Hoover responded to Assistant Attorney General J. Walter Yeagley on January 19, 1968:

> Two incidents, one at the Kit Carson national Forest in October 1966 and the other at Tierra Amarilla, New Mexico, in June, 1967, have illustrated the willingness of the AFDM to resort to violence in seizing U.S. lands or in taking over established local government in furtherance of its objective . . . prosecution under Section 2384 . . . under 2385 . . . Section 2386 (Voorhis Act) might also be considered.

At bottom of the two-page memorandum, Hoover adds: "While no communist direction or foreign influence has been revealed, the proclivity to violence and revolutionary actions of the group appear to call for a countermove to negate its strength in New Mexico."

On January 30, 1968, the FBI director granted the Albuquerque SAC's request to investigate with intent to prosecute the Alianza members. It is a one-liner: "Authority is granted to conduct the investigation outlined in reairtel." Albuquerque notified the director on January 30 that the trial for the AFDM leaders had begun in Santa Fe the day prior. In this communication, the SAC refers to "various rumors being circulated by unknown persons that some type of violence will occur during the hearing; however, no concrete information developed to date."

FBI Response to State Police

The FBI promptly sent back to the New Mexico State Police the laboratory worksheet acknowledging receipt as of January 19, 1968 in a two-page letter with sixteen more pages of notes on preliminary findings. The state police followed up on January 23 with two more letters; one indicating a shipment of evidence and the other a listing of the contents of the crate. The crate contained four pieces of asphalt pavement from the murder scene on SR 112 where the car left the road, along with brake and clutch rubber pedals from a 1966 Mustang. The FBI was requested to see if they could determine traces of human blood or footwear or footprints on any of these items.

The day before, January 24, the FBI's Latent Fingerprint Section of the Identification Division not only returned by registered airmail to the New Mexico State Police the U.S. Treasury brown envelope they previously had received, item 13, but also the bad news that "no latent prints of value for identification purposes were developed on the envelope." J. Edgar Hoover's signature stamp was affixed to this letter.

On January 26, 1968, the FBI's laboratory worksheet reporting on the shoe prints found on the asphalt samples was forwarded to the state police. The shoe prints were important because the state "investigators determined that Salazar's body had been transferred to the front floor before his car was put into neutral and ditched down the steep embankment, bursting through a barbed wire fence."[18]

The FBI was able to estimate but not determine shoe sizes from the foot prints, and found no hair samples on the pedals. Fibers were from red floor covering of an automobile. On this same day, January 26, the SAC at Albuquerque requested of the director of the FBI "that certain individuals in the AFDM be closely scrutinized as candidates for the Rabble Rouser Index (RRI)." The names listed were redacted. Three days later, January 29, the FBI laboratory sent a four-page report under Hoover's signature stamp and one handwritten page with notations indicating that the hair and blood samples sent previously and paint chips had been analyzed. The blood was human. The hairs "do not possess enough individual microscopic characteristics to be positively identified as originating from a particular person to the exclusion of others" (p. 2). The basal ends of most hairs were missing, indicating "these have been forcibly pulled out by their roots" (p. 2). And there were no textile fibers found in the fingernail clippings. The wood splinters did reveal that they "are walnut, checkered on one side. They may have originated from a rifle, shotgun or pistol ... not sufficient physical characteristics for identification of the particular weapon (p. 3). The paint chips were run through the National Automotive Paint File by the FBI laboratory, and no match to an automobile was found. The FBI suggested, "Perhaps the source of these chips is a truck. Paint panels of trucks are not maintained in the National Automotive Paint File" (p. 4).

Who Murdered Eulogio Salazar?

During his incarceration at Montessa Park prison in 1969 awaiting the second trial on the Tierra Amarilla events, Tijerina learned of a new witness to be called by the prosecutors, Lee Woods. He was the rancher from Tierra Amarilla who claimed he came upon the body of Eulogio Salazar. Tijerina had tried to cross-examine him but was not allowed to by Judge Burks. Tijerina knew that "footprints belonging to a cripple" had been found at the murder site.[19]

On June 29, 1974, personnel from the U.S. marshal's office went to Tijerina's home to transport him to the federal penitentiary. This was his second prison term. "For the first thirty days of my term I was in quarantine...."

After the quarantine, I was placed in a dormitory with Blas Chávez. He had begun his political career with Senator Dennis Chávez."[20] Tijerina relates that his relationship with Blas led to startling discoveries because Blas knew many details about the murder of Salazar. Tijerina wrote that over the course of three months "Blas began to tell me detail by detail and fragment by fragment the entire story."[21] Tijerina knew that Blas was bitter toward U.S. senator Joseph Montoya and Emilio Naranjo, the U.S. marshal. He was the fall guy for many crimes he committed at their behest. Now that he was in prison doing a fifty-year sentence for a crime he did not commit, he was talking. Tijerina wrote:

> Blas felt he was a victim of politicians.... He had been used by the politicians. Blas told me of more than one hundred burglaries he committed for politicians, breaking into safes. I listened to all Blas had to say. Blas told me one day, "My brother José worked at state police headquarters and was able to steal the report Robert Gilliland made on the Salazar murder. William Fellion is an assassin that works for the state police and politicians of New Mexico. Max Sanchez, in my presence, paid $2,000 to William Fellion a few days before the death of Salazar. I was with Fellion in the red jeep, studying the layout in Tierra Amarilla for the assassination of Eulogio Salazar.[22]

Tijerina followed up on this revelation and admission of conspiracy to murder Salazar when he was released from prison on December 18, 1974, after serving only five months and eighteen days on a ten-year sentence. Blas Chávez had won his fight after three years for early parole and got out on December 10, 1974, eight days before Reies. On January 4, 1975, Tijerina looked up José Amador Gallegos, Blas Chávez's half-brother. According to Tijerina, "He confirmed everything Blas had told me while I was in prison."[23] Blas Chávez showed up on Tijerina's doorstep on January 8. "Blas Chávez came to see me. He told me he was ready. From the beginning, Blas had told me that he would only tell his story to a grand jury and not to reporters. He did not want to be killed beforehand."[24] Tijerina did the opposite of what Chávez wanted; he went to reporters Jerry McKinney and Ralph Looney at the *Albuquerque Tribune.* Nothing came out in the press. Tijerina explained in his book that the district attorneys in Rio Arriba, Castianos, and in Bernalillio, Brandenburg, were not his friends—they were with Senator Joseph Montoya.

The new governor of New Mexico, Jerry Apodaca, received Tijerina's delegation on February 27, 1975. They presented five items, one of which was "evidence about the death of Salazar and a request to publish the police report. . . . He accepted the agenda and promised to do what he could."[25] Months passed without any revelations about the true murderers. And on October 13, 1975, Robert Gilliland died of a heart attack after he killed two men in his bar. He was forty years old.[26] Tijerina sent copies of his own report on Gilliland and William Fellion to the local television stations. They did not report anything. Tijerina claimed that the FBI and state police knew all of these criminal activities on the part of Fellion. The FBI had given all this information to Gilliland. Gilliland even provided the FBI file number on Fellion, 3447790, in his report. Yet the FBI never moved a finger to stop Fellion's criminal activity.[27]

Tijerina went to the state legislature on February 2, 1976, and spoke with two legislators, David Salmon and D. J. Michaelson, about his findings on the Salazar murder, and they promised to help but did not. State Senator Michaelson told him by telephone the next day, "I can't, because there is a lot of opposition."[28] During the trip to Santa Fe to visit legislators, Tijerina also stopped at the office of the State Parole Board director, Santos Quintana, to tell him what he knew about the murderers of Salazar. Quintana told Tijerina, "Another FBI agent named Wirt Jones had already told him and Frank Garcia that 'In those days we cleared up the cause of Salazar's death.' But Santos said, 'We kept waiting for more explanation, but there was none.' To this day, agent Wirt has not explained anything about what he said to Santos Quintana."[29] The conspiracy to cover up Salazar's murder was much larger than Tijerina ever imagined.

Finally, on May 8 the *Albuquerque Journal* began to editorialize, three times, on the need to release to the public the police report on the death of Salazar and that a grand jury ought to be convened to investigate this death. The *El Paso Times* also ran seven articles on the death of Eulogio Salazar from June 27 to July 3, 1976. Then radio station KOB in Albuquerque called

Tijerina for comment on Governor Apodaca calling on the attorney general, Toney Anaya, "to investigate the death of Eulogio Salazar and convene a grand jury."[30] Hurriedly, Tijerina went to see the attorney general about this break in the case; they talked for over an hour and a half. AG Anaya had "boxes of information regarding the death of Salazar there."[31]

> In 1974 The governor announced that the investigative report on the Salazar murder would not be released. I decided the governor was implicated in the coverup and obstruction of justice of the murder. I felt rage but did not lose hope.
>
> It was clear the Anglos did not want the crime uncovered. They feared that Salazar's blood would end up on Anglo hands.[32]

CHAPTER 5

Poor People's Campaign

Maria Escobar, Reies López Tijerina's first wife, was the stalwart of the family. She co-pastored with him in churches, tents, street corners, and barns; gave birth to his children without a day off; walked by his side with children in tow on too many roads each time he gave away their possessions, including their car; tolerated the constant moving while he was a fugitive, and the frequent international trips to Mexico and Spain, leaving her and kids alone; had no help with the younger kids when he took daughter Rosa with him; and earned money to support the family, and Reies, for years. She had to homeschool the children as best she could, when she could, amid the turmoil and violence directed at them. Tijerina, oblivious to the economic hardship he placed on her shoulders, never once asked her about these serious problems. He never paid attention to the sacrifices his kids had to endure so he could fulfill his role as a religious man.[1]

While in Arizona and living in the Valley of Peace, Tijerina developed an abhorrence for the compulsory public education that he saw as obliterating the Hispanic identity, language, history, heritage, and culture. He and his followers erected a one-room building to serve as a school, and he obtained a permit from the State Department of Education to homeschool their kids. After Anglo juveniles from neighboring ranches burned the school to the ground, the commune children had to walk miles to catch the bus to attend the public schools nearby.[2]

> Now they were taking our right to educate our kids away from us. With the threat of jail and with guns they obligated us to accept a foreign education that perverts the honor of the sexes . . . what they called "sexual education." The Anglos got lost going in that direction.[3]

The members of the Valley of Peace decided to leave for New Mexico once he found his new cause, the land recovery movement. Shortly after forming the Alianza, the membership organization of land claimants, the violence began. There were always threatening phone calls, shots, rocks, and bricks thrown through the windows, bombings, arrests, jailings, and beatings directed at Reies, the family, his brothers, and the individual Alianza members. The violent episodes affected the Tijerina family. Reies himself had to take extreme precautions such as barricading the windows and installing iron doors; moving into the basement; recruiting his brothers as bodyguards and posting security guards in the home/office building around the clock. These new circumstances and events, on top of the economic hardships, was the proverbial last straw that broke Maria's back. In 1963, she broached the subject of divorce with Reies.

> My children were going hungry and doing without the necessities of life because of my life. I tried getting odd jobs, but within days my wife would see my spirit decline, as if I was a prisoner. My wife would tell me, "Your heart is not in this. It's better that you continue your mission." Finally, my wife went before Judge Paul Larrazolo and obtained a divorce. I did not appear. I still feared the power of the judges over my liberty. My wife took custody of the six children, our three boys and three girls. My wife continued helping me a lot in the Alianza, and my sons and daughters did not go far away from me.[4]

Tijerina got off easy; no child support payments and no health insurance for the kids, and he was awarded at-will visitation rights.

After he had learned enough about the land grant issue in the Southwest and in New Mexico, Tijerina began to make the connection with the fruits of the land to the sustainability of a people and their culture. The older land grant claimants would voice their complaints against the Forest Service and the Department of the Interior for cutting their grazing, fishing, and hunting rights; their rights to cut wood for lumber and fuel; and their access to water. Without those natural resources owned by them in perpetuity, their children would have to leave the family landholding and move to the city to work for wages. They could not feed themselves or their families. Tijerina also began to see the results of U.S. policies of genocide, removal, and holding Native American people prisoners on a reservation. While no Native American was forced to remain on the reservation in the late 1950s when Tijerina began visiting New Mexico, the prior forcing of a people off their homelands and holding them hostage on reservations had dire consequences for them, such as extreme poverty, chronic unemployment, alcoholism and drug addiction, domestic violence, depression, and suicide. When he visited Native Americans living on U.S. reservations in the Four Corners area of New Mexico, he began to understand the causes of poverty. He saw firsthand the role of government in either providing relief or promoting chronic poverty.[5] Now he was seeing the effects on his own people, the Indohispanos, especially in northern New Mexico, of having lost their lands. The land question was central to his analysis of development and sustainability among his people.[6]

Education also continued to be his concern. His older children, Rosa and Hugh David, worked in the Alianza office and stopped going to school. The younger ones did attend the public schools. On February 26, 1968, Raquel, another daughter, led a school walkout demanding the right to speak Spanish, learn of their history and culture, and have more teachers like them. The police came and beat the students. Tijerina concluded that "in the land of the free there is no room for our language."[7] In July following the walkout, Tijerina filed suit against the State Board of Education. He based his arguments on Article 2, Section 5, and Article 12, Section 8, of the New Mexico Constitution.

He invoked the rights to preserve and protect the Hispanic culture under the Treaty of Guadalupe Hidalgo. He equated the theft, abuse, and loss of the Spanish language to the theft of their lands.[8]

Meeting Elijah Muhammad and Dr. Martin Luther King Jr.

Alliance and coalition building had been one of Tijerina's agenda items to build a national movement among Indohispanos, Native Americans, and African Americans.[9] Previously, Tijerina had sought out the chieftains of various New Mexico tribal clans in an effort to build alliances. Some tribes had begun a working relationship with Tijerina's Alianza.

In 1959, Tijerina had read an article critical of Elijah Muhammad and the Nation of Islam (NOI) in *U.S. News and World Report*.[10] He found the story very biased, but of great interest; vicariously he developed instant admiration for the man, his courage, strength, and his struggle for his people. He made it a point to visit Elijah Muhammad, based in Chicago, someday. In 1960, while visiting his relatives in Chicago he called the NOI office and made an appointment to visit the religious leader. Tijerina felt they had a lot in common: the whites hated them; they had been imprisoned; they were religious leaders; they formed organizations to help their people; and they shared an unfavorable view of the Jewish people, particularly the Zionists. Tijerina went to see him at 4748 Woodlawn in Chicago while visiting with his sister Josefina and brother Margarito, just released from prison.[11] That meeting led to another and another over that week and resulted in a formal relationship; the two were moving forward with more frequent exchanges and discussions of joint projects between them.

In September 1967, Tijerina traveled to Chicago to attend the National Conference for New Politics.[12] Instead of looking up his fellow religious leader from the past, Elijah Muhammad, he sought out Reverend Martin Luther King Jr. (MLK), head of the Southern Christian Leadership Conference (SCLC). Dr. King was on Tijerina's radar screen as one of those to seek out while in Chicago during the New Politics conference. He had a moment to discuss with MLK an alliance between their respective organizations for participating in the upcoming Poor People's Campaign (PPC). Both Tijerina and Rodolfo "Corky" Gonzales of the Crusade for Justice in Denver sought out Dr. King in Chicago to discuss their collaboration with his proposal for the PPC. According to Ernesto Vigil, the FBI was monitoring them in Chicago, reporting on their presence, meetings, and discussions with Dr. King.[13]

The brief meeting with Tijerina and Gonzales apparently remained constant in King's mind. By telegram on March 5, MLK invited Reies and others, this author included, to an Atlanta meeting on March 14, 1968.[14] This gathering was dubbed the Minority Group Conference to discuss plans for the Poor People's Campaign. Corky Gonzales, Bert Corona, and Reverend Leo Nieto, among other Chicanos from the Southwest, were also invited and attended; notably absent was César Chávez. We heard Reverend King deliver a speech unlike any I had ever heard from him. He called for "the radical redistribution of political and economic power."[15]

As early as October 1966, MLK had been making public remarks about the need to bring economic demands on equal footing with civil rights. According to Amy Nathan Wright, MLK stated, "We have moved from the era of civil rights to an era of human rights."[16] She also credits Bayard Rustin as the author of the Southern Christian Leadership Conference paper on an Economic Bill of Rights, a condensed version of President Franklin D. Roosevelt's 1944 State of the Union address he did not live to implement.[17] The Rustin version became the economic plank MLK was looking for to coalesce the disparate minority groups into a Poor People's Campaign.

Reies López Tijerina sat at the right-hand side of MLK during the dinner welcoming all delegates to the Minority Group Conference in Atlanta. After the dinner, Dr. King suggested the various groups caucus and decide on their national representative to form a Committee of 100. Tijerina was unanimously elected the leader for the Chicano contingent, as we referred to ourselves.[18] When the Committee of 100 members regrouped after the caucuses, Tijerina audaciously presented conditions under which Indohispanos would participate.

We don't want scraps nor charity. We want justice. We want the government of the United States to swear by the Treaty of Guadalupe Hidalgo.

We want the return of the land stolen from our populations. We want our culture to be respected, and we want the foreign, compulsory education removed. Dr. King accepted our proposals. The other condition I presented to Dr. King was for the indigenous people, Native Americans, of all nations and tribes, to lead the march and that their rights be presented first; it would be like an arrowhead on the list of demands to be presented to the White House. Following them, the rights of Black people would be presented, and at the end of the list would be ours, Indohispanos [Chicanos].[19]

Before plans for the PPC could be further elaborated, however, Dr. King was assassinated in Memphis, Tennessee, on April 4, 1968. Tijerina, however, was being sought by the police and was finally jailed. The Albuquerque FBI sent an urgent teletype on April 30 to J. Edgar Hoover informing him that Tijerina was still incarcerated at the Santa Fe State Penitentiary as of that date. "No indications he or others in leadership of AFDM [Alianza Federal de Mercedes] planning to go to Washington, D.C., prior to time the Poor People's Group going by chartered bus." The FBI did not know what Tijerina was going to do with regard to the PPC.

Tijerina was released on bond and quickly made plans to fly to Memphis on May 2 at the behest of Reverend Ralph Abernathy, the heir apparent to MLK.

Would Tijerina Advocate Violence?

"A condition of subject's probation is that he refrain from advocating violence" is the opening line in the airtel from SAC, Albuquerque to the director of the FBI dated May 1, 1968. USA John F. Quinn, the federal prosecutor in Albuquerque trying Tijerina, requested that the SAC, Albuquerque monitor Tijerina, particularly his speeches, and that "copies of reports on Reies Lopez Tijerina be furnished him." USA Quinn knew and so advised the SAC in Albuquerque that Tijerina had filed an appeal on his conviction; hence his sentence and probation terms were all stayed while the matter was under appellate review. Therefore, nothing prohibited Tijerina from speaking about any subject in any manner he wished, including advocating violence. Nevertheless, the memo and its request were enough to trigger a constant surveillance of Tijerina for his movements.

The May 1 memo, based on human-gathered intelligence (HUMINT) is five pages, with page 2 entirely redacted under exemptions B1, B2, B7C, and D. The HUMINT content begins:

> The Special Agent who observed Reies Lopez Tijerina at Memphis, Tennessee, on 5/2/68 was SA [redacted].
>
> The Special Agents who observed Reies Lopez Tijerina at Albuquerque on 5/17/68 were SA [redacted] and SA [redacted].
>
> The Special Agents who observed Reies Lopez Tijerina in the Poor People's Campaign (PPC) March, 5/18/68, were SA [redacted] and SA [redacted].
>
> The Special Agents who observed Reies Lopez Tijerina and his daughter, Rose, at Albuquerque on 5/18/68 were SA [redacted].
>
> The Special Agents who observed Pat Blawis at Santa Fe, New Mexico, on 5/18/68, were SA [redacted] (p. 3).
>
> 1. Will maintain contact with sources who advise of activities of Reies Tijerina (p. 3).
>
> 2. Will attempt to monitor speeches and statements of Reies Tijerina.
>
> 3. Will follow and report prosecutive action in Federal and state courts. (p. 4)

The fifth page is without an FBI form number, but several boxes are marked with an X and some have additional information typed into the space allotted. Box 10 is X'd and reads: "Subject's SI card is tabbed Detcom," that is "Detention of Communists." The reasons for Detcom tabbing are "violent activities recently and the fact that he has indicated he may engage in violence in the future, as well as aligning himself with black militant forces."

Money to Tijerina for PPC

The SA in Albuquerque sent via registered mail a confidential four-page memo dated June 11, 1968, to many other intelligence agencies and the USA in Albuquerque. The agencies were OSI, Seventeenth District, Kirtland Air Force Base, New Mexico; U.S. Secret Service, Albuquerque; 112th MI Group, Fourth Army, Albuquerque; and the NISO, New Orleans. The "Synopsis" of the report on the first page is entirely redacted, as are significant spaces on the following page. The money trail is somewhat revealed. First are entries that suggest Tijerina asked for money, followed by entries that allege money was sent to Tijerina's organizational name, Federal Alliance of Free City States (FAFCS) as follows:

> Reies Tijerina, on May 15, 1968, requested William Rutherford, Southern Christian Leadership Conference (SCLC) office, 1401 "U" Street, Washington, D.C., to reimburse FAFCS for the following trips: Reies Tijerina to Los Angeles, California, April 17, 1968, in the amount of $94.50; Mr. and Mrs. Duran to Washington, D.C. in the amount of $124.00; Maria Varela to Washington D.C., in the amount of $231.50; Tijerina to San Francisco, California May 15, 1968, in the amount of $132.30. (p. 3)

Then follows the money coming in:

> R. Aronson, Western Poor People's Campaign, Denver, Colorado, sent $500 to Reies Tijerina, Albuquerque, New Mexico, on May 7, 1968; Reies Lopez Tijerina, FAFCS, 1010 Third Street, Albuquerque, New Mexico, received $1,000 from SCLC, Atlanta, Georgia, on May 4, 1968. (p. 3)

The bottom part of this same page indicates that Tijerina, according to the FBI, registered the FAFCS office as the office for PPC in Albuquerque "under the direction of Reies Lopez Tijerina."

**Incomplete FBI Report in Declassified Files from AQ 100-2567:
April 26–May 24, 1968**

The AQ 100-2567 report from the SAC, Albuquerque is at least thirty-seven pages long. Copies made available begin with page 5, which mentions that Tijerina would be traveling to El Paso with Cristobal, his brother, on the evening of April 26, arriving the morning of April 27, 1968. The day they left for El Paso, the *Albuquerque Journal* editorialized against Tijerina's leading Chicanos to Washington, DC, to participate in the PPC. The newspaper titled its editorial "Tijerina the Wrong Choice."[20] Tijerina was to address the New Organization of Mexican-American Students (NOMS) at El Paso's Downtowner Hotel (p. 27). The *El Paso Times* published quotes from his speech, and this source was made part of the thirty-seven-page report (p. 28). More importantly, this report tracks Tijerina's movements and media reports during the month-long period.

On May 2, 1968, a representative of the Federal Bureau of Investigation observed Reies Lopez Tijerina on the balcony of the Lorraine Hotel, 406 Mulberry Street Memphis, Tennessee, where a scheduled memorial service was being held in honor of the late Rev. Martin Luther King, Jr. (p. 9)

The lengthy report continued to list Tijerina's travel plans:

At 12:50 PM on that date Tijerina delivered a six-minute speech to the crowd assembled. He was one of fourteen speakers who participated.

On the afternoon of May 2, 1968, Reies Lopez Tijerina boarded one of the chartered buses engaged by SCLC to transport members of the PPC to Washington, D.C. He boarded the bus at Memphis, Tennessee and proceeded on the bus to Marks, Mississippi. (p. 9)

The report, however, was incorrect because the next paragraph reads:

[Redacted first sentence and first word of second line] advised that Reies Lopez Tijerina had returned to Albuquerque, New Mexico from Memphis,

Tennessee and would remain in Albuquerque until May 10, 1968, at which time he planned to travel to Washington, D.C., to meet with Ralph Abernathy and other leaders of the PPC. He is scheduled for an appearance in court in Stanta [*sic*] Fe, New Mexico, on May 13, 1968, and plans to be in Los Angeles, California, on May 15, 1968, to initiate the Southwest Segment of the PPC. (p. 9)

DA Sanchez had other plans for Tijerina: he jailed him. Instead of Tijerina flying to DC to join Abernathy, he came to be with Tijerina in Albuquerque. Together, after making bail and being released from jail, Abernathy and Tijerina marched five miles through the streets of Albuquerque's poorest sections and into downtown, ending at the Old Plaza, also known as Old Town Square. And Tijerina was jailed again upon return from a speech at the University of Texas–El Paso.

I was in solitary confinement for four days. They charged me with sixty-four counts for the takeover of Tierra Amarilla. The police harassed our people daily during 1967 and 1968. In those days, paid police spies trying to learn our every step plagued the Alianza. They wanted to find flaws. They did not let us rest. The police were waging a campaign of terror against the Alianza. Many people lost their jobs. Many others had to leave the Alianza.

During the four days, the judges kept me in jail, Reverend Abernathy and his followers surrounded the Department of Justice in Washington, asking for my freedom. . . . At the end of four days, I was released from the state prison. And, as I had promised Reverend Abernathy, I left for Memphis the next day. I was with Dr. King's widow and the Reverend Abernathy for two days. . . . Once the march officially began on May 2, I returned to New Mexico.[21]

Between May 8 and 9, the *Albuquerque Journal* and the *Albuquerque Tribune* reported contradictory statements in support of and in opposition to Tijerina's leading the Chicano contingent to the PPC. Apparently, Reverend Luis Jaramillo of San Felipe Catholic Church in Old Town Albuquerque supported Tijerina's plans to travel to DC and spoke to the press representing

Archbishop James Peter Davis, his superior. The archbishop and Ted F. Martinez, of the League of United Latin American Citizens, both spoke to the same media against Tijerina, claiming he was a bad choice as leader for being "an irresponsible self-appointed spokesman" (p. 8). However, at the Old Town speechmaking after the Albuquerque march, Archbishop Davis, "who had earlier questioned Tijerina's role, marched and called for people 'to look beyond Mr. Tijerina and what he stands for, to approve the march and hope it will be successful despite his connection to it.'"[22]

The thirty-seven-page report indicates that more incorrect information was being forwarded by SAC, Albuquerque to the FBI or, alternatively, Tijerina kept changing his plans to deceive FBI informants about his travel schedule. The report advised (from a redacted source) that Tijerina had made a TWA flight reservation from Albuquerque to Chicago on Mother's Day, May 10, departing at 2:00 a.m. He would change planes in Chicago and fly United to National Airport in DC and would return to Albuquerque from Friendship Airport in Baltimore on the afternoon of the same day. Instead, another redacted source "advised Tijerina departed TWA flight 169 at 5:45 pm for Albuquerque, New Mexico" (p. 10). Four days later, Tijerina is tracked by the FBI and its sources with plans to fly from Albuquerque to San Francisco on May 14. Three tickets apparently were bought, one by Fabian Duran, his future son-in-law, and another by him, plus his hosts in San Francisco sent a prepaid ticket to the TWA office too late for timely pickup (p. 10).

The lengthy report states Tijerina and Abernathy would be in the San Francisco area May 15-17 to make appearances together, recruiting persons to join them in traveling to the PPC events in DC The report states:

> Neither Reies Lopez Tijerina nor Ralph Abernathy appeared on the morning of May 16, 1968, at which time the buses carrying the PPC marchers departed from Oakland, California en route to Washington, D.C., although it was understood they were to be present. (p. 11)

Yet the paragraph following states that both the *Oakland Tribune* and the *San Francisco Chronicle*, on their front pages of May 16, carried stories regarding speeches made by Abernathy and Tijerina to groups. On the previous evening, Abernathy spoke at the Oakland Auditorium at an event called the "Poor People's Rally," where he concluded his speech by stating the Tijerina was giving his full and complete support for the PPC (p. 11). Tijerina has said the same thing at an earlier press conference held by both of them in Oakland (p. 12).

Tijerina and Abernathy then traveled to Albuquerque on May 17, arriving at Sunport Airport at noon. They met with Marlon Brando, the Hollywood star, and Bill Rutherford, the executive director of the SCLC, before proceeding later that evening to the Civic Auditorium in Albuquerque for another PPC Rally. "Among the speakers were two Indian chiefs, Marlon Brando, and Rev. Ralph Abernathy, and, of course, Reies Lopez Tijerina" (p. 12).

> Reies Lopez Tijerina was observed by Special Agents of the FBI as a participant in the Poor People's March in Albuquerque, New Mexico on May 18, 1968. He and his brother, Anselmo Lopez Tijerina, also active in FAFCS, led the march in Albuquerque, New Mexico, and they were accompanied in part of the way by Ralph Abernathy, President of SCLC. Reies Tijerina spoke briefly in Old Town Plaza, Albuquerque, New Mexico, at the conclusion of the march. Abernathy was the main speaker prior to the departure of the buses transporting the participants in the PPC to Washington, D.C. (pp. 12–13)

> Special Agents of the FBI on May 18, 1968, at Albuquerque, New Mexico, observed Reies Lopez Tijerina and his daughter, Rose Tijerina, and a third unidentified passenger departing Albuquerque, New Mexico at approximately 7:00 PM for Santa Fe, New Mexico driving a white Chevrolet pickup truck, New Mexico License 2-22811. (p. 13)

Then the same information is restated, but from FBI agents picking up the trail in Santa Fe. By then, the "third unidentified passenger" was identified as his wife, Patricia, and they must have run a check on the license plates to know that the Alianza owned the pickup truck by the time it arrived in Denver.

> Reies Lopez Tijerina, his wife Patricia, and his daughter, Rose Tijerina, departed Santa Fe, New Mexico, on May 18, 1968, for Denver, Colorado, and

Washington, D.C., in a white Chevrolet pickup truck, property of FAFCS. Reies Tijerina was driving. (p. 13)

The *Albuquerque Journal* reported on the May 19 front page that Tijerina was planning on flying from Denver to Washington, DC, and "remain during the duration of the Poor People's Campaign" (p. 13).

At the bottom of page 13 of the lengthy FBI report is a totally redacted paragraph, a redacted first line in the second-to-bottom paragraph, and, a quotation by an informant.

[Name redacted describes] Reies Tijerina as a "most erratic person, extremely strong willed. And it could be expected he will pull his people out of the PPC for the slightest provocation." [Name redacted considers] Tijerina to be unreliable and he hoped SCLC would be able to control Tijerina through Rudolfo "Corky" Gonzales, leader of the Crusade for Justice from Denver, Colorado. (p. 13)[23]

The POCAM program, FBI jargon for the Poor People's Campaign, was specifically aimed at recruiting informants to report on the PPC. Tijerina had his worries with state and local police informants; now he had FBI informants in his ranks, as well as those of all other groups involved with the PPC. POCAM was part of a larger and longer-lasting operation, the Ghetto Informant Program (GIP). The number of informants the FBI had working is astounding: in 1969, 4,067; in 1970, 5,778; in 1971, 6,301; in 1972, 7,402. Allegedly, GIP was discontinued in 1973, but oddly enough the FBI reported a new program, Operation TIPS, in 2002, according to Senator Patrick Leahy's inquiry on the subject during the Bush administration.[24]

The Buses Roll

Organizing across the Southwest by the various Chicano, Native American, and black organizations and those of white groups going to the PPC in DC began in earnest. Buses leased by these organizations and their supporters from Greyhound in Los Angeles, Denver, Albuquerque, and San Antonio converged in Kansas City, carrying the PPC participants into Washington, DC. The Chicano contingent alone totaled twenty buses carrying over five hundred activists; more arrived in their own cars and vans. The Colorado delegation was headed by Rodolfo "Corky" Gonzales of the Crusade for Justice; New Mexico by Reies Tijerina of the Alianza; and Texas by Reverend Leo Nieto, but mostly comprising members of the Mexican American Youth Organization (MAYO). California had a mixed contingency but no one leader; there were several youths involved with the Movimiento Estudiantil Chicano de Aztlan (MEChA), the Brown Berets (Los Angeles), and the Black Berets (San Jose). There also were countless other groups and local leaders from other states such as Arizona, Utah, Missouri, Kansas, and Nebraska.

Still reeling from the aftermath of the Chicano students' school walkouts in the early spring of 1968 at five high schools in Los Angeles, the leaders of the various groups supporting the students were slow in deciding on joining the bus caravan to the PPC. The former boycotting Chicano students were also reluctant to join the PPC after missing many days of school and with court appearances tied to their arrests for boycotting and protesting.

On May 15 as the buses left Will Rogers Park in the Watts neighborhood of Los Angeles, David Sanchez, Carlos Montes, Ralph Ramirez, Gloria Arrellanes, and three others literally had to run to catch up and get on board. The blacks already sitting in the front-row seats jokingly goaded the Chicanos that they had to ride in the back of the bus. Forty-seven Chicanos in all made the trip from Los Angeles to the PPC.[25]

The Western Caravan, as the buses and cars coming from the West Coast were referred to, headed from Los Angeles to Phoenix. The San Francisco / Oakland bus went to Denver, then Kansas City. In Phoenix, the money problems of financing such a massive number of people and the logistics of tracking the buses and the stops became evident. Reports were had that at least 80 people would not make the trip for lack of money and 123 climbed aboard more buses and private cars. Most of those turned away from getting a bus seat were other Chicanos; resentment and bickering between blacks and browns began, and Tijerina, later, gave voice to that disgust and demanded SCLC make good on its promises. Earlier, when Tom Houck of

SCLC made a trip to Albuquerque to plan the Western Caravan, Maria Varela, formerly a SNCC staffer, got into a heated argument about lack of resources being allocated to Chicano groups wanting to join in the PPC. Varela was now volunteering with the Alianza and helping Tijerina as a staff person.[26]

The Albuquerque march helped smooth over tensions and feelings because it was such a successful event, with more than twelve hundred persons marching in the streets. The speeches were motivational, uplifting, and emotional. Tijerina, as usual, stole the show with his passion and showmanship while speaking. The Native American speakers not only brought a new dimension to the amalgamated group of whites, blacks, and browns, but also a new perspective on what the PPC agenda should be; now reds joined in and got on the buses.

While the Albuquerque stop had been a multiracial rainbow of solidarity and group cohesion, El Paso became a nightmare. As they rolled down Interstate 10 into the city and over to the El Paso Coliseum, the buses were met by Texas state troopers and a company of Texas Rangers. The state police and Texas Rangers, augmented by more local city and county police, informed the Western Caravan leaders that their city march and rally were canceled. The police feared for their safety given several bomb threats that had been called into media outlets. The news media made sensational stories of these threats and repeated them over and over. Veterans of prior protests and marches voiced their displeasure with this police instruction; they knew a typical ploy was to invent a bomb threat to cancel protests and marches. And here it was playing out in front of hundreds of them.

The Texas Rangers and other police personnel led the bus riders into the coliseum and encircled the building to prevent their departure anywhere other than out of town the next day. Some bus riders observed the Rangers casually drinking beer and confronting them verbally: "Don't look at me in the eye; that's a challenge ... to get your head beat." The group spent a sleepless night on army cots and the arena floor, ate bologna sandwiches, and kept an eye on the police.[27]

The San Francisco bus caravan was as much fun for the bus riders as was the Albuquerque protest and rally. The Denver Crusade for Justice hosted them and held a rally on the capitol steps with a multitude of speakers representing different groups. Some folks from Albuquerque had gone in that direction rather than El Paso, and they stood out from the crowd with their cowboy hats, boots, faded jeans, and weathered look. They certainly were a contrast to the Oakland Black Panther contingent, who strutted about the crowd in black leather coats and black berets that could not fully contain their Afros. The white hippies, with their robust scent of patchouli, added color and distinctness to the crowd, especially the women with flowers in their hair, as the song lyrics go. There were few other whites in either of the bus caravans coming from California across the western states.

The combination of Tijerina and Corky, both speaking at the rally, really fired up the crowd, especially Chicanos and Puerto Ricans. The Native American speakers reminded all that "nobody knows what poor is like the Indians." Black Berets met Brown Berets, who met Black Panthers, who met Aliancistas, who also met the Crusaders from Denver. For many Chicanos, it was their first exposure to Corky and Reies and their rhetorical messages. Many of the Berets, both Black and Brown, left seats in other buses to ride with the all-Chicano buses and the Crusaders from Denver to Kansas City, six hundred miles down the road. The blacks, once again, felt segregated in the other buses until they reached Kansas City.[28]

The organizers of the Kansas City stopover planned it as an all-black event until Corky and his Crusaders showed up and pushed for Chicano and Native American inclusion, beginning with speakers. Regardless, the organizers, hearing the protests but not listening, kept with their program. They began the rally with a black preacher reciting a prayer, followed by more black leaders all addressing the plight of black Americans without mention of any other groups despite their very visible presence. Finally, Corky had enough and took over the microphone almost physically. He promptly shared the podium with Native Americans, who also shared their stories of poverty and need. When finished, Corky handed the microphone to his black host with the words, "You can have your program back now." Kansas City was the most poorly attended rally of the tour.[29]

Things got worse in St. Louis, where buses from San Antonio, Texas, carrying many more Chicanos, arrived and realized they were encroaching on an all-black program. Again the same jousting took place between Chicano leaders and black hosts about speakers and agenda. This time the blacks would not yield. Corky and the Crusaders began a walkout from the rally. Only then, with media attention all over the developing incident, did the hosts allow nonblack speakers access to the microphone. Shortly afterward, the agenda called for a historic march across the Mississippi River bridge. Blacks just assumed they would lead the march, but Corky again took the lead and demanded that Native Americans be the first in the line. The Black Panthers, the local chapter and the Oakland riders with some SNCC support, made a stand in opposition. They verbally insisted that blacks were the most deserving for being the most oppressed, a notion quickly attacked by Native American leaders and the Crusade for Justice members. Tijerina had from the beginning not only insisted on using the group term *Indohispano* to recognize the indigenous DNA within all Chicanos, but also had insisted that Native Americans be front and center, first always, in the PPC activities, agendas, issues, and presence. Only when the renewed threat of leaving the march was made did the blacks relent and allowed Native Americans to lead over nine hundred marchers to the apex of the bridge. There all sat for a few minutes in silent solidarity, then continued to waiting buses at the other end of the bridge.[30] But the riders were now carrying into the PPC a line of separation between blacks, on one hand, and the Native Americans and their Chicano progeny, on the other.

The SCLC logistical team responsible for Chicago fell short with housing and other resources, so the buses from the Western Caravan and the Indian Trail, as the buses from the Midwestern states bringing Indians was called, were rerouted to Louisville, Kentucky. There the housing was almost as bad as had been the cots in El Paso. The bus riders were sent to sleep in the barns of Churchill Downs, the Kentucky Derby race track. Word began to circulate among the blacks and the SCLC coordinators that Chicanos were making plans to house themselves at a location other than in the tents of makeshift Resurrection City (RC) in DC. Some of this was true; Tijerina had continued his protests to Abernathy and his lieutenants about how poorly Chicanos and Native Americans were being treated. He pointed out that at every stop the SCLC coordinators retired to motels and the private homes of other black hosts, while other riders endured what was made available at the last minute. He demanded he be given the SCLC resources allocated for these bus caravans and he would take care of logistics. He wanted the money to expense the Native American leaders up front and that it be given to them without further delay. He was not given any access to budget allocations, nor was he told what was available in dollar amounts. SCLC coordinators continued to stay overnight in motels along the way, and in DC Reverend Abernathy and the top SCLC leadership, including Andrew Young, stayed at the Pitts Motor Hotel.[31]

Tijerina Arrives at PPC and Gets Busy with His Agenda

Another lengthy FBI report, dated June 20, 1968, covers the arrival of Tijerina in DC on May 23 and all his activities through June 5. The accompanying memo is only two pages, but the report is twenty-one pages long. Tijerina spoke at a SCLC rally related to the PPC on May 29 held at the John Wesley AME Zion Church on Fourteenth and Corcoran Streets (p. 1). He spoke about the land grants and how documents to prove ownership were destroyed by the very government that took possession of their lands. He promised to get the job done, insinuating he would recover the stolen lands (p. 2). Heavy redaction blocks half the page. The bottom of the page reports that Tijerina did not move into Resurrection City and instead went to the Hawthorne School; and that about noon on May 31 "a Greyhound bus had been observed loading approximately 33 Spanish-Americans, with their luggage at the Hawthorne School, reportedly to return to New Mexico" (p. 2). The last pages of the report continued with details about the various protests led by various leaders, including Tijerina, at federal buildings housing executive departments, including the Department of Justice, where the group was trying to set up a meeting with the U.S. attorney general and secretary of state.

No sooner had the buses arrived at RC, Resurrection City, on May 23 and dropped off their passengers than the rains came. The PPC was to last from mid-May to mid-June, thirty-one days, in all; it rained for nineteen days. On the last two days of the PPC, June 12-13, it rained two inches in twenty-four hours. The balmy, summer-hot, humid place nicknamed "Tent City" became a mud pit. Winds knocked down the main dining hall; over one thousand persons had to be evacuated due to flooding of their tents; and, contaminated water flowed everywhere. Miraculously, no epidemic broke out. The SCLC's head of the medical committee, Dr. Edward Madzique, explained it this way: "It may have been the terrible conditions in which poor residents lived normally that prevented" an epidemic.[32]

The plan had been for all PPC participants to camp out in Resurrection City sleeping in tents, but after a week Tijerina and other Chicano leaders, with support from Puerto Ricans, moved out and housed themselves at the Hawthorne School, about two miles from Potomac Park.[33] Richard "Ricardo" Romero, Corky's brother-in-law, as advance man for the Crusade for Justice, had made an onsite visit to Resurrection City two weeks prior to the bus caravans arriving. He decided against Tent City as the spot for them to live for a month. He found help among local DC ministers and found the Hawthorne School ideal. In retrospect, Romero was right on target: the school had air conditioning, dry walls and floors, and full-service facilities and was safe and secure with windows and doors.[34] The relocation was not only due to the downpour of rain, wind, and mud and the poor coordination of services, but also the growing conflict with young blacks from DC, not part of the PPC, who were preying on nonblack females—white hippies, Chicanas, Native Americans, and Puerto Ricans. Particularly concerned were both Tijerina and Gonzales, who had family with them, including young adult daughters, Rosa and Nita Jo, respectively. Several of the Native Americans had brought their families on the trip.

Abernathy's lieutenants could not contain the young thugs or restrict them from Resurrection City.[35] To Tijerina and the Crusade people, the SCLC would not even try; they were black brothers. Mantler claims the Chicano groups and Native Americans never moved into Resurrection City, seeing the conditions at hand upon arrival; the five-hundred-strong mixed group went to the Hawthorne School right away. Some Indians went to St. Augustine's Episcopal Church, and poor whites such as Myles Horton of the Highlander Center opted to stay at both Hawthorne and St. Augustine, but not Resurrection City.[36]

"TV-Rina" Becomes His Nickname in DC

The prior June, in 1967, members of the Crusade and Corky Gonzales had traveled to Santa Fe to protest the jailing of Tijerina. Corky even attempted to help the Alianza with his leadership in Tijerina's absence and stayed over into July operating from the Alianza headquarters. This did not go well, and Gonzales was accused of being power-hungry and egotistical. He was also criticized for his poor command of Spanish. Gonzales, however, defended himself against the diatribes and accusations by producing a letter, according to Ernesto Vigil, wherein Tijerina had asked him to take over the New Mexico movement.[37]

A few months later, in September 1967, Daniel "Danny" Tijerina, was arrested in Denver. DA Sanchez was still hot on his trail and charging him with assault with intent to commit murder and kidnapping. Daniel, a juvenile, had been spending time with his mother, who had relocated to Denver after the Tierra Amarilla incident. Again, the Crusade activists and Corky came to the aid of Tijerina, providing for the legal defense with protests and lawyers for his son. Eventually, the extradition of Daniel Tijerina was dropped by Sanchez.[38] Tijerina was most grateful and accepted an invitation to address the Crusade at its November 19, 1967, first annual conference in Denver.[39]

At the Hawthorne School, however, differences arose between Tijerina and Corky Gonzales on many fronts, including the Chicano role within the PPC, management of the school building where they were staying, agenda items with Abernathy and his SCLC staffers, statements to the press, and what protests to carry out. Tijerina's flamboyance and his magnetism drew the media to him more than any other leader. Tijerina broke ranks with Abernathy in a public way by calling a press conference in front of Resurrection City. He had invited Abernathy to join him and explain to Chicanos, Indians, Puerto Ricans, and poor whites why the PPC was not living up to the agreements made with Reverend King. Instead, Rudolph Thompson, one of Abernathy's lieutenants, came and engaged in a shouting match with Tijerina, much to the delight of the cameras and reporters. Tijerina demanded that Abernathy come to the Hawthorne School to work things out.

They did meet and resolved some differences, but the pattern became clear. Tijerina, as the leader of the Chicanos, and co-leader for Native Americans, began calling more press conferences and engaging in protests of his own doing. Abernathy and the SCLC began viewing this behavior and agenda as a personal and private agenda, not part of the PPC.[40] The Crusade activists began calling him "TV-Rina" for constantly seeking out the television cameras.[41]

Robert Kennedy's Assassination

On June 5, 1968, Robert Kennedy was assassinated in Los Angeles while on the presidential campaign trail for the Democratic Party nomination. Sirhan Sirhan, a Palestinian with Jordanian citizenship, was the assassin. It was probably the first overt terrorist act by a Palestinian in response to the Israeli occupation of their ancestral lands. Senator Kennedy had been a strong supporter of Israel's right to a nation-state at the expense of the Palestinians throughout his political career. The RFK campaign was the reason why César Chávez stayed away from the PPC; he and his supporters were busy trying to win the California primary for RFK and cinch the Democratic Party nomination. Tijerina made a pointed observation about the assassination that fueled more charges against him of anti-Semitism:

> The Anglo does not recognize our right to demand justice for our property and for our culture. But it recognizes the right of the Jewish to reclaim their land two thousand years after they abandoned it. An Arab, one thrown out of Palestine, spilled Robert Kennedy's blood. That blood was part of the price the United States paid for wanting the land Jews claimed as theirs. And, that is what the Anglo must recognize: the land that I demand for my Indian and Indohispano people belongs to us in all truth. Just like the Anglo concedes reason and justice to the claims of Jews, he should concede reason and justice to us.[42]

Who Will Make the UN Claim?

While participating in the PPC activities in DC, Tijerina made time to present himself and his land claim cause before the Mexican and Spanish embassies, as well as the Organization of American States.[43] By 1968 he had learned that individuals cannot make or present claims before the United Nations, only member nations can. Tijerina was seeking help from the governments of Mexico and Spain; he wanted them to make the case of the stolen land grants in the Southwest before the UN.

The Mexican ambassador opened the doors to the embassy to more than three hundred of the people from the Southwest, part of Tijerina's Chicano contingent. "He greeted us with a hug and offered us delicious sodas." For over an hour, they exchanged views on the Southwest lands and the Treaty of Guadalupe Hidalgo. The Mexican ambassador offered his help with the cause. He sent an envoy to interview others in the PPC on this issue, and those findings were reported in the *Official Daily* of the Mexican government.[44] Ultimately, Mexico refused to present the case before the United Nations, much less repudiate the Treaty of Guadalupe Hidalgo as adopted by the United States after excising critical terms from the negotiated agreement.

Poor Becomes Black Again

Differences also arose between Tijerina and Abernathy's lieutenants on the purposes of the PPC, which were supposed to incorporate Tijerina's planks approved by Dr. King. The PPC was becoming more and more a black-led civil rights protest. Native American leaders were being pushed aside, and some had been jailed after they protested at the Supreme Court building over fishing rights. Ernesto Vigil and Reies's sons, Hugh David and Daniel, not only were arrested but beaten by police.[45] Tijerina also wanted to protest at the Supreme Court building, surround it, and demand the justices come out and meet with the protestors.

SAC, WFO (the Washington Field Office) sent a six-page report dated

May 30, 1968, to Hoover on the Supreme Court building takeover on the twenty-ninth by Tijerina's group with some participation by Abernathy's followers. Apparently, the Capitol Police, with backup from the Metropolitan Police, intercepted the protestors, numbering about two hundred, and informed them that unless they broke up into small groups of no more than twenty, no entrance would be allowed. The FBI report states: "This was done without incident" (p. 2). By 11:30 a.m., however, the protestors numbered about four hundred. Two members of the group, "Ray Johnson, Negro male, age thirtytwo [sic], WDC, and Cheryl Robinson, white female, both charged [with] disorderly conduct." They had lowered the U.S. flag to half-mast (p. 3).

More arrests followed: "Monte Washington, Negro male, age seventeen, of Cincinnati, Ohio, arrested and charged with interfering with officer." Then the windows of the building were broken by unidentified persons, and "participants departed area supreme court shortly after incident" (p. 3). At 6:30 p.m., some fifty protestors participants and police engaged again. This time, five were arrested for "disorderly conduct and subsequently released. Arrests stemmed from use of obscene and abusive language and with refusal to move from above location" (p. 4). These persons were Mark Jaramillo, Billy Joe Cheek, Ernie Vigil, Daniel Tijerina, son of Reies López Tijerina, and Miguel Jose Trujillo, according to the report (p. 4). Reverend Jesse Jackson, according to the report, had another group of some 150 to 180 coming to join Tijerina and Abernathy at the Supreme Court building, but never made it. They had departed May 29 at 9:00 a.m. for a first meeting at the Department of Agriculture, held in the cafeteria. The group ate and drank, running up a bill of $292.00 with Jackson only paying $72.

John Davis, the clerk of the Supreme Court, agreed to meet with four protestors, one from each of the groups—black, white, red, and brown. Tijerina insisted on at least twenty. Davis acquiesced and heard their demands. The next day Tijerina led the group to the State Department, where they insisted on meeting with Secretary of State Dean Rusk. Again, Rusk wanted four and they wanted twenty. Rusk also agreed to meet, but without the press present. They discussed Native American and Chicano concerns and land claims.[46]

It became clear, as the days went by, that the claims of the Indian, Puerto Rican, and Chicano delegations, which centered on land and property rights based on treaties and international law, were distinct from black concerns and claims, which centered on expanded War on Poverty programs. To blacks, poor was akin to black, not Chicano or Indian. The PPC was to be a black demand for more programs, services, and civil rights, not a multiethnic class event for land and human rights. Whites, particularly middle-class whites, viewed poverty in racial terms, as only a black issue; the War on Poverty was the solution to lift blacks out of poverty. To be sure, this was the view of President Lyndon B. Johnson and his vision for a Great Society. Whites were oblivious to poverty among Chicanos, Indians, Puerto Ricans, and even lower-class whites. To them, these peoples are mostly invisible. The class and racial binary in the United States is black and white. William S. Clayson makes such an argument about the views of whites regarding the PPC and War on Poverty:

Few Texans viewed "the poor" as a group needing a campaign. In terms of group identification, race trumped class. White Texans declined to participate in Johnson's War on Poverty. Even if they recognized their poverty, low-income white Texans showed little interest in taking advantage of OEO [Office of Economic Opportunity] programs because they associated the Great Society with the demands of nonwhites. The growing electorate of affluent or middle-class whites in the states, even those Harding [Bertrand Harding, head of OEO] described as "supportive" or "middle-of-the-road" in relation to civil rights or the War on Poverty, opposed the OEO due to its association with racial militancy and urban violence. Many African American and Mexican American Texans, under the influence of militant nationalist movements, determined that racial solidarity offered the best way out of poverty. The groups competed with each other over OEO funds and sought to exclude whites from programs. With scant support among white Texans and often bitter competition among nonwhite groups, politicians had little reason to defend the OEO. Indeed, attacking the OEO promised more political benefit.[47]

Time Running Out on the PPC

The permit issued by Capitol Police for use of the grounds adjacent to the Lincoln Memorial to erect the tents for RC was good until June 16. The Metropolitan Police, however, advised the FBI's WFO on June 11, 1967, that the permit had been extended one additional week, until June 23.[48]

Informants continued to plague all leaders and groups during the PPC, according to Gerald McKnight.[49] In mixed company, a Puerto Rican snitch could easily slide up to Chicanos and pass for an activist, or a black informer could pass as a wanna-be Black Panther among them, and the same with Native Americans. The FBI had plenty of informants and agents working double time during the months of preparation, travel, arrival, and departure from the city. In the lengthy thirty-seven-page report already cited, an informant let the FBI know that Tijerina had asked for $2,000 from the SCLC for his expenses but was not funded (p. 14). Many of Tijerina's comments to the press were forwarded to newspapers back in Albuquerque, such as the *Albuquerque Journal.* Several of these articles are included in the report, including coverage in both the *Albuquerque Journal* and *Washington Times Herald* of the meeting between Abernathy and Tijerina to iron out differences after Reies threatened to pull out of the PPC (pp. 15–18). Even Abernathy's rebuttal to Tijerina in articles published in the *Albuquerque Tribune* are included in the report (pp. 21–22).

The demonstrations carried out by Tijerina and Corky Gonzales and their statements after the Supreme Court building takeover, when windows were broken, were reported in the *Tribune* and *Journal* in Albuquerque (pp. 23–26). The report lists chronologically all the court appearances pending for Tijerina, with outcomes for each. For example, a person whose name is redacted provides a summary description labeled as a "Characterization" of the National Lawyers Guild (p. 33), then provides information on the charges of kidnapping and armed robbery on Tijerina from June 5, 1967. He was arrested April 28, 1968, jailed at the state penitentiary, and released on posted property bond of $40,000 on April 30. "Beverly Axelrod, an attorney, came to the Penitentiary to post the bond" (p. 34). On May 13 the court date was set for June 24, but later on May 24 postponed to July 22 in Judge Paul Larrazolo's courtroom, not Judge Joe Angel's, on an order from the state supreme court dated April 30 (p. 35).

The report also notes that the Alianza's legal name was changed as of August 19, 1967, to Federal Alliance of Free City States (Alianza Federal de Pueblos Libres) (p. 36).

The next FBI communication in the declassified files is an urgent two-page teletype dated June 6 reporting that Tijerina had been in DC with POCAM since May 23 but was now leaving for Oklahoma City to raise funds from Native American groups (p. 1). The information on his travel plans was obtained "by source of MPD and confirmed by Wash. Field Office pretext interview member Tijerina group" (p. 2).

The huge rift between Chicano delegations and the SCLC was not helped when Tijerina and Reverend Hosea Williams of the SCLC engaged in a shouting match before a large audience of PPC participants and FBI informants, according to an LHM submitted on June 20, 1968. The pressure from SCLC on Tijerina to vacate the Hawthorne School and move into RC never stopped. He was threatened with a cutoff of funding and expulsion from the PPC. Hosea Williams was among the most vocal in accusing Tijerina of double dealing, that is, doing his own thing with SCLC money. The accusation was true, but justified, according to Tijerina, because the PPC, as he saw it, had an entirely black agenda led by blacks from SCLC.

Tijerina's first speech to the PPC audience was on May 28. He gave his standard Alianza speech on how the Southwest was occupied and taken by Anglos under fraud by violating the Treaty of Guadalupe Hidalgo. He kept making speeches and adding new information about property and land rights in the Southwest as the days went by (pp. 1–2 of the LHM). When protest marches started being organized, the fight began in earnest between Tijerina and the SCLC. Permits to march were obtained by SCLC leaders, who had provided information in advance to police authorities on the reasons for the march, how many they were, and what would be discussed in speeches. Problems began when Chicanos and Indians wanted to add agenda items to the discussion. They were denied by police and the SCLC. The Chicanos wanted the attorney general, Ramsey Clark, for example, to call on the LA police to release from jail Chicano students who had been arrested during the walkouts in the spring.

Hosea and Corky Gonzales got it on the first time at the attorney general's office. Gonzales wanted to force the police to arrest protestors for being too many and too loud; Hosea objected and ordered the group back to RC. The Chicanos and Indians refused. Close to midnight the AG's representative informed Gonzales that the LA student leaders had all been released and that the AG would meet with Gonzales and others on June 4 (p. 5).

Across town at the Ebenezer AME Church, Tijerina was challenging Reverend James Bevel and Ralph Abernathy of the SCLC on the role of the church as being hostile to poor people and accusing the United States of a conspiracy by violating the Treaty of Guadalupe Hidalgo. He told the audience the U.S. government had done the same to Indians and blacks. The solution he proposed was to make citizen's arrests of those in power and guilty of perpetuating these crimes. Tijerina brought the crowd to its feet in enthusiastic applause when he retold the story of the lion and the cricket (pp. 5–6), previously mentioned in the introduction. (The LHM erroneously reported that Tijerina used the metaphor of a flea instead of a cricket. The reaction by Bevel and Abernathy and any informant present was redacted for an entire paragraph on this page.)

Hosea Williams at a press conference outlined the agenda for the June 4 meeting with AG Ramsey Clark. According to the LHM, the SCLC had previously submitted an agenda to the AG's office for a meeting at 3:15 p.m. The news infuriated Corky Gonzales, who felt sidestepped, ignored in his demands and scheduled appointment time. The Chicanos and Indians and others organized themselves into a march and walked from Hawthorne School to RC and then toward the DOJ building, arriving at 2:40 p.m. Hosea Williams, Father James Groppi, and Tijerina met them at the front entrance and began entering the Great Hall at 3:05 p.m. Another 150 protestors could not be accommodated in the auditorium, so they remained outside and began singing. Hosea Williams introduced the AG when he walked in at 3:15 p.m. Hosea reminded the AG that they wanted a response to the SCLC requests for action presented to him on employment discrimination, school segregation, housing discrimination, police brutality, alien strikebreakers, and hunting and fishing rights of Indians. The AG "then pointed out what USDJ [U.S. Department of Justice] is doing in these areas to achieve equal justice for all Americans" (p. 7). Corky then took the microphone and repeated the reasons for the LA school walkouts, the cultural and racial discrimination against Chicanos, and inferior education and insufferable conditions. Gonzales demanded an executive order enforcing the terms of the Treaty of Guadalupe Hidalgo. Several other speakers took the microphone and made specific demands of the AG.

Instead of the AG responding, Hosea Williams explained that "there are certain things the Attorney General can do personally," implying that it was not what the speakers had demanded (p. 8). AG Clark quickly explained he could not issue executive orders but would investigate the Los Angeles walkout student arrests, and he left at 5:10 p.m.

On the fifth Tijerina marched his group over to RC to ask Abernathy and the SCLC to join them in meeting with the State Department. The SCLC, through Hosea Williams, refused. Tijerina marched on with about seventy persons and was met by Assistant Secretary of State Covey Oliver and Peter Krough, from the secretary's office. They were told the secretary of state, Dean Rusk, would meet with them at a later date. Tijerina, unfortunately, had allowed a crude, hand-made leaflet to circulate calling for the celebration of the Tierra Amarilla "June 5th Revolution" (pp. 10, 19). According to the LHM, this was the real reason the SCLC had refused to participate with Tijerina's march to the State Department. The LHM also quoted the *Washington Post* of June 6, which gave the details of the shouting match between Williams and Tijerina at RC. The article was entitled "Marchers' Rift Breaks into Open."

On June 5 Tijerina and Williams took a position on a raised platform across from each other to address two hundred persons at Resurrection City (p. 11). The speakers courteously passed a bullhorn back and forth to direct their insults to each other. Hosea started it by saying that as director of demonstrations, he was not authorizing the march on the State Department; they were marching on the National Rifle Association (NRA) to protest the shooting of Senator Robert F. Kennedy. Tijerina took the bullhorn from Williams to tell the crowd they had previously announced the State

Department march and that he knew nothing of the march on the NRA. Williams then took the bullhorn from Tijerina to say he knew nothing of the State Department march and repeated he was the one in charge of demonstrations and direct action for the SCLC. Tijerina countered with, "It was discussed Tuesday at the PPC steering committee meeting." The two continued for more turns with the bullhorn, ensuring that the crowd would divide into blacks and Mexican Americans who began to glare and grumble at each other. Tijerina accused Williams of humiliating Mexican Americans by leaving them out of decision-making. Williams countered with, "Brother, we need to coordinate" and he announced he was taking the matter up to the city council for RC (p. 12). Tijerina pointed out the city council was made up of SCLC staff people and continued his criticism of the PPC leadership. Williams and other SCLC staffers began moving the crowd away from Tijerina for another activity. Tijerina closed with a statement that "we need unity, and I want that." The *Washington Post* article and LHM both quoted that comment. Two days later, on June 8, the *Washington Post* carried another article cited by the LHM stating that Secretary Rusk would meet with Mexican Americans "but made it plain in advance that he thought they had nothing to protest about" (p. 13).

The LHM is silent as to the outcome of any meeting that may have taken place, but it does report that Tijerina took off for Oklahoma City in the early morning of June 6 to drum up support among Indian groups (p. 14). It also has a direct order from Abernathy to Tijerina, according to a "sixth confidential source" who learned that Tijerina had been given an ultimatum: either "move into RC or leave town" (p. 15).

This LHM also has the source of information about death threats against Tijerina as himself, by way of comments he made to a Metropolitan Police Department officer—nothing specific, just a mention he had received several threats. The officer ["was of the opinion Tijerina made this statement boastingly in order to attempt to prove his importance" (p. 16). After Oklahoma City, Tijerina did return to DC and the Hawthorne School. He announced that a meeting with Secretary Rusk was now scheduled for June 13. The next paragraph is redacted entirely, so no other information on this rescheduling is available (p. 18).

Death Threat by Interview?

The next urgent one-page teletype sent on June 7 from Oklahoma City to Hoover and the WFO advises that Tijerina, according to American Airlines, left DC that day and arrived in Tulsa, Oklahoma,

> to recruit more Indian support for POCAM and subject's life reportedly has been threatened by persons identifying themselves as members of John Birch Society. Dick Gregory stated he has assumed leadership of the Indian contingent of POCAM. (p. 1)

On June 8, at the crack of dawn, 5:26 a.m., the director of the FBI sent an enciphered, priority, two-page teletype alert to the president, the Department of the Army, the Department of the Air Force, and the White House Situation Room, to the attention of the Secret Service, that Reies López Tijerina had arrived in Tulsa, and the FBI had received information from the Military Intelligence Group in Oklahoma City that Tijerina's life reportedly had been threatened by persons identifying themselves as members of John Birch Society, though a "reliable source Tulsa, Oklahoma, states unaware of Tijerina's arrival and know of no threats against Tijerina's life" (p. 1).

Perplexing as these two transmissions are, the more intriguing content is the second-guessing by Hoover. On the one hand, the Military Intelligence Group out of Oklahoma City is reporting Tijerina is in Tulsa and has been threatened by John Birch Society members. But on the other hand, Hoover reports to the White House's Situation Room that his reliable source is not aware of Tijerina being in Tulsa, much less threatened. Hoover adds that he has communicated with numerous reliable sources in the state of Oklahoma and none are able to report on the whereabouts of Tijerina. Hoover must have been livid all day at his agents and informants not being able to locate Tijerina. Hoover also reported that he advised sheriff's offices and police departments in Tulsa, Ponca, Muskogee, Norman, and Oklahoma City of the alleged threats to Tijerina, including the area director of the Five Civilized Tribes, and is asking to advise Oklahoma FBI if they spot Tijerina (p. 2).

The Domestic Intelligence Division (DID), coincidently, issued an informative note dated June 8, 1968, a copy of which is in the file, that repeated the air flight departure from DC and arrival of Tijerina into Tulsa, Oklahoma, and the death threats. While Hoover and his network of contacts did not know much of the Tulsa travel by Reies López Tijerina, William Sullivan, head of the DID, was fully aware, for he issued his note the same day, June 8. Sullivan added that it was the American Nazi Party that had made threats, according to Metropolitan Police Department, Washington, DC. The last sentence of Sullivan's note reads: "As local authorities are source of this threat information and pertinent local authorities have been advised, no action is being taken by Bureau to advise Tijerina."

Fortunately, nothing did happen to Tijerina while in Tulsa, and he probably slept soundly. The FBI did nothing to alert him of the grave danger he faced from the American Nazi Party and John Birch Society members; local authorities were reporting this information to themselves. The FBI washed their hands of this affair. From the documents supplied, I do not see that any local authorities were aware of the danger to Tijerina. They were not made aware by the FBI of the death threats. The FBI was inquiring of them as to Tijerina's whereabouts. This internal chasing by the FBI and police of the proverbial dog's tail never advised Tijerina that his life could be in danger. It is sheer waste of government personnel at all levels to spread reports on for empty threats no one but Tijerina knew about.

Tijerina or one of his traveling companions was the source of the information on the death threats, according to both the first notice from the Metropolitan Police Department and the Washington FBI field office of June 6, 1968, which clearly listed them as sources. The DID note concurs in that the local authorities knew about this, but the FBI did not.

Another long LHM report, twenty pages, dated June 12, 1968, tracking Tijerina's movements from Albuquerque to DC and his activities at the PPC was sent from SAC, Oklahoma to the director of the FBI with accompanying two-page airmail memo. The report was sent to several other intelligence agencies, mainly military ones: USA, Secret Service, 112th MIG, OSI, and NISO, New Orleans, plus ABQ, WFO, and Oklahoma POCAM, according to the listing on the first page of the cover memo. The second page reports that car rental agencies at the Tulsa airport had nothing on a Tijerina rental. The LHM begins with a review of Tijerina's flight plans from Washington to Oklahoma City, with travel to Norman. The next paragraph states he was flying to Tulsa rather than Oklahoma City. Airline records show he landed in Tulsa (p. 1). The next page discusses at length the trail of comment on the death threats. Apparently, it began with the Metropolitan Police Department, which claimed that Tijerina told them of the threats during an interview. The MPD, in turn, told the 116 Military Intelligence Group in DC, which reported to the U.S. Army Intelligence Command in Fort Holabird, Maryland (p. 2).

No actual threats were known by any of these agencies; they just forwarded a comment obtained from Tijerina himself in an interview with MPD. Tijerina and a traveling companion named Romo not only arrived in Tulsa but left for Chicago the next day and then for Washington's Dulles Airport on June 7, 1968 (p. 3). The FBI's POCAM program in Oklahoma began to monitor who was holding meetings for the purpose of recruiting participants in the PPC. For example, the FBI learned from informants and possible agents present that at the Tulsa Council of Churches meeting held at 225 East Fifth Street in Tulsa, Tijerina recruited fourteen people to travel on a Greyhound bus, number 2831, that had a capacity for thirty-nine riders. The drivers of the bus and of private cars to be traveling with the Tulsa caravan was unknown. The Tulsa travelers were scheduled to arrive in DC on May 22, 1968, at 8:00 p.m. and be off-loaded at the Lincoln Memorial (p. 5). An appendix was provided with background information on the National Socialist White People's Party, aka the American Nazi Party; American Nazis; the World Union of Free Enterprise National Socialists; and the George Lincoln Rockwell Party. Included in the information was that George Rockwell was assassinated in Arlington, Virginia, and that his replacement as of August 28, 1967 was Matthias Koehl Jr.

SCLC Blacks in Charge

Tijerina constantly raised the issue of SCLC control of everything associated with the PPC. He complained that this was not the agreement he had reached with Dr. King for their participation or that of Native Americans. He stressed that their collective concern, Chicanos and Indians, was over their loss of homelands and property rights, not more government services. The specter of SCLC control of everything surfaced most visibly on June 10. The SAC, WFO in the twelve-page memo previously cited lists on page after page the presenters at this meeting of the groups participating in the PPC; all were black leaders except for Tijerina. It also reported on contributions to the SCLC for the expenses of the PPC; all were by black organizations such as Urban League (p. 1), Coretta King Day Care Center (p. 6), Dr. William Holmes Borders, Baptist minister from Atlanta (p. 7), Mrs. Mary Logan, SCLC representative from New York City (p. 7), Frank Sullivan, American Federation of Teachers, Philadelphia (p. 7), and Reverend Walter Fauntroy, vice chairman of the City Council, Washington, DC. (p. 10).

At 9 p.m., Tijerina was the first of the non-black presenters to speak before the POCAM groups on June 10. He first attacked the churches, "[Both] Catholic and Protestant in the U.S. have exploited the poor and the causes of poverty in this country have been locked in the refrigerators of Wall Street and Congress" (pp. 8–9). The reporting agent paraphrased Tijerina's continuing speech as mentioning the treaty between Mexico and the United States and how it has been violated, and that the culture and property of the Spanish-Americans would be protected by the people themselves: "If it is violated, the U.S. would be trespassing on the Southwestern section of the country and the Spanish-Americans would have a right to arrest the president if he went to the Southwestern section of the country" (p. 9).

Tijerina told the group he was going to meet with Secretary of State Dean Rusk to discuss the treaty and its violations on June 13. Next to speak was Corky Gonzales, who launched into the extent of racial inequality in this country (p. 10). Not to be outdone by the Chicano militants, Reverend James Bevel, an SCLC staff official, spoke to the group and accepted that the PPC "has had its conflicts within it and in RC, but these were inevitable." He left his best inflammatory rhetoric for last: "We are going to turn Washington into RC. RC is going to tear Washington up. When Johnson runs us out of RC we are going to come back and tear the whole town apart" (p. 10). Abernathy somewhat echoed the Bevel message: "We are not going to let anyone run us out of RC" (p. 10). The last speaker was Reverend Jesse Jackson, who "served as City Manager for RC." He made mention of the general status of the poor in America, the aims of the PPC, and closed with a discussion of the fishing rights of the American Indians (p. 11).

Just before the Solidarity Day event, perhaps June 18 or 19, a three-page telegram was sent from the FBI in Atlanta to the director of the FBI and the WFO to report that a reliable source had informed them that the senior officials within SCLC

> continued to be concerned with the attitude of the Mexican American people participating in SCLC's Poor People's Campaign. . . . These people through their leader Reies Lopez Tijerina continue to demand a definite voice in planning PPC strategy and resent being "dictated" to by SCLC concerning . . . [the top of page 2 is redacted and most of the bottom half]. (p. 1)
>
> On June Four Rev. Ralph D. Abernathy, president, SCLC; Andrew J. Young, Executive Vice President, SCLC; and Hosea Williams, Director of Voter Registration and Political Education, SCLC, arranged to meet with Tijerina and Rudolph Gonzales to discuss these problems. Source could not advise the results of this meeting. (p. 3)

Solidarity Day, Wednesday, June 19, 1968

When Dr. King was planning the PPC, he consulted Bayard Rustin about how to end the month-long event in a dramatic but enduring fashion. Rustin came up with the idea for a Solidarity Day on June 19 at the Lincoln Memorial. The problem became most acute after King's death when Rustin failed to consult with anyone about the agenda for Solidarity Day and drafted a litany of "demands" for Congress to take up to help black Americans. He left out mention of all other groups and left out the land

and property rights issues of major concern to Chicanos and Indians, even some *Independista* Puerto Ricans. Worse yet, Rustin held a solo press conference to announce the plans for Solidarity Day. In Texas, June 19 is known as Juneteenth Day, the day in 1865 after the end of the Civil War when slavery was finally outlawed in the state. This commemoration by itself without mention of other historic dates in the struggles of Native Americans and Chicanos made matters worse between the groups. Calamity ensued, and the end result was the resignation of Bayard Rustin from anything having to do with the PCC and, in the future, with the SCLC.

Reverend Abernathy's leadership in SCLC and over the PCC was immediately called into question. The greater idea that a class-based, multiracial/ethnic coalition was feasible and desirable was almost completely dashed. In Tijerina's mind it certainly was. He wrote:

> I considered the march and the Poor People's Campaign one of the best opportunities to give our own version of our history, not the Anglo version, to the world. The Anglo knew what I wanted. And that is why he twisted the truth and deceived the public on everything related to the events in the capital of the United States.[50]

Puerto Ricans also disengaged and organized their own Solidarity Day on a Saturday the week before. They argued that it was not possible to get their folks into town on a workday. Both Corky and Tijerina attended and spoke at the Puerto Rican, *Boricua,* rally. The Chicano duo and others did appear at the PPC Solidarity Day; however, they again forced themselves onto the agenda speaker's podium after Abernathy concluded his headlining speech. The one hundred thousand persons gathered there listened to Tijerina speak of cultural genocide. Corky unveiled his Plan del Barrio, consisting of policy goals in socioeconomic areas and land reform. And women of all races and economic classes spoke to the crowd. Not speaking, but present, were Senator Eugene McCarthy and Vice President Hubert Humphrey.

On June 23, four days after Solidarity Day, heavily armed city and military police in full SWAT gear, flak jackets, and riot helmets moved into Resurrection City to forcibly evict the tenants. Most were already gone;

Reverend Abernathy and many others still standing on the edge of the U.S. Capitol grounds were arrested, cuffed, boarded into paddy wagons, and taken to jail, where they remained until mid-July.

The Aftermath of the PPC

Reies went home to face court battles with a new attorney in tow, William "Bill" Higgs.

> When the campaign for the poor was coming to an end, an Anglo approached me and offered me legal help. I did not have any money to pay lawyers and so I accepted this Anglo's help. . . . Patricia told me from the beginning that she did not trust Bill Higgs, but I convinced her that there were some good Anglos in the world. . . . While I was in Washington, Beverly Axelrod had represented me in the New Mexican tribunals. She had not appealed Judge Bratton's sentence of December 15, 1967. That was the main reason I accepted Bill Higgs's offer in Washington. . . . Bill pulled us out of that one.[51]

Corky Gonzales also went home to plan the first Chicano Youth Liberation Conference, to be held in Denver. Carlos Montes and other Brown Berets, like Tijerina, returned to Los Angeles to face court charges stemming from the school walkouts. Corky had proposed that a Catholic priest, James Groppi of Milwaukee, head a coalition of groups from the PPC to keep the movement going, before the Committee of 100 was proposed, according to the SAC, WFO report dated June 10, 1968 (p. 2). The report also mentioned that Corky volunteered information that he and Tijerina would hold a rally at San Jose State College in California (p. 3). The FBI took note of that information for future monitoring of the two Chicano leaders.

Despite their best efforts to keep the momentum alive and moving forward, nothing much happened or lasted with these efforts. In Olympia, Washington, Tulalip tribal members built their tent city, Resurrection City II, on the capitol grounds and carried out demonstrations for three months.

The camp was demolished, as had been the one in DC by the police after ninety days.[52]

Perhaps it was too much to have had Reverend King and Robert Kennedy killed just prior and during the PPC, depriving it of their leadership. Perhaps the SCLC was not eager to continue funding an operation it clearly could not completely control. Not everything was for naught, however; the OEO obtained more funding for War on Poverty programs, according to the June 10 FBI report cited. Abernathy was quoted during a press conference he called to list the PPC's accomplishments as of that day while the FBI was listening:

> [The USDA] would release food to the neediest counties in the country; two hundred seventy million dollars had been released ... twentyfive [sic] million dollars had been released by the Office of Economic Opportunity for the poor; a housing bill had been passed by the Senate; and that hearings of the Ad Hoc Committee [of Congress] would be held at RC. (p. 4)

More minorities, mostly blacks and women, were hired into top-level positions as a result of demands made by SCLC. School lunch programs were expanded, as was Head Start, with jobs opened primarily for blacks. San Antonio's Head Start has been led by a black woman ever since, even though the children served then and now are overwhelmingly of Mexican ancestry.[53] Chicanos and Native Americans remain the lowest percentage of federal employees across all agencies, even in the face of executive orders and affirmative action plans designed to correct this imbalance. In some agencies, blacks hold a greater percentage of the jobs than they comprise in the general population, for example, the United States Postal Service.

FD-376 Due Again

FBI reporting every six months to the Secret Service on persons potentially dangerous to the president was done timely via LHM on January 30, 1969, with copies to the usual agencies: Secret Service, military intelligence units, NISO in New Orleans, USA, and other FBI affiliates. The material is of interest due to new items being reported, such as the fact that late in 1968, Tijerina had wired the U.S. Commission on Civil Rights, according to the FBI's reading of a local Open Source newspaper the *Albuquerque Tribune* of December 16, to hold hearings on the land grant issue in New Mexico.

In the *Albuquerque Tribune* edition of January 7, 1969, Tijerina is quoted as having been given ten minutes on the agenda of the State Board of Education to speak during its meeting on January 6 (LHM, p. 4). Allegedly, he denounced the board for not letting him speak earlier and longer. Typically, the clippings cited are made part of the report, but not this time. Only the hearsay of the FBI agent reporting is available. Supposedly using two textbooks as props for his "arm waiving oration," "the land grant leader made a stinging attack on school board policies and school text books" (p. 4). The books did not "tell the truth about Indo-Spanish history and culture." They are "part of an organized criminal conspiracy against Spanish-speaking people"; Tijerina predicted that there would be 600 million of them by the year 2000. The school board attorneys had advised against permitting Tijerina to speak since he had filed lawsuits against the board and the Albuquerque schools in federal courts (p. 5).

Petition to Spain

Tijerina learned from his dealings with the U.S. State Department and the government of Mexico during the 1968 PPC that international relations were complicated, almost impossible for individual interlopers such as himself to affect. Nevertheless, Tijerina began work on a document after he left the PPC. He drafted a petition to Generalissimo Francisco Franco of Spain that also landed in the hands of the SAC, Albuquerque. According to an FBI communication, Tijerina

> requested of Spain, "the mother of our blood," bring this matter up before the United Nations, alleging that the Treaty of Guadalupe-Hidalgo between the United States and Mexico had been violated. He concluded by

stating, *"la voz de la sangre se atiende primero que la voz de la ley"* (the voice of blood comes before the voice of law).[54]

By the end of the month, Hoover was writing to various military intelligence units and the Secret Service about Tijerina as an internal security matter. Hoover included a photograph of Tijerina along with his eleven-page memo. Hoover stated that "Mexico had already refused to present their case, Tijerina reported in fear of retaliation from the United States. Spain would probably refuse, too, for the same reason" (p. 3). Supposedly Tijerina asked his supporters and Alianza members if he should approach Cuba to present their case if Spain refused.

No somos Comunista, pero necesitamos alguien—una nacion hermana—que pueda presenta [sic] neustro [sic] caso [We are not communists, but we need someone—a sister nation—that can present our case]. The Latin American countries have told us they cannot do it. But Cuba does not owe a cent to the United States. We aren't going to get involved with ideologies. (p. 4)

CHAPTER 6

Local Police and Hoover's Hand

When Hoover became director of the FBI in 1919, his first domestic surveillance program targeted "Negroes," black writers, and other writers like James Joyce, actors on stage and in Hollywood, and entertainers of all types.[1] Political leaders were of special interest, as were gays and lesbians.[2] He hired persons to read black literature. William Maxwell calls them "Ghostreaders" in his definitive work on the FBI's interest in African American literature as evidence of subversive activity.[3]

Military Intelligence Paves the Way

The files Maxwell obtained confirm what was first learned from former intelligence agents—that army intelligence, in the name of preparedness and security, had developed a massive system for monitoring virtually all political protest in the United States. In doing so, it was not content with observing at arm's length. Army agents repeatedly infiltrated civilian groups. Moreover, the information they reported was not confined to acts or plans for violence, but included much private information about people's finances, psychiatric records, and sex lives.[4]

Maxwell opines that demonstrators and rioters were not regarded as American citizens with possible legitimate grievances, but as "dissident forces" deployed against the established order. Given this conception of dissent, it is not surprising that army intelligence would collect information on the political and private lives of the dissenters. The military doctrines governing intelligence, counterinsurgency, and civil affairs operations demanded it.[5]

Hoover Puts Out His Long Arm

The nature of mass surveillance of people by the U.S. government has evolved over time. During World War I most people relied on the postal service and telephones to communicate with each other. The FBI in order to monitor the surveillance had it easy at first. Only a quarter of the population had telephones and local police numbered 350,000; the thousands of postal service personnel inspected the first-class letters for any word, sign, or display of un-Americanism. By World War II, more people in the United States, about 40 percent of all, had phones, had more mail inspected, and more police officers were hired. The FBI's ranks of agents grew by the thousands, from 650 in 1924 to 13,000 by 1943. Hoover began his wiretapping programs and collecting paper from field offices on the behavior of the FBI's political targets. And what Hoover began as a practice and pattern of domestic surveillance was soon eclipsed with the advent of the internet and later smartphone.[6]

The 9/11 attack on the Twin Towers in New York propelled the National Security Agency (NSA) ahead of the FBI into the forefront of electronic surveillance. The Patriot Act of 2001 created the Foreign Intelligence Surveillance Courts (FISA). The FISA court permitted collection of personal communications by the billions of records of U.S. persons, not foreign operatives, under the PRISM program. FISA's order and subsequent orders required Verizon, Google, Yahoo, and other service providers to turn over daily data to the NSA.[7] And these companies did.

Tijerina Got the Last of Hoover's Hand

Nathan Theoharis, noted student of the FBI, opined,

> Since the 1940s, FBI officials had regularly briefed the White House about those activists and organizations that they deemed subversive. In addition, they had covertly and on an ad hoc basis leaked information about these organizations and their leaders' plans and personal character to reliable reporters, editors, and columnists.

In a note, Theoharis elaborates:

> FBI officials divided reporters into two categories: "Special Correspondents," i.e. those deemed reliable, and "Not Contact," i.e. those deemed unreliable. The former was favored with leaks and had their requests for assistance honored.[8]

By the mid-1950s, Tijerina was a target of the FBI based on reports coming from law enforcement and the district attorney, Sanchez, in New Mexico. He was a person of interest.

> Throughout the 1950s, Hoover regularly briefed the Eisenhower administration about the plans and personal morality of both the left- and right-wing activists and also about individuals as prominent as the former first lady, Eleanor Roosevelt, the Democratic presidential candidate Adlai Stevenson, Supreme Court Justice William Douglas, the *New York Times* reporter Harrison Salisbury, and the syndicated columnist Joseph Alsop. These briefings elicited no protest from the Eisenhower White House over why the FBI was monitoring and then disseminating information about radical activists and prominent Americans.[9]

Hoover reached the mandatory age of retirement, seventy, on January 1, 1965, when Lyndon Johnson was in the White House. To keep Hoover, Johnson issued an executive order waiving the mandatory retirement.[10] Johnson and Hoover collaborated well in monitoring dissidents of his policies, mainly the liberal Democrats in the Democratic National Committee and at the 1964 Democratic National Convention. LBJ also wanted any information Hoover had on members of Congress who had contact with Soviet and Soviet-bloc embassies "documented through FBI wiretaps of these embassies."[11]

Court Cases

Tijerina was embroiled in almost continuous courtroom battles from July 1957 to 1976. The federal investigations carried out by the FBI and passed on to the U.S. attorney usually resulted in a court case. Hoover had three ways to track Tijerina: (1) have SACs investigate him and his supporters; (2) pass investigative results to the U.S. attorney for prosecutorial action, and (3) monitor Tijerina's prison sentence and stay abreast of parole conditions and terms. Court hearings on Tijerina's or the U.S. attorney's motions or pleadings were the prime subject matter sent to Hoover during these years. And while Tijerina was incarcerated during part of these years, his writs, appeals, and new motions kept SACs in Albuquerque and other places very busy reporting to Hoover.

SAC, Denver on January 19, 1971, sent a one-page memorandum to the director with the information that "[name redacted] Clerk, U.S. Court of Appeals, Tenth Circuit, Denver, Colorado, advised that no opinion has been filed in this case. Denver will follow." Copies were also sent to the Albuquerque FBI office. On January 28, 1971, SAC, Albuquerque followed up on the same matter: "[name redacted] U.S. Attorney's Office, Albuquerque, New Mexico, advised that as of that date she had not received an opinion of the 10th Circuit Court of Appeals concerning captioned matter." The captioned matter was "Reies Lopez Tijerina; et al Assaulting a Federal Officer; DGP OO: Albuquerque Appeals in Bureau Cases."

THE GAG ORDER EXCEPTION

Back in October 17, 1966, Tijerina and Jerry Noll had been placed under a gag order by federal judge Howard Bratton, ordered not to discuss any aspects of the charges, case, witnesses, and evidence stemming from the Echo Amphitheater trial with anyone until all appeals were exhausted. Federal judge Ewing Kerr of Wyoming was brought in to hear a criminal contempt charge against Tijerina of violation of the gag order. The contempt case was based on a tape recording made by undercover police and other informants during the October 16-17, 1967, annual Alianza convention. On the recording were the voices of Tijerina and Noll making mention in their speeches to the assembly of land grants, citizen's arrest, Spanish laws, and the theft of lands in the Southwest. The defense attorneys for Tijerina and Noll, Charles Driscoll, Beverly Axelrod, and Larry Tapia, argued that the recording had been illegally obtained by parties not Alianza members trespassing into a private meeting open only to members and without authorization of either Noll or Tijerina to be recorded. Judge Kerr was not convinced and found both defendants guilty of violating the gag order. He sentenced each one to thirty days in jail and a $500 fine.[12]

MARIA STILL UNDER SURVEILLANCE

Maria Escobar, Reies's first wife was still under surveillance in 1972. The FBI used telephone taps and human intelligence sources to monitor her and what she knew of her former husband's activities and those of her grown children. She had married a man named Robert Kenworthy after the divorce from Tijerina. "He was a communications consultant with the telephone company. He would do tappings [wire taps on phones] . . . wherever it was needed for the government."[13] She was introduced to Kenworthy, the FBI's human intelligence source (HUMINT), by a lady friend.

He was a very nice man, of course. We stayed about two years before we . . . get to know more, get to know him more . . . *Entonces* [Then] after that

he asked me to marry him so, I got married. He was transferred to this job
here, Mountain Bell to Farmington. There's where we got married.[14]

The marriage would only last one year.

> He was a top-secret worker for the government. He came home very drunk
> and left his papers there on top of the coffee table. And he would never do
> that. But I guess he had been drinking too much so he forgot them there.
> I got up early and I saw them. . . . Well, it said, "Top Secret." . . . Putting tap-
> pings in the homes.[15]

The surveillance of Reies and Maria Tijerina began much earlier, as
discussed in the opening chapters of this book. Hoover's hand was also
involved in the affairs of the Tijerina families, including his brothers and
ex-wives, from the mid-1950s until he died in 1972. The FBI surveillance
extended to the many attorneys Tijerina employed during his legal battles
with the U.S. government and State of New Mexico. Several of his attorneys, such as William Kunstler of Chicago Seven trial fame, had their own
FBI files. One such attorney of special interest to Hoover was William L.
Higgs. During the Poor People's Campaign, Higgs ingratiated himself with
Tijerina and joined in the Alianza cause, even moving to Albuquerque and
setting up office in the building on Third Street where Tijerina had rented
space.

Hoover's Early Hand in Shaping Training and Culture

There are several exposés on Hoover's character and illegal behavior by
prominent journalists and scholars. There are a handful of books written
by ex-FBI agents who served under Hoover and by FBI directors who succeeded Hoover. Books written by rookie FBI agents such as Vincent Sellers
discuss conditioning, discipline, and values drilled into trainees to ensure
the proper person graduates into the ranks of special agent, the lowest rung
in the hierarchy of field operatives.

The FBI is made of extremely competent, dedicated people, but the culture is all blue-collar military and police mentality. Leadership comes from the ranks, which frequently meant that forward-think people with significant cultural diversity and business knowledge are scarce and undervalued. The FBI's slow transformation to fighting terrorism, white collar, and cybercrime is no surprise, considering the mentality for the DT [Defensive Tactics] program at the FBI Academy.[16]

An FBI agent is a federal law enforcement officer. Therefore, knowing how the law works is critical for an FBI agent to be effective in the field. A large block of time in legal training is spent on the Constitution and constitutional amendments.[17]

Knowing what the law is and what is required when in the exercise of duties may be a training component, but the review of FBI activities with regards to Tijerina and the Alianza membership suggests that knowing the law is one thing and following the law is another. Some training never took place, such as learning the criteria for electronic surveillance and break-ins of homes, offices, and businesses. Neither did the instruction on the use of firearms follow the law, as Sellers, a new FBI recruit, notes:

Allen [Hobart, supervisory special agent] instructed all agents on the squad to acquire an extra weapon that would provide more firepower than our standard issue Glock handguns. I chose to carry an MP5 which ... is a submachine gun that can shoot about 30 rounds in two seconds.... I carried this weapon for the remainder of my time in the FBI; if I did not have it in my passenger seat, I had it locked up in my trunk so that any time I was called out for an operation I would be armed and prepared.[18]

William Sullivan, Hoover's director of the Domestic Intelligence Division and thirty-year veteran of the FBI, wrote:

Although the subject of electronic surveillance never came up in FBI training courses, two months after I became a Special Agent, I found myself listening in on a Communist cell meeting as the first announcement of the Japanese attack on Pearl Harbor came over the radio.... During the war, very few FBI agents stopped to ask for official authorization before tapping the telephone of a possible Nazi spy.... Years later, the FBI was still listening in on other people's conversations without the authorization of the attorney general, but now it was because we were afraid that his knowledge of some of our programs could prove publicly embarrassing.[19]

The FBI under Hoover was shaped into a top-down rigid structure with strict control by superiors ending down the ladder with the field agent. Sellers, the recruit, certainly saw it this way:

> The FBI's operating structure follows a rigid model that is similar to that of a military organization. A Supervisor position has great power and importance, since all activities that agents perform must be approved by a supervisor. All documents and papers must be reviewed by a supervisor. Short of going to the bathroom, anything an agent does has to be discussed with a supervisor.[20]

Obstruction of Justice

In one of his first trials over the Tierra Amarilla Courthouse citizen's arrest, Tijerina subpoenaed the FBI SAC in Albuquerque, Thomas J. Jordan, as a defense witness. In response, the FBI with conspiratorial help from the U.S. attorney went into lockdown and man-all-battle-stations mode. On November 26, 1968, William C. Sullivan received a memorandum from his underling, D. E. Moore, reporting that Tijerina had subpoenaed Jordan for the morning of November 27, 1968. Moore contacted the U.S. attorney in New Mexico, John Quinn, and asked that he accompany Jordan and seek to quash the subpoena before Judge Paul Larrazolo and if all else failed urge Jordan to refuse to testify. The FBI would have the U.S. attorney file a writ of habeas corpus in the event Jordan was found in contempt of court and jailed. According to the correspondence, mainly teletypes from SAC, Albuquerque to the Hoover, Tijerina was going to question Jordan on the role FBI had played in the "alleged bugging of his headquarters and to show racial imbalance in government and business." Jordan did not testify, nor did any other federal or state employee because the judge granted the government's motion to quash the subpoena and eleven other subpoenas served on other state police officers.

Tijerina had mentioned his desire to represent himself at a meeting at the Alianza headquarters the night before the first day of trial. The next morning Judge Larrazolo and the prosecutors all knew of his plans, but not the defense attorneys. During the arguments before the court on the subpoenas, one of Tijerina's attorneys, John Thorne of San Jose, California, made that point. A government agency was electronically bugging the Alianza offices, and his attorneys had a right to discover which police agency was responsible: FBI, state police, county sheriff, or local Albuquerque police. The judge did not agree. He refused Tijerina the right to question any of the police officers, much less expose any wrongdoing on their part.

Tijerina Fires His Attorneys

Judge Paul Larrazolo, upon motion by the state, severed the other ten defendants from Tijerina and announced he would be tried first on the Tierra Amarilla charges. This prompted Tijerina to ask for a continuance, which was denied. He then asked to represent himself because not all lawyers at his table were representing him; some represented other defendants. The *Albuquerque Tribune* reported that Tijerina stood in open court and told the judge he had been thinking about his freedom and constitutional rights and that he found himself in jeopardy. Now it was just him on trial: "My lawyers became obsolete when they were cut off completely from the other defendants. We prepared for months and months together."[21] He was allowed to represent himself.

When the trial began, Tijerina had his choice of attorneys, Beverly Axelrod, John Thorne, William Higgs, and Gene Franchini. Franchini, an Albuquerque lawyer, was appointed by Judge Larrazolo because Tijerina had pled and signed an affidavit of poverty in open court. Judge Larrazolo also appointed Axelrod to assist Tijerina. Thorne and Higgs were there without pay. According to an LHM dated December 13, 1968, from the SAC, Albuquerque to Hoover, Tijerina had affirmed he had been unemployed since 1960 and solely did social work at the Alianza for no pay in exchange for his apartment in the building (p. 14). Judge Larrazolo instructed Franchini and Axelrod to make themselves available to Tijerina for assistance. Tijerina, nevertheless, kept Thorne for a few days more. Thorne took the lead in making objections and demanding rulings to perfect an appeal should it become necessary. Judge Larrazolo continued to deny almost all motions by Tijerina and his attorneys: declaring a mistrial due to extensive media prejudice; granting more than twelve preemptory challenges to the jury panel; and being tried on all ten charges against him, not just three in this trial and the remaining charges later.[22]

The state rested its case the afternoon of December 3, 1968, after putting thirteen witnesses on the stand. The trial was to resume the next day at 9:00 a.m., with Tijerina presenting his defensive case.[23]

Tim Chapa's Illegal Activity

During an oral history interview I conducted with Tim Chapa, the undercover state police officer, he confessed that he stole records from Tijerina and the Alianza headquarters whenever he could. He took books, papers, and notes Tijerina made. On one occasion, he took the notes Tijerina had made on the eve of one of his trials.

> He had a lot of notes, . . . lot of things underlined, you know, that he would use for his own defense. And I stole them—the book, and I turned it over and showed it to Jack Love, the prosecutor, and he made copies of it. And that was his defense, you know. And then returned the book. (p. 47)[24]

Chapa was able to do this when they took breaks for lunch or recess ordered by the judge. Tijerina was careless in leaving these items lying around in the Alianza office, but leaving his trial notebook on his defense table inside the courtroom, while the trial is in progress, was reckless. The prosecutor, being an accomplice in this theft, would have been subject to prosecution and mistrial if the judge had been informed this behavior. Tijerina and his lawyers were oblivious of the pirating of his notes until he sat in my interview with Chapa in June 2000. Perhaps Chapa stole more private trial notes and communications between him and his lawyers during other cases. Regardless, this blatant disregard for private property, personal privacy during which Tijerina's liberty was at stake, and professional rules of ethics and conduct for lawyers in an adversarial setting was cast aside by the state in the blind pursuit to convict Tijerina and lock him up for decades.

"Reyes Hugh Tijerina" Makes It into the Ranks of Armed and Dangerous

Hugh David Tijerina is the birth name of Reies Tijerina's oldest son, now deceased. Seldom did anyone call him "Hugh"; occasionally it was "David"; usually he answered to "Reies Jr." He also would substitute an *x* for the *j* in Tijerina because his father had told him that was the ancient spelling.[25] His FBI file number is 105-173626 and the Albuquerque FBI case number is 105-1573. The number 105 is used for subversives, typically foreign-influenced subversives. It can perhaps be justified as appropriate given the FBI did consider him "Armed and Dangerous."

Nevertheless, David Tijerina was the subject of a two-page memorandum from SAC, Albuquerque to Hoover dated December 4, 1968, which is accompanied by a photograph of him taken on June 10, 1967, just after the Tierra Amarilla Courthouse citizen's arrest incident. Most of the document is redacted (p. 1). On the last page, however, is the SAC's comment that he "is believed to be completely dominated by his father." The last sentence of the description reads: "He is considered armed and dangerous inasmuch as he participated in an armed raid on a courthouse and was armed at the time." At bottom of the memorandum is the notice that "Reyes Hugh Tijerina's visit to New York City, as well as pertinent information concerning the 'Poor People's Embassy' and/or 'Poor People's Association' is of interest to FBI Albuquerque; please furnish" (p. 2).

Acquittal in the Tierra Amarilla Courthouse Trial

The month of December 1968 was exciting for all those tracking King Tiger and for him as well. By teletype SAC, Albuquerque on December 13 informed Hoover that Tijerina had been "acquitted in state district court on all charges of kidnapping, false imprisonment, and assault on jail in connection with the raid on Tierra Amarilla, New Mexico Courthouse." It took the jury of six women and six men three hours and fifty minutes to reach a verdict. Tijerina still faced other court cases, but for now, he was free to start up where he left off.

Hoover, however, had not waited for the verdict; he promulgated an FD-376 form to the U.S. Secret Service that same day. Hoover was asking for Detention of Communists (DETCOM) tabbing of Tijerina's Security Index (SI) card to continue and gave as a reason that Tijerina had engaged in violent activities recently "and the fact that he has indicated he may engage in violence in the future, as well as aligning himself with black militant forces."[26] A twenty-one page LHM on December 13, 1968, appears to have contained a (redacted) list of informers.

Beginnings of the People's Constitutional Party (PCP)

In the long LHM are found tidbits of information not reported elsewhere, such as the formation of the People's Constitutional Party (PCP). The LHM cites two newspaper articles, from the *Albuquerque Journal* of July 28 and August 4, as containing the information on the PCP. He became the PCP's nominee as candidate for governor on August 4. He had publicly announced his intentions to run for governor on July 27 (p. 3). The New Mexico secretary of state, Ernestine Evans, and the attorney general, Boston Witt, kept Tijerina off the ballot. On appeal of this decision to the state supreme court Tijerina lost the fight, and a further appeal to the U.S. circuit court to postpone the election until this matter was resolved was denied (p. 11). The legal basis for these actions was a ruling by Witt that Tijerina's federal conviction on November 11, 1967, although on appeal, made him ineligible to run for public office or vote under the New Mexico Election Code. The opinion by the Supreme Court of New Mexico in *State Ex Rel. Chavez v. Evans,* 446 P.2d 445 (1968) upheld Witt's argument that a conviction is a conviction despite being on appeal.

On December 30, 1968, a new six-page LHM was submitted by SAC, Albuquerque to the Director, FBI on the PCP. Of interest is the disclosure of another FBI file on the Alianza Federal de Mercedes (105-127538). Apparently, the Alianza organized PCP chapters primarily in the northern New Mexico counties and qualified candidates in five of these counties. The PCP candidate for lieutenant governor, Jose Alfredo Maestas, was removed from the ballot for running with a felon. New Mexico's constitution "requires candidates for Governor and Lt. Governor to run as a team, and since there is no candidate for Governor, there can be no candidates for Lt. Governor" (p. 2). Preston Monongye, the PCP candidate for district attorney, was also ruled off the ballot, because he was not a licensed attorney, as required by the state constitution (p. 2). In a rearguard action, the PCP members decided to nominate others to replace Tijerina and Monongye; they picked Jose Alfredo Maestas of San Juan Pueblo in Tijerina's place and Crusita Chavez to replace Maestas. The PCP also had candidates for president and vice president of the United States, Ventura Chavez and Adelicio Mora. Various last-minute motions to federal courts to postpone the election so as to add these names to the ballot were all denied. The secretary of state did acquiesce in that "the names would be placed on the ballot by means of gummed stickers" (p. 2).

In the general election held November 5, 1968, Republican David Cargo beat Democrat Fabian Chavez by only 2,910 votes. On the ballot was also a measure to extend the term of office for governor from two to four years, and it passed. David Cargo, the newcomer from Jackson, Michigan, who arrived barely ten years before, was the youngest person to win the office, at age thirty-seven.[27]

Jose Alfredo Maestas of the PCP obtained almost half a percent of the vote, 1,540 votes, refuting the view that if the PCP had not been on the ballot and their votes had gone to Chavez, he would have won. The PCP's vote was irrelevant in the gubernatorial race of 1968. The other interesting question raised by these low vote totals for the PCP is how many members the

Alianza had who voted. Ventura Chavez, candidate for president, received
1,330 votes; Jose Alfredo Maestas, candidate for governor, obtained 1,540
votes; William Higgs, candidate for the Northern Congressional District,
received 714 votes; Wilfredo Sedillo, also running for the Southern District,
received 631 votes (p. 4).

Given all the attorneys Tijerina had at his disposal, it is startling to
learn that he never asked any of them to check the laws on elections and
qualifications of candidates before filing anyone for any public office. Especially of interest in this matter is William Higgs, an attorney for Tijerina
since the Poor People's Campaign days, who was a PCP candidate himself.
Tijerina, after this experience, was soured on any alternative political party
effort and voiced those opinions during the 1972 National Raza Unida Party
Convention in El Paso.

The Dirt on William L. Higgs

Patricia's intuition about William L. Higgs, which she expressed to Reies
during the Poor People's Campaign when Higgs signed on to be an attorney for the Alianza and Tijerina, turned out to be correct. On July 26, 1971,
a few days after Reies was released from federal prison, Reies's daughter,
Rosa, was entrapped in an attempted rape. This incident was detailed in
chapter 7. After Rosa managed to escape her would-be rapists, she and
her mother, Maria Escobar, told Higgs about the incident and wanted
charges filed against the perpetrators. Higgs advised them that he and
Reies thought it was best to do nothing. Rosa revealed her feelings in her
interview with me:

> My father had a lot of faith in that creep and he was up to no good. I figure
> if my dad doesn't think anything has to be done, I guess not. So nobody
> ever said anything about it anymore. He was up to no good. He comes and
> takes over and because he's educated, my father put his faith in him, laid
> the books in Bill Higgs's hands and says, "Do what Bill says." Then, when
> my dad tells him, "Get out of here," when he finds out what he's all about,

then Bill Higgs takes all the funds with him. Left the Alianza penniless. And my dad put the signature of the checks and everything in him.... And he brainwashed Anaya and took Anaya with him. From there the Alianza never picked up again. Bill Higgs just wanted to do away with the money, so the Alianza would end up back on the ground. Sure enough, we did. He took the money, and ... I hear he took many, many trips to Mexico. It was $50,000.[28]

David Tijerina, Reies son, also suspected Higgs. When I asked him if he knew of any other police agents or informants, he was quick to name William L. Higgs.

I never trusted Bill Higgs. He ... Xeroxed a book on how to build bombs, homemade bombs, and gave it to me, you know, so that is insinuating, you know. "You've got to do something, David." And he was always trying to impress me.... He would take me with him. And what I hated the most was that my father would make me go. I got arrested in Chicago one time. And my father had told him when we left here, he said, "Give David $200." And he never gave it to me. So we ended up in jail that night and they scared Bill. So he starts crying. "I got enough money to get out, but only one of us. And I think I should be the one to get out because I can help the rest of us." The next day came and [he] called on one of his friends, and they came and bailed us out.[29]

The Chicago arrest came as a result of a traffic stop while David was driving a truck camper through the city en route to Washington, DC. The police looked at David's New Mexico license and insurance papers, then looked inside the camper. They saw knives and forks used to eat while on the road. The police insisted on citizenship papers and proceeded to arrest David. After finally making bail, David continued to DC and on his return appeared in Chicago for trial. The judge read the charges and scolded the policemen for not realizing New Mexico was a state, not another country, and said, according to David, "If you went to their state you would want them to give you a little slack. You don't know the rules they have in their state." The judge dismissed the charges, refunded the bail money, and let them go on their way.[30]

ANOTHER THEFT BY HIGGS

Tijerina in his memoirs wrote about the treachery Higgs perpetrated on him and the Alianza immediately after the Poor People's Campaign. Tijerina had obtained a grant of $30,000 to the Alianza while they were in DC with the PPC. Tijerina wrote, "I have known that the Anglo does not have good intentions. Even among the better Anglos, the one I brought back with me from Washington, D.C. after the Poor People's Campaign stole the $30,000 donated to our cause by the Catholic Church."[31] This theft was corroborated by a SA, Albuquerque report dated January 31, 1974 to the SAC, Albuquerque and FBI headquarters covering eighteen months of activity by Tijerina and the Alianza. In this sixteen-page report, it is noted that "the Alianza has split into two factions and at present both are inactive" (p. 2). It also mentions that the *Albuquerque Journal* of July 12, 1972, quotes Robert Carvajal, associate director of the Catholic Church's grant-making foundation, the Campaign for Human Development, as stating that "the grant to the splinter group of the Alianza led by Bill Higgs is being cut off." According to the newspaper article Higgs had resigned and was unavailable for comment.[32]

THE FBI DIRT ON HIGGS

The FBI apparently had a lot more dirt on William L. Higgs that Tijerina never knew about. Some five years prior to his showing up at the Poor People's Campaign and befriending Tijerina, he had been convicted in Mississippi. While Tijerina was in prison the first time and Higgs was running the Alianza's and Tijerina's legal affairs, a FBI top official (whose is redacted) sent an LHM to C. D. Brennan, another top FBI official dated February 8, 1971. The second page of this memorandum contains the dynamite disclosure that on July 3, 1963, William L. Higgs was disbarred after having been convicted in Hinds County Court, Mississippi on February 15, 1963. Apparently,

Higgs was charged with having committed immoral acts with a minor male. The report continues with information from the *Clarion-Ledger* of July 4, 1963, that described Higgs as "a white, civil rights attorney who fled the State of Mississippi following his arrest on a moral charge" (p. 2). The bottom half of this page is entirely redacted.

William L. Higgs was tried in absentia in Hinds County, Mississippi, before County Court Judge Russel Moore and was found guilty on February 15, 1963, of contributing to the delinquency of a minor, a misdemeanor offense, by an "all white jury mostly composed of businessmen" after thirty-five minutes of deliberation. The testimony by ninth-grader William McKinley Daywalt III of Collegeville, Pennsylvania, detailed that Higgs offered him a home, food, money, clothes, and his bed. The boy said in open court that "they engaged in unnatural acts." Judge Moore promptly sentenced Higgs to six months in jail and a $500 fine. In the courtroom were members of the Mississippi Bar Grievance Committee, who within six months of the trial proceeded to disbar Higgs from the practice of law in the state. Chancery Judge Stokes L. Roberson heard the disbarment proceedings and ordered the disbarment. Higgs was also absent for this hearing.[33]

Higgs never took the New Mexico State Bar examination, according to the records, but he was able to practice in federal court despite the disbarment in Mississippi. Yet no mention is ever made by the FBI or any other New Mexico state official of Higgs's criminal history and disbarment. On a prior occasion, Hoover did not hesitate to tarnish Bayard Rustin, aide to Reverend Martin Luther King Jr. for his convictions on moral charges involving white men.[34] Is it possible that this did not happen with Higgs because he was a state police informant? Perhaps that was the case. At this point in time, however, the investigations over the break-in at the Watergate building diverted attention away from Higgs and Tijerina.

Was Fellion's Hand Also Hoover's Hand?

In April 1968, a dynamite explosion at the Alianza building at 1010 Third NW Street in Albuquerque left a lot of damage and one right hand. The blown-off hand belonged to William Fellion. Minutes after the bomb blast, City Patrolman Gil Gallegos stopped Fellion for erratic driving at speeds up to 70 mph in Albuquerque streets. Fellion refused to answer any of Patrolman Gallegos's questions. The police report made out by Gallegos on Fellion when arrested stated he had a loaded .22 caliber Magnum revolver and a stick of dynamite stashed underneath the front seat of his car. Given the gravity of this crime and other explosives and weapons found, Fellion was charged and tried in the municipal court of Albuquerque. The loaded gun charge was dismissed by the judge because the gun was not loaded. The municipal judge dismissed possession of the stick of dynamite as not being a crime. He did cite Fellion for reckless driving and ordered him to notify the driver's license authorities that he now drove with one hand.[35] The district attorney studied possible felony charges against Fellion but never filed any. The FBI never investigated or recommended prosecutorial action against Fellion by the U.S. attorney.

Fortunately, the three occupants of the Alianza building at the time were not hurt at all. The three, including Cristobal Tijerina, surveyed the damage outside the building and helped police find a hubcap, a hat, and the hand that belonged to Fellion, the bomber.[36] Another crew of bombers were caught and charged. They were Jose A. Romero, Agapito Jose Vigil, and Salomon B. Velasquez, all of Canjilon, New Mexico. These men were seen leaving the scene when the first explosion occurred and were stopped by city police officer Joel Dunlap. They had one stick of dynamite in their car when apprehended.[37] The municipal judge did convict Vigil of possessing a stick of dynamite without a permit, but gave him a thirty-day suspended jail sentence. The charges against the other two were dismissed because they did not own the dynamite and it was in Vigil's car not in their possession.[38] Following this bombing, obtaining insurance for the Alianza building was difficult, but with State Insurance Department help, the Firemen's Assurance Company finally offered some coverage.[39]

A Short List of Attacks on Tijerina and the Alianza

The police sometimes investigated, but the district attorney never filed charges against anyone committing crimes against Tijerina, his family, Alianza members or their office. The same applied to the FBI, which sometimes investigated but never recommended prosecution to the U.S. attorney. For example, the first bomb was set off by ex-Deputy Sheriff for Bernalillo County, William R. Fellion on April 16, 1968; three others perhaps tried that same day but did not explode their dynamite. The night of October 17, 1968, was the tenth in a row of windows broken at the Alianza building, tires slashed on vehicles parked in front of the building, and car windows smashed. On December 5, 1968, bullets were fired into the building's windows and front doors. Police found .38 caliber slugs inside the building. Thereafter, all windows were sealed with concrete blocks and the front doors replaced with metal ones. On January 23, 1969, another bombing took place, but this time it was at the rear door of the building. Patricia, Tijerina's wife and two children escaped injury, as did Juan Roybal, who was lying on a couch near the door. The bomb remnants were sent to the FBI for analysis. On March 15, 1969, two more bombs were set off, one at the Alianza building while a meeting was in progress and another at the home of Thomas Gallegos, an Alianza official. On both locations, witnesses reported seeing four white males drive off in a late-model red car. Again, no one was hurt and the bomb fragments were sent to the FBI for analysis. On June 24, 1969, more bullets were fired at the Alianza building while a meeting was in progress. No one was injured. The police found shell casings outside the building. And in a most ingenious method, nine Aliancistas were gassed while driving their cars after an Alianza meeting. The criminals placed powdered tear gas in the air vents of the automobiles that blew into the interior when the car reached a certain speed. On the occasion of these gassings, hospital attention was required because the powder was poisonous carbon dioxide. Upon inquiry by the media, the police, local and state, said they were investigating each of these incidents. The main state police officer in charge of investigation was none other than Robert Gilliland, the same Gilliland that testified in open court that he really hated Tijerina, that he had aimed a loaded shotgun at Tijerina's head, and that he wanted to kill Tijerina. Gilliland never visited the site of any of these incidents to investigate. The FBI was more candid and said it was not investigating any of these incidents.[40]

Bombings are illegal and violation of 18 U.S. Code 837 and 245 (a) (5)—a federal offense.[41]

A three-page teletype dated January 24, 1969, to the director of the FBI from an agent in the field informed Hoover that a second bomb was set off at the Alianza building and the local police were investigating: "Found at the scene of the explosion were two pieces of safety fuse . . . no request has been made for Bureau investigation. . . . Because of the controversial nature of the organization and the pending prosecution in state court of several of its members, it is recommended that no investigation should be conducted" (p. 2). Yet active investigation of the AFDM was being conducted in both these files. In other words, the FBI would investigate Tijerina for wrongdoing but would not investigate any wrongdoing against him or the Alianza. Later that day, the SAC, Albuquerque forwarded a memorandum with attached police report on the bombing. The SAC listed the damage and persons inside the building when a recent bomb was set off: Patsy Tijerina, Rosita Romero, Juan Roybal, and two children of Reies and Patsy, ages two years and four months, respectively.

Word about the bombing got to Jerris Leonard, assistant attorney general of the Civil Rights Division of the Department of Justice. Leonard, in turn, asked Hoover for a report on what happened. Hoover, by a two-page airtel on February 14, 1969, to the SAC, Albuquerque, sent copies of some "self-explanatory Departmental letter," which probably was the DOJ request for an investigation. Hoover expected a response in ten days. Hoover checked off the boxes that read, "State in the first paragraph of the details of your report that it contains the results of a limited investigation and underscore the word limited" (p. 1).

The Limited Investigation

On February 25, 1969, the SAC, Albuquerque sent his twenty-seven-page report on the limited investigation to Director Hoover: the explosion occurred on January 23 about 8:00 p.m. at the rear entrance of AFDM in Albuquerque, New Mexico. In the apartment on the second floor of the Alianza building were six occupants previously listed. No injuries occurred to the occupants. The dynamite bomb was placed approximately six feet from the outside wall of the building and two feet from an adjoining building in the alley. The explosion blew off the rear door, caved in the garage door, and broke numerous windowpanes in the neighborhood. Investigations failed to develop suspects. Investigations were being conducted by the local police and fire departments (p. 1).

Beginning on page 2 the title is "THIS IS A LIMITED INVESTIGATION." The local police received a call at 8:10 p.m. reporting the bomb explosion, and the caller provided basic information to the police officer. The next day, January 24, a physical investigation of the blast area by the local police found two pieces of the safety fuse; one piece was six inches long and the other four inches long. Because the Alianza building is made of concrete block, little damage was done to the structure, outside light, and electric meter (p. 2). Tijerina was in San Diego, California, making a speech, but upon return he advised the police he had no suspects in mind or any idea as to who may have committed the bombing (p. 3). *El Grito del Norte,* the community newspaper published by Betita Martinez, Maria Varela, and Beverly Axelrod, carried a story on the twenty-ninth about the bombing, and the article was attached to this report. This article contains a revealing piece of information about a possible suspect. Mrs. Tijerina reported to them that "an Anglo voice telephoned 3 times that evening. Each time he asked, where is Reies? On the third call, she finally told the man, 'He's not here.' About 20 minutes later came the explosion." The article also mentions that Patsy Tijerina and baby son had been standing by a window that was blown away; they barely missed serious injury from the flying glass (p. 4).

The report takes a secret turn on pages 6 through 15. Nine of these pages were entirely withheld under exemption (b) (7) (d). This exemption is to protect the identity of a confidential source and the confidential nature of the information.[42] First, the SAC, quoting an Albuquerque police officer (whose name is redacted), advised that "he had not been able to develop any suspects in this matter" (p. 16). No mention is made in this report of William Fellion or the other three persons caught after the first bombing or interrogated as to their activities at the time of this second bombing. Second, the SAC advises that several people were in the building before the bomb went off besides those mentioned previously: William Higgs, Myles Horton, Wilfredo Sedillo, Filipe (*sic*) Santillanos, and another by surname of Pacheco. The Albuquerque police interviewed some of them but not all. Santillanos supposedly reported he drove in behind the building just minutes before the blast and found the back door partly open and no alley light on. He informed Juan Roybal of this situation, who promptly closed and locked the doors after Santillanos, and his wife left. These interviews are on pages 17-24. The interview that follows is with Reies López Tijerina, the day before this report was filed on February 24. He only offered one new piece of information on a car he saw about a week or two before the bomb. It had out-of-state license plates and was driven by a young man with another male passenger. They looked away from him as they passed him standing in the back doorway "as if trying to hide their identity . . . the letters "Man" or "Men" were on the right-hand side of the car . . . three to four inches high . . . they came by about 10:00 or 11:00 in the morning" (p. 25).

The report then reads as follows:

[Redacted name] advised that while he was there on the night of January 23, 1969, Reies Tijerina called from San Diego, California, and was talking with one of the people in the building. This person called [redacted] to the telephone and [redacted] told Tijerina what he had observed and all he knew about the explosion. After this, Tijerina made the statement that it looked like two or three sticks of dynamite had been used. [Redacted name] advised that he thought it odd Mr. Tijerina should make such a statement particularly since later demolition experts had estimated that two or three sticks of dynamite had been used. (p. 26)

The report does not elaborate on what action was taken by the local police, fire department, or FBI on the information about the odd statement.

On March 15 and 16, Tijerina sent two telegrams to the president imploring him to protect them from these bombings. He specifically referenced the bombing of the home of Alianza member Thomas Gallegos. Fortunately, his wife and four children were at an Alianza meeting with him at the time of the blast.[43] The second telegram demanded the bombers be arrested and prosecuted. He accused the local police of failing to protect their rights and alleged they "conspire against them" (p. 12). These telegrams are reproduced entirely in the March 1, 1969, sixteen-page report from SAC, Albuquerque to the director of the FBI. A few questionable omissions in this report are the local police's report on the second bombing, and that of the Sheriff's Department, both in their entirety (pp. 3–9). The photograph of Santiago Anaya's car blown apart while parked outside the Alianza building did not make front-page news in the *Albuquerque Tribune;* it was buried on page C-3 on March 17.

The FBI did continue attempting to incarcerate Tijerina and his wife, Patsy. The General Investigative Division circulated an undated letterhead note initialed by "JJB" authorizing the arrest of Tijerina for trying to effect a citizen's arrest on James H. Evans, Forest Service agent, on June 10, 1969. And JJB also wrote that the USA Albuquerque "will attempt to file motion to revoke Tijerina's appeal from a conviction in U.S. District Court growing out of an assault on 10/22/66 on Forest Rangers and conversion of two Government trucks" (penciled p. 505, left bottom).

Patricia Tijerina's Turn to Take Hoover's Heat

On June 9, 1969, SA, Albuquerque reported by telephone to the SAC, Albuquerque and Hoover that he had received information about a group including Reies and Patsy Tijerina as being "in the process of burning a U.S. Forest Service sign valued at approximately $2,000" (p. 2). The narrative in this report states that James H. Evans in his capacity as special agent of the Forest Service saw the "Redwood sign ... burning in the area ... by one Patsy

Ann Tijerina and Carol Jean Watson." Instead of arresting Patsy and Carol, Special Agent Evans tried to arrest Tijerina for "participating in the destruction by fire of a U.S. Forest Service sign." He was prevented from doing so by several others identified as Jose Marcelino Aragon, Rudy Stanley Trujillo, Ramon López Tijerina, and Reies López Tijerina. Reies Tijerina did more than resist arrest by Evans; he tried to citizen's arrest him by pointing a .30 caliber rifle at him (penciled p. 515, left bottom). There were others present who also got arrested by Forest Service agents: "Reyes" (*sic*) Hugh Tijerina and Kerim Thaddeus Hamarat (penciled pp. 510, 516, 520, 521, 532, and 571, left bottom). Eventually, the Forest Service agents were able to restore order and arrest Reies, Patsy, and Carolyn, who on the ride into the Federal Building in Albuquerque stated to her federal officer captors that "the burning of the sign at the entrance to the Coyote Ranger Station was planned and executed by Patsy Tijerina" (penciled p. 535, left bottom and number 35 in black ink, bottom center). Another informant was interviewed June 10 and advised the sign burning took place at 3:00 p.m. He saw Patsy Tijerina "piling paper, rubbish, and deadwood under the sign and poured some liquid on it. She then struck a match and threw it at the sign and it went up in flames" (penciled p. number 571, left bottom, dated June 11, 1969, top right).

Within days of the incident on June 11, 1969, attorney John Murphy, representing Patsy Tijerina, was being contacted by the FBI to have his client give a statement to them. At first, Murphy agreed, provided she approved, and he wanted to be present. The next day, June 12, Murphy declined to allow the interview (penciled p. 529, left bottom). However, by the beginning of February 16, 1970, by one-page airtel from SAC, Albuquerque to Hoover, he was responding to an earlier proceeding referred to on December 22, 1969, about her mental competence. She was given a psychiatric examination by Dr. Henry T. Penley in Albuquerque on that same day, February 16. About the same time Judge Howard Bratton was moving the wheels of justice to try Patsy and ordered Reies Tijerina be transferred to a federal mental hospital, still a prisoner, in Springfield, Missouri.[44]

Patsy was given a clean bill of mental health and found fit to be tried for her federal crime. Federal Judge H. Vearle Payne "set case for immediate hearing and jury selection was completed by 1:00 p.m. Court was recessed until 2:30 p.m." (p. 1). The trial continued, according to another one-page airtel dated February 18, 1970, and ended this day with jury instructions given and sent to deliberate at 4 p.m. The deliberations were quick, only six and a half hours. The jury was unable to agree on the indictment involving the sign at Coyote, and a mistrial was declared. The jury did find her guilty on the first count "alleging the destruction of a U.S. Forest Service sign at Gallina, New Mexico, on June 8, 1969." This sign-burning at Gallinas was not referenced or mentioned by anyone in these files. "Sentencing of Patsy Ann Tijerina was set for March 6, 1970," the airtel reads in its last sentence.

Meanwhile in Corpus Christi, Texas

Ramon Tijerina, Reies's older brother and resident of San Antonio, Texas, worked with the head of the Mexican American Youth Organization, Carlos Guerra, to organize a "Free Reies" rally on June 13, two days after Reies was arrested and imprisoned. On June 11, 1969, Reies López Tijerina had been arrested again and put in prison by Judge Howard Bratton to begin serving his two-year prison sentence on the assault on forest rangers. An informant advised SAC, Houston that a handbill was being circulated in Corpus Christi announcing this rally. SAC, Houston teletyped Director Hoover the night of June 11 at 9:23 p.m. with that information. The rally would be held at Ella Barnes Junior High school at noon. SAC, Houston followed up with another teletype at 8:39 p.m. after the rally's conclusion. He reported some 150 persons had attended and that no violence occurred, and all proceedings were peaceful.

KUNSTLER VERSUS GILLILAND

On June 17, 1969, Judge Bratton revoked Tijerina's $50,000 bond.[45] Tijerina felt that Peter Adang, the second lawyer appointed to represent Patricia, did a very poor job at defending her.[46] The first attorney appointed was David Kelsey, an ex-CIA agent, according to Tijerina, who recommended she fire him.[47] During the bond revocation hearing before Judge Bratton, Tijerina was represented by William Kunstler from New York, the famed civil rights attorney. But before the hearing could commence the twelfth and thirteen floors of the federal building in Albuquerque on Fifth and Gold Streets were evacuated due to a bomb threat called into the U.S. attorney's office. No bomb was found after a two-hour search of the premises.[48] Once the hearing resumed, an exchange occurred between Kunstler and Robert Gilliland of the state police, the prime witness against Tijerina and Patsy during the sign-burning event at Coyote, Kunstler asked Gilliland if he had threatened Tijerina with a loaded shotgun during that occasion. Gilliland responded, "If Reies pulls that trigger, I'm going to shoot him." Probing more, Kunstler asked Gilliland, "You really hate this man, don't you?" Without hesitation Gilliland put on the record, "Yes sir, I do."[49]

The wheels of justice can move extremely fast when a federal judge wants to move them faster, as in this case. And justice can be selective. Once Tijerina and Patsy were embroiled in their respective cases, all federal charges against Carol Jean Watson and Kerim Thadeus Hamarat were dismissed on July 1, 1969. Those against "Reyes" Hugh Tijerina Jr., Ramon López Tijerina, Rudy Stanley Trujillo, and Joseph Marcelino Aragon were dismissed on July 8, 1969. The FBI lab confirmed that the M-1 carbine used by Tijerina was operable. In other words, if Tijerina had fired, he probably would have killed Evans. This evidence and testimony by other state and federal officers was enough for Judge H. Bratton to find Tijerina to be a danger to others.[50]

Tijerina, while he sat in prison, hoped for a reversal of his conviction on the attempted citizen's arrests of Forest Service agents. He was released from federal custody on July 26, 1971, but still had pending the state sentence for the Tierra Amarilla incident,[51] He was out of prison temporarily on a $10,000 bond. Leonard E. Davies was Tijerina's attorney. Tijerina's hopes to be vindicated on the federal appeal were dashed on August 4, 1971. The SAC, Albuquerque sent Hoover a copy of the thirteen-page U.S. Court of Appeals Tenth Circuit opinion, No. 138-70, July 1971. While this appeal was denied, Tijerina still had an opportunity to seek review by SCOTUS. SAC, Denver so informed the director of the FBI on September 24, 1971, by one-page memorandum: "The time for filing a writ of certiorari has not yet expired." A month later, on October 29, SAC, Denver advised the director that "no further action has been taken in the appeal of this case and the time for filing for a writ of certiorari to the Supreme Court of the U.S. has expired." One of the many lawyers Tijerina had at his disposal had dropped the ball in filing the writ.

While Tijerina was out on bond waiting for the state sentence, he renewed his travels and organizing, but with a new theme that fit his parole conditions of not being an Alianza officer, not advocating violence, and not being armed. The FBI was still tracking his every move and that of other Chicano militants. SAC, Albuquerque on October 22, 1971, was trying to play catch-up with Hoover by alerting him that Tijerina had gone to San Antonio, Texas, and was now en route to Washington, DC, to attend a demonstration by the People's Coalition for Peace and Justice. Tijerina would be lodged at the Hospitality House, and that phone number was 70392. SAC did not have an address. Later that night the SAC provided the director with more information on one page, which is entirely redacted. The Domestic Intelligence Division was already on Tijerina's trail. R. J. Gallagher sent a memorandum to Mr. Bates, a top-ranking FBI administrator, with copies to all the other top FBI administrative guns, such as Felt, Rosen, Shroder, Bledsoe, Miller, and Bishop, that some redacted source had informed the FBI on October 22 that "a party of four Latin Americans are passengers on Eastern Airlines Flight 146 [were] scheduled to arrive at National Airport, Washington, D.C. at 12:09pm today." Having identified Tijerina, the memo gave the

remaining passengers as First Name Unknown (FNU) Guttierez [*sic*], President of the San Antonio, Texas, Chapter of La Raza (not further identified); (FNU) Compean, head of the Mexican American Youth Organization; and (FNU) Pena.

Security Supervisor [name redacted] of our Alexandria Office was alerted to the above information as was Domestic Intelligence Division Supervisor, R. H. Horner.

SAC, San Antonio followed up on October 27, 1971, on Tijerina with a five-page memorandum on the speech he gave at the University of Texas on October 19, 1971. Copies of this memo also made it to the CIA, State Department, DIA, and the Albuquerque FBI office. Tijerina, according to the informer, discussed the rights of Indohispanos under the Treaty of Guadalupe Hidalgo and how comparable they are with the rights guaranteed in the U.S. Constitution. He elaborated on the themes that caused a new awareness in him while he sat in prison for two years. He shared his thoughts about love, hate, justice, law, organized religion, and social welfare. He now saw that hate was growing while harmony and brotherhood were diminishing. He also said the United States was losing friends and must look for support from South Americans, who in turn would see how the United States treated the Chicano in the Southwest to evaluate the Anglos on their attitude toward brotherhood and justice.

Presidential Pardon

Tijerina was rebuffed by Governor Bruce King in seeking a commutation of his state sentence in time to avoid the federal penitentiary. The governor wisely deferred long enough to make the request moot by seeking public comment on whether or not he should grant Tijerina's request. Daughter Rosa was also politely put off by the governor's staff when she came to his office with a dozen citizens asking that he pardon her father. Tijerina had to serve his state jail time.

Several years later, Tijerina sought a presidential pardon of sentence and have his civil rights restored to be able to vote. In 1979, he began by getting the three required sponsors on his notarized application. His first notarized document was a loyalty oath to the United States, which he signed on January 9. The two sponsors were Ben Chavez and Richard Manzanares, who signed their documents affirming their belief as to his good character on January 9 and February 1, respectively. The entire application packet was notarized on March 6, 1979. The third sponsor was late in signing off; not until June 10 did Antonio Mondragon submit his notarized document. His application churned slowly. The SAC, Albuquerque submitted some of the paperwork to the FBI headquarters on March 21, 1979 and requested an investigation into the content of the documentation. Earlier, John R. Standish, attorney with the U.S. Board of Pardons and Parole, also directed his request to the FBI director for his "authorization of the usual clemency investigations and sending two copies of the report to his office." The Phoenix and Albuquerque FBI offices got busy verifying data on all prior arrests and dispositions to see if all fines and fees had been paid and also the new character references submitted, such as retired archbishop Peter Davis in Nogales, Arizona and the new archbishop in Albuquerque, Roberto Sanchez; the new governor, Jerry Apodaca and lieutenant governor, Roberto Mondragon; the last probation officer and one of the sponsors, Richard Manzanares; former mayor of Albuquerque Harry Kenney; World War II hero Guy Gabaldon; and Albert Mora of Chilili, New Mexico. There were seven pages of files, documents, records listed by file number to be checked and crossed out as they were checked. Phoenix FBI reported on May 2 that its investigation had concluded that Archbishop Davis only "recalled Tijerina's last name. Unable to make any recommendation." The police arrest records stemming from activity in Arizona all checked out as closed, and any pending arrest warrants had been quashed. Albuquerque FBI reported on May 7, 1979, that Tijerina's record showed he complied with all conditions of his sentences and added: "References and acquaintances consider applicant sincere in the cause, a devoted family man, and a good loyal citizen with no reason to question his character, associates or reputation. Applicant's credit rating satisfactory. No arrests noted since conviction" (p. 1).

Albuquerque FBI also added that it could not do a neighborhood investigation where Tijerina had lived at 1010 Third Street NW because that location "is surrounded by junk auto yards and junk part houses" (p. 2). His probation officer, Richard Manzanares, recommended "the applicant for pardon" (p. 5). Gabaldon, the war hero, considered the "applicant to be a loyal American devoted to the American way" (p. 6). Ex-mayor Harry Kenney concurred with Gabaldon's opinion. The recommendations from the governor and lieutenant governor were also in favor of a pardon. Archbishop Roberto Sanchez was out of town during the vetting of references and could not be reached for comment. An astonishing comment was attributed to Governor Apodaca, who stated that "he pardoned Reies Tijerina, who was convicted in New Mexico for more serious crimes, and feels the Federal Government should pardon both the Tijerinas" (p. 7). This is the only statement on this issue found in all the records at my disposal. Even Tijerina does not reveal this pardon in his memoirs. He did leave state prison early without explanation; perhaps it was that he was pardoned by Governor Apodaca. The two state officials, state police director and District Attorney Sanchez, declined to comment on Tijerina's application for a pardon (p. 7).

On June 4, 1979, an additional five-page report was filed by the Albuquerque FBI office containing some of the prior material just listed and one new contribution, that of Richard Martinez, the U.S. chief probation officer. Some factual errors in the Martinez statement were made by him or taken down in error by the reporter. Martinez is supposed to have said, "Applicant was born in Laredo, Texas" and "Applicant is of low mentality, he was manipulated." Martinez did recommend that Tijerina's "civil liberties be restored" (p.5).

The FBI files released on Tijerina end in 1979, and there is no indication he ever received a presidential pardon, nor did he ever mention having been pardoned by any president.

Tim Chapa: The Informant

Spying and the use of informants is as old as humankind if we believe biblical stories and the narratives on battles and wars by Marcus Tullius Cicero. Use of snitches and informants remains a full-time preoccupation of local police and federal agencies such as the FBI. Alexandra Natapoff's work brings those interested on the subject up to date.[1] In chapter 5 on the Poor People's Campaign, the role of the FBI in creating a new COINTELPRO to destroy and disrupt that event is mentioned as well as the by-product, the Ghetto Informant Program (GIP). On orders from AG Ramsey Clark to FBI director Hoover, the GIP was implemented, using some 7,000 informants passing information on protestors and dissidents to the FBI. The GIP was made an integral part of the disruption of the Poor People's Campaign in 1968 utilizing the code name POCAM.[2] These informants were employed in GIP by the FBI during 1967 to 1973 to get information to be used in the various COINTELPRO operations during the apogee of the civil rights era involving many different ethnic and racial groups, including Chicanos.[3]

230 ■ Chapter Seven

Some Informants Named

The Chicano civil rights movement of the 1960s into the 1980s was plagued with informants, snitches, decoys, undercover police, and agents from all types of federal agencies. Eustacio Martinez, originally from Brownsville, Texas claimed he had infiltrated at least five Chicano groups from July 1969 to 1972, including Casa de Carnalismo in Los Angeles, the United Farm Workers Organizing Committee, and the Mexican American Youth Organization in Texas. He prompted a police raid on the Chicano Moratorium committee headquarters in Los Angeles by parading with a shotgun in front of the building. He was recruited in Houston by a federal agent from the Alcohol, Tobacco and Firearms Division of the Internal Revenue Service.[4] When California governor Ronald Reagan was to speak at the Biltmore Hotel in Los Angeles, April 24, 1969, Fernando Sumaya, a recently graduated police officer from the police academy of the Los Angeles Police Department (LAPD), infiltrated the Brown Berets, which had plans to set fires and create disturbances in the hotel to disrupt the governor's presentation.[5] At trial, some of the Brown Berets charged with planting the bombs and arson testified it was Sumaya who was the provocateur. On one occasion he urged the group to kill Chief Thomas Reddin of the LAPD.[6] Another undercover informant within the Brown Berets from inception was Richard Valdemar from Compton, California, who was enrolled in the Los Angeles County Sheriff's Department training academy. He was assigned intelligence duty and infiltration of the Brown Berets (BBs). He posed as an AWOL army soldier with a fake identity card. He was accepted into the BBs and soon rose to become a squad leader. He participated and informed on all the BBs were doing to the LA County sheriff, who passed on the information to the FBI.[7]

Rodolfo Acuña wrote about these Chicano undercover agents, as well as about Louis Tackwood, a self-proclaimed police informer in August 1969, inside the Black Panther Party for the LAPD's Criminal Conspiracy Section intelligence officer Ronald G. Farwell.[8] A former Drug Enforcement Agency special agent and former Miami Police Department narcotics sergeant, Dennis G. Fitzgerald who joined the defense side of the criminal bar, wrote

"Inside the Informant File," an insider's tip on what defense attorneys can use in the discovery process of a case to unlock the data he calls "detonator" material "to blow the government's case against your client out of the water." He details what typically is found in the informant file, such as the contract, the amount of money paid, what to expect in return for snitching, and "blacklisting." Blacklisting is the documentation prepared by the control agent for the informant that contains guidelines on misconduct, credibility, and deactivation. Fitzgerald claims that "the DEA, the FBI and Customs are the largest federal consumers of informant services. Federal agents and local law enforcement are equally dependent on informants."[9] The use of informants and protection of their identities is the most closely guarded secret of the FBI.[10]

Becoming an Informant in New Mexico

In June 2000 I interviewed an undercover police officer and informant utilized against Reies López Tijerina and the Alianza.[11] Tim (Timoteo) Chapa's brother Antonio "Tony" Chapa was killed in bar in a shootout over a drug deal gone bad in Albuquerque (p. 3). The Chapas were a close-knit family, and the seven siblings, four sisters and three brothers, looked out for each other. Tim quit school when he was sixteen years of age. His family members were cotton pickers living in Tahoka, Texas, the home base, as they moved around West Texas in search of work. Tired of that life, Tim quit school to join the U.S. Army in the 1950s. In those days, the army took anybody who signed up. He obtained his GED while in the military.

During that time, he married Clara Bell and divorced her before his military service was over in 1959 (p. 4). When discharged, he headed to El Paso with dreams of becoming a professional wrestler like his older brother Domingo, or "Mingo," as the family called him. The wrestling school he wanted to attend to learn the culture and business tricks of the trade, such as the holds, bouncing off the ropes, and hitting, was in Juarez, Chihuahua, Mexico, where Mingo had learned the wrestling moves of the professional sport. Tim's professional name became El Demonio de Tahoka (The Demon from Tahoka). For eight years, he traveled the wrestling circuit from El Paso to other border cities and deep into central Mexico in search of matches. To make ends meet, he became a butcher and worked between wrestling tours. His meatcutter trade took him to jobs from Lubbock to El Paso (p. 5). Tim Chapa also became a snitch for the federal government when he was a professional wrestler working out of El Paso.[12] While a wrestler, he observed drug deals carried on by wrestlers, promoters, and dealers, time and again. He started working as an informant for the Federal Bureau of Narcotics to bust the drug traffickers and dealers.[13] A lot of drugs were trafficked by the wrestlers and their teams, back and forth, from Mexico to the United States, according to Chapa (pp. 5-6).

When he learned of Tony's killing, he left for Albuquerque to help his sister-in-law with the funeral arrangements and to help her move back to Texas. He wanted to find out who had killed his brother and take revenge. Mingo, after he no longer could wrestle against younger men, became an ordained Baptist minister and moved to Albuquerque, along with three sisters. Tim also decided to stay in Albuquerque (p. 3). Just sister Lily stayed in Texas, moving to Del Rio.

In pursuit of revenge, Tim questioned local and state police officers about the shooting. He was befriended by Robert Gilliland because Chapa volunteered that he knew "some people that were dealing drugs. So he recruited me, put me under payroll. So I started working with him for . . . a couple of years, I guess" (p. 8). He was recruited and joined the New Mexico Mounted Police as an informant.[14] Chapa moved to Cuba, New Mexico, and got a job cutting meat at the Trading Post. The state police had an intelligence division and a target, Reies López Tijerina, and his organization, the Alianza.[15] Tijerina was not unawares of the police surveillance of his activities and that of the membership. "By June 1966, our offices were full of visitors, day and night. Some we knew were police spies and ears for local politicians," he wrote.[16]

Gilliland came up to Cuba and asked Tim to infiltrate the Alianza. He would earn $500 a week. In El Paso, the Bureau of Narcotics only paid him $250 a week (p. 7). His training as a mounted police officer, basically a seminar each week conducted by a former state police officer, covered procedures of arrest, search and seizure, traffic control, patrolling, self-defense, gun safety and qualifying with a .38 caliber handgun, and chemical use (Mace and other pepper sprays).

The intelligence-gathering portion of the training was done by an FBI agent out of the Albuquerque office. The agency with the greatest change in its application of undercover operations was the FBI. The attitude changed from viewing their snitches and paid informants as too risky and costly to seeing them as an important crime-fighting tool. And surveillance could not be done without the use of informants and snitches, as well as covert agents doing undercover work.[17] Chapa had some experience with intelligence gathering as an informant and undercover agent while in Albuquerque.[18] He had already been recruited to infiltrate and monitor the activities of a university campus group, Students for Democratic Society (SDS) earlier by the Albuquerque police (pp. 7-9). When he moved to Cuba, the first undercover assignment was changed from Tijerina to Elizabeth "Betita" Martinez.

First Target: Betita Martinez and *El Grito del Norte*

Tim's orders were to infiltrate the newspaper *El Grito del Norte* and report on the staff's radical women, principally Elizabeth "Betita" Martinez.[19] She had shown up in Española, New Mexico, one day with two other women, Beverly Axelrod and Maria Varela. Together, they started the newspaper for Reies López Tijerina in 1968. It was to be the voice of the Alianza. The women were documented as radicals in FBI files, and that information had filtered down to the state police in New Mexico.

Betita was formally Elizabeth, or "Liz," Sutherland. Her father, Manuel Guillermo Martinez, immigrated from Mexico in 1917, dating to the Mexican Revolution years. In time and with some formal education at Georgetown University, he became a professor of Spanish literature. Manuel married an Anglo schoolteacher and social activist; they settled on the outskirts of Washington, DC, where Elizabeth was born. She graduated from Swarthmore College with a degree in history and literature in 1946, the first Mexican American to graduate from Swarthmore. In 1947, she took a job at the United Nations as a translator because she knew Spanish. By the early sixties, she was working as an editor at Simon & Schuster and took a trip to Cuba in 1961, where she experienced a political awakening: "When Cuba declared itself socialist, so did I."[20] In 1964 she learned of the Student Non-violent Coordinating Committee (SNCC) in New York and joined their "Freedom Summer" campaign, going with them to Mississippi. Upon return, she promptly became the organization's New York office manager, the only nonblack with authority in SNCC. She began traveling more and more with SNCC leaders to the South, where she met another Chicana, Maria Varela; "we were the only two Chicanos."[21] In 1966, SNCC voted to be all-black organization; Betita was replaced. Undaunted, she continued to volunteer with SNCC and in 1967 traveled with Stokely Carmichael, Julius Lester, and George Ware to Cuba once again for a gathering of Latin American revolutionaries. The 1966 SNCC all-black policy change was cathartic for her, however, and she also had an epiphany.

> In June of 1967, she sent a paper called "Black, White, and Tan" to SNCC's Atlanta headquarters. She wrote, "One day I found myself unable to vote in SNCC because I was 'white.' When I was a child, the girl next door wasn't allowed to play with me because I was Mexican." She signed the paper Elizabeth Sutherland *Martinez,* using her father's last name for the first time in SNCC.[22]

Betita moved to New Mexico to help Tijerina with his communications to the public and membership in the Alianza. The relationship did not last long, but the newspaper, free and independent of Tijerina, did publish for an additional five years, until 1973.[23]

THE TWO OTHER COLLABORATORS

Mary "Maria" Varela, like Betita, was of mixed parentage; her mother was Irish and father Mexican. She was born in Newell, Pennsylvania. She enrolled in Alverno College in Milwaukee, Wisconsin, graduating in 1961 with a degree in speech and secondary education. A staff position with the National Student Association's Civil Rights Leadership Project in Atlanta, Georgia, connected her with SNCC. She stayed on with SNCC as a photographer and curriculum writer for adult literacy until the purge of 1966. By the next year, 1967, she was in New Mexico and became "Maria" full time. She joined Betita and another radical woman, Beverly Axelrod, in founding *El Grito del Norte*. Varela also helped form a wool-weaving cooperative and a health clinic.[24] In 1990, she received a "genius award" from the MacArthur Foundation for her organizing work.[25]

Beverly Axelrod was the third leg of the trifecta in the founding of the newspaper. She was an experienced lawyer who before defending Reies López Tijerina had already cut her legal teeth by defending other prominent and notorious activists of the 1960s. She was a volunteer lawyer for the Congress of Racial Equality (CORE) and defended hundreds of those jailed in Louisiana on various trumped-up charges. The reality was they were being jailed for promoting voter registration among blacks. Another of her clients was Jerry Rubin, who was called to testify before the House Un-American Activities Committee in 1966. One of her most notorious clients, and later defendant in her lawsuit against him, was Eldridge Cleaver of the Black Panther Party.[26] In 1965, while in Folsom Prison in Represa, California, Cleaver wrote to Axelrod asking for legal assistance. They exchanged letters and she visited him. They fell in love, both claimed. She not only helped him write his material and edits, making it suitable for publication, but also did his legal work, appeals and book contracts, such as *Soul on Ice* and "Prelude to Love—Three Letters."[27] Her other most notorious client became Reies López Tijerina. She was part of the battery of lawyers he employed over the years fighting criminal charges, but he fired her. He wrote,

> While I was in Washington [for the Poor People's Campaign], Beverly Axelrod had represented me in the New Mexican tribunals. She had not appealed Judge Bratton's sentence of December 15, 1967. That was the main reason I accepted Bill Higgs' offer in Washington. It was already late, and Beverly still had not prepared the motion. She was embarrassed and even cried once. Bill pulled us out of that one.[28]

Beverly had previously worked for César E. Chávez and the United Farm Workers Organizing Committee. After *El Grito del Norte* ceased operations in 1973 and physically moved its operations to Albuquerque to restart under a new name, the Chicano Communications Center, she moved back to California and served as an administrative law judge for the California Agricultural Labor Relations Board.[29] She died on June 19, 2002, in Pacifica, California.[30]

CHAPA TRIES TO FIT IN

Tim Chapas told me about Betita. "My first assignment was to get close to a lady by the name of Petita [*sic*] Martinez ... Who was funding her? What was her goals ... her contacts ... just general information gathering, who attended her meetings? Where she was getting these write-ups and everything?" (p. 10). Chapa named another informant, Esequiel Sandoval, who also watched Betita and her staff (p. 11). Chapa stated, "That was part of the job. Steal notes, steal address books, you know" (p. 11). "I was assigned just to follow her. I even stayed in her office there.... We used to sleep in her office in Española, another guy from the Alianza. Well, sometimes it was Quelo [Esequiel] Sandoval's stepson. His name was Mike Soto" (p. 17).

Killing of Two Black Berets

In New Mexican history during the period from September 9, 1850, when it was a territory, to January 6, 1912 when it became a state, much violence took place between the land claimants and their heirs and the newly arrived Anglo thieves of their lands. Around 1889 a vigilante group formed in San Miguel County to fight against the white, land robber barons. They called themselves Las Gorras Blancas (The White Caps).[31] During the Chicano Movement years, some activists in New Mexico had heard of the newly formed Brown Berets in Los Angeles and liked what they read about their mission and purposed. The New Mexican activists opted to form their own version of such a group, but with the name Black Berets, as the opposite color of their caps worn by Las Gorras Blancas. Among the founders of this group in the late 1960s were Jeanne Guana, Richard Moore, Placido Salazar, Nita Luna, Joaquin Lujan, and their spiritual leader, Catholic priest Luis Jaramillo.[32] By 1972, the Black Berets had more members, including two who were murdered, Antonio Cordova and Rito Canales.

Chapa claimed he provided dynamite to several of the Black Berets, one of whom was Cordova, a staffer for *El Grito del Norte* (p. 52).[33]

> We were up one time in Santa Fe, and there was some local nightclub owner here in town that wanted to eliminate competition. So they wanted the [Black] Berets to torch other clubs. So one of the state policemen said, "Well, I've got some dynamite at my dad's house," a guy by the name of Ted Drennan. So we went to his dad's house in Santa Fe, and they gave me a sack full of dynamite to give to the Black Berets. (p. 52)

The FBI and the ATF were in on the operation beginning with the first theft of the dynamite set up by Drennan. He had been debriefed by the FBI and ATF afterward (p. 60)

I asked Chapa point blank to tell me how he participated in the murder of Rito Canales and Antonio Cordova. He related the story with these words: "They needed more dynamite, you know, the Black Berets, to blow up some more nightclubs. You know, they had blown up one or two up Central [Street, Albuquerque], you know, torched everybody there, you know" (p. 55). Ted Drennan supplied Chapa with more dynamite to take to the Black Berets.

Drennan suggested Chapa tell them where they could get additional dynamite themselves—setting them up to be killed.

> So I went up there and stole the dynamite, the first time. Okay, the second time after that, they had some bombs and done some shit. They made it, all three or four of us made a, made a bomb out of fifty sticks of dynamite. . . . This was supposed to be rolled down the ramp into the police station, the Sulley. (p. 56)

Chapa informed his state police handler of the plan to roll the bomb down the entrance to the police station known as the Sulley. He in turn told the city police, and Chapa was ordered to make certain he knew where the bomb was at all times, day and night.

> So I had to stay with them, you know, living with them. . . . So I came up with a plan to tell them that Corky Gonzales up north, you know, would pay $500 for a case of dynamite. . . . [State Police Officer Leroy] Urioste [said] "You go tell the Black Berets that." I didn't trust Urioste. . . . I would have to hear it from a higher-up. . . . And we would make a special trip up north to talk to [director of the state police Hoover] Wimberly. [He said] "Hell yes! It's all right with me. . . . Yes, I said so." You know, if you say so. . . . Every time they would come up with a new idea, I didn't want to do it. Maybe that's why they started not trusting me so much either. . . . So they were going to steal three cases [of dynamite], you know, so we could make $1,500. They had the right view of the clubhouse [at the construction site where the dynamite was kept] and everything else, you know. So, yeah, they agreed to it. So again [Robert] Gilliland went up there and told the guard to leave the area. (pp. 57–58)

The state police, "six or seven" in number, and city police, "the second in command and five others," set up the ambush to kill Cordova and Canales at the construction site off South Coors Street. "It was Gary Miller, assistant chief of police, Wayne Larson, Polo Rios, and Manny [David] Salazar from the city . . . from the state was Lieutenant Albert Graves, Bob Carroll, Leroy Urioste, Ted Drennan, and Ralph MacNaught" (p. 58).[34]

Chapa then related to me the events that transpired to execute the plan. He and David Salazar changed the plates on Salazar's pickup truck, and Chapa took over the use of the pickup. Once all the state and city police officers were in place at the construction site where the dynamite was located, Chapa went to the Black Beret headquarters on Twelfth Street. It was about midnight. Canales, Cordova, and another man were there, but he had a cast on an arm and begged off in going because he could not carry a box of dynamite. Chapa suspected this man was another informant. Chapa had used the fake-cast routine himself to avoid being involved in a caper he did not want to get into (p. 59).

Chapa and the two Black Berets, Rito and Antonio, took off in the pickup down South Coors toward the construction site. The problem was that Rito wanted a gun and Chapa had lied about having one, but Rito found one in the pickup. Chapa had some explaining to do: it was a police-issued gun. He got out of it by claiming he meant he did not have a gun on his person, that it was in the truck. They arrived at the South Coors Street construction site and Chapa told them where to go up the hill to find the clubhouse where the dynamite was stored. He convinced them that he should keep his gun and stay below. In case someone else showed up, he could keep him away. Once Rito and Antonio had the dynamite, they would signal him with a flashlight. He then would drive up to the mesa to load the dynamite onto the pickup. Chapa was stationed behind some debris at the bottom of the hill when the following occurred:

> I heard several shots, bursts of gunfire, you know. And I knew the plan had taken place, you know, it happened. . . . And then I noticed flashlights flash-ing. . . . Well, it could probably be [finished] unless all the policemen are dead, and they are flashing me to go up there and retrieve the dynamite. I just didn't know what to think, and . . . I did nothing. (p. 62)

While Chapa was pondering what to do next, he saw policemen rushing up the hill in a car. He decided to leave the scene and wait it out at a Casa Grande motel room the police had rented where they could meet up and debrief or just get their stories straight. Some three or four hours later, Urioste and Salazar arrived, cussing and angry at him for not helping them shoot Rito and Antonio. They said they had been signaling him with their flashlights to come up and help.

> Well, I wasn't supposed to go up there. That wasn't part of the plan . . . to go up there. . . . Then we took the truck back to Salazar's house and they drove me to Isleta to my house. It was almost daybreak. Either way, the bodies stayed up there somewhere almost twelve, fifteen hours before they

brought them down. And I didn't hear nothing from the state police.There
was no news release of nothing ... about the killing till twelve, fourteen
hours later.(p. 63)

A day or so later, Chapa was called by Urioste to meet him at the corner
of Coors and Blake. He was met by five officers sitting in an unmarked state
police car. He had to get in the car and they drove him out two or three miles
to a ravine on West Mesa. They started threatening him with serious bodily
harm; one said to "smoke him," meaning kill him. They were afraid he
would reveal that the killings were premeditated. Leroy Uroiste played the
good cop, defending him. Polo Rios played the bad cop, threatening to blow
up his house, harm his family, and smoke him. Chapa defended himself by
saying, "I'm one of you. I planned it. We carried it out. I'm just as guilty as
you guys are" (p. 63).

Chapa identified the killers in the interview. I asked him, "Urioste
and Drennan were the shooters upstairs, on top of the hill?" And Chapa
responded,

Yeah ... cause they were bragging about how he thought he hit him on
the side and the other guy was crawling and trying to get away. . . . And
still that's when they got him. . . . They were, they were just bragging ...
Drennan, you know ... Drennan and Urioste both. Drennan said how he
shot Cordova after he was down just to see ... How do they put it? Just to
see him twitch or jerk or something, to see if he would jerk or something
like that.(p. 64)

Chapa had been promised by the state police director, Hoover Wimberly, lots of money if any of the Black Berets were killed. "If you pull this off
...we'll see that you get quite a bit of money and compensate you" (p. 64).But
he wasn't given any money; Urioste kept it all. Chapa signed vouchers for
his part of the work and Urioste turned them in and never made a payment
to Chapa. Cheated out of his share of the money, $1,500, Chapa started to
break contact with those involved. He would not return their calls or meet
with them.

He instead went to work with Robert Gilliland in Corrales, New Mexico, where he had opened a bar, the Territorial House. Chapa worked on remodeling the place for nine months. He shared many jobs with Gilliland, some legal, some not. They did a buy-bust drug job once in Las Cruces. Gilliland shot the Mexican drug dealer on that deal and left his body in the Rio Grande. Chapa was with him and kept the money, but not the marijuana. Gilliland used to get the drugs from evidence lockers. The sales of drugs taken from evidence lockers were not official sting operations, just extra money on the side (p. 68). On one occasion while at the Territorial House, Drennan and Urioste showed up, and the subject of the money payment due to Chapa came up. Drennan asked Urioste if he had ever paid Chapa. Urioste winked at Chapa and said, "Yeah, yeah."

During this prolonged stay while working for Gilliland, they talked a lot about everything they had done together in years past. From these talks, Chapa learned that Eulogio Salazar was not killed by Tijerina or his people; it was Gilliland and others. Reportedly, he said to Chapa, "We took care of him. We took care of that." Chapa felt this was his way of saying, "I killed him" (p. 65).

Back to Target Number 1: Reies López Tijerina

Chapa worked his way into the Alianza membership by hanging around the building, attending meetings, and being of help when asked to do something by Tijerina or one of the brothers. While Tijerina did not suspect Chapa, he did have concerns about spies:

> Police agents infiltrated the Alianza. We knew our telephones were tapped. We spied on these police agents and informers, while they kept vigilance on us. The FBI kept close watch on the Alianza members. They had the membership list. Judge Payne has forced us to turn it over to the police. Each of the thirty thousand members were visited by the police and with lies and falsehoods they tried to get the members to break with the Alianza. In the Albuquerque area alone, we had over 9,000 members.[35]

Tijerina was right on target with his observations on the surveillance
and the real reason behind the police getting the Alianza membership list.
Chapa was one of those undercover agents that got into the Alianza and
close to Tijerina.

Chapa began full-time surveillance of Tijerina right after the Tierra
Amarilla incident in June 1967. In order to do this, he had to quit his
meatcutting job and stop wrestling, so he could be at Tijerina's side constantly. He asked the state police to pay him $500 a week, to pay for his
insurance coverage, and to give him a car. They also gave him a gun and a
radio that he kept in the trunk of the car. The gun was hidden behind the
car radio mounted on the bottom of the dashboard. He would contact his
handler with the portable radio or just talk directly when he could with
the higher-ups in the state police, usually Hoover Wimberly. He did a lot
of note-taking, jotting down names, license plate numbers, and names of
people who came to the Alianza offices. His handler was Robert Gilliland,
head of investigations, and his boss was Hoover Wimberly, second in command at the state police headquarters (pp. 13-14). "Wimberly was the head
of the snake," said Chapa (p. 16).

Chapa's statement is a realistic assessment of the political hierarchy,
in that Wimberly was a career man, a professional, whereas Joe Black, the
actual director of the state police, was a political appointee of the governor.
Tijerina did not think much of the director of the New Mexico State Police.

Joe Black is a Mexican with an Anglo name. He was called a *"coyote."* The
people in New Mexico called those Mexicans with Anglo parents or names
"coyotes." And they consider them more dangerous when they were uni-
formed police with guns at their side.[36]

Chapa would report to Gilliland and Wimberly, whom he saw two or
three times a month. "He was the one that was giving the orders of what to
do …[I] got orders from him to cut fences or burn haystacks, or …during the
Coyote incident [the burning of the Forest Service sign] one of my jobs was to
take out a black militant …if he pulled his gun out of his pocket" (pp. 14-15).

The black faces among the crowds during the annual convention or at Alianza activities such as the taking of Echo Amphitheater and the Forest Sign burning were members of SNCC. They participated with Tijerina more than other black groups that Tijerina reached out to, such as Ron Karenga's US, the Black Panthers, or Elijah Muhammad's Nation of Islam.

Wimberly's Order: Kill Tijerina

When I was recruited to go surveil Tijerina ... I asked for full commission. I wanted insurance.... They took me to Hoover Wimberly. They said, "Now we got to get rid of this guy. We've got to. We've got to ... get Tijerina. Come up with some dirty laundry work. We've got to get him, ah, anything, anything you can on him." (p. 20)

Then the orders got more explicit: "After a while, after a while it got so bad that ... between Gilliland, Jake Johnson, Hoover Wimberly, that we got to find a way to smoke the guy, you know ... that means killing, that means kill" (p. 19). On another occasion in Coyote, Chapa was asked by Gilliland, "Why don't you push Tijerina over the cliff? Why don't you lure Tijerina to the cliff and push him over?" (pp. 24–25).

During the confrontation at Coyote over the burning of the Forest Service sign by Patricia Tijerina, Chapa accompanied Reies, along with many others. Also present were many more police officers of all types, state police, sheriff's deputies, Forest Service agents, and undercover police like Chapa. They watched the burning take place. While they did arrest Patricia, they wanted to arrest Tijerina who was just a bystander. Two police officers, Jack Johnson and James Evans, and one state police officer, Robert Gilliland, tried to shoot Tijerina. Chapa himself was there on orders to shoot Tijerina if he pulled a gun: "He wasn't supposed to walk away from Coyote, no matter what." Tijerina did pull a rifle from his car. Chapa thought, "Oh this is it. The man is gone. The man is history" (p. 25). Tijerina pointed his rifle at Evans, but Evans turned and ran away.

I thought it was chicken of Evans to run away. He had the chance to shoot him and he didn't do it. The next one that came close to him to shoot was Gilliland. . . . They pointed rifles at each other. I don't know why, why nobody pulled the trigger. Johnson did pull the trigger: "I fired at him. I fired at him. And it didn't go off." (p. 26)

Chapa adds, "The only law that was broken there was when Patsy burned the sign, you know" (p. 27). Would not the huge police conspiracy in motion for days emanating from the state police headquarters in the office of Hoover Wimberly and the head of investigations, Robert Gilliland, to commit murder break the law? How about the attempt to murder Reies by Gilliland, Evans, Johnson, and Chapa? Or the plan to kill the black man he stood next to?

The New Mexico State Police and the U.S. Forest Service that day were the law, prosecutors, jury, and judge onto themselves, accountable to no one. And if there were FBI undercover agents present, they also made themselves part of this unjustifiable criminal conduct by the police.

The Rape of Patricia Tijerina

According to Chapa, State Police Officer Frank Tenorio bragged of seducing Patricia, of what he had done with her when Tijerina was imprisoned. He had nude photographs of her, he claimed. Chapa never saw them but heard Tenorio and other police officers make comments about the nude photos. Tenorio did not admit to rape; he implied it was consensual. I asked Chapa if he thought it was rape. "I think it was the guy's ego . . . but then again, I would not put nothing past Wimberly. It was a joke around the station . . . about how he had sex with Tijerina's wife" (pp. 39-40). No charges were ever filed against this state police officer.

Chapa had his own role that he played in the life of the Tijerinas: not to help them but to hurt them, to get information to report to Gilliland and Wimberly, and to kill Reies. "I drove Patsy to Anthony [Texas, the location of La Tuna Federal Prison] and checked her in at the . . . Capitan or the Gavilan,

Gavilan maybe, Gavilan motel there.... I stayed with her ... Never had sex with Patsy." Chapa would volunteer not only to drive her in his car, but also to babysit the kids while she visited with Reies inside the prison. Patsy had to take their two kids, Harmonia and Carlos Joaquin, with her since she had no money for babysitters. On the return trip, he would debrief her about what Reies said about his ideas, plans, and events, anything about him or the Alianza. Chapa reported this information to Gilliland and the FBI (p. 39).

Chapa left the state police after the killing of Rito and Antonio because the other police officers' threats against him and his family. He then became an investigator for Sandoval County.

A lengthy thirty-page report dated November 8, 1971, to Hoover to comply with the rules of forms FD-376 (Secret Service) and FD-305 (Security Index Program) contains much information on Tijerina in the prior months. An article taken from the *Albuquerque Journal* dated May 26, 1971, indicates that the parole board approved Tijerina's release from federal prison as of July 26 of that year. He was still facing time in a state jail pending the outcome of his appeals of those convictions (pp. 2-4). The report confirmed that Tijerina had been released on parole from the federal prison in Springfield, Missouri, on July 26, 1971 (p. 5). By September 1971, he was making the rounds of public speaking. On September 8, he addressed the Albuquerque Press Club (p. 15). On September 16, he addressed students at Eastern New Mexico University (p. 17). This invitation was controversial and blocked temporarily by the university president, Charles Meister, but overturned by the regents at a special meeting. On October 3, a Sunday, he was speaking before junior high students and parents at John F. Kennedy Junior High school in Española, New Mexico (p. 25). A controversy arose over his speech and honorarium scheduled for October 10 at New Mexico Highlands University. He was accompanied by Patsy and their four-year-old daughter Isabel and received a standing ovation upon introduction from the two thousand students in attendance (p. 22). By October 21 he was in Austin, Texas, speaking before more than one thousand students at the University of Texas (p. 25). Before the end of the month, Tijerina was in Washington, DC, to speak at another conference, along with other grass-roots Chicano leaders and members of Congress, including those from New Mexico. His statements at this conference generated more controversy because he announced his wife had been raped by state police while he was in prison (pp. 25-29).

Interestingly, the material from local newspapers in Albuquerque covered the rape allegation, but not the fact that the Tijerinas were getting divorced. The FBI, however, noted in its report that Tijerina "filed for divorce proceedings in San Miguel County District Court, Las Vegas, New Mexico, against his wife, Patricia. He is basing his divorce on the fact that Patricia, while he was away, was consorting with other men, including State Policemen" (p. 30).

The FBI report concludes that on Sunday, October 24, 1971. At a press conference in Washington, DC, Tijerina "publicly announced that he was withdrawing his divorce action against Patsy" (p. 30). Nothing more is found in the FBI files concerning the divorce. Tijerina's memoir reveals the marriage was still intact in February 24, 1974: "My wife Patricia and other women served food all day. Many people came to congratulate us." The occasion was the eleventh anniversary of the Alianza held in Santa Fe.[37] Again in 1976 he mentions that Patricia is still part of his family: "My family and I left for Mexico."[38] The year 1976 was the last year Tijerina wrote about in the memoir. Sometime after that year he divorced Patricia and moved to Mexico again. He eventually remarried, this time to Esperanza Garcia Valladares, his third wife, on June 9, 1993.

The Rape of Tijerina's Son Noe

Albert Vega, another state police officer, was given the responsibility to care for the security and safety of the Tijerina family while they were held in custody for trials. In March 1973, Vega kidnapped Noe Tijerina, then fourteen years of age and raped him.[39] Chapa learned of the rape while working in Sandoval County.

> Yeah, the one I felt most sorry for was his kid, you know, because I thought the guy was a mental case. They put in a sick guy. It happened because this guy was just a pervert, Albert Vega. And that wasn't the first time he

had pulled something like that. Another incident he exposed himself to some women . . . on the road or something like that. He got demoted or reprimanded. I worked with him. We were working surveillance together in Sandoval County. He was the state police assigned to that county. To this day I don't know . . . I don't see why they didn't hang him to this day. (pp. 40-42)

For months Tijerina was unable to make the police—local, state, federal—take the criminal charges he and his minor son wanted to make against Albert Vega. He also had not been able to make them take the criminal charges for the rape of his wife. The noncooperation of intake police personnel at the three levels—local, state, federal—who refused to take the information despite the media providing ample reports on each incident. Instead, the three police levels wanted to charge Tijerina with crimes, try him, and lock him up forever. It was not until much later that he contracted an attorney to file a civil suit against Vega. On March 18, 1974, that the case was called. "My son's lawsuit against Vega began today. The case was not filed to make money, but to open the investigation into Vega's higher-ups and the state police. We alleged that this crime was part of a larger conspiracy to force us from the state."[40]

Nearly a decade later, in 1982, Tijerina released a press statement on state-sponsored and instigated violence:

My wife was violated by police. My daughter Rose was kidnapped by police. My son Noé was kidnapped and raped by police. My home and office were bombed four times by police. . . . And why all this terror? What is the motive for all this terror? The State and Federal Government will stop at nothing to cover up the ruthless raping of all our municipalities that were created under the Governments of Spain and Mexico. The stealing of our property rights is the real motive behind all this terror. This is the reason for denying me and my wife our constitutional rights.[41]

The Attempted Rape of Rosa

Tijerina recounts the story his daughter, Rosa, told him when he came home from federal prison about her kidnapping on or about July 17, 1972, by undercover police officers posing as Black Berets. According to Reies, a call came into the Alianza office informing Rosa of an emergency meeting taking place where Reies was needed. The caller asked if in his absence she could come. The man promised to drive by the headquarters and pick her up to go to the meeting. She agreed and, when he arrived, got into the back seat of the car with three men dress as Black Berets. She did not recognize any of them and did not believe they were Black Berets. At first opportunity when the car slowed, she opened the door and rolled out onto the pavement. She ran into a bar and called for help. Other than bruises and scrapes, she was unharmed.[42] When I interviewed Rosa, she corroborated the story.[43]

Chapa did not reply during the oral history interview about any specific actions taken by him or others against Rosa." He simply stated that "all of them were targets." He did point out that "the son-in-law [Rosa's future husband, Fabian Duran] was more of a target." Fabian was one of Reies closest bodyguards (p. 37).

Burning Haystacks and the Clinic

Chapa and others on the payroll as undercover police or informants or just black-bag job operatives had instructions from Wimberly to do anything that would implicate Tijerina and his Alianza members in wrongdoing. He suggested they burn barns, cut fences, shoot cattle, Chapa remembers. They did so at Bill Mundy's place. Mundy was a modern-day, ophidian land thief, a real snake. Born and raised in New Mexico, he was familiar with the land grant contestation. He and his wife, Ethel, bought the family's first 11,000 acres in 1949 from descendants of the Tierra Amarilla land grant, a communal land grant that could not be sold. In 1878, this grant had been surveyed by James K. Proudfit, the U.S. surveyor general, at 472,737 acres. In 1886, another surveyor general cut it down to 166 acres. In 1894, the U.S. Court of Private Land Claims confirmed 1,423 acres as the new grant size, and the U.S. Supreme Court affirmed this acreage in 1897. Chief Justice Melville Weston Fuller stated that communal lands became public lands when the United States took over as the new sovereign.[44]

Ethel Mundy, Bill's wife, became a real estate agent and helped grow the family ranch, doubling the land spread to 27,000 acres. She bought land from descendants of communal lands who had no authority to sell.[45] The local land grant heirs of the Tierra Amarilla communal land grant sued the Mundys and ultimately lost after appeals up to the New Mexico Supreme Court. This court ruled that communal lands became private lands or public lands after the United States took possession of the Southwest, citing Fuller's opinion for the U.S. Supreme Court. Therefore, anyone claiming ownership interest in the Tierra Amarilla land grant could sell their share to Mundy. No more communal land grants were to be in New Mexico, only public or private ownership. In 1953, Mundy went to the local district court and obtained a restraining order against some of the local people to keep them away from his property and person.[46]

From that day on, Bill Mundy resisted with force anyone attempting to take back any piece of his grasslands, trees, water, fencing, and livestock. Vigilantism, as in the days of the Gorras Blancas and the Mano Negra, returned to northern New Mexico and the Mundy Ranch in Tierra Amarilla. He fought back by working with the state police officers Robert Gilliland and Jack Johnson and the local sheriff, Emilio Naranjo, and deputies to destroy his own property to frame Tijerina. They burned haystacks (pp. 21, 22), salt boxes (p. 32), and homes and trailer homes (p. 33), bombed buildings (p. 21), cut fences (p. 22), poisoned fish (pp. 27, 31) and water supplies (p. 34), and shot livestock (p. 21). They also went after the Alianza directly, tear-gassing members' cars (p. 21) and burning a health clinic in Tierra Amarilla tied to the Alianza (pp. 21, 23, 44). "They wanted the clinic burned down so it wouldn't help the people" (p. 44), said Chapa. Gilliland and "his federal agent, some Indian," drove the arsonists to the clinic and left them. After starting the fire, they had to run across creeks, streams, wooded areas, and a great distance to get to Mundy's ranch house. Mundy loaned them a truck to get back to Albuquerque because Gilliland and the Indian federal agent never showed up at the ranch to pick them up (p. 45).

The poison for killing fish and contaminating water supplies came from Kirtland Air Force Base (p. 34). The explosives Chapa and others used in these crimes were also supplied by the air force, "Kirtland, perhaps Sandia" (pp. 27, 44). Once they went to Abiquiu Dam with a demolition expert, a sergeant from Kirtland, to reconnoiter the area for the possibility of blowing up the dam (p. 27). On another occasion, Chapa and another undercover agent, named Kevin, were about to firebomb a trailer home when they realized a lady and a kid were inside; they did not light the fuse (p. 33).

Mundy's hired thugs were the undercover cops Chapa, Esequiel Sandoval, and George Chavez, a state police investigator, among others, including agents from the ATF (pp. 21-24). In the winter of 1960, seven homes were burned in that area; one was Mundy's. "The suspects were various land grant activists, although no one was charged with the arson."[47] Given the admissions by Chapa, the practice and pattern of committing crimes to be imputed to Tijerina and the Alianza members, it's clear, were ordered and authorized by the second-in-command of the state police, Hoover Wimberly. "A rich family also donated one of those mansions, one of the big ranches up there.... Well, they were afraid he [Tijerina] was going to use it for some kind of study center, a school or whatever, so they burned it. [Jack] Johnson burned it down.... Sandoval and Soto did" (p. 32). Those with home insurance obtained replacement value on the burned homes. The point was to cast a dark light on Tijerina and his members; "Blame it on Tijerina. Thought we would ruin Tijerina" (p. 27). "I never saw him poison the water or shoot a cow or burn a haystack. I never saw any of Tijerina's bunch do that. We were doing that" (p. 21).

Another accomplice in bombings of Tijerina, his family, homes, and of the Alianza members and headquarters was William Fellion, whom we have already encountered in chapter 4 and 6. This man was an ex-deputy sheriff in Bernalillo County who was fired by Sheriff Lester Hay in 1962. The sheriff found out there was an arrest warrant for his deputy from Arizona for assault with a deadly weapon dating to 1961 and that burglary tools were found in the trunk of his car. On April 16, 1968, Fellion, a paid assassin and

demolitions expert based in Española, New Mexico, placed a huge bomb at
the Alianza building. The bomb made an enormous hole in the street, but
it also tore off his hand. Many vehicles and glass windows were destroyed
up and down that street. No one was hurt inside the building, fortunately.
Fellion was hospitalized, then jailed for fifteen days and released. He never
was charged with any crime.[48] The man in charge of the investigation into
this crime was Robert Gilliland. According to David Correia's article, Fellion,
as well as members of the New Mexico State Police, several County sheriffs, District Attorney Alfonso Sanchez, and State Attorney General Boston
Witt at that time were members of the John Birch Society, a right-wing
organization.[49]

Chapa claims that funding for his criminal activity while an undercover police agent was obtained from private sources. That way his payroll check would not have the state imprint and be traceable, just in case
something went wrong with the illegal operations. He named four major
sources: Mundy; an unnamed woman ("this lady rancher from Southern
Colorado gave them a grant to keep my salary up," p. 22); the First National
Bank in Albuquerque (pp. 48, 66); and the George Maloof family (pp. 48, 66,
84). Maloof was the president of the First National Bank and a very well-
connected public figure. He was chairman of several important statewide
commissions, including the Racing Commission and the State Fair Commission. "He was a pretty powerful person here. . . . He used to finance the
state police quite a bit or give them money. . . . At least he paid my salary"
(p. 84). The funds paid by check were drawn from an account at the First
National Bank (p. 85).

Framing Jobs

The police targets were any and all of the core Alianza members, Tijerina and
family, including his brothers, Cristobal and Anselmo. Hugh David, Reies'
first born son, was targeted several times by Chapa in an effort to frame him
with a crime. The state police gave Chapa a check-writing machine taken in
a robbery. Chapa was to get David to hold it to get his fingerprints, then raid

the premises to find it and frame him and others, perhaps, with the robbery. It did not work; David refused to touch the machine even when it was being thrust into his stomach (p. 29). Gerardo Borunda, an Alianza member, was driven by Chapa to Montoya's Restaurant on Lomas in Albuquerque to rob the cash register of its contents. Inside were two undercover cops waiting for him to attempt the robbery so they could shoot him. Borunda must have smelled a setup because he refused to get out of the car and carry out the heist (pp. 30–31).

Anselmo Tijerina, one of the Tijerina brothers, had set up a summer camp-style operation on the outskirts of Tierra Amarilla for youth as part of the health clinic programs. Anselmo had been able to get donations of shoes, clothes, and the like for the youthful participants. The goodwill being generated by the health clinic and this summer camp made it a target for destruction by the state police. Chapa and his cohorts poisoned the water supply at the summer camp and made everyone sick (p. 34).

On instructions from the Albuquerque FBI, they tried to frame Cristobal Tijerina with a stolen vehicle. The operation involved Chapa taking a car for a test drive from University Volkswagen, an Albuquerque car dealer, and not returning it. Chapa and his partner, "this black guy," drove to El Paso and crossed into Juarez to locate Cristobal and give him the car. They were going to say that Reies had sent it for him. They called Cristobal and arranged to meet, but he didn't. Like Gerardo Borunda, he may have smelled a setup because no one except Chapa had called him about this gift. Instead, Chapa's companion "got caught, and the car was kept over there" (p. 35). Chapa crossed back to the United States and notified the FBI as to what happened. The FBI threatened to arrest him for stealing the car, but Chapa got Gilliland on the phone, and they let him go (p. 35).

Chapa also admitted during the oral history interview that he and Leroy Urioste also arranged for Larry Casus, a Native American student activist at the University of New Mexico, to kidnap the mayor of Gallup. Not only did Casus kidnap the mayor, he paraded him around town with a gun to his head. He took the mayor to a sporting goods store to hide from the police. A gun battle took place, and Casus was killed. Chapa and Urioste had driven Casus to Gallup to commit the hostage-taking (p. 84).

Chapa Gets Stonewalled

Chapa married Daisy Montoya, a Native American woman, as his second marriage, but kept her in the dark about being an undercover police officer (pp. 4, 69). She only knew him as a meatcutter and wrestler. That was his cover when he left for extended periods of time. "A lot of times I left her home crying with the kids, you know" (p. 69). The day finally came when, feeling guilty about what he had done to so many people (p. 70), he could no longer justify his actions to himself, and he told her what he really did. He told her he was going to take all his notes and recollections to the FBI. First he turned to Larry Barker, an investigative reporter with the local Channel 7 station in Albuquerque and showed him his records. Chapa then went with his box full of notes to the FBI. "The guy that oversaw the FBI when I went there was a Chicano guy by the name of Perez. I don't know, I forgot his first name" (p. 70). "Perez" was Bernardo Matias "Matt" Perez, who had sued the FBI in 1983 for discrimination against Hispanic agents and won in 1988. Chapa "talked to . . . a guy by the name of, agent by the name of . . . last name was Robin. . . . I didn't talk to Perez. I wanted to talk to Perez. . . . I didn't get past Robin, you know." Chapa recollected this happened in 1994 or 1995 (p. 71). Chapa also talked to his superior, Charlie Daniels, when he worked for the inspector general's office. Neither Robin of the FBI or Daniels of the inspector general's office ever got back to him on his whistle-blowing allegations (p. 72).

During all these years of undercover work, Chapa was often wired so a record could be made of conversations with targets. "I was wired most of the time with a—a lot of the time with Tijerina, other times [in] my surveillance work, half of the time I was wired" (p. 73). Despite the fact that Chapa said he wanted to obtain his FBI file and state police records, he has not done so or authorized anyone else to do on his behalf (p. 71). My requests about Tim Chapa were refused by the state police, whole claimed no such person was ever their employee.

Tijerina Gets Stonewalled by the Cover-Up of the Cover-Up

The Eulogio Salazar murder hung around Tijerina's neck like the proverbial albatross.[50] He was always requesting that the police authorities and
high-ranking politicians release the investigative report done by the state
police's Robert Gilliland on the murder. In 1969, Edward Schwartz of the
New Mexico Review, based on his own journalistic investigation, identified
the potential killers. No one followed up on this exposé. Finally, Bob Brown,
Tijerina's nemesis from the *Albuquerque Journal,* sent word through his assistant, Jerry Crawford, that the newspaper was going to call for the release
of the state police investigative report.[51] On March 21, 1974, Tijerina and a
delegation of his supporters, including Dorothy Orrison, met with Governor
Bruce King. They presented him with a letter signed by some thirty-nine
prominent persons asking Governor King to force the release of the investigative report.

> Dorothy Orrison told the governor, "Mr. Governor, I am an Anglo and live
> among Anglos that believe Mr. Tijerina is responsible for the death of
> Eulogio Salazar. That is why I came to speak with you today. I believe it
> is very necessary that the investigation into this death be made public
> and this unjust suspicion be cast aside." The governor said, "By God, let us
> publish this investigative report so the people will know the truth. They
> have a right to it."[52]

A week later the governor announced he would not ask the state police
to release the investigative report. Tijerina wrote in his daily diary, "I felt
rage but did not lose hope."[53]

Patricia and Reies made plans to move out of Albuquerque and relocate
to Mexico. In the meantime, he moved his family to a remote little town in
another part of the state.

> I now live on a ranch in Madera, New Mexico. I had taken Isabel out of
> school for our move to Madera at a good time. I had taken her to school
> daily and noticed strangers following us. My wife told me of threats she

had received over the telephone regarding our children. They wanted me to stop investigating the death of Salazar.[54]

Tijerina experienced a glimmer of hope on June 4, 1974, when the primary election returns for the Democrats indicated that Jerry Apodaca had won the nomination for governor and Toney Anaya had won for attorney general. "All the Anglo opponents lost. It was a complete Indohispano victory."[55] Changing white faces for brown faces, however, does not guarantee any major policy change or reform. Still, Tijerina held out for hope as he was taken on June 29, 1974, to the state prison to do his time for the crimes he had been convicted of in state court. While in prison, Tijerina heard the news that Apodaca and Anaya had won their offices in the November general election. Upon release from prison on December 18, 1974 he secured an invitation to Apodaca's inaugural ceremony, to be held January 1, 1975. During the swearing-in ceremony, a radio station asked for Tijerina's comments. "I said that I was very happy to see one of our community members taking control of state government and that now we could expect to have more justice for all of the oppressed."[56] It was not to be.

Tijerina courted Governor Apodaca as best he could; the governor was a keynote speaker at his Fourth Annual Fraternity and Harmony Conference. He had met to discuss issues with the governor within a month of his taking the oath of office. Among the items for discussion was again the release of the investigative report being withheld by the state police on the Salazar murder. "He accepted the agenda and promised to do what he could."[57] A state senator, D. J. Michaelson, had also promised Tijerina that he would do all he could to get the report released. "The next day he called me and said, 'I can't, because there is a lot of opposition.' Now my supporters and I realize that the conspiracy to cover up this death has grown much larger."[58]

On June 27, 1975, the *El Paso Times,* according to Tijerina, began the first of a seven-article series on the Salazar murder and cover-up written by Richard Bowman. The articles provided names of the most suspicious people implicated in the murder and cover-up: former U.S. marshal, former sheriff, and former state senator, Emilio Naranjo; U.S. Senator Joseph Montoya; state police officers Freddie Martinez, Robert Gilliland, and William

Fellion; and others such as Max Sanchez and Carlos Jaramillo. On July 11, the *El Paso Times* carried a cartoon labeled "Salazar's Assassination," featuring a can of worms coming out with a hand trying to put the lid on the can. A sign pointing to the hand said, "State Officials."[59]

On August 16, 1977, Attorney General Toney Anaya announced to the press that his 150-page report on the 1968 murder of Eulogio Salazar would be released the next day.[60] The next day he reported to the media that he had conducted a thirteen-month investigation into Salazar's murder and could name the killers of Eulogio. He said he believed they were followers of Tijerina, but not Tijerina himself. But he said his investigation also disproved all the conspiracy theories that a cover-up had ensued. All the allegations made by Tijerina as to the murderers were dismissed as unfounded. He had given a copy of the full report to Governor Apodaca, he said. Anaya concluded his press announcement this way:

> No public official at that time or currently is under suspicion by this office. Although there is evidence that former U.S. Marshall Emilio Naranjo infringed on the original investigation, there has been no "factual basis" to pursue accusations of wrongdoing by Naranjo.[61]

CHAPTER 8

Prison Years

O n June 11, 1969, Tijerina convicted of burning the forest sign became Federal Inmate 45707-146. With this incarceration, he became part of the national U.S. prison history involving Mexicans and those of Mexican ancestry. Tijerina was released from federal prison on July 26, 1971, and re-imprisoned for his state sentences beginning on June 29, 1974 until December 18, 1974. After serving five months and eighteen days, he was released on parole.[1]

Tijerina added to the huge increase in the prison population in the US for persons of Mexican ancestry and other Latino nationalities. "Starting in the 1970s, the U.S. legal system underwent a drastic shift by incarcerating more offenders and placing more people under surveillance for longer periods of time. . . . In fact, regarding the 'race/ethnicity factor,' Latinos are the fastest growing group being imprisoned."[2] The Bureau of Justice Statistics compiled data on state and federal prisoners from 1925 through 1986 and reported that in 1972 there were only 21,713 federal prisoners, and 174,379 were in state facilities. By 1986, these numbers had begun to grow dramatically higher, with federal prisoners totaling 33,135 and state inmates jumping to 470,659. In New Mexico, only 597 federal prisoners were counted in 1972, growing to 2,198 by 1986.[3] Obviously, the U.S. population had increased over the sixty years from the mid-1920s to the mid-1960s, but the prison population grew at an even faster rate. By 2001, according to the Sentencing Project, citing federal statistics, there were 283,000 Hispanics in federal and state prisons and local jails, making up slightly over 15 percent of the inmate population.[4]

Hispanics, like Black Americans, became the prime target for incarceration because the movement to privatize prisons found echo in the legislative halls of states and the U.S. Congress. In 1971, adding fuel to the privatizing fire, President Nixon declared war on drugs, and in New York Governor Nelson Rockefeller pushed for and obtained severe sentences for drug offenses: life sentence, no parole, no probation. By 2015, federal prisoners totaled 1,526,600. In 2012 the publicly traded company Corrections Corporation of America and the GEO Group, combined, received $2.3 billion in revenue, more than half of the private prison business. Corrections Corporation of America was founded by Tom Beasley, John Ferguson, and Don Hutto from Texas and began contracting with the federal government to house undocumented immigrants held in detention for pending proceedings or deportation.[5] The adding of political emphasis on immigrants as criminals took firm hold as of 1980s. Between 1991 and 2007 federal immigration laws became a growing priority and immigration-related offenses, according to the Pew Hispanic Center, represented nearly one-quarter (24 percent) of all federal convictions, up 7 percent from 1991. Hispanic immigrants accounted for 80 percent of those arrested and detained.[6]

Criminalization of the Mexican Identity

Urbina and Alvarez have termed the process over one and a half centuries "the criminalization of Mexican identity."[7] The criminalization of Mexicans continues to this day, nearly half a century after Tijerina's attempt at a citizen's arrest at Tierra Amarilla. In 2015, presidential candidate Donald Trump's views were indicative of this perspective declaring: "When Mexico sends its people, they're not sending their best . . . they're sending people that have lots of problems, and they're bringing those problems with them. They're bringing drugs. They're bringing crime. They're rapists."[8]

This man is now the president of the United States. He is in complete control of the executive branch of government, which houses all the components for the administration of justice. He appoints the attorney general; the justices to all federal courts; the U.S. marshals; the director of the FBI and all other directors of the intelligence agencies, including Homeland Security; the director of the Bureau of Prisons; and the Joint Chiefs of Staff, who lead the branches of the military, all of which also have an intelligence unit. He is the commander in chief, and as such can order the National Guard, the domestic army, to duty and action anywhere in the country at any time for just about any reason. President Trump has declared war on Mexicans by bringing the full force of these systems of social control to bear upon a people and the individuals.

The Border Wall and the National Guard

As president, Trump, still on campaign mode, repeated in speeches across the country that he was going to build a wall on the southern border that Mexico would pay for and ultimately signed an executive order on January 25, 2017, toward that end.[9] Another set of executive orders signed that day allowed an increased in the size of the Border Patrol by five thousand agents plus five hundred more air and marine agents to patrol the U.S.-Mexico border. The other executive order prohibited cities from declaring themselves "sanctuary cities," where local police are not authorized to inquire about immigration status of those persons stopped by them.[10]

The news media produced estimates of the costs for such an immense construction project as the border wall. CNN's Chris Isidore and Jeanne Sahadi estimated it would cost about $3.9 million per mile.[11] President Trump also began a series of tweets in early March 2018 indicating he was thinking of sending federal troops to the Mexican border to help seal the boundary, in addition to building the impenetrable physical wall the length of the

U.S.-Mexico border, which spans 3,145 kilometers or 1,954 miles. On April 4, 2018, President Trump ordered use of the National Guard forces to report for duty at the border "to stop the flow of deadly drugs and other contraband, gang members and other criminals, and illegal aliens into the country."[12] As president, however, without congressional approval, he cannot commit federal troops for any engagement beyond sixty to ninety days, according to the War Powers Resolution of 1973.[13] Moreover, Congress can withhold funding any such effort by the president, but has not done so in decades past. In this case, President Trump is asking border governors to send in National Guard personnel.[14] Past presidents, namely George W. Bush in 2006 and Barack Obama in 2010, also sent National Guard troops to the U.S.-Mexico border, six thousand and twelve hundred, respectively.[15] Additionally, President Trump is prohibiting actual contact between National Guard personnel and immigrants detained or apprehended. They are being used to support the Border Patrol and other agents from Homeland Security in their border enforcement duties.

To be sure, more police and now military action will result in more arrests of Hispanics, legal or otherwise, not just along the U.S.-Mexico border but across the country now that the president has made the hunting and removal of Mexicans one of his highest priorities. Symbolically, every Mexican immigrant crossing into the United States is restating a right to enter what was and is occupied Mexico. This cause of land recovery is what Reies López Tijerina championed during the Chicano Movement and ultimately had him incarcerated given the actions he took toward that goal.

Tijerina Incarcerated for Land Recovery Movement

Tijerina spent many days in city jails and state and federal penitentiaries, not for drugs or his citizenship but for his land recovery movement. He repeatedly was charged and arrested for numerous offenses, state and federal, and in some cases found guilty. He spent ninety days in jail and without trial in Florence, Arizona, for example.[16] He was imprisoned twice in Mexico for a couple of days and once was deported to the United States.[17] His second wife,

Patricia, and daughter Rosa were also jailed shortly after the Tierra Amarilla incident in June 1967 but were released after a few days in the case of Patricia, who was pregnant, and a month in the case of Rosa. Tijerina remained behind bars for thirty-five days, first at the Santa Fe jail, then the state prison, before his bail was set.[18] When Eulogio Salazar was found murdered on the January 3, 1958, Reies and a dozen others had their bonds immediately revoked and were rearrested and jailed. They were not released until February 8, 1968, just over a month of incarceration on mere "suspicion" of that homicide.[19] During the time Tijerina was shuttling back and forth from Memphis, Tennessee, preparing for the Poor People's Campaign (PPC). He was rearrested again in April 1968 and formally charged with sixty-four counts stemming from the Tierra Amarilla incident. He spent the first four days in solitary confinement, until he made bail, and resumed his travels to participate in the PPC.[20] His children, Daniel and Raquel, were jailed and beaten by police while in DC during the takeover of the Supreme Court building. Tijerina was not arrested because he was restrained by his companions from going after the police as he witnessed their misconduct toward his children.[21]

Right after his wife, Patricia, burned the Forest Service sign at the entrance of the national forest in Coyote on June 8, 1969, both she and his son, Hugh David, were arrested and jailed until released on bail. Within days, federal judge Howard Bratton revoked Tijerina's bond because of these new charges against his wife and son. Tijerina, though he wasn't the one who burned the sign, went back to jail on June 11, this time to the federal penitentiary named La Tuna.[22] He spent two weeks in solitary confinement when he arrived at the federal prison to begin his first-year prison sentence.[23] In February 1970 he was transferred to the state prison in Santa Fe. The trial on the burning of the sign got him a nine-year sentence from Judge H. Vearle Payne. Tijerina wrote about his harsh punishment:

> During the time I was in prison, a couple of Anglo kids stole a forest park sign like the one Patricia had burned. They were tried by one of my judges and fined $25. My people sent Nixon another telegram with this information and offered to pay $25 for the sign that was burned. They received no response.[24]

In October 1969, Tijerina was temporarily transferred to Montessa Park prison in Albuquerque, awaiting trial on another charge. "I was taken in shackles to my fifth trial on November 15."[25] He was found guilty. "I was now sentenced to twenty-six years in prison from all the trials combined. I made a motion to Judge Garnett Burks to reduce my sentence. He rejected my motion."[26] He was sent to La Tuna prison to serve his remaining federal sentence.

Dissension in the Alianza Ranks

On November 7, 1969, the Albuquerque FBI's special agent reported to J. Edgar Hoover that the Alianza Federal de Mercedes (AFDM) had reelected Tijerina as its president at the October 1969 annual convention (p. 1). Then Tijerina "publicly resigned over actions of organization. His brother RAMON TIJERINA elected to act as President while REIES TIJERINA serving sentence on prior Federal conviction which had been upheld by all appellate courts" (p. 2). At issue was the petition to the U.S. government, approved by the membership at this convention, "to create '*Republica de Aztlan*' (a new nation) in United States consisting of Colorado, New Mexico, and southern parts of California, Arizona, and Texas" (p. 3). Tijerina, within a week following the convention, according to the *Albuquerque Journal* of October 22, 1969, "angrily resigned as President of the Alianza he founded and said he was completely severing ties with that organization." Tijerina wrote in his biography,

> The Alianza membership . . . passed a resolution calling for the creation
> of a new nation in the Southwest. Those who pushed for this resolution
> wanted to show they were more militant than I. The judges, however, were
> not afraid of mere words. I was not imprisoned because of my words, but
> for my deeds.[27]

Erroneously and carelessly, the report also stated, "At this convention, PATSY TIJERINA, wife of REIES TIJERINA, set fire to two large Forest Service signs and she and REIES TIJERINA arrested for destruction of Government property" (p. 2). That incident had happened many months prior, not at the convention.

Many pages were redacted from another lengthy fifty-page or more report from FBI, Albuquerque to Hoover. A heavily redacted page mentions that the resolution for the creation of an independent nation, Aztlan, was passed unanimously (p. 10). It also quotes another local newspaper, the *Albuquerque Tribune* of October 22, 1969, with the same announcement of Tijerina's resignation from the Alianza over this resolution. The report provides more details.

His daughter, RACHEL TIJERINA, delivered a statement from REIES TI-JERINA which is quoted as follows: "I, REIES L. TIJERINA, from this day of October 21, do and forever resign my post or office of President of the Alianza Federal de los Pueblos Libres. Reason: I don't believe nor support the present course of the (Alianza) administration. My motto is justice but not independence nor revolution against the present Government of the United States. I have been blamed for too much and too long for other people's ideas or inclinations. I am tired of paying the debts of others." (p. 37)

More pages were withheld from this report, which may have added information to an entry that is not redacted:

On July 24, 1969, [two lines redacted] advised that during the morning of July 23, 1969, SANTIAGO ANAYA, Vice President of AFDM, had reported to the Police Department that sometime during the night of July 22-23, 1969, someone had shot three bullets through a second story window at the headquarters of the AFDM. (p. 40)

As had been the practice and custom, the local police found no one to charge even though they had the Alianza members and building under surveillance.

The shooting into the building did not do as much damage to the prospect of early release for Tijerina as the resolution on creating Aztlan. The

FBI and all other intelligence agencies receiving the reports making this mention now had proof that the Alianza, while not a communist organization or under communist influence, was a separatist, revolutionary group, irredentist to say the least. The American Immigration Control Foundation, a John Birch Society-sponsored organization, was to make that charge in a booklet on the land recovery movement and U.S. immigration policy.[28] A letter from the Alianza to President Nixon asking for a pardon did not help.

Santiago Tapia y Amaya Letter

In Tijerina's stead as leader of the Alianza stepped in Vice President Santiago Tapia y Amaya, his most trusted confidant among those comprising his inner membership core. On December 3, 1970, Tapia y Amaya wrote a letter to the president of the United States; it was in Spanish. The content is important because Tapia y Amaya was not helping Tijerina obtain early release from his prison term. He is not helping because his language was perceived as threatening.

> Creemos que usted esta con su encarcelamiento poniendo en peligro la seguridad de muchos oficiales, embajadores, cónsules en paises Latino-Americanos y aqui senadores y gobernadores y otros oficiales en Washington y Nuevo Mexico.
>
> [We believe that you with his continued imprisonment are putting in danger the security of many officials, ambassadors, consuls in Latin American countries and here senators and governors and other officials in Washington and New Mexico.]

The translated letter was forwarded by Robert C. Mardian, assistant attorney general, Internal Security Division, to the director of the FBI on January 22, 1971. Both the translation and the forwarding Mardian letter contain erroneous information identifying "Santiago Tapia y Amaya, President of the Federal Alliance of Free Countries." Tapia y Amaya, as previously noted, was the vice president of the Alianza, and the Alianza name does not contain the words "of Free Countries." The director of the FBI in turn sent the original letter, the translation, and the Mardian letter to the SAC, Albuquerque, on January 28, 1971, with instructions to "immediately interview [name redacted] determine the basis for his communication to the President." Obviously then, the name redacted is Anaya—who else communicated with the president? "If he should indicate he intends this letter to be a threat, facts should be discussed with the appropriate United States Attorney. In any event, Secret Service should be advised locally" (p. 1).

Tijerina's Prison Letter

Tijerina wrote in his autobiography about his experiences while in prison.[29] And in 1971 he published a "letter" from prison in an anthology.[30] This piece is insightful about Tijerina's experiences in prison and the reasons he accepted imprisonment. It was probably written while at the Santa Fe state penitentiary rather than at La Tuna, given the publication year. It could have been earlier, as indicated by the title given in his autobiography: "My Letter from Prison: August 15–17, 1969."

> When I wrote this letter, I had been in prison for sixty-five days. My crime is defending the rights of my people under the Treaty of Guadalupe Hidalgo. I am in prison because of our land and our rights. Our claim is as legitimate or more so than that of Israel. Yet, many in New Mexico will support Israel's petition, but will not acknowledge our rights. And, what's more, they are helping those who cover up Salazar's death. With one hand, they hid the killers of Salazar, and with the other hand, they point at me.
>
> The letter I wrote in prison was more than thirty pages long and I had great difficulty getting it out. One of the guards confiscated it, but another helped me get it back. My letter was published in *El Grito del Norte* newspaper.[31]

The letter he refers to is probably the one that is published in the Ludwig and Santibañez anthology. Tijerina does state in this letter that "for

40 days, since my arrest and incarceration in the New Mexico State Penitentiary, Cell #49, Block 3, I have been without communication with the offices
of the Alianza (Confederation of Free City States) or with its officials." These
are some thoughts he recorded on being imprisoned:

> For the first time in all my life, I feel a deep satisfaction and conviction
> that I am serving my people with all my energy and strength of my heart.
> For the rights of my people I am being held captive. Because of the rights of
> my blood brothers to their property, their culture, and their inheritances, I
> suffer imprisonment. And, I shall suffer it again if necessary. In the future,
> people will not underestimate the Hispano community.
>
> Here in prison I feel very content—I repeat, very content and very
> happy because I know and understand well the cause I defend. My con-
> science has never been as tranquil as it had during these days in prison
> because, as I have said before and now repeat from prison: For the land,
> culture, and inheritance of my people I am ready not only to suffer im-
> prisonment, but I would, with pleasure and pride, sacrifice my life to bring
> about the justice which is so much deserved by my people—the Spanish
> American people.[32]
>
> I do not feel like a prisoner here in my cell. I am not sad, like a de-
> feated criminal—on the contrary, I see and feel that the one being judged
> by the whole world is the Federal Government of the United States which
> has failed to respect its obligations and has robbed the Indian and the
> Hispano of their lands.[33]

Tijerina in this letter reiterates his favorite clauses and language found in
the Law of the Indies, U.S. Constitution, and the New Mexico Constitution
to buttress his arguments for the primacy of the land claims made by the
Alianza. He also rebuts the often-stated argument that the Spanish Crown
also stole the land from the indigenous peoples, just as the United States
had done. He cites the applicable Law of the Indies:

> We have not robbed the Indians, as some accuse us, nor do we seek harm
> for the Indian. The Indian is our brother, and that same law of the Indies

commands us to live as brothers with the Indians. Law 7, Title 17 of Book 4 reads thus: "The mountains, pastures, and waters of the places and the mountains contained within the grants which may be made or that we may make dominions in the Indies should be common to the Spaniards and the *Indians,* and thus we command the Viceroys and *Audiencias* to protect them and to comply."

The ejido or pasturage of the land grants is for the Indian and for the Hispano.[34]

Tijerina's letter writing may have helped him spend his days focusing on their content but it did little in terms of results for a possible clemency or pardon. In prison for the long haul, he began not only to acquaint himself with his surroundings and schedule but also to make contact with fellow inmates. With respect to some, like his cellmates, he had no choice; others, in the yard, the dining areas, and workplace he could pick and choose.

La Tuna

His longest prison stay was at La Tuna correctional facility in El Paso. La Tuna is the short name for the Federal Correctional Institution (FCI) operated by the Bureau of Prisons (BOP), which is part of the Department of Justice.[35] It is a low-security penitentiary for male inmates known as FCI La Tuna, with an adjacent federal prison camp for minimum-security prisoners known as the FPC. A third component located at Fort Bliss, a U.S. Army post just east of El Paso, is known as the FSL, for "federal satellite facility." The main facility is at 8500 Doniphan Road, near Anthony, Texas, which straddles Texas and New Mexico, about eighteen miles from El Paso. FCI La Tuna opened in April 1932 as a "detention farm." In 1938, it acquired its current name, and together, the FCI and the FPC, situated on 635 acres of land, housed 1,059 inmates. In 1970, at FCI there were 780 inmates; 260 at FPC; 191 at FSL. The total number of inmates in 2017 was 1,240, probably less in the 1970s.[36]

The violence, both from guards and from other inmates, was severe during Tijerina's time at La Tuna, to be sure. Reform for to reduce physical assaults, mainly male-to-male rape, was slow in coming. To this day, the public will not concern itself with prison reform as a priority. To begin with, people do not believe that more males than females are raped in the United States. Those making this claim count prison rapes in their statistics. "In 2008 it was estimated that 216,000 inmates in detention were sexually assaulted while serving time, compared to 90,479 rape cases outside of prison."[37] In March 2011, the *New York Review of Books* ran a series of articles by David Kaish and Lovisa Stannow on the subject that called for investigation into inmate allegations and stricter compliance with legislation already in place.[38]

In 2003, with passage of the Prison Rape Elimination Act (PREA), each Bureau of Prisons facility has to undergo an audit for meeting standards, which include male-on-male sexual assaults. Women prisoners had, without success, for years sought protection from rape, mostly by guards, not other female inmates. Male rape in jail and prisons became a sensitive topic despite the growing number of studies indicating this was a most serious epidemic within the prison walls. As early as 1974 Carl Weiss and David James Friar projected that forty-six million Americans would one day be incarcerated and that ten million of those would be raped. Others opined that most of the rapes were in state jails and only 10 percent in federal facilities, but no one had hard data. It was not kept for the record by the BOP. Christine Peek provided hard data in her law journal article, and finally, Congress enacted the PREA, which called for an annual PREA report.[39] The annual audits help, but the problem remains. The *Atlantic Monthly* once again stoked the fire of reform in an article in 2015.[40]

Inmate violence, other than sexual, is a major problem. Gang fights, revenge attacks, ordered hits, and emotional frustration with captivity lead to inmate violence, not to mention the psychosis among those in mental facilities who are in the general inmate population and should not be. FCI La Tuna passed its PREA audit with flying colors in 2014. It met forty standards, failed to meet none, and exceeded two standards required of all facilities.[41] In fact, the PREA audit found the two standards that deal with inmates reporting rape and disciplinary action for abusive staff were met. The auditor wrote, "There were no investigations to review for notifications being made since La Tuna has not had any allegations made." And, for staff conduct, the auditor wrote, "In the past 12 months there have been no staff from the facility that have violated agency sexual abuse or sexual harassment policies."[42] Therefore, La Tuna is a relatively safe place to be imprisoned in current times, according to these sources. But how about the time when Reies López Tijerina was imprisoned there as a forty-year-old? There was no information I could find for the status of La Tuna regarding inmate violence of any kind in those years. But he did survive the incarceration despite harrowing experiences he may have. He did have some notorious inmates at La Tuna, some in his cell. Over the years, the facility has housed many celebrity inmates.

Celebrity Inmates: Curcio, Jung, Valachi, Peyson, and Tijerina

Anthony Curcio masterminded a $400,000 heist of an armored car. It was an almost perfect crime. Curcio, from Monroe, Washington, became a golden boy to his family by breaking several records in football at his high school and going on to be a celebrated wide receiver at the University of Idaho. But he got hurt playing the game and got addicted to Vicodin, a medicine prescribed by his doctor. After his injury healed, he began stealing furniture from the university and selling the goods to afford his habit. He married his college cheerleader sweetheart and paid for four rehabilitation programs that did not help him kick the addiction. Soon he was needing $15,000 a month to pay for his drugs, which now included cocaine. He expanded his business from the life of crime to real estate and was good at that as well. Flipping homes, buying waterfront properties and fancy cars was providing good profits, but then came the housing bust, and he was forced to look for another angle.

He came on to it while biting down on a burger at a Jack-in-the-Box located across the street from a Bank of America branch as a Brinks truck drove up. He returned to that spot at that same time for the next three months to monitor the money pickup and drop from the armored truck. As with the Thomas Crown affair, he hired day laborers wearing the same kind of clothing to meet him at the bank's parking lot the day of the robbery. He dressed the part, faked the robbery by almost going up to the Brinks truck, then backed off and hid his disguise behind a dumpster. A homeless guy watched him and became curious. When Anthony came back to retrieve the items, the homeless guy who lived by the dumpster confronted him. He wanted the clothes stashed behind the dumpster. He also took down his license plate number.

The actual day of the robbery went as planned. The laborers were in the parking lot, all looking alike, picking up debris. Anthony, once he saw the money being put into the truck, came up to the guard, sprayed him with Mace, took the bags of cash, and ran across the street. He went past the laborers and down the street to a creek. He had hidden a yellow inner tube which he used to float down the water to his parked car. And he was gone.

Had the homeless man not called 911 to report the strange men working in the parking lot of the bank where the truck was robbed and the guy he saw earlier wearing the same clothes, the police would not have obtained the license plate number and tracked down Anthony Curcio. He was arrested November 8, 2008 and convicted in 2009 for the crime. He served five years of his six-year sentence at La Tuna.[43] After his release Anthony Curcio went on to more fame and fortune. He wrote a book, *Heist and High,* with Dana Batty and even taped a TED talk.[44]

GEORGE JUNG

George Jung was another celebrity at La Tuna. He continued his celebrity status after release from prison with a book and two movies, all about a life of drugs and dealing. His book was the basis for the films *Blow* (2001) and *Heavy* (2014).[45] Jung became a major player in the cocaine trade from 1970s to the 1980s as part of the Medellín Cartel. Allegedly, this group at one time controlled up to 90 percent of the drugs being smuggled from Colombia into the United States. Jung started dealing marijuana and doing drugs in Southern California during the 1960s. He graduated to taking Winnebago RVs full of marijuana to the East Coast. But then he was caught in Chicago's Playboy Club while waiting on his buyer for the marijuana he had. The buyer was arrested and ratted him out to reduce his sentence. Jung was convicted and sent to prison in 1974. While in the penitentiary in Danbury, Connecticut, his cellmate was Carlos Lehder Rivas, a drug lord from Colombia who taught him the ways of the cocaine business. At that time, the cartels were making $60,000 from every kilo of cocaine. After his release he continued trafficking drugs and was arrested again in 1987 but skipped on his bail. In 1994, he was caught again, tried, and sentenced to twenty years. His sentence began in Kansas; he was transferred to New York then to La Tuna.

His smuggling methods were audacious and daring. He first convinced his flight attendant girlfriend to bring drugs in her luggage; he paid tourists to bring the drugs into the United States in their luggage; he paid to put drugs in the tires of airplanes flying into the United States; he got his own airplane and began daily flights with Carlos Lehder Rivas, who by then had bought an island in the Bahamas, Norman's Cay, which was their headquarters and private airport.[46]

JOSEPH VALACHI

While Curcio and Jung are the more recent celebrities, two others at La Tuna were jailed with Reies López Tijerina at the same institution and cell. One of these, Joseph Michael "Joe Cargo" Valachi, was a famous crime mobster connected to the Mafia; the other was a white supremacist, Walter Patrick Peyson. Valachi had other nicknames and aliases, such as Charles Charbano and Anthony Sorge, over the years as a criminal, mostly in New York. The five Cosa Nostra families operating in the city constituted one-third of all organized criminal activity in the nation, a business that grossed more than $40 billion a year, according to Peter Maas, Valachi's biographer.[47] Prior to Attorney General Robert Kennedy, the FBI took little interest in investigating organized crime. "In 1959, for example, only four agents in its New York office were assigned to this area. On the other hand, upwards of four hundred agents in the same office were occupied foiling domestic Communists."[48] Valachi also has a book and movies to his credit. Unlike Curcio and Jung, he did not live to see them; he died of a heart attack at La Tuna on April 3, 1971, at age sixty-seven.[49]

Vito Genovese and Valachi served time together in an Atlanta federal prison, but Don Vito believed "Joe Cargo" had become a traitor to the Genovese family and his former capo, the boss. Word had gotten to Don Vito that the Bureau of Narcotics had put the hard squeeze on Valachi when he was taken to testify in a trial in New York. He was told by Narcotics Bureau agents that Don Vito had ordered a hit on "Tony Bender," a former lieutenant in the Genovese family whose real name was Anthony Strollo. When he was returned to Atlanta, Genovese asked Valachi to share his cell. At that time, up to eight men could request to bunk together in a cell at the Atlanta facility. Valachi accepted but heard that Genovese had put out a $100,000 bounty on his head, which remained uncollected to the day he died.[50] Shortly thereafter he agreed to testify before a congressional subcommittee on the workings of Cosa Nostra, aka the Mafia. He was the first mafioso to do so. Speculation still circulates as to his motives for testifying, knowing this was a self-inflicted death sentence. Peter Maas makes mention of two theories about why Valachi turned "snitch."

> One theory is the Bureau of Narcotics, convinced he had a lot more to say about the movement of heroin across U.S. borders, deliberately spread the word to bring enough pressure on Valachi to break him down completely. A second theory, which Valachi, among others subscribes to, is that his accuser, a codefendant in the same narcotics case, did it to divert suspicion from himself.[51]

From Valachi's perspective, he would not get out of prison alive unless his sentence was reduced, so he sought ways to get that done; testifying was a gamble, but he took it, knowing he was a walking dead man. Valachi did murder another inmate on June 22, 1962. Valachi assumed that inmate, Joseph DiPalermo, was the one who was supposed to kill him in the Atlanta prison yard.

> At approximately 7:30 a.m. on June 22, 1962, at the U.S. Penitentiary in Atlanta, Georgia, prisoner number 82811, a convicted trafficker in heroin named Joseph Michael Valachi, seized a two-foot length iron pipe lying

on the ground near some construction work, and before anyone realized what he was up to, rushed at a fellow inmate from behind and in a matter of seconds beat him to a bloody, dying pulp.[52]

Unfortunately, the dead inmate was not DiPalermo; he had killed a different inmate named Joe Beck.[53] Valachi asked to be put in solitary confinement to stay alive.[54] Then he went on a hunger strike until they transferred him to La Tuna in July 1968.[55] The following year Valachi shared his cell with Tijerina. Of this experience Tijerina wrote:

> While in La Tuna, I had another interesting experience. I became a cell-mate to Joseph Valachi. He was the Italian mafia member that testified against them. Valachi's cell was carpeted and large. I thought it was strange that I would be in such luxurious cell. Prison staff that befriended me told me not to eat my food. I was being placed in Valachi's cell to eat poisoned food, so they could then say someone tried to kill Valachi and poisoned me. Our people would blame the Italian Mafia, and the Anglos would be free of any guilt in this. I believed this because all my cells have barely been the size of a bathroom. I had to eat my meals right next to the toilet hole on the ground. My cells usually had no windows or sunshine. I didn't eat any of the food and drank only water in Valachi's cell ... other inmates would give me candy and food tidbits while I went through this situation. Mexicans were eighty-five percent of the inmates in La Tuna.[56]

WALTER PEYSON

The other celebrity, a young man named Walter Patrick Peyson, was the protégé of Robert Bolivar De Pugh. De Pugh was founder of a white supremacist organization in the 1950s based out of Norborne, Missouri. The white hate group was called the Minutemen. De Pugh was an extremist's extremist with a flair for the sensational. He wrote diatribes, published thousands of copies of polemical booklets, and circulated them widely. At one point, he published the names of twenty congressmen he wanted dead; AG Robert Kennedy ordered the FBI to watch him closely and infiltrate his organization. His goal was terror and his purpose was to use guerilla warfare to repel the on-coming imminent Communist invasion. He and the Minutemen were going to save the United States from communism. To that end, he found ways to acquire numerous weapons he stashed in various places along with his cache of explosives. He financed his operation with his business, which was the manufacturing of a vitamin pill for dogs that lengthened their lifespan. What dog lover does not want his pet to last forever? While he bragged of fifty to one hundred thousand members in the Minutemen, Laird Wilcox, an expert on extremists, knew it was a few hundred, less if you take out the FBI undercover agents and informants.[57] "Some members of the Minutemen, a tiny but militant anticommunist group that stockpiled arms, conducted paramilitary exercises, and, by the late 1960s, bombed leftist establishments, also received attention, especially if they held cross-membership in Klan organizations."[58]

A journalist for the *Kansas City Star* newspaper, J. Harry Jones Jr., wrote about these Minutemen.[59] On September 26, 1967, De Pugh and his protégé, Walter Peyson, were caught by the federal authorities in Bellevue and Lake City, Washington. They were charged with violating the National Firearms Act and convicted.[60] But they jumped bail and hid out in New Mexico for two years. While they were on the run, appeals were filed in their case and were denied in 1968.[61] Peyson was involved in another case with William Carey Edwards Jr., and both were charged with and convicted of perjury. Their appeal of this case was also denied.[62] When De Pugh was brought back before federal judge William R. Collinson, he told him that if he "had been tried as a revolutionary, I would have pleaded guilty"[63]

De Pugh wrote about a book about making bombs and another on being imprisoned. Eric C. Beckmeier also wrote a book on De Pugh.[64] Peyson has yet to write a book or have one written on his exploits. He does have a wanted-by-FBI poster and a photograph for sale.[65] In 1969, Peyson and De Pugh were both caught in Truth or Consequences, New Mexico, where they were tried and convicted in 1970. When caught at their compound they had two former Minutemen confined in crates for being traitors to the cause. Peyson was sent to La Tuna, where Tijerina was doing his time. Tijerina wrote his memory of that experience in these words:

One time, I was taken back to Albuquerque. While there, the FBI had arrested one of the white militia members called the Minutemen, an extreme right organization. Robert De Pugh and Walter Payton [*sic*] were arrested five kilometers from Truth or Consequences, New Mexico, about 150 miles south of Albuquerque. The FBI confiscated some five tons of weapons and ammunition. The next day, for the first time in my prison life, I had a cellmate: Walter Payton. I was unaware of his identity and talked with him for more than four hours. Walter was about twenty-five years old. Payton told me a most interesting story about being processed in Albuquerque. According to Payton, one of the arresting officers asked him, "Do you know whom we have in jail here? Reies Lopez Tijerina, King Tiger." Payton said to me that he had told them, "Well, you better not put me in there with him because I'll kill him." I asked him if he would make that declaration before a court of law in the future. He said he would. When the jail officials realized that we were getting along and that he had not killed me, they transferred him out of my cell. I never saw him again.[66]

ANOTHER CELEBRITY AT SPRINGFIELD

Alben William Barkley "Bill" Truitt was a fellow inmate with Tijerina at Springfield's Medical Center Facility for federal prisoners. Why he was there is not known other than he was part of the federal inmate population due to the commission of some crime. And he was in Springfield because he needed medical attention for some malady, maybe even mental illness. Tijerina liked him; he called him a friend. "Bill was not a regular Anglo. He believed as I did. He thought that Anglos were headed in the wrong direction and that they would soon fall as a people. In Bill I saw the mentality of the Anglo youth rebelling against their parents."[67]

Bill Barkley Truitt came from a very political family with a history of accolades and accomplishments. He was the grandson and namesake of former vice president Alben William Barkley, who served under President Harry S. Truman. He also was the nephew of General Douglas MacArthur. It is said by some historians that Truman's victory from the sure signs of defeat in 1948 at the hands of the Republican candidates, Thomas E. Dewey and Earl Warren, came from the campaign work of Bill Barkley.[68] In 1905, Bill's grandfather started his political career by getting elected as a county attorney, and quickly rose to become a member of Congress in 1912. Within a dozen years, in 1926, he was elected U.S. senator from Kentucky. His oratory and debating skills won him the honor of being the keynote speaker at four Democratic presidential nominating conventions, 1932, 1936, 1940, and 1948. In 1937 he became the Senate majority leader and collaborator with President Franklin D. Roosevelt in enacting the legislation of the New Deal. He lost out to Truman as FDR's vice president in 1944 because he opposed the president's Supreme Court–packing scheme, which angered Roosevelt. Truman finally made him vice president. Together, the Truman-Barkley ticket obtained 49.55 percent of the vote in the general election and with that came 303 electoral votes, more than enough to win the presidency. Like others, Barkley helped carry most of the South despite Strom Thurman being on the ballot as candidate for the presidency for the newly formed Dixiecrats. Thurman received 2.41 percent of the vote. Barkley had presidential ambitions of his own. In 1952 he announced his bid for the Democratic Party nomination but was promptly blocked by the AF-CIO. He was much older than Truman and at seventy years of age, most pundits thought he was too old to be president. He stayed in the Senate and died on April 30, 1956, while giving yet another rousing speech.[69]

Tijerina and Bill Truitt spent many hours discussing current events and the "hippie" movement, as Tijerina called it. Both were convinced that white youth were so countercultural in opposition to their parental upbringing that they would not serve the country well as leaders. Eventually, both of them were released and had no further contact. Bill Truitt, Tijerina's friend at Springfield, died April 2, 2003. He was seventy years old.

The World of Prisoners

According to Tijerina, being in prison is hell. If he encountered personal violence from an inmate, he did not write about that. He did write about what it was like to be captive in the world of prisoners:

I had known life as a fugitive and had gotten used to being hunted like an animal. I had not known the horrible world of prison life. While my appeals were in progress, I had hope of Liberty. While I had this hope, prison life was tolerable. I began to lose my appeals and my hopes were dashed. The weight of facing twenty-six years in prison began to press on my mental faculties. I lost my faith and lost my feelings. Only the prisoner knows how much he suffers in prison, especially his mind and his spirit. I began to lose contact with my reality. I was in limbo. But I learned that the human body will adjust to everything given time. The prisoners lose all rights, and the guards take advantage of that power they have over them. On the outside, those that control the land and have power oppress the poor and the ignorant. But the oppressed can at least rebel. In prison you can only tolerate your situation. The guards can with impunity increase your terror every minute, every hour, every day. Time is on the side of the guards. Time for the prisoners is on hold. The guards develop an appetite for brutality and agony.[70]

In prison, I had to step softly like a cat. I had to live in peace with my oppressors, the guards, and have contact with others, but avoid the dangerously insane. I had to be alert day and night, but not arouse the suspicion of my jailers. Many times, inmates provoked me. I'm sure superior authorities goaded them. This happened to me in all of the prisons that I was in: Santa Fe, Albuquerque, Montessa Park, La Tuna in Texas, and now here in Springfield, Missouri.[71]

The Time in Springfield's Medical Center for Federal Prisoners

For years, Tijerina had complained of chronic throat problems.[72] Warden Loy Hayes at La Tuna signed the order to transfer Tijerina to Springfield, Missouri, on January 14, 1970. The facility at Springfield is the medical center for all federal prisoners. A caseworker's analysis of Tijerina at the time was mostly negative and, in an undated report, provided these recommendations:

It is felt that Tijerina should be placed under supervision and it is further recommended that he be considered for a transfer to another institution.

The latter recommendation is made in view of the fact that this institution has a high Mexican and Mexican-American population and because
of Tijerina's notoriety it is felt that for the protection of the individual
as well as for the protection of the institution that he should be located
elsewhere.[73]

When he arrived at the Springfield prison, he was promptly evaluated
for his "mental condition" despite his main complaint about his throat.
He was scheduled to take the Stanford Achievement Test. The results were
entered into a document titled "Educational Data." Tijerina did well on
the test. He scored tenth-grade level or slightly better on word meanings
and paragraph comprehension; eight-grade level on English; between
sixth- and seventh-grade level on spelling, and almost sixth-grade level on
arithmetic comprehension. His battery median was recorded as 8.5; it was
recommended he upgrade his education. For work duty, he was assigned to
food service. Apparently, Tijerina did not like how he was received or treated
at Springfield. He and others wrote letters making serious allegations to the
governor of New Mexico and the U.S. attorney in Kansas City, Missouri.

Acting Director C. F. Campbell of the Springfield facility wrote to Governor David F. Cargo on September 17, 1970, refuting Tijerina's allegations
made via a newspaper source. Campbell denied Tijerina was ever in solitary
confinement at Springfield and denied that officials delayed in allowing
him to apply for parole, that they urged him to drop his appeals and that
he had not been treated for his various medical conditions. Campbell did
inform the governor doctors had operated on his throat. In the meantime,
the director of the Bureau of Prisons, Myrl Alexander, received a letter dated
September 23, 1970, from the chairman, a doctor, of the Medical Committee
for Human Rights in Philadelphia, Eli C. Messinger, concerned about the
treatment of Tijerina. He mentioned that "they have noted a serious weight
loss," which was not correct. The medical records show his weight while at
Springfield fluctuated between 175 pounds on his admission date in January 22, 1970, to a low of 169 pounds on October 5, 1970. His weight stayed at
about 170 lbs. for the remainder of 1970, and he was last weighed on February 8, 1971, at 171 lbs. Dr. Messinger requested that a private physician, Dr.

Leonardo Garcia-Bunal, assistant professor of psychiatry at the University of New Mexico School of Medicine, be permitted to examine him. Nothing in the medical records indicates this occurred or that Alexander called Dr. Messinger, who not only provided his address but also his phone number and asked for prompt reply to his letter.

TIJERINA'S MEDICAL RECORDS

Tijerina later claimed he had lost thirty pounds while at Springfield, which the weights recorded for him indicate was inaccurate. He wanted to go there for medical attention to his throat problems but was ignored. He figured out a plan. He prepared a legal document.

> I finally decided to write a writ of habeas corpus and file it with the court in Kansas City, Missouri. In this writ I detailed my seven months in solitary confinement, the attempts on my life by guards and other police. I also cited the lack of medical attention and my being housed with mentally ill prisoners as evidence of cruel and unusual punishment. I provided a list of ten or twelve witnesses, including Walter Payton [sic] and Robert De Pugh. The news of filing my writ of habeas corpus was publicized throughout the United States.[74]

Handwritten notes in his medical record read "Hysterical Personality?" and "Hypomanic?" Under the line "Treatment orders and management precautions pending examination by Ward Surgeon" is the handwritten entry "Routine Care." In next line reads, "Records and findings indicate that this patient should be classified ... ," and there are five choices. The one circled is "Psychiatric Service."

After the intake, he underwent a physical examination by "M Seal MD. The doctor found him normal for the most part, no hernias or prostrate problems, "heart not enlarged," normal hearing. He needed eye glasses for "reading only"; the doctor noted a couple of scars, one on his right knee and another on his abdomen from a surgery. Doctor Seal made two handwritten entries besides these findings: "43 y/o Mexican male who sighs & clears his throat periodically & describes his throat complaints in a somewhat histrionic manner." He ended his evaluation with this entry: "Imp 1. Globus hystericus 2 Hysterical Personality." After this exam, Tijerina was given a referral slip that scheduled three types of examinations or evaluations, one of which was a "Psychiatric Exam. And/or Staffing." Under "Remarks" at the bottom was noted: "Schedule pt. for Early Staff—does not need to remain on psychiatric."

Tijerina must have realized he was in for difficult and trying times, possibly without relief for his throat. He wrote:

> Psychiatry is useful to the one that applies it. Psychiatry is in the hands of the enemy of the people; so, they destroy the powerless. I studied psychiatry fundamentally so that the government psychiatrists would not declare me a psychopath. What is psychiatry? Is it a science? When and where did it begin, how is it used, who uses it? What's the correct interpretation of a psychopath? I had to find answers to these questions. I had to, because psychopaths and psychiatrists surrounded me. My total environment was penetrated with the agony of these inmates. Some would laugh at themselves all day; others cried incessantly. Every prisoner was a sad mental case.[75]

The study of psychiatry by Tijerina led him to the conclusion that the Anglo "as a race, he is psychopathic."[76]

> The origins of the Anglo psychopathy began when the English were excluded from the Treaty of Tordesillas, signed June 7, 1494, between Spain and Portugal. The treaty was a deal brokered by the Pope. It was at this time that the Anglo not only rejected the legitimate body of the era, but also the religion that went against them. The Anglo, without respect for authority and religion, and to get back into the colonization game, legalized piracy. They had to operate outside the law to become the law. Over the last 480 years, the Anglo complex of psychopathy has worsened. His conscience torments him and his thinking grows demented for having violated his own religion, his own law, and humanity.[77]

The stay at Springfield exceeded the torture he had experienced at other facilities. Given the cruel treatment being given to his wife, Patricia, by the police and judges, which she related to him during her visits and in letters, it is amazing how he managed to cope with the daily challenges of being locked up in this prison. He put it this way:

I began to listen to the strange stories told to me by the psychiatric patients and psychopaths in the prison. Day and night, I heard these prisoners cry out. This was a strange world to be in. Not only was I in jail, but I had to live among truly insane inmates. To survive in this environment, I had not only to listen to the insane, but to the psychiatrists, and accept their medications. If I didn't, I'd be put in solitary confinement. The stories I heard from the inmates were incredible. Some told me they could see their brains on the wall. Others told me that Mrs. Richard Nixon, the president's wife, had come to visit them in prison. These prisoners who had committed serious crimes—bank robberies, murders—and many of them had more than ten years in that prison. Others, I discovered, became mentally ill and unstable because they had been in prison for such a long period of time. This is a reality and the judges know that better than anyone else.[78]

While in the Springfield prison, Tijerina continued to claim he lost thirty pounds and continued to demand medical attention for his ailments. He complained to his family that these prison doctors would only give him tranquilizers and no medicine for his throat. The doctors, Tijerina believed, thought it was all in his head, that he had a mental condition. He wrote these observations on that subject:

Psychiatrists surrounded me while at the Springfield, Missouri, prison. Day and night, day after day, one would come, and another would leave. They all thought highly of themselves. They bored me with their questions. I had to answer their questions. And they were not true to themselves. Some of them were homosexuals that took perverted liberties with their patients. I had to tell them my life history against my better sense. Over and over, I had to repeat my life story, from childhood to confrontations with the White House. They wanted me to relate a life story that was not real. For example, I told them of my childhood poverty and how that was not unpleasant because I lived in the midst of love, joy, happiness. I told them of how I got food from garbage cans but thought that was normal at the time. They would ask me if I harbored ill will toward the rich. My child-hood did not now influence my view of the world. They wanted falsehoods. They wanted to know my childhood fears and how many fights I had. I told them that I was afraid of the dark until I was about fifteen years of age. I told them I never had a fight as a child, but I did love wrestling. I was asked if I was afraid of lightning. I told them that lightning, and storms made me feel happy and extraordinarily joyful. I told them my mother taught me not to fear snakes by handling them in her hands.

Once I had a psychiatrist from Dallas, Texas. He taped everything we discussed about my family. I suspected he was a White House operative, and friends in the prison hospital control room confirmed my suspicions. This is how it is in prison. I had to watch myself against the psychiatrists, guards, and inmates. Often, I had dangerous, insane inmates in my cell. On those occasions, I would not sleep. The cowardly Anglo guards did not want to hurt me with their own hands. They wanted another inmate to do the job for them.[79]

CLINICAL RECORD AND NURSING NOTES

The most thought-provoking entries are about the transfers among cell units.[80] On "1-23-70 Physical completed. OK for transfer to F 10-G"; then again on "1-26-70 Transferred to 10-A," but then the change did not occur because the recommendation was to place him in 10-G. Three months later, he is transferred again, "3-12-70 Transfer from 10-G to 3-1 W." Within two months, he is transferred again: "May 11 1970 Trans. From 3-1-W to 10-A-1." A week later, "5-17-70 Transferred 10-a-1 to 8-2 for surgical treatment" and he was returned in two days: "5-19-70 8a Trans from 8-2 to 10-A-1 or exam done." A day and a week later, "5/27/70 Transfer to 8-2 order of Dr. Rhoads." Then, on "6-9-70 Trans from 8-2 to 10-A-1, surgery completed." Late July, "7-20-70

Tran. to Ward 8-2" for a second surgery. "Patient refuses spinal Anesthesia." He was operated again on "7-21-70 . . . Repair of right inguinal hernia" by Dr. Cohen and Dr. Slade. On the medical records titled "Clinical Record Consultation Sheet" May 26, 1970, Dr. J. Rhoads wrote, "Feels a sharp pain when he rises from a sitting position or turns over on his side in bed. Possibly a slight impulse was felt on palpation." A week later he is transferred back to 10-A-1. His weight on October 1, 1970, was 171 lbs.; it was not true he had lost thirty pounds while at Springfield.

All in all, Tijerina had three operations at Springfield. The first was an esophagostomy on May 18, 1970, for the throat problems. The second surgery was "exploration of right cervical area with small Penrose drain inserted" on June 2, 1970. The third for the hernia was on July 21, 1970.

TIJERINA'S VISITORS AT SPRINGFIELD, MISSOURI

Patsy came to visit her husband almost every month. The hardship this posed can only be estimated. She owned no car, had no job, had no savings, had two children, did not know how to read or write, and had her own legal cases against which to defend herself. On the day Tijerina went to press charges against Jack Johnson for attempting murder by pointing a rifle at him, his bail was revoked. The U.S. marshals took him in and confiscated $4,241.75 cash Tijerina had on him. "Chief Duffy refused her the money. My wife had to ask for welfare assistance to survive."[81] Then, he adds, "It was now five months since the money I had left for my family had been confiscated and not returned."[82] Moreover, she was borderline mentally challenged with a low IQ. "When I was tried in September, the people learned that Patricia had a low IQ, a 69, which is below average."[83] Furthermore, Tijerina wrote:

> Judge Payne and his wolves took advantage of my wife, despite the fact
> that several psychiatrists testified that Patricia was not in a condition to
> be tried because she could not read or write. She did not understand even
> the most rudimentary elements of law, much less what was said in court.
> They tried her anyway. The jury was an all-Anglo jury. They were more

embarrassed than Judge Payne and refused to condemn my wife. Judge
Payne wanted the jury to find Patricia guilty of the destruction of the forest sign in Coyote. Regardless, the jury refused to condemn my wife. She
was the principal person charged with the crime. Peter Adang, my wife's
lawyer, represented her in these matters very poorly. Patricia came to
Springfield, Missouri, and told me all that was going on.[84]

Frank Tenorio, whose actions were related in chapter 7, offered to help
her get the money back.

When the media reported on the money I had when arrested, Frank Tenorio, a state police officer, approached my wife. Tenorio assured her he was
not like the other police agents. He promised to help her obtain the money
she was entitled to. We had a secret Alianza member employed as a U.S.
Marshal, Edwin Berry. He kept me informed of what was being plotted
against us. Tenorio was lying to Patricia in order to gain her confidence.[85]

Patricia never got the money that was confiscated by the police and promised by Tenorio.

Toward the end of June, Patricia told me a story that hit me like a bomb.
Three men had raped her. Patricia went to the state police, someone
named Sanchez, but he didn't listen to her. When Patricia insisted on
police protection, they threatened to put her in jail. Patricia told me there
were witnesses to what had happened. Neighbors came to her side and
offered protection. The neighbors loaned her a gun. Within days, an officer,
Richard Martinez, came and took the gun away from Patricia.[86]

Patricia would not tell Reies who had raped her for fear he would seek
revenge and be returned to prison.

I had to threaten her with divorce if she didn't tell me who raped her
and almost killed my son. I finally got the names from her and began to
place them in the larger conspiracy out to destroy me.[87] On March 29,

1973, I received a telephone call informing me that my son Noé had been kidnapped and was being treated at a local hospital. I went immediately and found out that some men had attempted to rape my son. The perpetrator was a police officer, Albert Vega. He and Frank Tenorio had been the two officers assigned to assist my wife during my trials. At first, Vega pled not guilty before Judge Gerald Fowlie and then changed his plea to guilty before Judge Roger Sanchez. At the urging of my son, David, I wrote to Judge Sanchez and recommended clemency for Vega. Vega has a wife and six children. I know how the wife and children suffer when the father is in jail.[88] They protect Frank Tenorio and other puppets that have violated my wife, while they keep me in a mental institution.[89]

The distance from Albuquerque to Springfield, Missouri is approximately 1,328 miles, at least a two-day drive. The costs include an overnight stay at a motel, unless you sleep in the car, plus lodging and meals while visiting Reies at the prison. Patricia and others came regularly. The medical records from Springfield took note of "Approved Visitors" on a log. The two-page record indicates that "Patsy Tijerina, wife" signed in for thirty-four visits from February 5, 1970, to July 23, 1971. "My family was broken. Patricia's last court-appointed attorney was encouraging her to divorce me," wrote Tijerina in his memoir.[90]

She only missed visiting for an entire month in April 1970, and four months in 1971, February to June. In 1970, Patsy brought one of the children, Isabel, to see him on March 17 and 18, then again August 20, 21, and 22, and once a month for several days the remainder of 1970. "Witnessing my wife's agony and suffering further broke my spirit. She was being broken and used by Frank Tenorio on orders from Judge Payne," he entered in his autobiography.[91]

In 1971, Patsy again brought Isabel on June 17, 18, 19, 21, and again the 22 and 23 to visit her father. The visits impacted Tijerina: "My wife and children came to visit me from time to time. Her visits always left me sad because I could see how they were using her. She would tell me things that bothered me a great deal. I could not tell Patricia what evil lurked around her; she would not understand."[92]

Rosa, the daughter from Maria, and her husband, Domitilio Duran, came to visit him on three occasions during his stay at Springfield. Cristobal Tijerina came to see him once, on July 1, 1971. His son, Hugh David, and wife, Jo Ann, came twice on March 16, 1970, and July 1, probably with Cristobal. Hugh David signed in as "Reies, Jr." for visits for seven months, May 1970 to January 1971. Reies was very proud of his son: "My son David was my right hand ... He was the one to come and tell me that at a conference in Denver, Colorado, the delegates passed a resolution designating me the first national hero of Aztlan."[93] Patricia, however, was the one who regularly kept coming to visit him during his incarceration.

The National Hero and Holiday of Aztlan

The SAC, Albuquerque notified Hoover on May 28, 1970 about a woman using the "IS-Spanish-American" and "IS-Cuba," which indicate she was thought of as an internal security risk (p. 1). The content of the LHM is heavily redacted on the second page because these are the informants relied upon. On the fourth page of the LHM is an article obtained from a public source, *El Grito del Norte,* the newspaper published by Enriqueta Vasquez of Espanola, New Mexico (p. 3). The article is reporting on activities that took place during the second annual Chicano youth conference held in Denver during March 25-29, 1970. Among the events that took place was making "TIJERINA: NATIONAL HERO The conference declared that Reies López Tijerina is an official hero of the nation of Aztlan. June 5 was recognized as a national holiday in Aztlan" (p. 6).

In mid-November a law student, Phillip A. Martinez, wrote Tijerina in Springfield with a series of questions about the land grants to which he sought answers for a research project pending his graduation in December. The student letter was intercepted on November 18, 1970, at the medical center and sent to Director Pasquale J. Ciccone, who in turn replies to the law student and returns his letter. He advises the student to write the director of the Bureau of Prisons because "inmates are not permitted to provide interviews such as you are requesting."[94] Dr. Ciccone also sent copies of all the letters and his denial to Norman Carlson, director of the BOP.

More Visitors at Springfield

The other visitors who were approved by "Mr. Melnick" for only one visit and came to Springfield were Alianza members and core loyalists: Juan Roybal, Santiago Anaya, Cespiridiona Amaya, Camila Armijo, and Jose O. Armijo. Roybal came on June 5, a most symbolic day, and the others on the 16.

Tijerina's attorneys or persons signed in as attorneys also came to visit on two occasions. "John Thorne Att Case McGowan [Att. Sec.]" came to visit October 1, 1970. Thorne apparently had communicated with the warden's office at Springfield about coming to Missouri on a weekend. C. F. Campbell, the acting director the Springfield Medical Center, responded to John E. Thorne in San Jose, California. He advised him to come during the week if not able to come on a weekend, but that the visiting room facility was crowded then. Bill Higgs came on July 16 and 17, 1970. And "specially approved by Ben Wright" were G. Davis on June 25 and John T. Dunn on April 10. On May 19, 1970, Tijerina had three visitors, "John C. Wheeler and Jack Moore" signing in as attorneys and "Mr. Eldridge M.U. Legal Aid M.U. student."

The Last Medical Records from Springfield

There are three sets of records germane to the medical treatment Tijerina received while at Springfield: doctor's orders, progress notes, and a clinical record consultation sheet. The progress notes indicate he was operated for removal of esophageal mass on May 18, 1970; had the flu on April 1, 1970; had an operation on his neck that was only exploratory, nothing removed or found, on June 2, 1970; and had a hernia repaired on July 20, 1970. By September, he was still complaining of pain and problems with his throat, so the doctors began making entries on June 6, 1970, that "he appears to have Globus Hystericus type symptoms" and on August 19, 1970, "Note: Psychiatric Dx-Schizophrenia." On September 25, 1970 the doctor's entry is very specific: "The man's defenses are rigid and internally felt . . . he appears psychotic. It may represent two somewhat different approaches, but it appears to me that the patient is basically schizophrenic and probably has been for some time." He was referred to "one of our consulting psychiatrists [that] speaks Spanish fluently. If so I will prevail upon him for additional help."

Tijerina reported ailments about strain of a tendon; pain in the right knee and foot discomfort; along with his leg muscles tightening. He had been given crepe-soled shoes April 4, 1970, and eyeglasses finally on September 9, 1970; he had requested them on July 17. The X-rays taken in March 1, 1971 and again on July 7 showed no abnormalities. "Has normal xrays of L-5 spine and has had orthopedic consult in past. Will encourage to continue to work." Doctor Cornwall noted on July 16, 1971, that Tijerina was "not actively participating in community. Many somatic problems. Just begins in group therapy. Plan-Evaluate on 10A, in group therapy."

The notations in the doctor's orders are consistent with the progress notes. Regrettably, the doctor's orders contain many entries for medications and or drugs, names of which do not mean anything to me other than Tylenol, Sudafed, Benadryl, Cherry cough syrup, Mylanta, Valium, Maalox, Codene, and morphine administered several times in June 1970, which is when he was operated on. There are many drug names I do not recognize such as Thorazine, Atrophine, Tetracyeline, Stelazine, Zactrin, Melloril, Methylpyrilone, Maslex, Strazine, Artane, Sod Salicylate, Haldol, Nasalicilate, Dulcolax, Compazine, Hale, Darvon, Vdrlin, Xylocaine, Ampicillin, Demerol, and Nembutol. Tijerina, perhaps took this mix of drugs as antibiotics and for psychotropic treatment.

According to the consultation sheets, Tijerina began to complain in October 1970 about his right knee "jumping out of place." And the consultation sheet dated May 15, 1971, makes mention of his complaint regarding the right knee still jumping out of place; pain in his neck; and trouble sleeping. Dr. Rhoads, chief of surgery, references Dr. Jameson's consultation: "His neck has been very thoroughly evaluated by 2 consultants. I believe there is nothing further to be done for the neck. I suggest we treat the scar with cocoa butter."

Clinical Record: Narrative Summary

Dr. Thomas P. Cornwallis entered the final notes without a date as follows:

> Mr. Tijerina was admitted 1/22/70 to the Medical Center. He had psycho-
> logical testing which was reported as finding no psychiatric problems.
> He was then discharged 1/17/71 after many surgical procedures—see old
> records. This time he was admitted 1/24/71 and has been on the psychiatric
> ward. He has worked well at his job & taken part and in the community. He
> has no evidence of thought disorder at this time. Discharge Diagnosis—1.
> Schizophrenia, paranoid type in remission. 2. Unstable R Knee.

The explanation for what appears to be an error in dates of discharge and admissions is due to detainers filed by other authorities wanting Tijerina to be moved from one institution to another or for court events. The two pages on detainers among the medical records indicate he was moved twice in 1969, July 10 and December 30, on writs of habeas corpus from El Paso to Springfield. On July 20, 1970, Dr. Ciccone, the director at Springfield, wrote a note to himself about an AP reporter from Kansas City who indicated that Tijerina was now "alleging that tumor in throat had become malignant." Then, the director adds: "My response[:] This allegation neither admitted or denied. Individual recently had surgery and has made satisfactory recovery from his surgery. Prognosis considered good." Later, on October 7, 1970, Dr. Ciccone wrote to the director of the BOP, Norman A. Carlson, about Tijerina. Apparently, someone persuaded Carlson to inquire on September 21 about any additional developments on Tijerina because "Senator Bennett" had requested information. There was a U.S. senator from Colorado named Michael Bennett, but there is not enough information in this one-page memo to confirm this identity. Dr. Ciccone repeats the history of throat problems and his referral for psychiatric evaluations. He concludes the memo with

"[It is] the staff's opinion that Mr. Tijerina's present problems are chiefly in the area of mental health at the present time, and that his physical problems have been adequately taken care for [sic]."

Special Progress Reports

The two special progress reports in the medical records dated October 7 and November 5, 1970, are critical of Tijerina's maladies and his mental status. The October report states:

> The initial diagnostic impression was that he suffered from an anxiety neurosis. Since July 7, 1970, the patient has received very extensive psychiatric workup. This will be summarized in a later report. The diagnostic impression should be changed to schizophrenia, essentially paranoid with grandiose and persecutory ideation. A major component also includes semantic [sic, somatic] delusions. The patient functions on borderline psychotic status. Two Board Certified Consulting Psychiatrists, one from Dallas, Texas, and one from the University of Missouri Medical School, Columbia, Missouri, agree with the psychiatric diagnosis of schizophrenia. The psychological examination by a Consulting Psychologist defined the personality structure compatible with its diagnosis, although the psychologicals themselves do not reveal an active psychotic process.

This document was reviewed signed by Dr. H. Wayne Glotfelty, chief, Psychiatric Service and Dr. G. Thomas Wallender, staff psychiatrist.

The November report is even more damaging to Tijerina. It repeats the first four lines of the prior report but adds new material, especially in the concluding paragraph. These are the significant parts:

> A major component also includes somatic delusions. The patient has been extensively studied, particularly by the department of surgery in regard to the patients' throat complaints. At the present time it may be said that the patient throat complaints appear to the psychiatric service to consist of

somatic delusions. At present the patient is on Stelazine in moderate doses as a trial. Objectively he appears to have benefited somewhat. The subject denies this. He admits that he is very afraid that if he is on psychiatric medication he will be refused parole. At the present time the patient is also being evaluated for a knee condition. Orthopedic consultation had been obtained, however at the present treatment plans are not known.

It is probable that continued psychiatric hospitalization does not offer much hope of improving the patient. The patient's "SET" toward this hospitalization at the U.S. Medical Center for Federal Prisoners is that it is part of a plot by federal officials to harm and discredit him. It is thought that the patient will seek and will indeed requires some supportive psychiatric care on release. It is not thought present therapy or future therapy will require hospitalization of patient more than two or three months.

This document was reviewed and signed by the same doctors as the prior report. It never occurred to these professional medical and psychiatric specialists that the paranoia attributed to Tijerina was based on his reality for the past twenty years.

Tijerina was aware of what was going on with his treatments. He worked in the kitchen while he was an inmate and made friends with many staff members, "including an Anglo psychologist who befriend[ed] me. He would tell me what other psychiatrists were saying behind my back and what was coming in my future."[95] It certainly helped Tijerina cope with prison reality because he knew some of the events, reports, comments, and recommendations being made by those who had his life in their hands; he somewhat knew what was happening around him. Knowing one's situation is a path to coping.

In 1971, the assistant U.S. attorney in Kansas City informed the Springfield authorities that Tijerina was to be transferred "back to the Committing Court."[96] A reply was had from Dr. Ciccone of the Springfield facility to the chief judge, U.S. district court in Kansas City, William H. Becker, that Tijerina had been transferred back on January 24, 1971, to New Mexico. On July 26, 1971, Tijerina was given federal parole. However, the attorney general for State of New Mexico had filed a detainer notice to hold him for transfer to New Mexico, where he still had a "two to ten years, New Mexico Penitentiary" warrant pending. On this occasion Tijerina wrote,

> I was in prison for 775 days, when suddenly I was taken from Springfield, Missouri, to the Albuquerque airport and released. . . . The White House set me free on July 26, 1971. I was not completely free. I had difficult and hard conditions of parole. I was to be on parole for fifteen years and had to report monthly to Richard Martinez. I could not hold any leadership position in the Alianza for three years.[97]

Sentence Data Summary

Prison sentences are imposed by judges, federal and state, and are stated in numbers of years; two to five years or ten years, for example. Tijerina was sentenced to twenty-six years total time in both prison systems, state and federal.[98] His federal sentence began on June 11, 1969, for computation purposes. For the crime of assault on a federal officer he was sentenced to five years in a federal penitentiary by Judge Bratton on December 15, 1967. Judge Payne gave him three years for destruction of government property, aiding and abetting on October 10, 1969. And he received thirty days for contempt of court from Judge Kerr on February 27, 1968.[99] The sentences were tabulated to run concurrently; therefore, Tijerina had five years to serve. These computations are done at the Designation and Sentence Computation Center (DSCC) in Grand Prairie, Texas. Tijerina's sentence was to be computed under 18 U.S.C. 4208 (a) (2), and any possible parole would be determined by another section of the 18 U.S. Code, 3050, Subpart A.[100]

There is provision for earning credits toward the federal sentence term. The Sentence Data Summary form prepared by Bureau of Prisons indicated he would serve until June 9, 1974, but with credits, release could be as early as February 14, 1973.[101] The state system for New Mexico works much the same way, with more generous credits for good behavior; three days for every one served without incident. The state time can be greatly reduced for that cause, and it was. He was fortunate that he did not violate parole conditions and return to the federal or state prison system. Six years later, on February 2 and 3, 1980, the New Mexico State Prison had the worst prisoner riot in its history, second in violence only to the Attica prison riot of 1971.[102]

U.S. Board of Parole

On April 2, 1970, the U.S. Board of Parole received an application for parole by inmate 45707-146, "Reis [sic] Lopez Tijerina." The action taken was to "continue with an Institutional Review Hearing in January 1971 with psychiatric evaluation."[103] Six months after the hearing, the parole clerk for the board of parole stamped "Jun-1 1971 RECEIVED" on the notice of action for inmate Reies López Tijerina, register number 45707-146 (also his federal prisoner number). Tijerina's case was heard en banc by the U.S. Board of Parole.

> On the date shown below, the following action with regard to parole, parole status, or mandatory release status was ordered: <u>Parole to the actual physical custody of</u> the detaining authorities in the State of New Mexico ONLY effective July 26, 1971.
>
> Special Condition:
> Should he be released by New Mexico authorities prior to June 9, 1974, a special condition of parole is that he not hold official office or position in the Alianza Federal de Pueblos Libres (Federal Alliance of Free Countries).[104]

The Alianza did not fare well while Tijerina was in federal prison and worse once he was released given the condition he not hold any office in the organization. The Alianza provided him with housing and some money for daily expenditures. He had no automobile or other income. He had to exercise leadership and seek control via surrogates. Moreover, he had to conceptualize a new strategy to stay in the public eye. He went on speaking tours to raise funds and let everyone know that the rumors of his having been lobotomized while in prison were totally false.

> **Brotherhood Awareness, Cultural Awareness,**
> **and Peace and Harmony Conferences**

The three themes of brotherhood, cultural, and peace and harmony were the names Tijerina gave his conferences. These conferences took place during 1972 and 1973; officially they were billed as Fraternal Harmony conferences. The FBI was not fooled by this appearance. The SAC in Albuquerque notified the director of the FBI in a two-page LHM memo dated February 20, 1973, that Tijerina was still unemployed; living at the Alianza building; and traveling the country extensively while he was on parole and his state convictions were on appeal: "Even though ... he is not to be an official of AFDM, he is, in fact, according to sources, who have furnished reliable information in the past, running the activities of the AFDM" (p. 2).

A sixteen-page report from the SA Albuquerque to the Bureau and various military intelligence agencies is dated January 31, 1974, but is reporting on material from June 1, 1972, to January 30, 1974, basically eighteen months. This report included the FD-376 periodic report now signed by the newly appointed FBI director, Clarence M. Kelley. He is still checking the boxes as Hoover did, and as Gray did while acting FBI director, indicating that Tijerina is potentially dangerous and has participated in anti-U.S. demonstrations and civil disturbances. For this reason and perhaps others not noted, Kelley checked box 9, which keeps Tijerina on the ADEX list because "he still directs activities of Alianza Federal de Pueblos Libres, the activities of which in the past have led to violence." The other parts of the FD-376 are marked "Confidential" but the reasons are redacted, and the following page is entirely withheld. The LHM report of the thirty-first has a one-line entry without any other comment or attachment advising, "Subject's conviction on state charges stemming from the 1967 raid of the Rio Arriba County Courthouse in Tierra Amarilla upheld by New Mexico Supreme Court." It also states that "the Alianza is still split into two factions and at present it is inactive." At the bottom of this page, under the capitalized and underscored headline SPLIT BETWEEN REIES LOPEZ TIJE-RINA AND SANTIAGO ANAYA, the three to four lines of content that follow are redacted. A newspaper article from the *Albuquerque Journal* of July 12,

1972, has a front-page story by Chuck Anthony, but not about Anaya. Instead it is titled "Splinter Alianza Unit Loses Catholic Funds" and tells about the ouster of William Higgs from the Alianza (p. 3). The news story related that the U.S. Catholic Church's funding mechanism, the Campaign for Human Development (CHD), had frozen the funding the Alianza until Higgs was removed. Reportedly, Higgs gave his resignation from the program to Robert Carvajal, the associate director of the CHD. Carvajal reiterated support for the work of the Alianza and its four CHD-funded programs, one of which was La Escuela. Carvajal is quoted in the article that the CHD did not fund the Alianza, it funded programs; it did not fund personalities, it funded the original applicants for the grant (p. 4).

The first fight Tijerina had when he was first incarcerated was with his brother, Ramon, whom he left in charge in 1969. At that time, the Alianza membership passed a resolution espousing the name "Aztlan" for the Southwest, recognizing that term as synonymous with the homeland, the grant lands taken by the U.S. government in the West. Tijerina branded that term as separatist and a Chicano nationalist agenda that he wanted no part of. His daughter Raquel personally delivered his message to the Alianza, as reported by the SA, Albuquerque report to the FBI director, on November 7, 1969, a report covering the period from March 5 to November 2. Tijerina's statement in this report is as follows:

> I, Reies L. Tijerina, from this day of October 21, do and forever resign my post or office of President of the Alianza Federal de Los Pueblos Libres.
>
> Reason:
>
> I don't believe nor support the present course of the (Alianza) administration. My motto is justice but not independence nor revolution against the present Government of the United States. I have been blamed too much and too long for other people's ideas or inclinations. I am tired of paying the debts of others. (p. 37)

There is a paragraph immediately following this statement as if to indicate it was part of the statement but entirely redacted, about eight to ten lines.

The Lobotomy Rumor

This abrupt action taken by Tijerina made possible the speculation that something was going on in prison that was harmful to him. In the most provocative and totally unsubstantiated assertions, Betita Martinez and others at *El Grito del Norte* wrote under the headline of "Torture of Tijerina" that two writs of habeas corpus had been denied; that Reies had been held in solitary confinement for seven months; and that "there have been fears that the government is preparing to perform a 'lobotomy' on Reies." David, Reies's son, said: "Reies has not mentioned this possibility to him."[105] But the rumor was set loose and repeated by those seeking answers as to why Tijerina was not talking about the land grants anymore and instead was talking about harmony, brotherhood, peace, justice, and culture.

In April 1972, the next fight was with Santiago Anaya, who was the elected head of the Alianza but challenged by Tijerina's choice of candidate, Eduardo Chavez, the existing secretary-treasurer. Anaya, a longtime loyalist and strong supporter of Tijerina was ousted and Chavez remained president of the Alianza from 1974 into 1976 without any intervening election of officers. The third fight was with Alfredo Maestas, Pedro Archuleta, and Moises Morales, who led about fifty others out of the organization. They were questioning the finances and lack of support for their projects under the framework of La Alianza: La Clinica and La Cooperativa del Pueblo. They also had formed a chapter of the Raza Unida Party in 1973 and were fielding candidates in 1975.[106]

Back to State Prison

Once his appeal of the conviction stemming from the second trial over the citizen's arrest at Tierra Amarilla Courthouse was denied, Tijerina was picked up and began serving his two concurrent sentences, one to ten years and one to five years, in the state penitentiary. Tijerina still had to serve his state prison sentence. "Emilio Naranjo's agents came to take me to Santa Fe to begin my second prison term."[107] The date was June 29,

1974, seven years since the event. Tijerina, however, got time off for good behavior. Governor King never got around to deciding whether to grant him clemency or not. By the time the state released him under its own procedures, Jerry Apodaca was now the governor of New Mexico. "I walked out of [state] prison on December 18, 1974 and went to celebrate with my family and community."[108]

CHAPTER 9

Mexico: Love It and Leave It

Over the years, Tijerina traveled in Mexico and developed a love for its life, culture, language, and the old traditions still maintained by families he stayed with, visited, and observed. What he saw and experienced in Mexico coincided with his worldview on many fronts. In 1956, he just knew he wanted to remove himself from Anglo society and began his communal experience at the Valley of Peace.

Here I would take my family and those who accompanied me in this great adventure ... they knew, as I did, that we had left behind the cities, with all their vanity and corruption. We had abandoned a form and a style for life that we considered evil and opposed to the road to justice that had been indicated to us by the man from the Holy Land.[1]

What most pushed us to relocate to the desert were our children. We wanted to liberate them from the bad influence that was eroding family and spiritual unity. This influence, I was convinced, came directly from Anglo education. The Anglo believed that was possible to discipline everything, except the family. Discipline the police, discipline the military, but they did not believe in discipling the family. . . . Another thing that repulsed us about Anglo education was the perversion of the sexes. What they called "sexual education." The Anglos got lost going in that direction.[2]

He liked the strict roles ascribed by the culture for women and men in Mexico.

I found that the Constitution does not offer a single provision or safeguard to the family. Moreover, it does not offer deal specifically with corruption and the degeneration of the sexes that was destroying society.[3]

Tijerina always wanted to be in charge. His oldest son, Hugh David "Reies, Jr.," made this observation:

Well, the way he brought us up, you know, he was the boss. He was strict. And he was the leader of the family. Always taught me that the educational system was a lot of lies. So when they took me to school, I told the teacher that. I wanted to get out of there. I was afraid, I guess. She told the other kids to block the door so I couldn't get out, Then I started fighting and kicking, and somehow I broke her glasses. . . . I skipped some grades. So, that was the last time I went to school [eighth grade].[4]

Women were supposed to follow the man, be submissive and accept what came their way. Rosa, during my interview with her mother, Maria Escobar, interjected that Reies delivered Ira de Ala, acting as the midwife because "he was so jealous he didn't want doctors seeing you or touching you." Maria did not controvert that surprising misogynistic behavior, just added, "I never saw a doctor."[5] His oldest son also learned some of his father's views. David wanted to marry but did not want to have children because, if he went to prison like his father,

My wife's gonna find somebody else, and I don't want to have to worry about that. . . . I saw my father and mother get divorced under pressure from the U.S. government. . . . And once they got divorced, my mother felt free. Women are like that way. And slowly they became further and further apart.... I was afraid something like that was going to happen to me.[6]

Tijerina disliked any public display of affection and discussion of sex. He certainly was opposed to any instruction on the subject in the public schools. He did not want his children exposed to any of that, nor did he want them learning the history, language, and traditions of Anglos at the expense of their own. He wanted them to learn in Spanish. On many occasions, he withdrew his children from the public schools and resorted to home schooling. While in Arizona at the Valley of Peace, he built and began a school for the children. In a way, he sought to reconstruct his own upbringing; after all he managed to become literate, informed, knowledgeable, and effective. He wrote,

As you read this book, do not forget that I never had an education. I was not educated in any Anglo school or college. I learned at home. My greatest education came in the struggle against injustice that the Anglo perpetrated against my people.[7]

Santana and Carmela Vergara

Tijerina found many supporters who unselfishly gave of their time, money, and lodgings, not only during his first trip to Mexico in 1956 but also many future trips: "I was thirty years old when I left for Mexico. I did not know anyone in the Mexican capital city. I stayed in Mexico for three months."[8] Santana Vergara was his early patron who boarded him at his home for most of this time and again when he returned in September 1958. This time, "Mr. Santana Vergara built a small three-room house for me and said, 'Bring your family. Here you have a home that isn't going to cost you a thing.' Don Santana had a lot of sympathy for our cause."[9] During this prolonged stay in Mexico he approached the secretary of foreign relations and formally requested political asylum. He was rejected: "I was told that the United States was not pursuing me and therefore I was denied."[10] He should have

known then he no longer was a fugitive and could safely return to his family in New Mexico; instead he sent for them. Together they spent another
three months in Mexico, until May 1959, when Maria and the kids returned
to pick cotton in Texas. Reies did not join them until mid-September 1959
to help pick cotton. Before returning to Texas, however, Reies stopped at the
archives in Guadalajara, Jalisco, to research land grants in New Mexico. He
presented himself and asked for those archives only to learn that they had
been stolen by a woman and the photographer from the United States hired
by the Mexican government to copy them. The woman was an Anglo from
Albuquerque.[11]

By January 1960, Tijerina was longing to return to Mexico; he crossed
at El Paso into Juarez, then took a bus to Mexico City. This time the trip
was full of horrors. First, he carried in his satchel a five-hundred-signature
petition addressed to the president of Mexico, Adolfo López Mateos, and
other documents showing the theft of their land grants in New Mexico. In a
moment of carelessness, he left the satchel on the counter at the main post
office in Mexico City to ask a clerk for information. It was taken along with
his money within seconds. Second, he met Lombardo Toledano, renowned
member of the Mexican Communist Party, who agreed to discuss the land
grant issue with him.

> [Toledano] promised to use his influence to see what he could do so that
> the government of Mexico would take responsibility for people in the
> United States of Mexican ancestry. He would try to see what Mexico could
> do to obligate the United States to fulfill its obligations under the Treaty of
> Guadalupe Hidalgo. But he asked me for twenty-five thousand dollars for
> his services and expenses. I left his office shamed.[12]

Dolores Diaz de Rebeles

He returned to Mexico again in late 1961 with Rosita, his daughter, and his
brother Cristobal. They stayed with Mrs. Dolores Diaz de Rebeles, a new
contact. Don Santana and Carmela Vergara had since passed away. On this

trip, he met with General Lázaro Cárdenas, former president of Mexico, to discuss the land grant issues. General Cárdenas was most forthright in his advice. "Well, I do not promise I can do everything, but I promise to do the best I can. Independent of that, I should tell you one thing. That is, if you are not willing to see blood spilled, forget about all this."[13] The following year, in 1962, Tijerina again sought out Cárdenas. And again Cristobal and Rosita also made the trip. Its purpose was to discuss communal land rights since Cárdenas, as president, had returned lands to the native tribes to form *ejidos*. It was Cárdenas's opinion that communal lands are the perpetual property of a community or city.[14] This coincided with Tijerina's views on the communal land grants in New Mexico. Three months later, in September 1963, he and Rosita traveled to Mexico again and stayed three months. In January 1964, he and Rosita were back in Mexico City. He met with labor unions and sought out the Mexican secretary of state. The assistant to the secretary, Donato Miranda Fonseca, received him. Rosita stayed at the home of Dolores "Lolita" Rebeles, while Reies returned briefly to Albuquerque to finalize plans for the car caravan into Mexico later that year. Rosita celebrated her quinceañera at the Rebeles' home; Reies returned for that event. In July 1964, Reies, with Rosita in tow, made another trip to Mexico City, but he was jailed in Chihuahua City, Mexico while en route. He was released the next day, and immediately sought out the Mexican attorney general, Luis Echeverría Álvarez, when he arrived into Mexico City.

Deported from Mexico

Echeverría listened to his plans for a car caravan, its purpose, and took the documentation Reies had on the land grants, including the memorandums earlier presented to President López Mateos in 1959 and 1964. He was deported the next day, August 8, 1964, to San Antonio, Texas. Reies sent David, his son, to bring Rosa back from Mexico. The same Echeverría that had deported Tijerina became president of Mexico in 1970. As president until 1976, he made it possible for Tijerina to travel to Mexico despite the restrictions of his parole.

President Echeverría extended a written invitation to him to come to Mexico City and meet with him. With that letter, Tijerina was able to obtain his parole officers permission to leave the state in August 1975. On that occasion, near the city of Texcoco, he and Rosita were involved with the making of the commercial film on his exploits, *Chicano,* directed by Jaime Casillas.[15] While on this trip he also made time to inform the Mexican presidency that he was going to organize another automobile caravan from the United States into Mexico. He prepared a memorandum on that event and presented it to President Echeverría on October 28, 1975. The memorandum asked him for three things: (1) establish an office at the executive level to coordinate Chicano/Indohispano affairs; (2) study the land grant claims and the validity of those titles with a legal opinion; and (3) approve the car caravan into Mexico. Tijerina wrote, "The president told us that night all three items were viable."[16] The requested report on land grant claims was prepared by Dr. Sergio Garcia Ramirez, the assistant secretary to the attorney general of Mexico, and forwarded to Tijerina, who received it December 26, 1975. He thought "the report was favorable to our claims. The Mexican report has lifted the spirit of our people."[17]

Despite many letters from Tijerina, no U.S. president invited him to meet and discuss his concerns over land grant claims. He was consistently ignored and only once received a form letter of acknowledgment. Now, on the eve of 1976, he knew what he wanted for his family.

Tijerina's Thirty-Day Fast

Tijerina decided to start a thirty-day fast with in the new year, 1976. During the fast, he also began to write about his struggles for the land for the last twenty years.

> I would limit myself to talking about the struggle for the land, the land
> that belonged to my people since the signing of the Treaty of Tordesillas
> on June 7, 1494. If I wrote about my struggles with the church, I wouldn't
> finish by 1976. I'd have to add ten more years, and I wanted to finish this
> work by 1976. I will reach the age fifty in September 1976.[18]

Tijerina explained what he wanted to write in his memoir. It is worth repeating the words he penned between January 20 and 31 in their entirety:

In this month of fasting, my mind and spirit helped me reflect and meditate on the justice and true liberty that I seek for my brothers. During this time, I reviewed the history of my people, the injustice and the theft of our land; the clash of our cultures; the Anglos' mentality; the destructive direction that the United States is taking, its sexual liberties and use of drugs; and family disintegration. The Anglos, through the various corporations they control, had put the entire nation in danger. Given the conditions we find ourselves in, we must choose the road most convenient to us so that we do not perish along with the Anglos. We must think about ourselves. This is a very critical hour. We should not pay for the crimes of the Anglos in the United States. It is time for us to chart our own course and mark our own time. We must totally repudiate the mentality and lifestyle of our oppressors. The Anglo has used his best tactics and secret agents to destroy the spirit of our people's movement. He tries to take our courage away and make us forget the significance of our victories in New Mexico: June 5, October 2, and June 8.

He made a maximum effort to break up my family, to make me pay for Salazar's blood, to poison the blood of my brothers so that they would hate me, but he failed in all of that. The spirit of courage and justice is still firmly growing in the community.

I offered my fast of thirty days for this great victory against the government and its agents. During the fast, I lost forty pounds, but my health is in good condition. Every day, during the fast, many of my supporters came to see me from the north, south, east, and west. I had fasted up to eleven days before, but never had done thirty. During my fast, I only drank water. Just before I finished my fast, Felipe Santianes suggested we all gather and celebrate the last day of my fast. And, on January 31, in front of my supporters, I had my first meal, chicken soup.[19]

The probes he sought the authorities to make into Salazar's murder did not materialize. He continued to be plagued by that albatross around his neck. He continued to receive death threats, even relayed via his siblings such as his sister, Josefa, who had also received a call urging her to get Reies to stop looking into that murder.[20] His children were harassed in school. He took Isabel out of school on February 16, 1976. He began thinking it was best to move to Mexico and away from this terror and oppression.[21] Near the closing of his autobiography, Tijerina made his feelings known about his travails with the courts and his struggle for land recovery.

> The White House has had me tied down for eight years. Since June 1969, I have been in prison, I have not been freed completely. I am only free on parole, but they watch my every move, hoping I make a mistake.... For the past twenty years, Anglo power has sought to paralyze me, but it has failed. As I finish this work of reflection on my life of struggle for twenty years, I feel strong and sure. My people are ready. They are not the same timid and cowardly people I met when I first met them. There are few brave ones, but the few are the ones that make the struggle. The majority just follows the brave ones. The movement is on from Texas to California, with New Mexico as the axis.[22]

On February 21, 1976, Tijerina headed to Mexico to stay with Don Pepe Trejo in San Juan del Rio, Querétaro:

> My family and I left for Mexico under the cover of darkness so none of my enemies would detain us. We got as far as San Juan del Rio, where I have good friends. One of them, Don Pepe Trejo, had an empty house available. He offered it to my family without accepting a penny for rent. I stayed there with my family for two months. Here in San Juan del Rio, Queretaro, I feel very secure and safe with my family, except for the CIA.[23]

The reference to the CIA stems from a *New York Times* article of August 3, 1975, reporting that the agency had a secret list of fifteen hundred organizations it considered enemies of the United States; included in that list were the Alianza and its leader, Reies López Tijerina. Supposedly, Senator Frank Church with support from Congress had ordered the CIA to destroy such a list, but it still existed—in Tijerina's mind, to be sure.[24]

On September 22, 2000, I wrote the CIA requesting under 5 U.S.C. Section 552, as amended, and 50 U.S.C. Section 431, (FOI/PA) any documents on "Reies Lopez Tijerina, founder of the Alianza Federal De Pueblos Libres in New Mexico." The CIA response from Kathryn I. Dyer, information and privacy coordinator, dated September 6, 2001, was "No records responsive to your request were located." There was no indication that any possible relevant files had been destroyed, as has been the case with other files at other times for other subjects.

The CIA's Project CHAOS

While Tijerina was battling with DA Sanchez, culminating in his mid-1967 citizen's arrest effort at the Tierra Amarilla Courthouse, President Johnson was busy with two major developments. First, U.S. intelligence, namely the National Security Agency (NSA), was monitoring the impeding Israeli war with three Arab nations, the Six-Day War. Second, the opposition at home to the Vietnam War was escalating and fueled by the media. The *New York Times* had begun to report on CIA activities around the world. Beginning in early February 1967, *Ramparts* magazine in a series of articles exposed the CIA-funded National Student Association and infiltration of the AFL-CIO via Jay Lovestone, a union official. Antiwar rallies were increasing and were now being joined by notables such as Reverend Martin Luther King Jr. and noted philosopher Bertrand Russell. Then the riots began in U.S. cities, some 160 of them just in 1967. In Newark, New Jersey, local police and the National Guard killed twenty-three people. In the Detroit blowout, thirty-four more people were killed by police, National Guard, and U.S. Army paratroopers called in to quell the rioting. President Johnson suspected a conspiracy orchestrated by foreign powers using white and black radicals. He called on Richard Helms, director of the CIA, for help.[25]

The CIA had for years engaged in domestic surveillance. It had opened domestic mail, tapped phones, broken into homes and businesses, and spied on individuals in the United States. In August 1967, President Johnson pressured the CIA for more extensive intelligence-gathering on domestic targets; and, the CIA began Operations CHAOS, MERRIMAC, and RESIS-TANCE.[26] These three programs were aimed at U.S. citizens, residents, and organizations. By the time they ended this in 1974, some thirteen thousand people were in the CIA's files; seven thousand were U.S. citizens. A thousand organizations had CIA files. Under Project 2, agents targeted student organizations and students. The CIA went as far as to create and fund a front, the National Student Association, as the umbrella to attract these radical students and monitor them up close. When *Ramparts* magazine first looked reported on the National Student Association's funding from the CIA, Richard Ober, the director of Special Operations Group with oversight of CHAOS and the other programs, directed the Internal Revenue Service to audit the magazine and placed all the writers, editors, publisher, and associates of the magazine under surveillance.[27] More of this history and the CIA's domestic activities were uncovered by the Church Committee on Intelligence during its hearings in the middle to late 1970s and reported in several government publications.[28]

Frank Rafalko, a CIA operative for nearly four decades, worked on MH/CHAOS from its inception and has a different opinion on the nature and scope of this program. He claims the CHAOS targets were limited to certain Americans: radical leftists and black militants.[29] The purpose of MH/CHAOS was "to determine if the American Left or black militants were under foreign control."[30] His last assignment during late summer 1974, under orders from William Colby, then CIA director, was to destroy all soft files, computer tapes, and FBI reports compiled under CHAOS. The destruction continued until it was reported by the *New York Times*.[31] He also claims that the number of targets of CHAOS listed by the Rockefeller Commission was incorrect, that Colby's numbers given to the president of the United States was more accurate: 6,629 files on Americans, known by CIA insiders as the "Family Jewels."[32]

Both Presidents Johnson and Nixon, in light of increasing domestic unrest and specific opposition to the Vietnam War, believed, according to Rafalko, that foreign agents were prompting these subversives and agitators. "Between 1963 and 1968," during the Johnson administration, "there were 369 civil rights demonstrations, 239 black riots and disturbances, 213 white terrorists attacks, 104 antiwar demonstrations, 91 campus protests, 54 segregationist clashes with counterdemonstrations, and 54 anti-integration demonstrations," all of which prompted the formation of the Kerner Commission to find the root cause of these disturbances.[33]

Jefferson Morley claims the CHAOS program indexed the names of three hundred thousand Americans in the agency's Hydra computer system. "CHAOS opened files on 7,200 individuals and more than 100 organizations. More than 5,000 reports were sent to the FBI."[34] Rafalko lists twenty important areas of CIA operational interest around the world to ferret out and monitor U.S. citizens engaged in conduct that might rise to the level of being under the control of foreign governments; among these cities were "Mexico City, Santiago, and [CIA CENSORED]."[35]

> Principal concern was for coverage of foreign involvement in the extremist antiwar movement; extremist student/youth/faculty groups; black, Chicano, and Puerto Rican extremism; deserter/evader support and inducement; and international aspects of domestic underground media. We were interested in various organizations, which included, among others, the People's Coalition for Peace and Justice, the National Peace Coalition, the Student Mobilization Committee, the Black Panther Party, the Puerto Rican Socialist Party, the Students for a Democratic Society, Dispatch News Service, Newsreel, Liberation News Service, and *Ramparts*.[36]

What about MH/CHAOS Interest in Chicanos?

I made a FOIA request for files held by the CIA under my name, not Tijerina's, and received a ten-page document with copies of articles (four pages) dated November 21, 1972, at the top left with a caption "PRIORITY (EYES ONLY)" and a handwritten entry on top right of the page, "HQS-2485 21 Nov 72." Below the caption were three lines: CHAOS, then redacted information; and toward the bottom more redacted information. The next page, page 2, had my name and titles, all in capital letters, as chairman, Crystal City, Texas, School Board and a leader of La Raza Unida Party / (redacted). On this same page is more redacted information; and lower on this page another number "3. Appreciate any CHAOS-Related INFO able proved re this activity." Page 3 just has the caption "END OF MESSAGE." The remaining three pages are legal size and labeled "Dispatch" and are dated at bottom right December 12, 1972. Just below this entry is a stamped block with this wording: "Approved for release Date: 16 JUL 1976." This dispatch in the subject line reads: "CHAOS Visit to Mexico City of Chicano Delegation." There follows "Forwarded as Attachment 1. Herewith, are newspaper clippings covering the 21-25 November 1972 visit to Mexico by a Chicano delegation headed by Reies Lopez Tijerina and Jose Angel Gutierrez." A few lines are redacted, and then comes the conclusion by the preparer of this document:

> [Redacted first words], it was apparent they failed to generate any groundswell of local support for the Chicano "cause" in the United States. It was also obvious that, even within the space of two or three days, there was division among the various self-proclaimed leaders of the Chicano movement who put in an appearance.

Page 2 of the dispatch contains a list of the Chicano delegation (redacted) and in items 3 and 4 is information on the conference held at the National Autonomous University of Mexico, (UNAM) with names of speakers: "Arturo Sanchez Rodriguez, Director of 'La Raza' magazine; Antonio Rodriguez, a lawyer from Los Angeles; Olga Villa, from Notre Dame; Dr. Juan Gomez and Prof. Narciso Aleman (identified in paragraph 2. above)." This is a reference to the entirely redacted item on prior page. The last page of the dispatch is more CIA agent observations on the event, other activities, and more names, "Jose Angel Gutierrez, Mario Cantu, Bert Corona . . . Isais Rojas Delgado."

The point of this departure in the narrative is to provide documentary evidence that the CIA lied about the existence of any files on Reies López Tijerina. The CIA disclosure also has stamped on its pages a notation that the information had been approved for release since July 16, 1976.[37]

Meetings in June 1976 at Los Pinos with President
Luis Echeverría Álvarez

Undaunted by CIA surveillance, Tijerina traveled to Mexico City to meet with President Luis Echeverría.

I met with the Pres of Mex at *Los Pinos* [the Mexican White House] to confirm the last details of the international caravan scheduled for June 5. Harmonia, my daughter, was four today [March 8]. The president took her in his arms and gave her a kiss.[38]

Upon his return to Albuquerque to continue organizing and planning the international caravan, the FBI was waiting.

An FBI official, Sam Jones, called me to ask details about the caravan. I got very irritated. I reminded him that he had detained me once in 1964 and that they would not be able to do this again. He lied to me. When I asked him where he was from, he gave me the name of another state. But his Anglo friends told me he was from here. In other words, he was educated in New Mexico.[39]

Tijerina made these entries in his autobiography about this trip.

Today [June 5, 1976], our caravan left for Juarez. We crossed the border at five in the afternoon. June 12 the president of Mexico received our eighty-six delegates at the presidential residence, Los Pinos. The Attorney General [*Secretario de Gobernación*] Pedro Ojeda Paullada ... was with the president. During our presentation, we talked about the protections we felt we deserved under the Treaty of Guadalupe Hidalgo. The President ordered the Attorney General to conduct a study on the issues presented. In summary, what my brothers and I asked the president was for Mexico to take our complaints to the United Nations. This treaty was an international one, between the United States and Mexico, and limited jurisdiction applied in that forum only to nations. In 130 years since the United States signed the treaty, it has not done justice and has violated our human rights. That's why it was natural that we would come to Mexico and ask this country to present our case before the United Nations and to form a special international commission to investigate our complaints. Attorney General Ojeda Paullada made an appointment with me that very night.[40]

We met with the President again at Los Pinos [on July 9, 1976]. Pedro Ojeda Paullada explained why the land in Texas was off limits in Mexico. Supposedly, Mexico and the United States had signed a treaty on September 8, 1923, covering the land grants in that state, 433 of them. Because of this, Mexico could not open new discussions about these properties. Upon listening to this explanation, the president interrupted and said, "I plan to discuss this with the president of the United States, because taking it to the United Nations could result in delay and possibly even losing the request." He began talking about trying to resolve our problem by tying it to discussions that were coming in the near future about the salinity of the Colorado River. He asked me to stay another week to work with the attorney general on the content of these negotiations and to prepare a textual narrative about the issues. I accepted.[41]

I returned to Mexico [on July 15] to meet with the president and finalize what we had started to work on. I stayed there until July 24.[42]

The FBI's Watchful Eye

In early 1976, February 23, the Bureau requests of the SAC, Albuquerque that the office "ReAQteletype 2/23/76 captioned as above. Promptly submit contents of referenced teletype in form suitable for dissemination." The "referenced teletype" is in "RE: Reies Lopez Tijerina Mexican American Militancy EM-SA"; and this is a game changer. The subject matter: Mexican American militancy was now a new program being conducted by the FBI.

The teletype sent to the director of the FBI and SAC, El Paso from the SAC, Albuquerque has the designation of "Mexican American Militancy" also. The first three to four lines of the message are redacted. The next full paragraph verifies that Tijerina still resides at the Alianza address but adds that the building now has another sign posted outside: "Institute for the Research and Study of Justice." The transmission continues with some favorable narrative:

> No information has come to the attention of the Albuquerque Division that Tijerina has been involved in any acts of violence or that he has carried firearms since his imprisonment in 1974. [Three lines redacted] advised Tijerina completed his parole and imprisonment on June 9, 1974. The subsequent probation expired on November 11, 1974. [One line redacted] Tijerina has not been involved in any violence nor has he carried firearms since [redacted block of information at bottom left, about six short lines] that time. [Redacted first words] Tijerina has found "Peace Activities" more lucrative than his former violent activities. Tijerina has been very much involved with the Brotherhood Awareness programs which are reportedly for the purposes of creating peace and brotherhood between peoples. Tijerina has met often with Governor Jerry Apodaca of New Mexico; the Attorney General of New Mexico; the Archbishop; and in addition, he has received a great deal of newspaper publicity because of these activities.
>
> [Three lines redacted] advised Tijerina was sentenced to the New Mexico State Penitentiary at Santa Fe, New Mexico, on June 26, 1974. He was released from prison December 18, 1974 and is still on parole. [Redacted] Tijerina has obtained from the New Mexico State Probation and Parole Director, Santos Quintana, written travel permits to travel to Mexico to act as consultant for movies being produced by the brother of Luis Echeverria, President of Mexico. In this regard, Tijerina has met several times with the President of Mexico. (p. 2)

Tijerina did make a trip to Mexico during late 1975 and returned to the United States in 1976. (p. 3)

President Echeverría Visits San Antonio, Texas

Before his term was up, however, President Echeverría again came to San Antonio, Texas, to promote trade and the establishment of a branch of the national university of Mexico, Universidad Nacional Autónoma de México (UNAM). The occasion was also a prelude to the annual celebrations held in Mexico and in many U.S. cities on the anniversary of Mexican independence, Las Fiestas Patrias, around the second week each September. Texas governor Dolph Briscoe and city officials from San Antonio sponsored a breakfast in honor of the Mexican president on September 8, 1976. I had invited Tijerina as part of my delegation from Zavala County, Texas, to this event. I notified the Mexican presidential staff that Tijerina and I would both be at the breakfast.[43] Once before in 1973, President Echeverría had visited San Antonio and I had wrangled invitations for Tijerina and myself and others to be in the audience for a breakfast held in his honor.[44]

Reies López Tijerina was seated at the dais next to President Echeverría at his request, much to the chagrin of the San Antonio mayor and Texas governor. Tijerina took the opportunity to again ask for a meeting with him to discuss the September 8, 1923, treaty involving Texas land claims. Tijerina had a copy of the fifty-three-year-old treaty and another agreement signed in 1941 involving a land exchange. After the breakfast, President Echeverría invited Tijerina to the Palacio del Rio San Antonio Hilton hotel to review the terms of these agreements. The Mexican president "assigned Jose Gallastegui to meet with me and find a solution to the problem that I posed. He asked me to come to Mexico, but I could not." Tijerina did return a month later to meet with the Mexican deputy secretary of state, Jose Gallastegui on October 15. "A ten-person delegation accompanied me, and we presented our claims for land in Texas to him. I felt good about this meeting. It was the first time we had actually made a claim and been listened to."[45]

The United States and Mexico Change Presidents

1976 was the year of transition in the Mexican presidency and in the United States. Jimmy Carter won the presidential election in November, as did José López Portillo in Mexico. In July 1977, Carter named Cyrus Vance as his secretary of state and soon thereafter Julian Nava as ambassador to Mexico—a historic first to have a person of Mexican ancestry in that role. There were problems with this appointment in that another ambassador for trade with Mexico, Robert Krueger from Texas, had been appointed shortly after his defeat for a U.S. Senate seat in 1976. The Mexicans wanted to know who the real ambassador was and if Nava really had the ear of President Carter or was just a token appointment. Secretary Vance also named Chicano scholar Ralph Guzman to be deputy assistant secretary for inter-American affairs, another first.[46]

Dr. Guzman knew his Chicano politics and its diverse array of activists and politicians and quickly recommended that a Hispanic advisory group be named for relations with Latin America, namely Mexico. Such a group, comprised of influential Hispanics from all quarters, would surely blunt and derail the growing Chicano-Mexican relationship that had developed since the Echeverría years. This dialogue had been initiated during the first months of creating the Raza Unida Party in Texas with later help from Tijerina.[47]

José López Portillo, the New Mexican President

While the Mexican presidents did listen to Chicano concerns Tijerina and I expressed to them, they did not act as Tijerina had hoped. President Echeverría had chosen as his successor as his party's nominee for president José López Portillo, and he made it a point to have him meet with us on several occasions during the presidential campaign. One of those occasions was in Juarez on November 15, 1975. Tijerina and I both felt that Portillo, while he was not like Echeverría in demeanor or character, was genuine in assuring us of continued relations with the both of us. He promised me that as soon as he was president, he would increase the number of scholarships for Chicanos to study medicine, which he did. And he promised Tijerina he would review the reports made for Echeverría on the land grant question and reopen the talks with him at first opportunity as president.

President López Portillo in early 1978, about a year after having taken office on December 1, 1976, informed Tijerina that Mexico would not pay Texas land grant heirs any settlement money over the 1941 agreement or any other treaty arrangement.[48] Tijerina antagonized the new Mexican president by his remarks at a press conference in Mexico City severely criticizing President Jimmy Carter as a hypocrite for not investigating the scores of murders of Mexicans and Mexican Americans at the hands of U.S. local police. Tijerina also implied that President Portillo was complicit in that laxness by not calling on Carter to have the FBI investigate murders of Mexican workers in the United States.[49] President Carter may have listened to the criticisms from Tijerina and other Chicano leaders about his concern for "human rights" in other countries, but not in the United States.

Another area of hot friction between the United States and Mexico, at this time, involved Carter's energy secretary, James Schlesinger, who served the first two years of this administration, until August 13, 1979. Mexico was awash with natural gas that was being mostly flared and not consumed, in order to get to the crude oil below. The United States proposed Mexico build a pipeline to supply needs for natural gas directly into the United States. Mexico began building and by the time the pipeline reached Ciudad Victoria, Tamaulipas, some 250 miles south of Brownsville, Texas, Secretary Schlesinger dictated to Mexico the price the United States was willing to pay for the natural gas, which was not near the market price. Mexico diverted the pipeline west toward Monterrey and continued to flare much of its natural gas.

To Carter's credit, in 1978, he proposed for the first time in the history of the FBI a charter to limit the powers of the agency and govern the scope of activities it engaged in as part of investigating crime. Carter also proposed a separate charter for the foreign intelligence and counterintelligence functions of the FBI. The charters were presented to Congress on July 31, 1979.[50]

The U.S. State Department Strategy: Divide, Intervene, Neutralize

Dr. Ralph Guzman's recommendation to create a group comprised of influential Hispanics to advise the secretary of state on Latin American affairs and, specifically, the relations with the government of Mexico (GOM) was accepted by newly elected Jimmy Carter. The purpose of such a group with regard to Mexico was to blunt and neutralize the growing Chicano dialogue with the GOM, which had begun during the Echeverría administration in 1968. At that time, under the organizational name of the Mexican American Youth Organization (MAYO), we organized one-day issues summits, usually on a Saturday, across the state of Texas. The format was efficient and action oriented; in the morning we discussed problems faced by our people in that area of the state and prioritized them. After lunch, the local participants proposed solutions to those problems, and by late afternoon an action agenda was agreed upon to tackle those issues and problems. MAYO had a reputation for doing direct action, typically school walkouts, farmworker protests, antiwar demonstrations, and teach-ins and sit-ins on various topics and issues. When we took on the action agenda of the issues summits, we usually were most successful.

At one such summit, a representative of the GOM was present, Jorge Agustín Bustamante, a PhD from Notre Dame and a lawyer in Mexico City. His doctoral dissertation was his experience in crossing into the United States as an undocumented worker. He knew firsthand the issues involved in immigration and farmworker organizing, which were beginning to make headlines in both countries at that time. Dr. Bustamante, in turn, reported to the GOM on his impressions of our event, which drew great interest in Mexico, and at the Autonomous University of Mexico (UNAM). Eventually, UNAM developed a Chicano studies curriculum, and the Mexican foreign relations secretary created a Chicano desk to monitor the growing militancy of our community in the United States. Given this context, I was able to approach the Mexican president when he visited San Antonio in 1970.

One MAYO group protested his presence in the city for his role in the massacre of students at Plaza Tlatleloco in downtown Mexico City during the Olympics of 1968. Another MAYO group, but under the name of the

Raza Unida Party (RUP), led by me and working in collaboration with Dr. Bustamante, sought to meet with President Echeverría. It was no magic that he chose to meet with my delegation and not the other one, led by Mario Cantu. In typical Mexican presidential fashion, he promptly asked why we wanted to meet with him and not the U.S. president; what could Mexico possibly do for U.S. citizens? My response was quick and to the point: "Not a photograph." His staff and the U.S. Secret Service detail assigned security for him did take plenty. Instead I asked for full scholarships to study medicine in Mexican universities and for him come back and attend to the medical needs of his Mexican citizens living among us. He was taken aback by my reference to his responsibility. He queried me as to why we did not enroll in U.S. medical schools. For the next few hours instead of a few minutes we had been told was allotted for this meeting, I related the history of segregation and violence directed at both Mexicans and their progeny, the Chicanos; the denial of basic services to both communities; and the violence at the hands local and state police we constantly suffered. He was most intrigued and interested in learning more. Toward the end of our meeting, he asked for how many scholarships I wanted. I responded with fifty. He then signaled for someone in his entourage to get my contact information and arrange for my travel to see him in Mexico City. After the meeting we immediately began to make plans and arrangements for this first group of recipients, *becarios,* to arrive and be placed in universities across the country. It was my turn to be taken aback at how quickly this relationship in unchartered waters began to unfold.

This was the beginning of many other programs with Mexico, but specifically the Becas Para Aztlan program. It was expanded to fifty per year during the López Portillo administration and leveled off during the presidency of Miguel De La Madrid and ended with the last graduate during the administration of President Ernesto Zedillo.

I basically represented Chicanos before the GOM in early 1970 after our electoral victories in three South Texas cities and counties in April and May that year under the banner of our Chicano-based political party, the RUP. After the 1972 national RUP convention, Tijerina joined me in traveling to Mexico to meet with the president. César Chávez refused my overtures to join the Raza Unida Party and visit the GOM. Chávez always claimed he was a Kennedy Democrat and that Mexican scabs were his enemy in organizing farmworkers in the United States. Our arguments to go speak with Mexican unions about helping educate the Mexican worker who was contemplating crossing into the United States fell on Chávez's deaf ears. Rodolfo "Corky" Gonzales and others shared his views of Mexico's president, such as Bert Corona of the Mexican American Political Association, the Rodriguez brothers with Casa Hermandad of Los Angeles, Dr. Juan Gomez Quiñonez of UCLA's Department of History and Chicano Studies Program, and Mario Cantu of San Antonio, who continued to see Echeverría as the assassin of student protestors and not the new Mexican president. Moreover, Corky Gonzales could not speak Spanish.[51] When Tijerina and I traveled to Mexico, he pressed the land claims and monetary reparations from Mexico, while I proposed national projects such as the Becas Para Aztlan scholarships for Chicanos to study medicine, supplying bilingual education materials, economic development projects, intensive seminars on Mexican government and society, and, Mexican government purchases of U.S. products through Chicano agents. We also established communication with the various Mexican political parties, their leaders, and some of the national elected officials. Our visits soon drew the attention of other Chicano organizations and the U.S. government. One of our biggest assets in this dialogue was that, unlike some other Chicano leaders, and many of the Hispanics, Reies and I were fluent in Spanish. Tijerina's stories delivered in Spanish grabbed the attention of all, particularly President Echeverría who could not believe the extent of violence directed Tijerina and his family. Echeverría, in my presence, offered Tijerina a haven in Mexico for the safety of his family, specifically a large home in Ciudad Satelite, a growing suburb at the northern limits of Mexico City. I never knew if he ever took possession of this home, but I do know he took title. Tijerina's non-Mexican citizenship had to be brokered to own property in his name. Tijerina asked for my advice and help with this matter. I was also present on October 28, 1975, when Tijerina who was in Mexico City consulting with the filmmakers of his movie, *Chicano,* was invited over to the presidential residence, Los Pinos, to join President Echeverría and me. On that occasion, Echeverría suggested very emphatically that Reies had to write his autobiography so the movie would be closer to Tijerina's version of events than just fictionalized portrayals of what had happened to him. He promised him the book would be published in Mexico. "I guarantee it," the president said.[52]

U.S. Embassy, Mexico City to State Department Teletypes

From a FOIA request to the Department of State, I obtained three documents that indicate the active role the U.S. embassy played in relaying information on the Chicano Connection, the group Tijerina and I had been developing with the Mexican government. The first is a three-page teletype dated October 29, 1979, from the U.S. embassy in Mexico City to the secretary of state. These documents do not show redacted material, as the FBI used to do with words or lines blacked out and entire pages withheld; now the FBI places boxed spaces where text would have been.

In this first State Department-released communication the person sending the transmission begins with this underscored narrative:

> The Mexican Government is apparently going forward with plans to enhance relations with Mexican-American (Chicano) groups in the United States. Coming in the wake of occasional Mexican presidential meetings over the past several years with Chicano delegations, the establishment of an institutionalized GOM-Chicano means of consultation reflects a gradual lowering of the traditional Mexican inhibitions against involvement in U.S. internal affairs.[53]

Following this opening statement is a blank space of about six lines. Then follows,

> Following up on initial contacts made during the Echeverria administration, President Jose Lopez Portillo (JLP) has met a number of times since the beginning of his administration with representatives of Mexican-American organizations. The primary tangible outcome of these meetings,

besides public expressions of sympathy for Mexican undocumented worker rights, has been the establishment of a modest scholarship program for Mexican-American students here and the formation of an office for special projects and bilingual education in the Secretariat of Public Education to facilitate cultural-educational activity among the Chicano community. (See Reftel for background on GOM-Chicano Contacts.)

Unfortunately, the FOIA disclosure does not contain the "Reftel" with those contacts. The transmission continues with four more numbered paragraphs of content. Number 3 informs on recent meetings held between JLP and Mexican American groups in Mexico City on September 20, 1979: National Association of Farm Workers Organizations (NAFO); Mexican American Legal Defense and Educational Fund (MALDEF); National Peace Council; Hispanic Affairs Office of the Catholic Conference of the United States; La Raza Legal Alliance; Migrants Legal Action Program, and the National Coalition for the Hannigan Case. JLP also met separately with representatives of the United League of Latin American Citizens (LULAC).

Item 4 discusses another meeting JLP held in New York City prior to meeting with President Carter. In addition to meeting again with LULAC, NAFO, and MALDEF, there were leaders of the Raza Unida Party. JLP promised these Chicano representatives to discuss with Carter protections for Mexican undocumented worker human rights and that he would form a mechanism to maintain contact with Chicano groups. In item 5 mention is made that upon returning to Mexico, JLP made the centerpiece of "his highly nationalistic October 1 report to the Nation that he had not hesitated to raise the undocumented/Chicano rights issue in Washington." Item 6, the last full entry, advises that JLP had named Pedro Ojeda Paullada, his labor secretary, to coordinate contacts with Chicano organizations. There could have been more information which was redacted.

The following page states that Secretary Paullada named Guido Belsasso as the coordinator for such meetings with Chicano organizations. Belsasso is the director of INET, an acronym not fleshed out with a full name anywhere in the teletype [*Instituto Nacional de Estudios del Trabajo*]. Interestingly, items 8, 9, 10, and 11 are blank but begin with these type of words: "Belsasso told us ...," "Belsasso told us that ...," "Belsasso also indicated ...," "Belsasso explained ..." It seems that Belsasso became the voice of the GOM that the CIA turned to for information via some agent, either an FBI Legat or a CHAOS operative in the U.S. embassy.

The last two numbers, 12 and 13, contain opinion that Paullada's work with Chicano groups would be in conflict with Alfonso Rosenzweig Diaz, as the head of the intersecretarial group on migratory workers; and, that the Electrical Workers Union in Mexico, joined by two dozen Mexican American leaders of U.S. trade union locals, were circulating a petition with their signatures demanding the president's political party, the Partido Revolucionario Institucional (PRI), support their demands for protection of migratory workers. Rosenzweig Diaz is simply described as the "FONSEC Undersecretary." The rest of the narrative is blank.

The State Department's second two-page record is dated November 10, 1979, from the U.S. Embassy in Mexico City to the secretary of state. The subject is "GOM Committee Meets with Chicano Group." The content consists of ten numbered paragraphs, however, numbers 1, 3, 5, 6, 7, 8, 9, and 10 are entirely or partially blanked out. Item 2 summarizes that a Mexican American organization asked the GOM to intercede with USG on education of children of undocumented workers and the Hannigan case.[54] "Mexican government tentatively agrees with this request but plans to raise issues only through working groups of bilateral consultative mechanism ... not through special demarches. End summary."

Item 3 advises that representatives of LULAC and some from NAFO had met with three Mexican secretaries, "Foreign Relations, Labor, and Education—but not the President of Mexico" October 29-November 1 in Mexico City: "The meeting received no press coverage." Item 4 begins with a divisive note regarding an alleged "controversy with LULAC over which group shall have leadership role in GOM-Chicano dialogue." Apparently, the report states, most of the organizations that originally had met with the Mexican president on September 10 in Mexico City and September 27 in New York were not at this meeting. The U.S. embassy writer notes that the reference to the "Forum" in the transmission is not to be confused with the American G.I. Forum, which "did not participate in recent contacts with the GOM." Item 5 continues reporting that LULAC was very expressive in stating the appreciation it had for the contact with the GOM in that it enhances the "organization's political status in U.S." LULAC mentioned that at its 1979 national convention it had "four U.S. Cabinet members and Senator Kennedy" in attendance and extended an invitation to "President Lopez Portillo to attend February 1980 convention in San Antonio. But GOM sources believe [about four blank lines follow]."

Extensive redaction is in item 6, which begins "LULAC, we have been told by GOM officials present" and is then redacted for about ten lines. Item 7 has only one word, GOM, and then the entire paragraph is blank for about eighteen lines. Item 8 states:

Begin Comment: GOM apparently has now taken first tentative action, under newly institutionalized GOM-Chicano means of consultation (See Reftel), to accept—at least tentatively—human rights complaint from Mexican-American organization for discussion with USG. (In addition [blank after this word for about twenty-five lines to end of column on this first page].)

Item 8 mentions

President Lopez Portillo's raising of such complaints in September with President Carter. GOM sources point out that Labor Secretary Ojeda, in his previous post as Attorney General, periodically raised Chicano complaints with his U.S. counterpart.

Item 9 turns to State Department analysis of these events. First, the author is quick to point out that the human rights complaints raised by JLP involve "Mexican citizens, not Mexican Americans." Second, "This fact coupled with apparent decision of GOM both to avoid publicity for LULAC meeting and to raise human right complaints in routine working group meetings—rather than through publicity—generating special demarches or presidential messages—[the rest is blank for about five lines]." Item 10 ends this transmission with a few words: "with regard to substance of LULAC-raised rights issues, [blank for remainder of the page]."

The last of the three files released on this request, dated March 17, 1980, is from the U.S. Embassy to the secretary of state. The subject is "Mexican Government Policy Toward the Mexican-American Community: An update (Post Reporting Program)."

Item 1 is blank. Item 2, "Summary," begins with

> Mexican government welcomes the formation of a unified "Commission" of Mexican-American organizations to dialogue with the GOM—a development that the GOM hopes: (A) will enhance relations with the Mexican American community and limits complications for the GOM flowing from Mexican-American Inter-Organizational rivalry, and (B) will permit management of the dialogue with the Mexican-American community in a manner that will avoid unintentional aggravation of U.S.-Mexican Relations. While the Mexican Government now intends to maintain contact primarily with Mexican-American groups represented in the new "Commission," left elements of the PRI-affiliated trade unions, leftist opposition parties (including those that receive some financial help from the GOM), and communist-affiliated groups will probably continue to cultivate more militant Mexican-American groups and seek to exploit Mexican-American and Mexican undocumented worker grievances for domestic political gain. End Summary.

Item 3 discloses that, according to U.S. embassy staff opinion,

> after heated discussions among visiting Mexican American and Hispanic organizations in Mexico City, February 18, officials of the GOM Secretariat of Labor . . . were successful in mediating an agreement. . . . under rotating chairmanship . . . as an implicit trade-off for this unification the new "Commission" would be the GOM's principal interlocutor with the Mexican-American community.

The State Department's pursuit of intelligence about this new commission and the GOM's position continued to be the subject of concern as reflected in item 4's content. Apparently, U.S. embassy representatives met with Guido Belsasso on March 12 "to discuss GOM relations with the new commission. But item 5, which follows, is blank but for the first three words, "Dr. Belsasso indicated," and the entire right side of the page is blank as well. It could be that item 5 continues the narrative on this right side and it is redacted, or that item 5 ends quickly after the first three words because there is only space for another two to three lines on the left column. The next page is entirely redacted and blank.

Role of Dr. Ralph Guzman against the Chicano Connection with Mexico

Dr. Rafael Cortez Guzman, born in Moroleon, Guanajuato, Mexico, in 1924 and brought to the United States as a child during the Depression of the 1930s, was raised in East Los Angeles. He became known as Ralph in the barrio as well as in school. Like many others of his generation, he joined the navy during World War II and served with distinction. Unlike others of his immigrant background and heritage of the time, he used his earned military benefits to pursue higher education. He obtained both a BA and master's degrees in political science by 1960. His PhD was obtained from the University of California at Los Angeles while working with others on the first comprehensive study of the Mexican American people, published in 1970.[55] He also served as associate director of the Peace Corps, doing stints in Venezuela and Peru. Utilizing his academic credentials, he served as associate professor of politics and community studies at the University of California at Santa Cruz until 1977. He took leave and became part of the administration of President Jimmy Carter. In 1980, he returned to Santa Cruz. He suffered a massive heart attack and passed away at age sixty on October 10, 1985.[56]

During his doctoral work, he visited Crystal City, Texas, and interviewed me, first on our Winter Garden organizing project in 1968-1969, then after our first municipal victories under the name of Ciudadanos Unidos, United Citizens, and last after my first election as county judge for Zavala County, Texas, in 1974. I assumed then that he was conducting research as any other political scientist would do given this second coming of Chicano control of a Texas city. The first electoral victory by Chicanos in Crystal City had been in 1963; and both events had been documented by John Shockley in his book *Chicano Revolt in a Texas Town.* In 1977, Guzman was now inside the State Department and working against what Tijerina and I were doing with Mexico.

The Fight with Texas Governor Dolph Briscoe

Our efforts at economic development once Raza Unida Party officials held almost all the public offices in Zavala County by 1976 were varied, but one caught the attention of Texas governor Dolph Briscoe. We were trying to buy twenty-five hundred acres of land to farm under a cooperative venture comprising ex-migrants. We already had successful chicken and hog cooperative ventures going; now we needed farmland for animal feed and fresh produce. This same governor on a prior occasion had called on President Richard Nixon to stop any federal funding for our health clinic without success in 1970. In 1975, Governor Briscoe called on President Jimmy Carter to stop federal funding of our OEO grant application, which had received high grade points for full funding from all review panels. Briscoe was successful in lobbying Carter against us, and he ordered OEO to not fund our grant. We sued the government in Washington, DC, and lost. Our case file before Watergate judge John Sirica was, and is still, kept under seal due to national security concerns. We felt we had proved the collusion between Briscoe and Jimmy Carter to deny us approved funds from OEO with telephone logs, correspondence, and public comments made and reported in the press; we still lost the case. We also lost the ability to obtain the case file because it had been classified and executive privilege invoked in blocking admission of evidence on the collusion. I am sure that if we ever obtain this file, the handprints of the FBI, CIA, and State Department will be all over the pages of evidence withheld.

The Guzman Plan

The gist of Guzman's multifaceted plan while working for the State Department in 1978 was to discredit the Chicano Connection group Tijerina and I had developed with the Mexican presidents. One first step was to legitimize one of the two other groups working on creating a new Hispanic Commission to dialogue with Mexico as an alternative group to ours. Guzman began to recruit members from these two groups to become an advisory group to the secretary of state as a way to legitimize them as persons with access to the top levels of the U.S. government. At the same time, he would make them part of the State Department's community outreach and transparency. He succeeded at all three purposes is short time. To accomplish these goals, Guzman had identified his targets for recruitment into the web he was spinning for creation of the advisory group.

Early on, Dr. Guzman began casting about for people who could supply him with information about the meetings Tijerina and I had been having with the Mexican presidents. He found Rodolfo Balli Sanchez and Al Perez. They both met with Guzman at various times in DC to list the organizations and the dynamics at play between individuals and the groups, to coalesce them into a group as the principals in forming the Hispanic Commission. The name "Hispanic Commission" changed at different times to the "Bilateral Commission" and the "U.S. Hispanic-Mexican Commission," renaming the group to obscure the "Chicano Connection," as they referred to Tijerina and my efforts, even inside the halls of the State Department.

Guzman wrote at least three memorandums that I obtained from the State Department by FOIA request. The first two-page memo is dated February 11, 1980, and has as a subject heading "Conversations with Rodolfo Balli Sanchez and Al Perez on the 'Chicano Connection.'" Guzman reports that Balli Sanchez and Perez have formed a group called "a 'Bilateral Commission' per Lopez Portillo's Request." The second group Guzman reports on is "a competing group of Chicanos headed by Ruben Bonilla, LULAC President and Attorney Sandoval of Texas." Guzman opines that the "group headed by Sanchez appears to have the inside track to Lopez Portillo." And he concludes that this Bilateral Commission is an outgrowth of "visits made to Mexico by Chicano leaders who also belong to the National Forum of Hispanic American Organizations" (p. 1). The second page is confusing, or perhaps Guzman is confused as to his players. He begins the page with "I thanked Gonzales and Perez for bringing their concern to the Department." Who is Gonzales is not explained. Next, what concern were they bringing to the Department? An explanation or elaboration on these "concerns" is not elaborated upon in this memo. Then Guzman states:

> I detect a wish to work closely with the Department. These are serious, sophisticated Chicanos who mean well; they want to be responsible. If we, here in the Department, make special efforts to understand them serious international and domestic problems can be avoided.
>
> I strongly recommend that they be listened to with our usual courtesy and that they be thanked for their efforts to be responsible and for placing the interests of the United States Government above ethnic considerations. Both Gonzales and Al Perez represent a solid, moderate sector of Chicano society.

The second, two-page document is titled "Briefing Paper" just below the Department of State letterhead. The subheading is "THE CHICANO CONNECTION." I assume the author to be Guzman only because it was included in the packet of documents received from the Department of State under my FOIA request. It appears to be a report on what transpired in Mexico City on February 18, 1980, between the leaders of U.S. Hispanic and Mexican American organizations and Mexican secretary of labor and social welfare Pedro Ojeda Paullada and Guido Belsasso. The purpose of that meeting allegedly was to form the "commission" for dialogue with the GOM.

The author of this briefing paper begins with the usual and timeworn cliché that Mexico has been reluctant to maintain cultural and political linkages with Mexican Americans for concerns "that these contacts could be seen by the USG as Mexican interference in U.S. domestic politics." The pivot, however, is in the next sentence: "President Lopez Portillo seems to have broken with tradition last September when he met with Chicano leaders in New York, the day before his Washington meeting with President

Carter." The remaining paragraphs repeat much of what was teletyped from the US embassy previously on this matter. The competing groups agreed to a rotating chairmanship between LULAC and the National Forum; the GOM has designated Guido Belasso as the main contact; there was little time to discuss issues at the February meeting, so they were left for further discussion in April 7–8 when Belsasso would return to DC. "Leftist elements within the PRI-affiliated trade unions," "leftist opposition parties, and communist affiliated groups" could be expected "to continue to cultivate more militant Mexican-American groups and seek to exploit Mexican-American and Mexican undocumented worker grievances for domestic political gain."

The wording of this paper matches exactly that of the embassy teletypes of 1979 and March 17, 1980, previously referenced. Someone is simply copying prior statements.

In the closing of this briefing paper, Guzman or its unknown author suggest a hypocritical "TALKING POINT (IF A SUITABLE OPPORTUNITY ARISES)" with this forked-tongue statement:

> We are of course pleased by the courtesy shown by the Mexican Government in meeting with private U.S. organizations, especially Mexican-American groups. But we certainly agree that the proper channel for dealing with migration and other bilateral issues is through the intergovernmental process, in particular the working groups of the Consultative Mechanism. (p. 2)

Among the released documents is a two-paragraph response dated February 19, 1980, from "ARA/MEX-Everett E. Briggs" to "ARA/DAS-Ralph Guzman" that confirms Guzman as the author of the nameless memo previously mentioned. Briggs thanks Guzman for the memo and agrees that Balli Sanchez and Perez "can be valuable assets to our understanding of Mexico and U.S.-Mexico relations." Briggs urges Guzman to encourage them to "touch base with Bill Pryce at our Embassy in Mexico, since he is the individual who works most closely with Guido Belsasso and his staff." Attached to this one-page memo from Briggs without reference is another one-page listing of ten members of the U.S. Hispanic-Mexican Commission with an eleventh name, Rodolfo Sanchez, National Coalition of Hispanic Mental Health and Human Services Organization.

April 8–9, 1980, Meeting in Washington, DC

The three-page memorandum of conversation dated April 10 with additional two-page enclosure, probably written by Guzman, is an attempt to report verbatim what transpired and who said what at the two-day meetings. I assume it was Guzman who authored this report because only three persons are listed as participants Paullada, Belsasso, and Guzman. On the eighth Guzman attended a luncheon hosted by SER–Jobs for Progress, Inc., attended by U.S. labor secretary Ray Marshall and Ojeda Paullada, who spoke on Mexican training programs and "twice alluded to the need for social justice and the more equitable distribution of Mexico's wealth." The next day, April 9, a small reception-dinner was held for both labor secretaries with ambassador-designate Julian Nava in attendance. Curiously, Ojeda Paullada in his toast offered to friendship and understanding and "pledged his government's support of Ambassador-designate Nava even though there may be others who may not be ready to express a welcome" (p. 1). He added that the GOM saw Nava as "a representative of all the American people, not just a special cultural sector" and that he understood that in Mexico, Nava would represent the president of the United States.

Guzman inserted a personal note, writing that he knew Guido Belsasso from when he "worked with Chicano patients at UCLA," and from 1978, when both were at the Colegio de México. Guzman felt that Belsasso was "close to Ojeda and to Lopez Portillo." He added that "Guido probed for the following:—relationship between Krueger and Nava; who Krueger and Nava answered to in the Department"; and "who was higher in hierarchy, Nava or Krueger?" Guzman writes that he explained the different roles for Krueger and Nava, and that both worked closely; that Krueger worked a multiplicity of U.S. agencies; that this special job reflects the importance with which Mexico is held; that Krueger worked for the secretary of state and was staffed by ARA while Nava was an ambassador in ARA (p. 2); and, that he, Guzman, was one of two deputies without a regional responsibility working in three areas of congressional, human rights, and public affairs.

Whatever content followed this last statement is redacted until mid-page, which has the two closing paragraphs. In one is found a bit of information on the Wednesday meeting "between Ojeda Paullada and the members of the U.S. Hispanic/Mexican Commission (what some of us call 'the Chicano Connection'). They discussed nine points but reached no final decision (see copy of report). The group agreed to meet in Mexico at an early date." Guzman in the concluding paragraph enters his opinion on the Mexican labor secretary: "Ojeda can be characterized as an extremely cautious official. His overtures to the Hispanics were diplomatic and tentative" (p. 3).

The two-page enclosure, which may be the report alluded to previously, attached to the Memorandum of Conversation is from "Ruben Bonilla, Chairman-U.S. Hispanic Commission" to "Members of the U.S. Hispanic Commission." There is no date. The ten members of this group are listed in order as American G.I. Forum-Lupe Saldaña; ASPIRA of America-Mario Anglada; IMAGE-David Montoya; Mexican American Women's National Association (MANA)-Wilma Espinoza; Mexican American Legal Defense and Education Fund (MALDEF)-Al Perez; National Association of Farmworker Organizations (NAFO)-Dr. Sal Herrera; National Council of La Raza-Raul Yzaguirre; National Forum of Hispanic Organizations-Rudolfo Sanchez; SER-Jobs for Progress-William Bonilla; and League of United Latin American Citizens (LULAC)-Ruben Bonilla. Apparently, sometime during this weekend meeting the name for this amalgam of groups came up and it was decided to use the name "U.S. Hispanic Mexican Commission." MALDEF, together with MANA and American G.I. Forum, were charged with examining the legal ramifications of incorporating such a group in light of the Logan Act.[57] Dr. Belsasso sat in on the first meeting of these nine members. The group decided to meet again in D.C. on April 28 (p. 1). The last page of the enclosure lists seven items as recommendations. In ranked order, item 1 seeks Mexican funding for a scholarship program, Los Pinos Scholarship, item 2 seeks Mexican funding for two endowed chairs, Mexican American Study Centers, one at University of Texas at Austin and the other at the University of California at Los Angeles, for the study of U.S.-Mexico relations, item 3 seeks Mexico's support for the U.S. Senate initiative to establish a Center for U.S. Mexico Relations, item 4 requests of the Mexican government its position on the H-2 program, the education of undocumented children, and the Hannigan police brutality case, item 5 expresses the commission's strong support for Ambassador Nava and its concern that Mexico receive him in a manner reflect a positive and enthusiastic recognition of his credentials and heritage, item 6 asks the Mexican government to urge U.S. private sector representatives to include more Americans of Hispanic descent when doing business with Mexico, and item 7 seeks information from Mexico on the COPLAMAR Program utilized to address educational needs of other language groups in Mexico because the commission wants to see its applicability and replicability to the needs of Hispanic Americans in the United States. Lastly, the commission requests that the Mexican government provide a comprehensive overview of the policies and workings of the López Portillo administration to include briefings on health, welfare, housing, employment, economic development, administration, energy, foreign affairs, education, and other pertinent areas agreed upon by members of the commission.

Nothing that I am aware of in news accounts, academic works, or information exchange with Mexican officials and some of these organizational heads ever resulted from these requests.

The Department of State Meetings with Hispanic Leaders

On October 29, 1979, Secretary of State Cyrus R. Vance, at the urging of Hodding Carter III and Anthony Lake, met with two hundred Hispanic American leaders at the State Department building to discuss more regular meetings and relations. Included in the larger group of two hundred were Hispanics from various nationalities, primarily Mexican, Puerto Rican, and Cuban. The secretary agreed to meet with them quarterly and sought to have smaller group meetings sometime in the summer of 1980, according to an action memorandum dated May 20, 1980, from the same staff members already mentioned. Apparently, Secretary Vance moved up the smaller meeting schedule and met with some of them on April 2, 1980. The present-ers were top officials from the State Department. The day was structured around six roundtable discussions on Latin American, Cuban, Caribbean Basin, Mexican relations, affirmative action, and a session on develop-ments in the Persian Gulf and South Asia. The secretary made some closing remarks before the group filed out to the Henry Clay Room for a reception. The secretary was pleased with the meeting, I surmise, because the State Department continued, as recommended by Guzman, to have at least three such meetings with Hispanic leaders.

On September 17, 1980, Anthony Lake and William J. Dyess were again seeking a date from the Secretary to meet with about twenty Hispanic leaders to discuss issues of importance to them, particularly about Mexico and Cuba. They proposed October 16, 1980, as the meeting date for a quick forty-five-minute meeting followed by a reception to close the day of pre-sentations the Hispanic leaders would sit in for. Those that attended the one-day seminar at the Department of State were David Montoya and Raul Yzaguirre from the U.S. Hispanic-Mexican Commission; the mayor of San Juan, Puerto Rico; the vice president of Pan American University in Edin-burg, Texas; the dean of instruction, Eduardo Padron, of Miami-Dade Com-munity College; Al Zapanta from ARCO Venture corporation in Los Angeles; National Urban Fellows president Luis Alvarez of New York; Eduardo Avila of NALEO; Domingo Garcia, president of the Puerto Rican Coalition; Jose Longoria, the CEO of LULAC; Diana Munatones, director of community rela-tions for KNX-TV in Los Angeles; Diana Torres of COSSHMO in Washington, DC; Juan Manuel Garcia-Passalacqua, of the Fundación Educativa Ana G. Mendez in Rio Piedras, Puerto Rico; and David Lizzarraga, president of the East Los Angeles Community Union (TELACU).

The all-day sessions these Hispanic leaders were to listen to were led by top-ranking officials in the State Department, including every top level Hispanic employee in the building: Francis Gomez, the deputy assistant secretary for the Bureau of Public Affairs, was the proposed moderator for the meeting, and to open the session were three welcome speeches by Wil-liam J. Dyess, assistant secretary for the Bureau of Public Affairs, Warren Christopher, the deputy secretary of state, and Esteban Torres, the special assistant to the president at the White House. An overview of Latin American relations, human rights and the Caribbean was to be given by another trio: W. Anthony Lake, director of Policy Planning Staff, Patricia Derian, assistant secretary of the Bureau of Human Rights and Humanitarian Affairs, and William G. Bowdler, assistant secretary of the Bureau of Inter-American Affairs. More sessions with top-level officials would continue through the day and include these Hispanic officers: Edward Coy, George Del Valle, Mari-Luci Jaramillo, and Roy Flores. The secretary of state would make an appearance and offer quick remarks just before the reception was to be held in the Diplomatic Reception Area.

The third in a series of meetings with the Hispanic leaders occurred on October 16, 1980, as planned. Newer additions to those previously invited had to be made. Those newly invited who did attend were Ruben Cruz of ABC-TV in Chicago; Maurice Ferre, mayor of Miami; Carmen Junco, president of the National Association of Spanish Broadcasters; Angel Manzano, acting director of MALDEF; Hernan Padilla, the new mayor of San Juan, Puerto Rico; Mara Patermaster, director of the National Puerto Rican Forum office in Washington, DC; and Jorge Zapata, acting director of the National Coalition of Hispanic Mental Health and Human Services Organizations.

The reception was held in the Thomas Jefferson Room, and additional Hispanic employees from other federal agencies were invited, swelling the number to over one hundred guests at the reception.

President Portillo Ignores the Hispanic Commission

In 1976 Tijerina continued organizing car caravans into Mexico to dramatize his agenda and sought appointments with the Mexican president requesting help that he could render on the land claims. Tijerina still wanted to have some nation present the demand before the United Nations for a return of these lands to rightful Indohispano heirs.

On more than one occasion, President Portillo expressed negative comments about the State Department's Hispanic Commission to me and Tijerina. For example, he asked us both why Mexican Americans would want to mix Puerto Ricans and Cubans as members of the Hispanic Commission when they should know he had no interest in the Cuban or Puerto Rican communities. He also complained that the members of the Hispanic Commission only wanted a photo opportunity with him and that they had trouble articulating their positions in Spanish. He told me after the first visit with members of the commission that he no longer would make himself available; his staff could meet with them.

President Portillo also never funded a single proposal submitted under the name of the Hispanic Commission. He did ask me to include one or two of them in my projects, so they would know whom he favored. I did invite and begin to work with Ed Morga, national president of LULAC, and Abel Amaya, then with the University of Southern California, in selecting *becarios* for the program. Years later, under the Zedillo administration, a Mexico-U.S. Solidarity Foundation, led by Graciela Orozco, was formed to continue the work we started with the Colegio de México on seminars to teach Chicanos/as how Mexico worked. Principal players in this organism became Raul Yzaguirre of NCLR and the American G. I. Forum. Tijerina and I were excluded. The foundation closed its doors at the beginning of this century.

Tijerina and I also began to be pushed out, not by the State Department or the Hispanic Commission members or any other group, but by Mexican presidential politics. Each potential aspirant for the presidency has a team that manages their network of contacts and loyalists. Discipline and loyalty are extreme virtues to have from top to bottom. When the leader moves up in position, so do members of his or her team. When the leader loses out, the team stays in place and waits; there are no defections. Defecting is the kiss of political death. Aspirants just wait their turn. With the election of Vicente Fox, not a member of the PRI, this slow team ascendency came to an end. Since then, new factions have emerged within and without the major political parties. Tijerina and I simply did not keep up with who was with whom over the years. And the "Chicanologos," or experts on Chicanos in the United States, died, retired, and moved on, such as Dr. Agustín Bustamante, who became the university head of Colegio Frontera Norte (COLEF), and did not reside in Mexico City anymore. He spent more time as a visiting scholar at Notre Dame and administering the COLEF in Tijuana, Baja California, than in Mexico City.

The "Chicano Connection" with Mexico's presidents and other components of the GOM was completely lost with the election as president of Vicente Fox. None of our Chicano groups or members of the Hispanic Commission that I knew had personal ties to any of the new officeholders in the Mexican government. President Fox named Juan Hernandez, a Fort Worth, Texas, resident and the son of his ranching neighbor in Guanajuato, Jalisco, to a post heading outreach to Mexican nationals in the United States. This was the beginning of what had now become the Consejo Consultivo del Instituto de los Mexicanos en el Exterior (CCIME) within the ministry of foreign relations. The CCIME comprises elected and appointed representatives from the United States who attend quarterly meetings in Mexico to discuss issues relevant to the Mexican-ancestry community in the United States and Canada. Chicanos have been replaced in the dialogue with the GOM by Mexican nationals and U.S. citizens or residents.

Chicano Activist Reunion, 1989

When Tijerina participated in the Chicano Activist Reunion held in San Antonio, he was again talking about moving permanently to Mexico. His marriage to Patricia Romero was not going well, and his children were almost fully grown. The youngest child from Patricia, Donna, named Danitha, was sixteen years old, Harmonia was seventeen, and the others were over twenty-one years of age. His attempts at organizing around Brotherhood Awareness, Harmony and Peace never got traction with the younger generation who now called themselves Hispanics. His trip to Palestine/Israel and his views on that lost homeland made him anti-Semitic among his critics. His income was reduced from his budget during the Alianza years, limited to an occasional speaking honorarium at U.S. colleges and universities. Yet he had substantial money in a New Mexico bank.

The FBI files obtained on Tijerina do not go beyond 1980, except for one document from the Comptroller of the Currency (OCC) dated in 1990.

This five-page document is yet another criminal investigation of Tijerina. The first four pages explain the authority of the agency to monitor national banks, particularly violations of the law involving financial transactions (p. 1). The second page is the actual intake form listing the First National Bank in Albuquerque as the location of the questionable financial transactions for accounts 727-601-149 and 759-791-945. The first one was under the name Reies L. Tijerina. The second account was under the name of "Reiese" Tijerina. The account holder's address is listed as Box 863, General Delivery, Coyote, New Mexico, 87012-0863. The third page, titled "Continuation Sheet," is the detail of the questionable transactions. In summary, on July 31, 1990, Tijerina cashed a $5,000 check drawn on his first account, at the Sandia Plaza branch of the First National Bank (FNB). That same day he cashed another $5,000 check on the same account at the Manzano Branch of FNB. The next day, August 1, he went to the Del Norte branch of FNB and cashed a $5,000 check drawn on the second account. Then he cashed another $5,000 check at the Montgomery branch of FNB, presumably on the second account, but the report does not state. He then went to the Manzano branch of FNB and cashed another $5,000 check. The total from the two accounts withdrawn was $25,000.00.

On August 2 he made out two checks for $10,000 each payable to (redacted name) and that same day the person went to the West Central branch of FNB and cashed a check for $10,000. The person also went to the Adobe branch of FNB and cashed another $10,000 check, a total of $20,000 drawn on this second account. On Friday, August 3, Tijerina went to the Montgomery branch again and cashed another $5,000 check and then, at the Del Norte branch of FNB, another check for $1,000. Later that day, Tijerina made a check for $20,000 out to (name redacted), who went to the main office of FNB in Albuquerque and cashed the check. During these four days, a total of $76,000 was drawn out in cash from the Tijerina accounts (p. 4). The last page, page 5, contains only the statutory listings for various crimes and the physical addresses of OCC district offices across the country.

No disposition of this investigation into a possible financial transaction crime was reported subsequently. And only Tijerina and perhaps the person with the redacted name—his current widow, Esperanza—knew what was done with this large sum of cash money.

Exile into Mexico

Tijerina moved permanently to Mexico sometime during the early 1990s; there he met his third wife, Esperanza, in Uruapan, Michoacán. When he divorced Patricia Romero is not clear, nor is the date he left for Mexico. I surmise he did so sometime after the $76,000 was withdrawn from his accounts in 1990 and before 1993. He married Esperanza by proxy in Albuquerque in 1993 and again in Uruapan the following month, on July 19. In 1994, after his home was bombed again near Coyote, New Mexico, he had enough. He lost all his possessions, library, and many of his books. Because Esperanza could not lawfully cross into the United States, he had left her in Michoacán; after his insurance claim was denied—according to him, because it was a criminal act and not accidental or due to any negligence—he left for Mexico. This firebombing, like others in years past, was never fully investigated or resolved.

In April 2005, nearly a decade and a half later, he and Esperanza moved to live on the Mexican side of the border in Juarez, Chihuahua, across from El Paso. Tijerina was sick and needed medical care and financial assistance. The folks at Centro de Salud Familiar La Fe health clinic in El Paso, Sal Balcorta and Estela Reyes-López, opened immigration law doors and helped him legally cross Esperanza into the United States. They also helped obtain the naturalization papers for Esperanza and get him medical attention for his diabetes and prostate cancer. The following year, in 2006, they moved their residence from Juarez to El Paso to be near La Fe clinic. Reies López Tijerina died in El Paso, Texas, on January 19, 2015.

Presidents, Attorney Generals, FBI Directors, 1945–2019

YEAR	PRESIDENT	ATTORNEY GENERAL	FBI DIRECTOR
6/27/45	Harry S. Truman	Tom Clark	J. Edgar Hoover
7/27/49	Harry S. Truman	J. Howard McGrath	J. Edgar Hoover
4/4/52	Harry S. Truman	James P. McGranery	J. Edgar Hoover
1/21/53	Dwight D. Eisenhower	Herbert Brownell, Jr.	J. Edgar Hoover
10/23/57	Dwight D. Eisenhower	William P. Rogers	J. Edgar Hoover
1/21/61	John F. Kennedy	Robert F. Kennedy	J. Edgar Hoover
9/4/64	Lyndon B. Johnson	Nicholas Katzenbach	J. Edgar Hoover
11/28/66	Lyndon B. Johnson	Ramsey Clark	J. Edgar Hoover
1/20/69	Richard Nixon	John N. Mitchell	J. Edgar Hoover
2/15/72	Richard Nixon	Richard Kleindienst	J. Edgar Hoover
5/3/72	Richard Nixon	Richard Kleindienst	L. Patrick Gray*
4/30/73	Richard Nixon	Richard Kleindienst	Wm. D. Ruckelshaus*
5/25/73	Richard Nixon	Elliott Richardson	Wm. D. Ruckelshaus
7/9/73	Richard Nixon	Elliott Richardson	Clarence M. Kelley
10/20/73	Richard Nixon	Robert Bork*	Clarence M. Kelley
1/4/74	Richard Nixon	William B. Saxbe	Clarence M. Kelley

1/4/75	Gerald Ford	Edward H. Levi	Clarence M. Kelley
1/20/77	Jimmy Carter	Richard L. Thornburg	Clarence M. Kelley
1/26/77	Jimmy Carter	Griffin Bell	Clarence M. Kelley
2/15/78	Jimmy Carter	Griffin Bell	James B. Adams*
2/23/78	Jimmy Carter	Griffin Bell	William H. Webster
8/16/79	Jimmy Carter	Benjamin Civiletti	William H. Webster
1/23/81	Ronald Reagan	Wm. French Smith	William H. Webster
2/25/85	Ronald Reagan	Edwin Meese	William H. Webster
8/12/88	Ronald Reagan	Richard L. Thornburg	John E. Otto*
8/15/91	George H. W. Bush	Richard L. Thornburg	William S. Sessions
8/16/91	George H. W. Bush	Wm. P. Barr	William S. Sessions
1/25/93	William Clinton	Stuart M. Gerson	Floyd I. Clarke*
3/12/93	William Clinton	Janet Reno	Louis J. Freeh
1/20/01	George W. Bush	Eric Holder*	Thomas J. Pickard*
2/2/01	George W. Bush	John Ashcroft	Robert S. Mueller, III
2/3/05	George W. Bush	Alberto Gonzales	Robert S. Mueller, III
9/17/07	George W. Bush	Paul Clement*	Robert S. Mueller, III
9/18/07	George W. Bush	Peter Keisler*	Robert S. Mueller, III
11/9/07	George W. Bush	Mike Mukasey	Robert S. Mueller III
1/20/09	Barack Obama	Mark Flip*	Robert S. Mueller III
2/3/09	Barack Obama	Eric Holder	Robert S. Mueller III
9/4/13	Barack Obama	Eric Holder	James B. Comey
5/9/17	Donald Trump	Jeff Sessions	Andrew McCabe*
9/14/17	Donald Trump	Jeff Sessions	Christopher Wray
11/7/18	Donald Trump	Matthew Whitaker*	Christopher Wray
2/14/19	Donald Trump	William Barr	Christopher Wray

*Acting

Notes

Chronology

1. Document is on file under my name with the papers on Reies López Tijerina, Special Collections, Michigan State University, East Lansing, Michigan.

Introduction

1. See Felipe Fernandez-Armesto, *Our America: The Hispanic History of the United States* (New York: Norton, 2014), for a review of this history dating back to the 1400s.

2. Among the best to chronicle these years and the struggle by land grantees to hold title is Maria Amparo Ruiz de Burton's historical novel *The Squatter and the Don*, first published in 1885 and republished in 2004 by the Modern Library. See also Leonard Pitt and Ramón A. Gutiérrez, *Decline of the Californios: Social History of the Spanish-Speaking Californias, 1846–1890* (Berkeley: University of California Press, 1999).

3. See an examination of the making and terms of this treaty by Richard Griswold del Castillo in *The Treaty of Guadalupe Hidalgo: A Legacy of Conflict* (Norman: University of Oklahoma Press, 1990).

4. A basic reader on this resistance is Robert J. Rosenbaum, *Mexicano Resistance*

in the Southwest (Dallas: Southern Methodist University Press, 1998).

5. See a very well-documented narrative of the 1915 Plan de San Diego (Texas), which called for the retaking of the U.S. Southwest by Mexicans, in Benjamin Heber Johnson, *Revolution in Texas: How a Forgotten Rebellion and Its Bloody Suppression Turned Mexicans into Americans* (New Haven: Yale University Press, 2005).

6. Rep. Steven Pearce (R-NM) on July 13, 2018, filed H.R. 6365 to create a commission to investigate land grant claims stemming from the Treaty of Guadalupe Hidalgo; it was referred to Committee on Natural Resources. In Texas, the State Historical Commission has authorized the placement of a historical marker near the site of the Porvenir Massacre of 1918 in Presidio County. The male members of the community were murdered by Texas Rangers and U.S. Army cavalry troopers. Their homes and possessions were burned and the lands they owned, over two thousand acres, taken by others.

7. See Armando Navarro, *Mexican American Youth Organization: Avant-Garde of the Chicano Movement in Texas* (Austin: University of Texas Press, 1995), for a first scholarly look at this organization. And see Juan Sepulveda, *The Life and Times of Willie Velasquez: Su voto es su voz* (Houston: Arte Público Press, 2005). See the PBS documentary *Willie: Your Vote Is Your Voice,* produced and directed by Hector Galan in 2016 for the Latino Public Broadcasting. See www.lpbp.org and www.pbs.org/video/2365837935/.

8. In 1970 Ralph Guzman, professor at University of California at Santa Cruz, published an article that became a monograph given the demand for its content, *Mexican American Causalities in Vietnam* (Santa Cruz: University of California, Santa Cruz, 1970). He estimated 20 percent Mexican American casualties from 1961 to March 1969. In 1970 the U.S. census reported that Mexican Americans comprised 10 percent of the U.S. population. These statistics and data are elaborated upon in Lee Ibarra's *Vietnam Veteranos: Chicanos Recall the War* (Austin: University of Texas Press, 2004), p. 4. Other works on Chicanos in the Vietnam War are Charley Trujillo, *Soldados: Chicanos in Viet Nam* (San Jose, CA: Chusma House Publication, 1993), which is a narrative based on oral histories; and John C. Trejo, *Carnales: A History of Chicano Vietnam Veterans* (New York: Leeds and York, 2013).

9. The Selective Service system was put in place in response to World War I on May 18, 1917 (40 Stat. 76). It is authorized by Article 1, Section 8 of the U.S. Constitution, which permits Congress "to raise and support Armies. To provide and maintain a Navy." SCOTUS in *Butler v. Perry* (1916) held that the draft did not violate the Thirteenth Amendment's prohibition against

"involuntary servitude." The next modification was the Selective Training and Service Act of 1940, passed on September 16, 1940, and ended on March 31, 1947. The Selective Service Act of 1948 created the system in place during the years covered in this work. Several changes were made, such as lowering the age from nineteen to eighteen and a half for conscription, creating exemptions for students, married men with children, only children, those whose service would cause hardship to their family (typically used by farm owner for agricultural need), divinity students, and conscientious objectors. In 1969 President Nixon signed an amendment to the Military Selective Act of 1967 to modify the draft to have young men selected based on a random selection process (lottery system). This system was scrapped on March 29, 1975, by President Ford, whose own son, Steven Ford, failed to register as required. The system was reintroduced in July 2, 1980, by President Reagan in response to the Soviet invasion of Afghanistan. On April 27, 2016, the National Defense Authorization Act extended the authority for draft registration to women. From 1980 to the present there have been twenty-three exemptions from military service registration. See www.sss.gov/ for the system's website that contains facts, figures, and some legislative history.

10. Ibarra, *Vietnam Veteranos*, p. 10.

11. These two names for the organization are used interchangeably throughout the secondary literature. Even Tijerina used both names. They both refer to the organization Tijerina incorporated in New Mexico to champion the rights of the land grantees and empower the land recovery movement. On occasion a third name was used by Tijerina: Alianza de Pueblos y Pobladores (Alliance of Towns and Settlers).

12. The Alianza helped publish a colorful booklet, *San Joaquin del Rio de Chama*, but with another title on the inside cover, *The Legend of the Town of San Joaquin del Rio de Chama*, with credit to translator Carlos E. Chavez, written by Kathelyn Koffman (Santa Fe: Synergetic Press, 1983). It relates the story of how their community grant was recorded by the U.S. surveyor but not approved by Congress. The narrative promises "the inevitability that the Liberty Bell, cracked and silent for 200 years, will again ring the words engraved on it: 'Proclaim Liberty throughout the Land unto all the inhabitants thereof.' (Leviticus 25.10)." This is the source of Tijerina's favorite speech on the Liberty Bell.

13. José Ángel Gutiérrez, "Chicanos and Mexicans under Surveillance: 1940-1980," in *Renato Rosaldo Lecture Series Monograph*, vol. 2, ed. Ignacio M. Garcia (Tucson: Mexican American Studies & Research Center, University of Arizona, 1986), pp. 29-58.

14. José Angel Gutiérrez, "Tracking King Tiger: The Political Surveillance of Reies
López Tijerina by the Federal Bureau of Investigation," paper presented at the
Twenty-Third National Association of Chicana and Chicano Studies Annual
Conference, Chicago, Illinois, March 20-23, 1996.

15. José Angel Gutiérrez, *The Eagle Has Eyes: The FBI Surveillance of César Estrada
Chávez and the United Farm Workers Union of America, 1965–1975* (East Lansing:
Michigan State University Press, 2019).

16. Richard Gardner, *Grito! Reies Tijerina and the New Mexico Land Grant War of 1967*
(New York: Bobbs-Merrill, 1971), p. 37.

17. Gardner, *Grito!*, p. 36.

18. There are some discrepancies in the birthdate reported. Tijerina himself,
in *Mi lucha por la tierra* (Mexico City: Fondo de Cultura Económica, 1978),
mentions "my birthday, September 21" (p. 36), and says that 1976 marked his
fiftieth birthday (p. 538). Michael Jenkinson, *Tijerina* (Albuquerque: Paisano
Press, 1968), p. 17, has his birth year as 1927; and Patricia Bell Blawis, *Tijerina
and the Land Grants: Mexican Americans in Struggle for Their Heritage* (New York:
International Publishers, 1971), p. 31, has the date as September 21, 1923.
    Busto spells the mother's name as "Erlinda," without the *H*. Rudy V.
Busto, *King Tiger: The Religious Vision of Reies Lopez Tijerina* (Albuquerque:
University of New Mexico Press, 2005), p. 35.

19. Gardner, *Grito!*, p. 31.

20. Gardner, *Grito!*, p. 36.

21. Gutiérrez, *The Eagle Has Eyes*, p. 36.

22. Peter Nabokov, *Tijerina and the Courthouse Raid* (Berkeley, CA: Ramparts, 1970),
pp. 194 and 197.

23. Hoover's report to the Secret Service mentions the two sisters, Maria de Anda,
married to Pablo de Anda, age forty-two, and residing in Michigan (p. 3); and
Josephina (née Josefa) Gallegos, age thirty-eight, divorced, living at 818 Fifth
Street, Albuquerque, New Mexico, at time of the report (p. 3).

24. Gutiérrez, *The Eagle Has Eyes*, p. 219; Tijerina, *Mi lucha por la tierra*, p. 541.

25. Gutiérrez, *The Eagle Has Eyes*, p. 218.

26. Blawis, *Tijerina and the Land Grants*, pp. 31-33.

27. Gardner, *Grito!*, pp. 41-42.

28. Interview with Maria Escobar, p. 2. Maria has different recollections than
did Reies about dates and events. For example, she claims they attended the
Bible school in Saspamco, Texas; married in "May of 1946"; and stayed in San

Antonio for "fifteen years" (p. 2).

29. Interview with Maria Escobar, pp. 42–47.

30. Daniel E. Tijerina, "Daniel E. Tijerina," in Alan Rinzler, ed., *Manifesto Addressed to the President of the United States from the Youth of America* (New York: Macmillan, 1970), pp. 189–193.

31. ABQjournal.com, obituaries, November 15, 2000. See also the author's interview with Hugh David Tijerina on June 28, 2000, in Albuquerque, four and one-half months before he died.

32. Gutiérrez, *The Eagle Has Eyes,* p. 197.

33. Telephone conversation with Esperanza Tijerina on July 27, 2017, arranged by Estela Reyes, media and communications director for La Fe Health Center. Information provided by Mrs. Tijerina on dates of marriage, her age, and citizenship.

34. See his book, Arnoldo de Leon, *They Called Them Greasers: Anglo Attitudes toward Mexicans in Texas, 1821–1900* (Austin: University of Texas Press, 1983), p. 1.

35. Rodolfo Acuña, *Occupied America: The Chicano Struggle toward Liberation,* 5th ed. (San Francisco: Canfield Press, 1972); Pitt, *Decline of the Californios;* Armando B. Rendon, *Chicano Manifesto* (New York: Macmillan, 1972); Luiz Valdez and Stan Steiner, eds., *Aztlan: An Anthology of Mexican American Literature* (New York: Alfred A. Knopf, 1972); and Matt S. Meier and Feliciano Rivera, *The Chicanos: A History of Mexican Americans* (New York: Hill and Wang, 1972).

36. Carey McWilliams, *North from Mexico: The Spanish Speaking People of the United States* (1948; new ed., updated by Matt S. Meier, n.p.: Greenwood Press, 1990; 3rd ed., updated by Alma M. Garcia, Santa Barbara, CA: Praeger, 2016).

37. George I. Sanchez, *Forgotten People: A Study of New Mexicans* (Albuquerque: Calvin Horn Publisher, 1968).

38. María Amparo Ruiz de Burton, *The Squatter and the Don* (San Francisco: [S. Carson], 1885); ed. Rosaura Sánchez and Beatrice Pita (Houston: Arte Público Press, 1997); with introduction by Ana Castillo (New York: Modern Library, 2004).

39. John R. Chavez, *The Lost Land: The Chicano Image of the Southwest* (Albuquerque: University of New Mexico Press, 1984).

40. Richard L. Nostrand, *The Hispano Homeland* (Norman: University of Oklahoma Press, 1992).

41. Frederick Nolan, *The Lincoln County War: A Documentary History* (Norman: University of Oklahoma Press, 1992).

42. "Treaty of Guadalupe Hidalgo: Definition and List of Community Land Grants in New Mexico. Exposure Draft," GAO-01-330 (Washington, DC: U.S. General Accounting Office, January 2001).

43. Roxanne Dunbar-Ortiz, *Roots of Resistance: A History of Land Tenure in New Mexico* (Norman: University of Oklahoma Press, 2007).

44. David Correia, *Properties of Violence: Law and Land Grant Struggle in Northern New Mexico* (Athens: University of Georgia Press, 2013), pp. 120–145.

45. David L. Caffey, *Chasing the Santa Fe Ring: Power and Privilege in Territorial New Mexico* (Albuquerque: University of New Mexico Press, 2014).

46. Mike Scarborough, *Trespassers on Our Own Land* (Indianapolis: Dog Ear Publishing, 2011).

47. Mike Scarborough, "The Dawes Act of 1887, Court of Private Land Claims Act of 1891 and GAO's Guadalupe Hidalgo Report of 2004 Are Mirror Images of the Government's Negative Attitude toward Indian, Spanish and Mexican Treaty and Property Right's [*sic*] during the Late 1800s and Early 1900s" (Santa Fe, no date, 14 pages).

48. See Scarborough, *Trespassers on Our Own Land,* figure 6, p. 51, for a map of the boundaries of this land grant. The original spelling of the family surname was with a *B,* as explained by the great-grandson (p. 56).

49. Scarborough located the original report by Justice Stone among the papers of New Mexico governor Miguel Otero. See *Trespassers on Our Own Land,* p. 251.

50. Scarborough, *Trespassers on Our Own Land,* p. 253.

51. Scarborough, *Trespassers on Our Own Land,* p. 234. Scarborough cites the Edgar Lee Hewitt file at the Fray Angelico Chavez History Library as the source of the document (p. 233).

52. See my *The Eagle Has Eyes.*

53. Reies López Tijerina, *They Called Me "King Tiger": My Struggle for the Land and Our Rights,* ed. and trans. José Angel Gutiérrez (Houston: Arte Público Press, 2000).

54. Jenkinson, *Tijerina,* p. 101.

55. These tapes are on file under his name in the Center for Southwest Research, Zimmerman Library, University of New Mexico, Albuquerque. The Nabokov papers, eight boxes, are also archived at the Zimmerman Library under his name and collection number MSS 93 BC. Box 5 of the Nabokov papers contains audio cassette tapes of interviews with Reies Tijerina and others involved with the Alianza. The masters of these tapes are locked in a vault controlled by the Center for Southwest Research and are in need of digitizing before they

crumble into nothingness.

56. Blawis, *Tijerina and the Land Grants,* pp. 178–181.

57. K. Gordon Mantler, *Power to the Poor: Black-Brown Coalition and the Fight for Economic Justice* (Chapel Hill: University of North Carolina Press, 2015).

58. Chavez, *The Lost Land,* pp. 139–141.

59. David Correia, "'Rousers of the Rabble' in the New Mexico Land Grant War: *La Alianza Federal de Mercedes* and the Violence of the State," *Antipode* 40, no. 4 (2008), pp. 561–583.

60. Maceo Martinez, *Chicano Movement for Beginners* (Danbury, CT: For Beginners, 2016).

61. Ramón A. Gutiérrez, "The Religious Origins of Reies López Tijerina's Land Grant Activism in the Southwest," in Howard Brick and Gregory Parker, eds., *A New Insurgency: The Port Huron Statement in Its Time* (Ann Arbor: University of Michigan Press, 2015), pp. 289–300.

62. Molly Boyle, "*Tierra o Muerte:* Remembering the Rio Arriba Courthouse Raid," *Santa Fe New Mexican,* June 2, 2017. See also the Associated Press article by Russell Contreras, "New Mexico Marks 50th anniversary of Chicano Courthouse Raid," printed in the *San Antonio Express-News,* June 5, 2017.

63. In 1967 Governor Reagan signed legislation, SB 53, that allowed the use of other languages of instruction in California. In 1973 Governor Dolph Briscoe signed into Texas law a bilingual education bill. The entire matter was legally settled by two SCOTUS cases, *Lau v. Nichols* (1974) and *Plyler v. Doe* (1981). In *Lau* the Court mandated education in the home language of the child, and in *Plyler* it required that immigrant children not only be allowed an education in public schools of all states across the country but also in the home language of the child. Opponents of bilingual education continue to propose English-only instruction and have not been successful at this writing to pass such federal legislation, but have had success in thirty-six states and territories requiring the business of government be in English only. In the southwestern states, only Nevada, Texas, and New Mexico have remained steadfast in not making English the only official language of government.

64. The *Plan de Santa Barbara* came about from a meeting called for that purpose by the Chicano Coordinating Council on Higher Education. Scholars in attendance, in addition to community activists primarily from Southern California, were Gus Segade, Jesus Chavarria, Juan Gomez-Quinones, Gracia Molina Enriquez de Pick, and Rodolfo Acuña. See Rodolfo F. Acuña, *The Making of Chicana/o Studies: In the Trenches of Academe* (New Brunswick, NJ: Rutgers

University Press, 2011), p. 59. See also *El Plan de Santa Barbara: A Chicano Plan for Higher Education. Analyses and Position by the Chicano Coordinating Council on Higher Education* (Santa Barbara: La Causa Publications, 1971); Pitt, *Decline of the Californios;* and Meier and Rivera, *The Chicanos.*

65. See Acuña, *The Making of Chicana/o Studies* for a history of the discipline and building of programs and departments in the country.

66. Rodolfo F. Acuña, *Anything but Mexican: Chicanos in Contemporary Los Angeles* (New York: Haymarket, 1996).

67. See Nicholas B. Lundholm, "Cutting Class: Why Arizona's Ethnic Studies Ban Won't Ban Ethnic Studies," *Arizona Law Review* 53 (2011), pp. 1041-1088, for an analysis of the litigation that ensued over the ban. On August 22, 2017, a federal district judge ruled the ban unconstitutional. He was upheld by a federal appellate court on December 27, 2017. The appellate court went further and prohibited the Arizona state school superintendent from interfering with the implementation of any new program.

68. Trial on the banning of Mexican American studies by the Tucson Unified School District is set for trial in Tucson, Arizona, on June 26, 2017.

69. Susan A. Roberts and Calvin A. Roberts, *A History of New Mexico* (Albuquerque: University of New Mexico Press, 1986), p. 137; on Tijerina, see pp. 309-310.

70. Roberts and Roberts, *History of New Mexico,* p. 310.

71. Roberts and Roberts, *History of New Mexico,* pp. 310-311. Personal anecdote in 2018: a history teacher, a young Hispanic male, at a Cameron County, South Texas, public school with excellent ratings on statewide assessment tests required his students, including my daughter, to write a research paper on a major event or person in history. She asked about a paper on Reies López Tijerina because her father was writing a book about him. The teacher asked her who this person was.

72. Roberts and Roberts, *History of New Mexico,* pp. 311-312.

73. John A. Garcia, *Latino Politics in America: Community, Culture, and Interests* (Lanham, MD: Rowman & Littlefield, 2003, 2nd ed. 2012, 3rd ed. 2017).

74. Kim Geron, *Latino Political Power* (Boulder, CO: Lynne Rienner, 2005) and Lisa Garcia Bedolla, *Latino Politics,* 2nd ed. (Malden, MA: Polity Press, 2014).

75. See Garcia, *Latino Politics in America,* 1st ed., pp. 283, 285.

76. See Garcia, *Latino Politics in America,* 2nd ed., pp. 258, 261.

77. See Geron, *Latino Political Power,* pp. 3, 43-50, 145, 151.

78. See Bedolla, *Latino Politics,* pp. 83-85.

79. See Bedolla, *Latino Politics*, p. 93.

80. See Meier and Rivera, *The Chicanos.* They used the term *Chicano* throughout their book in sections dealing with the Chicano Movement. In subsequent editions they dropped *Chicanos* from the title and reference to "Four Horsemen" and instead used our specific names. I assume this was deference to political correctness, to the fact that there also were women leaders in the Chicano Movement, and to preference for a less radical group identifier. A decade later the term *Hispanic* came into vogue, and the fallback term was *Latino.*

81. Dunbar-Ortiz, *Roots of Resistance*, p. 52.

82. *The Spanish Land Grant Question Examined,* no author listed (Albuquerque: Alianza Federal, 1966), p. 14.

83. *Spanish Land Grant Question,* p. 16. New Mexico became a territory of the United States with the Kearny Code, September 1846, then in Congress on September 9, 1850, and a state on August 19, 1911.

84. See Fernandez-Armesto, *Our America.*

85. I met with Rodolfo Alvarez, editor and publisher of the *Enciclopedia de Mexico,* a universal encyclopedia, in 1976 and convinced him to add a section on the other Mexico, in the United States, which he did in subsequent editions. The Mexican *secretaria de educación* also followed suit in textbooks for the public schools beginning in 1978. This change is significant because Mexican education is federal, meaning all students use the same textbooks in every school in every city and village.

86. Del Castillo, *Treaty of Guadalupe Hidalgo,* pp. 13–14.

87. Del Castillo, *Treaty of Guadalupe Hidalgo,* pp. 180–181.

88. See del Castillo, *Treaty of Guadalupe Hidalgo,* pp. 181–182 for a complete copy of its terms and some history.

89. See the appendices in del Castillo, *Treaty of Guadalupe Hidalgo,* for copies of the treaty and protocol and chapter 5, "Citizenship and Property Rights," for a discussion of Articles 8 and 10, pp. 62–86.

90. Del Castillo, *Treaty of Guadalupe Hidalgo,* pp. 55–58.

91. I discovered this attachment to the treaty consummating the land purchase and used the argument that it was a covenant running with the land in the federal case against the Tucson Unified School District (TUSD) when it sought to continue the segregation of Chicano students and a ban Chicano studies in 1998. The Spanish version of course has Article 10 but Article 8 is also intact

and protects and ensures the entitlement of those in the lands to "life, liberty and full enjoyment of their lands." I argued that, accordingly, these students of Mexican descent, probably descendants of these original *pobladores,* were entitled to live their heritage and culture and learn about their contributions to the United States, which meant their history and language. The court agreed and put aside the defendant's motion to dismiss plaintiff's petition for failure to state a claim and ordered the parties to settlement negotiations. That resulted ultimately in the realignment and reassignment of students, counselors, and beginning of Chicano studies at TUSD. This is the same program banned again by TUSD in 2010.

92. 10 Stat. 308.

93. Del Castillo, *Treaty of Guadalupe Hidalgo,* p. 87.

94. Del Castillo, *Treaty of Guadalupe Hidalgo,* pp. 88-93.

95. See 121 U.S. 325 (1887). Narciso was the son of Charles Bonaparte Beaubien and an unnamed Mexican mother and eligible to ask for a community grant, which his father gave in their names; others did settle on the land. Both Narciso and Stephen Lee were killed in the 1847 Taos Pueblo uprising. Charles inherited the land grant. He sold it to William Gilpin in 1863 despite the fact he could not sell a community grant, and new homesteaders lived there. Gilpin divided the land and later sold the southern half to Costilla Estates.

96. Christine A. Klein, "Treaties of Conquest: Property Rights, Indian Treaties and the Treaty of Guadalupe Hidalgo," *New Mexico Law Review* 26 (Spring 1996), pp. 201-229.

97. See 1876 U.S. Lexis 1423 and www.coutlistener.com, a project of Free Law Project.

98. 26 Stat. 85.

99. See *Kerlin et al v. Sauceda,* 263 S.W. 3rd 920 (2008) for a recent case validating claims to part of South Padre Island and mineral rights to the Balli family, more than 275 descendants of the heir Alberto Balli, nephew to original grantee, Juan Jose Balli. For the story on this claim see the article by Cecilia Balli, one of the beneficiaries, "Return to Padre," *Texas Monthly,* January 2001.

100. See Caffey, *Chasing the Santa Fe Ring,* pp. 18-21, 92-103; and Nolan, *The Lincoln County War,* pp. 450-451. There are more than a dozen discrepancies on dates and some name and places between Caffey and Nolan, but regarding the purpose of this book, nothing of major relevance—whether, for example, he married Julia A. Walz (Nolan, p. 451) or Sarah Jacobs (Caffey, p. 19)—is affected.

101. Caffey's appendixes A and B contains mini-biographies of all the participants in the public corruption schemes that led to dispossessing locals of their lands *Chasing the Santa Fe Ring*, pp. 238–258).

102. Wikipedia, s.v. "Western United States," last modified March 13, 2019, 16:24, https://en.wikipedia.org/wiki/Western_United_States.

103. Juan R. Garcia, *Operation Wetback: The Mass Deportation of Mexican Undocumented Workers in 1954* (New York: Praeger, 1980).

104. Chavez, *The Lost Land*, p. 1.

105. Chavez, *The Lost Land*, p. 3.

106. Chavez, *The Lost Land*, p. 4.

107. Chavez, *The Lost Land*, p. 5.

108. Gardner, *Grito!*, pp. 38, 44.

109. There are numerous sources on the history of the Liberty Bell dating back in time. The topic of its crack and why it does not ring is still of interest. Since 1986 it has been gently tapped annually on Rev. Martin Luther King Jr.'s birthday. A most recent article with a condensed history of the bell by Stephen Fried is "How the Liberty Bell Won the Great War," as the cover title of *Smithsonian* 48, no. 1 (April 2017), with an inside title of "Saved by the Bell," pp. 36–47, 90–94. The History Channel on A+E Networks created a show for television with accompanying article, "Why is the Liberty Bell Cracked?" in 2012; see www.history.com/news/ask-history/why-is-the-liberty-bell-cracked/. This documentary mentions that it cracked at first ring in 1752 after being cast in 1751 at London's Whitechapel Bell Foundry, then, again in 1824 and again later that year while tolling to signal a fire in Philadelphia. Another crack occurred during the funeral of Chief Justice John Marshall in 1835; and, finally it cracked for the last time when being tolled for George Washington's birthday in 1846. Thereafter it was taken out of service. The Abolitionists of the era gave it the name "Liberty Bell."

110. I witnessed hundreds of speeches during the time we worked together. This recollection about the Liberty Bell is from one of those occasions. The other favorite speech was "The Lion and the Cricket," mentioned later in this manuscript.

111. There was no celebration for the Declaration of Independence on the Fourth of July. Some places that got word of the Declaration did toll bells on July 8. It is possible that the Liberty Bell was hung on the eighth but it still could not ring due to the new miscasting. See "5 Surprising Facts about the Liberty Bell,"

at http://blog.efexploreamerica.com/author/adam/.

112. Article 6, Section 2 cases, laws, and treaties are the law of the land.

113. Busto, *King Tiger,* p. 1.

114. Tim Glynne-Jones, *The Book of Numbers* (London: Arcturus, 2007), pp. 26–27. See also Busto, *King Tiger,* pp. 164–165, for the influence of numbers on Tijerina's actions or analysis in hindsight.

115. Glynne-Jones, *The Book of Numbers,* pp. 42–47.

116. James M. Scott, *The Attack on the* Liberty*: The Untold Story of Israel's Deadly 1967 Assault on a U.S. Spy Ship* (New York: Simon and Schuster, 2009.)

117. "The Cost of Israel to the American People," p. 2. See www.IfAmericansKnew.org/202-631-4060.

118. "Cost of Israel," p. 2.

119. Sometimes I would have the foresight to record his conversation. These untranscribed tapes are at the Benson Latin American Collection, University of Texas-Austin, under my personal archival deposit.

120. Original copy of power of attorney is in my archival collection at the University of Texas Benson Latin American Collection under my name. It is dated August 20, 1994 and witnessed by Rees Lloyd, another attorney, Patricia Tober, and Fred Reade.

121. Busto, *King Tiger,* pp. 4–10. In chapters 3 and 5, pp. 77–114 and 142–171, respectively, he delves into the subject matter of his sermons and writings.

122. Seymour M. Hersh, *The Samson Option: Israel's Nuclear Arsenal and American Foreign Policy* (New York: Random House, 1991).

123. Michael B. Kelley, "How Much Does America REALLY Spend on Israel's Defense?," *Business Insider,* September 20, 2012. See www.businessinsider.com.

124. Jens Manuel Krogstad and Ana Gonzalez Barrera, "A Majority of English-speaking Hispanics in the U.S. are bilingual," Pew Research Center, March 24, 2015. The authors found that among U.S. Hispanics 38% speak Spanish, 25 % speak English, and 36% are bilingual. Pew Research (http://www.pewresearch.org/fact-tank) reported on August 13, 2013, that only 37.6 million Hispanics and another 2.7 million non-Hispanics spoke Spanish at home. Speaking (bilingualism) is not the same as reading (biliteracy) Spanish.

125. Busto, *King Tiger,* p. 4.

126. See Mike Wallace, "The Most Hated Man in New Mexico" and "The Hate That Hate Produced," two parts of a three-part series produced by WNTA television

(New York) that first aired July 13-17, 1959. For a favorable treatment from a Chicano perspective, see Jesus Trevino, "*Yo Soy Chicano*" (1972), a documentary also in English, and Jaime Casillas's commercial movie *Chicano* (1975), in Spanish.

127. Gutiérrez, *The Eagle Has Eyes*, p. 133.

128. Gutiérrez, *The Eagle Has Eyes*, p. 210.

129. Gutiérrez, *The Eagle Has Eyes*, p. 169.

130. Scarborough, *Trespassers On Our Own Land*, p. 130.

131. F. Chris Garcia, Paul L. Hain, and Harold V. Rhodes, *State and Local Government in New Mexico* (Albuquerque: University of New Mexico Press, 1979), pp. 7-10, 14-15.

132. Garcia, Hain, and Rhodes, *State and Local Government*, pp. 39-41.

133. Garcia, Hain, and Rhodes, *State and Local Government*, pp. 99, 101-102, 105-106.

134. See figure 2 in Garcia, Hain, and Rhodes, *State and Local Government*, p. 9.

135. Garcia, Hain, and Rhodes, *State and Local Government*, pp. 2-10.

136. Gutiérrez, *The Eagle Has Eyes*.

137. Michelle Hall Kells, *Vicente Ximenes, LBJ's Great Society, and Mexican American Civil Rights Rhetoric* (Carbondale: Southern Illinois University Press, 2018), pp. 211-214.

Chapter 1. The Years as a Fugitive

1. Tijerina wrote in *Mi lucha por la tierra* (Mexico City: Fondo de Cultura Económica, 1978), p. 27, that 160 acres of land were bought, and that seventeen families were the community of Valley of Peace. Richard Gardner in *Grito! Reies Tijerina and the Land Grant War of 1967* (New York: Bobbs-Merrill, 1971), p. 45, states that Valley of Peace consisted of 150 acres and seventeen families. Another description is provided by Patricia Bell Blawis in *Tijerina and the Land Grants: Mexican Americans Struggle for their Heritage* (New York: International Publishers, 1971); she states that the Valley of Peace was started in 1955 with nineteen families. Rudy V. Busto, *King Tiger: The Religious Vision of Reies Lopez Tijerina* (Albuquerque: University of New Mexico Press, 2005), corrects us all, claiming the number is nine men and their families, as recorded in an original handwritten manuscript. He does not tell the reader where this original manuscript is located. The commune thrived for at least two years, ending in February 1957, according to Busto (p. 132).

2. Reies López Tijerina, *They Called Me "King Tiger": My Struggle for the Land and Our*

Rights, ed. and trans. José Angel Gutiérrez (Houston: Arte Público Press, 2000), p. 3. This passage is found in chapter 1, "1956," of *Mi lucha por la tierra,* p. 29.

3. Tijerina, *They Called Me King Tiger,* p. 3.

4. Busto, *King Tiger,* p. 118; for the schoolhouse burning, see p. 131.

5. Tijerina, *They Called Me King Tiger,* p. 3, for both passages.

6. Gardner, *Grito!,* p. 46.

7. Gardner, *Grito!,* p. 46.

8. Tijerina, *They Called Me King Tiger,* p. 16.

9. Gardner, *Grito!,* p. 47.

10. Tijerina, *They Called Me King Tiger,* p. 16.

11. The FBI report is badly photocopied and most difficult to read. The FBI office of origin was Phoenix (PX) under file number 52-1230. Those arrested are listed as Sevedeo Martinez, Margarito López Tijerina, and Reies Tijerina, aka Reverend. The items mentioned in this lengthy report on page 4 were found by local police after searching the grounds of the Valley of Peace, including the dry water well. The search warrant was issued by Justice of the Peace Norman Murphy out of Eloy, Arizona. Many recovered items had the U.S. Forest Service inscription on them, and their description matched the report of theft of government property from Jicarilla Ranger Station in Dulce, New Mexico. A recovered government order invoice and voucher book was also listed but stamped "FS-8735 Forest Supervisor, Carson National Forest, Taos, New Mexico." This item was in the glove compartment of Tijerina's truck.

12. The report lists six airtels from Phoenix to Albuquerque and back, dating from March 23, 1957, to April 26, 1957, indicating that FBI files on Tijerina began earlier than this one. For reference to the FBI jargon, such as *airtel,* used in this narrative, please review the onomasticon.

13. File 52-69829-2.

14. Busto goes into great detail on Tijerina's dreams, visions, and imaginary thoughts in *King Tiger,* particularly chapters 4-6 and the epilogue.

15. Busto, *King Tiger,* p. 6.

16. Busto, *King Tiger,* p. 6.

17. Busto, *King Tiger,* p. 7.

18. Busto, *King Tiger,* p. 7.

19. Gardner, *Grito!,* p. 42.

20. The group's roots, however, date back to Spain and to the dearth of priests in

the eighteenth century. See Paul Horgan, *Lamy of Santa Fe: His Life and Times* (New York: Noonday Press, 1975), p. 147ff., for this constant problem with his Mexican subordinate priests. The Catholic Church of the United States and the Catholic Church of Mexico were at odds as to which had jurisdiction over the Southwest when the Treaty of Guadalupe Hidalgo was signed. The papacy had opted for Mexican church officials to continue exercising control over the vast land area by the bishop of Durango, some fifteen hundred miles from Santa Fe. But the politics of opportunity took priority among the U.S. bishops with a say on the issue. At stake was the phenomenal growth among the faithful in the Southwest, particularly New Mexico and California. Poverty was a concern, as was the physical condition of properties, including churches made of mud and sticks. However, the number of priests needed and positions of bishop to be filled was too attractive to the U.S. clergy to not intercede. They wrote letters to Rome with recommendations that Pope Pius IX accepted. On July 19, 1850, he created the vicariate apostolic of New Mexico and followed up with a papal bull, *in partibus infidelium,* on July 23 naming Father Jean Baptiste Lamy, a Frenchman, as bishop of Agathonica (Horgan, pp. 65-73).

When Bishop Lamy began his reorganization of his jurisdiction, he first had to inform his priests that they now owed allegiance to him and not Durango, Mexico. He spoke no Spanish, so translators were needed with his Spanish-speaking priests and nuns. Then he had to issue instructions as to how to administer his policies for the new American Catholic Church in New Mexico. None of this sat well with the orthodox practitioners of the faith or their priests. When the reassignments began of priests and nuns, those affected literally took to the underground and became what later was known as the *Penitentes,* a secret informal society of Catholics who continued to worship with their priests, their way, in hiding, and in Spanish. Other priests, such as Antonio Jose Martinez of Taos, fought with Lamy publicly. Father Martinez, son of Hispanos from New Mexico dating back to early 1700s, opposed the nomination of Lamy and resisted being removed from his parish in Taos. Father Martinez and his extended family members and supporters joined the *Penitentes.* Ultimately, Bishop Lamy began formal proceedings to excommunicate Father Martinez and Father Mariano de Jesús Lucero. Horgan, *Lamy of Santa Fe,* pp. 242-244. See also Antonio Jose Martinez, *Recollections of the Life of the Priest Don Antonio Jose Martinez* (Santa Fe: Lighting Tree, 1978); Fray Angelico Chavez, *But Time and Chance: The Story of Padre Martinez of Taos, 1793-1867* (Santa Fe: Sunstone Press, 1981); and a more recent work by Rey John De Aragon, *Padre Martinez and Bishop Lamy* (Santa Fe: Sunstone Press, 2006).

21. Tijerina, *They Called Me King Tiger*, p. 17.

22. Tijerina, *They Called Me King Tiger*, pp. 19–21.

23. Tijerina, *They Called Me King Tiger*, pp. 23–25.

24. Gardner, *Grito!*, pp. 80–81.

25. Busto, *King Tiger*, p. 56.

26. Busto, *King Tiger*, p. 51.

27. Busto, *King Tiger*, pp. 138–139. Peter Nabokov, *Tijerina and the Courthouse Raid* (Berkeley, CA: Ramparts, 1970), p. 201, claims Tijerina paid $9 an acre and confirms the location was part of the Peralta land grant. See a provocative exposé on Rockefeller money in politics by Gary Allen, *The Rockefeller File* (Seal Beach, CA: '76 Press, 1976).

28. Busto, *King Tiger*, p. 141, citing Tijerina's *Mi lucha* at p. 120. There is no mention on that page of any such theft by Addision Reavis; there is mention of nameless persons taking records pertaining to lands in New Mexico, but not Arizona.

29. Tijerina, *They Called Me King Tiger*, p. 37.

30. In fact, he was specifically named as a target in the first directives to twenty-three FBI field offices across the nation. FBI agents were directed "to expose, disrupt, misdirect, or otherwise neutralize the activities of black nationalists." See Kenneth O'Reilly with David Gallen, eds., *Black Americans: The FBI Files* (New York: Carroll & Graf, 1994), p. 48. The initial targets for this COINTELPRO operation included Martin Luther King Jr., Stokely Carmichael, Rap Brown, Maxwell Stanford, "and Elijah Muhammad of the Nation of Islam" (pp. 48–49). The FBI file on the Nation of Islam (NOI) and Elijah Muhammad is extensive and subject to FOIA requests because he died years ago.

31. Tijerina, *They Called Me King Tiger*, p. 37. In my possession I have such documents, not the entire file, but some preliminary documents. The first report is titled "the nation of islam (Anti-white, All-Negro Cult in United States)," is dated October 1960, and is eighty-nine pages long.

32. Tijerina, *They Called Me King Tiger*, pp. 26–28.

33. Tijerina, *They Called Me King Tiger*, p. 29

34. Gardner, *Grito!*, p. 94.

35. Gardner, *Grito!*, pp. 95–96.

36. Gardner, *Grito!*, p. 96.

37. Gardner, *Grito!*, p. 96.

38. This solo page file was given to me by Reies from his University of New Mexico archival deposit through the Center for Southwest Research, Zimmerman Library, University of New Mexico (CSWR). "MSS 93 (BC) Box 2 Folder 24" is stamped at bottom right. At top right is handwritten "#93, Box #2 Folder #45, Item #2-12."

39. Tijerina Archive, CSWR, MSS 93 BC, Box 2, Folder 45, Item 1.

40. Gardner, *Grito!*, p. 100.

41. Gardner, *Grito!*, p. 81.

42. Gardner, *Grito!*, p. 101.

43. This file is a copy from the Tijerina Archive, CSWR, MSS 93 BC, Box 2, Folder 45, Item 13.

44. Tijerina Archive, CSWR, MSS 93 BC, Box 2, Folder 45, Item 13.

45. Tijerina Archive, CSWR, MSS 93 BC, Box 2, Folder 45, Item 18, for the pages with Reies among the photos. The other page with Margarito's photo is not identified as to location in the Tijerina Archive.

46. Tijerina Archive, CSWR, MSS 93 BC, Box 2, Folder 45, Item 15. The item numbers are not in sequence, but that is the order in the files as obtained.

47. There are no identifying markings on this page. It can be found in the Michigan State Library Julian Samora Research Institute Archive under my name in the folder named "State Police New Mexico."

48. Tijerina Archive, CSWR, MSS 93 BC, Box 2, Folder 45, Item 19.

49. Tijerina Archive, CSWR, MSS 93 BC, Box 2, Folder 47, Item 1.

50. Map with underscored cities and words "Location of agents, Sept 65" is with files in my folder "State Police New Mexico."

51. See Plaintiff's Exhibit #2 marked "RA 9119" entered into the record of the hearing on the eviction notices in the file "State Police New Mexico."

52. This last requirement of the order would make for an interesting research project to verify service of process; otherwise the order was invalid and void as to those not getting served and document returned for filing. Regardless, these issues were not brought up in court.

53. Case no. 5928, Vol. 2., pp. 348–353.

54. See pages 1 and 2 of the seven pages of this enclosure found in either Tijerina Archive, CSWR, MSS 93 BC, Box 2, Folder 51, Item 15 or MSS 93 BC, Box 2, Folder 36 of the collection held by the Center for Southwest Research at the University of New Mexico. The first citation is written at top right of first

page; the left side of the border of the first page has the collection stamp with the location written in spaces.

55. Michael Jenkinson, *Tijerina* (Albuquerque: Paisano Press, 1968), pp. 44–45.

56. Nabokov, *Tijerina and the Courthouse Raid,* p. 26.

57. Nabokov, *Tijerina and the Courthouse Raid,* chapters 1 and 2, pp. 11–36; and Jenkinson, *Tijerina,* pp. 40–62.

58. See, for example, Nabokov, *Tijerina and the Courthouse Raid,* pp. 25–30, and Jenkinson, *Tijerina,* pp. 49–57. Nor are any FBI files declassified and released to me or Tijerina related to these FBI investigations, only DA Sanchez's file. Gardner's chapter 8 in *Grito!* is titled "File 43-1," and I have copies of portions of that file. I also have additional documents from the DA records, but these are titled "ALL OF FOLLOWING MATERIAL FROM FILE 50-51 DISTRICT ATTORNEY-ALFONSO SANCHEZ." Written on the face of this cover page is "additional material is available in this file in Mr. Sanchez' office—most of it relating to court procedures which ended in Judge Tarbett's order restraining the heirs—Also, there is available through Mr. Sanchez the court file. SH Sept 16, 1965." The last page of these documents is another handwritten note dated the day prior that reads, "Received Reies Tijerina File # 43-1 and Chama Land & Cattle Co. v. TA Land Grant Co. # 50-51." This is signed "Steward A. Hatch 827-2205," which perhaps was his phone number.

59. The last page dated "6-12-67" is the Notice of Partial Cancellation Item S-98 and Complete Cancellation Item S-64 of the warrant of arrest for extortion on "REIS [*sic*] LOPEZ TIJERINA."

Chapter 2. No Apology, No Compensation

1. Executive Order 9066 by President Roosevelt was rescinded by President Ford's Proclamation 4417.

2. See an extensive analysis of these reparations and comparisons to Hawaiian and African American claims in Eric K. Yanamoto, "Racial Reparations: Japanese American Redress and African American Claims," *Boston College Third World Law Journal* 19, no. 1 (December 1, 1998), pp. 447–523.

3. See Executive Order 13050, June 14, 1997, for the creation of this initiative on race and the *Houston Chronicle,* "Race Forum Comes to Town," June 28, 1997, p. 1.

4. Public Law 103-150, 103rd Congress, November 23, 1993. This joint resolution passed one hundred years after the occupation and taking of the Kingdom of Hawaii and forced acknowledgment by Queen Liliuokalani, yielding her

authority to the U.S. government.

5. The history of the Panama Canal has been detailed and recounted by many. Among those I consulted were David McCullough's *The Path between the Seas: The Creation of the Panama Canal* (New York: Simon & Schuster, 1977) and the work of John Lindsey-Poland, *Emperors in the Jungle: The Hidden History of the US in Panama* (Durham, NC: Duke University Press, 2003).

6. See "The Tuskegee Timeline," *U.S. Publish Health Service Syphilis Study at Tuskegee*, Centers for Disease Control and Prevention, last reviewed December 22, 2015, www.cdc.gov/tuskegee/timeline.htm/. The class action was filed in 1973 and settled out of court in 1974.

7. Since that time, I began researching that incident and have obtained valuable information, including an oral history with the son of one massacred, Juan Flores Bonilla, and am working on exhuming the bodies to match DNA with current descendants in order to file claims and seek return of stolen land, almost two thousand acres where the village of Porvenir once stood. There is also a group of professors who have initiated a movement and organization to place historical markers at sites of such massacres; see www.refusingtoforget.org.

8. Sam Houston, after he left Tennessee for Texas, spent nearly a decade among the Cherokee in East Texas. The Cherokee had been removed from Georgia, the Carolinas, and Tennessee in the late 1700s. The Spanish approved of their resettlement in what is now Missouri, Oklahoma, Arkansas, and Texas. As president of the Republic of Texas, Houston signed a treaty allocating this tribe a sizable portion of that region, but the legislature refused to ratify that treaty. In fact, it was nullified completely by his successor, Maribau Buonaparte Lamar. Houston became President of the Republic of Texas again in 1843-1844 and again signed a treaty despite the fact that the Cherokee Nation had been virtually exterminated and the few remaining persons lived in Oklahoma and Arkansas. After Texas became a state of the United States, the Cherokee and other tribes in the East Texas region sought compensation for their lost lands covered by that treaty. Under the name Alabama-Coushatta, the tribe filed suit against the United States and Texas. On June 19, 2000, a three-judge appellate panel of the U.S. Court of Claims ruled in their favor and ordered the parties to effect a settlement based on 109 years of trespass and use of these lands, 2,850,028 acres. The tribe had proved their aboriginal title was for 6.4 million acres in East Texas.

9. See Edward Lazarus, *Black Hills / White Justice: The Sioux Nation versus the United States, 1775 to the Present* (New York: HarperCollins, 1991), and Maria

Streshinsky, "Saying No to $1 Billion," *The Atlantic,* February 9, 2011, pp. 17-21.

10. The origin of the absolute right by government to take private property dates to Section 39 of the Magna Carta. That section declared, "No freemen shall be taken or imprisoned or disseized or exiled or in any way destroyed, nor will we go upon him nor send jupon him, except by the lawful judgement of his peers or by the law of the land." In U.S. jurisprudence, these words found their way into the Fifth Amendment. In *Barron v. Mayor and City of Baltimore,* 32 U.S. 243 (1833) these words were interpreted by the U.S. Supreme Court in applying only to the federal government and not the states, much less the creatures of the states, cities. After the passage of the Thirteenth, Fourteenth, and Fifteenth Amendments and the subsequent doctrine of "incorporation" being adopted by the U.S. Supreme Court these Amendments, particularly the Fourteenth Amendment, become the law of the land. The case on point is *Chicago Burlington and Quincy R.R. v. City of Chicago,* 166 U.S. 226 (1897). The Fifth Amendment does apply to the states, cities, and, one must assume, other local governmental entities, no cases on point notwithstanding. In the last fifty years, the SCOTUS case of *United States v. Carmack,* 329 U.S. 230 (1946) has been the guiding case affirming that the power of government on the use of eminent domain is essential for the public welfare.

    Every state has its own version of the law on condemnation and on eminent domain. Texas law, for example, is found in the Government Code, Chapter 2206, Eminent Domain. And in the Texas Constitution it is Article 1, Sections 17 and 19.

11. I do not know who is now in possession of this valuable collection of materials. Mr. Mares died and a realtor contracted to sell the property is reported by Reies's daughter Rosa to have removed all items and sent them to the dump.

12. President James K. Polk in his Inaugural Address of March 4, 1845 used these words. See also Roxanne Dunbar-Ortiz, *An Indigenous Peoples' History of the United States* (Boston: Beacon Press, 2014), pp. 197-201, and articles by Eric Kades, "The Dark Side of Efficiency: Johnson v. M'Intosh and the Expropriation of American Indian Lands," 148 *University of Pennsylvania Law Review* (2000), pp. 1065-1190; Blake A. Watson, "John Marshall and Indian Land Rights: A Historical Rejoinder to the Claim of 'Universal Recognition' of the Doctrine of Discovery," *Seton Hall Law Review* 36, no. 2 (2006), pp. 481-502; and "Colonial History: Theory of Christian Expansion USA Constitution and Discovery Doctrine," Cambridge Theological Seminary, 1977.

13. The Dawes Act of 1887, p. 2.

14. The Dawes Act of 1887, p. 3.

15. The Dawes Act of 1887, pp. 4 and 7.

16. Mark David Spence, *Dispossessing the Wilderness: Indian Removal and the Making of the National Parks* (New York: Oxford University Press, 1999).

17. Michael Jenkinson, *Tijerina* (Albuquerque: Paisano Press, 1968), pp. 39–41.

18. Reies López Tijerina, *They Called Me "King Tiger": My Struggle for the Land and Our Rights*, ed. and trans. José Angel Gutiérrez (Houston: Arte Público Press, 2000), p. 94.

19. Tijerina, *They Called Me King Tiger*, p. 29.

20. Tijerina, *They Called Me King Tiger*, p. 93.

21. Tijerina, *They Called Me King Tiger*, p. 94.

22. Tijerina, *They Called Me King Tiger*, p. 95 for both quotations.

23. Malcolm Ebright, *The Tierra Amarilla Grant: A History of Chicanery* (Santa Fe: Center for Land Grant Studies, 1980), p. 3.

24. Ebright, *The Tierra Amarilla Grant*, p. 3.

25. Ebright, *The Tierra Amarilla Grant*, pp. 51–52.

26. Ebright, *The Tierra Amarilla Grant*, p. 52.

27. Ebright, *The Tierra Amarilla Grant*, pp. 53–55.

28. See the volume edited by Robert J. Tórrez and Robert Trapp, *Rio Arriba: A New Mexico County* (Los Ranchos, NM: Rio Grande Books, 2010), for a compilation of articles on the history of the area that became one of the seven counties organized into the New Mexico Territory in 1852. The last chapter, "Politics in Rio Arriba," pp. 209-384, discusses the towns mentioned in this manuscript, such as Tierra Amarilla, Canjilon, Abiquiu, Espanola, Coyote, Gallina, Embudo, and Rio Arriba.

29. David Correia, *Properties of Violence: Law and Land Grant Struggle in Northern New Mexico* (Athens: University of Georgia Press, 2013), pp. 120-123.

30. Correia, *Properties of Violence*, p. 123.

31. Richard Gardner, *Grito! Reies Tijerina and the New Mexico Land Grant War of 1967* (New York: Bobbs-Merrill, 1971), p. 117, and *Newsweek*, January 3, 1966.

32. Gardner, *Grito!*, p. 94.

33. NMSA 1978 Sec. 30-38-2. Under the New Mexico statute any discussion, attempt, or action is enough to trigger the conspiracy charge. The act does not have to be completed, just contemplated.

34. 42 USC 1983.

35. Gardner, *Grito!*, p. 118.

36. Mike Scarborough, *Trespassers on Our Own Land* (Indianapolis: Dog Ear Publishing, 2011), pp. 109–110.

37. Tijerina, *The Called Me King Tiger*, pp. 72–73, and Correia, *Properties of Violence*, p. 132.

38. Gardner, *Grito!*, pp. 122–123. What Tijerina failed to understand was that the discovery process also requires the parties to produce records such as membership lists, bank accounts, and the like—anything leading to important and relevant material to the case. The Alianza would not want that to take place. The legal question would not have been whether land grants claims were valid or not.

39. Jenkinson, *Tijerina*, p. 58; Peter Nabokov, *Tijerina and the Courthouse Raid* (Berkeley, CA: Ramparts, 1970), pp. 217–218; Patricia Bell Blawis, *Tijerina and the Land Grants: Mexican Americans in Struggle for Their Heritage* (New York: International Publishers, 1971), p. 48; and Gardner, *Grito!*, p. 263.

40. Rudy V. Busto, *King Tiger: The Religious Vision of Reies Lopez Tijerina* (Albuquerque: University of New Mexico Press, 2005), p. 50.

41. Correia, *Properties of Violence*, p. 124.

42. *The Spanish Land Grant Question Examined* (Albuquerque: Alianza Federal, 1966).

43. News clippings of this meeting and many related stories on Tijerina and the Alianza are found at the Zimmerman Library, Center for Southwest Research, University of New Mexico, MSS 93 BC, Box 1, Folder 4 and are arranged by item number. These mentioned are listed as Items 1–4. There are similar articles in the Alianza archive at the same location under MSS 628 BC, Box 1, Folders 1 and 2; other articles are in oversize folders.

44. Correia, *Properties of Violence*, p. 132.

45. See Blawis, *Tijerina and the Land Grants*, appendix, p. 181, for some authority on the subject used in a case involving Tijerina.

46. This case is more focused on what constitutes a lawful search and seizure based on the Fourth Amendment's prohibition against that type of event after an arrest of a woman for not wearing her seatbelt while driving a car in Lago Vista, a resort community just outside Austin, Texas. The case opinion, however, makes mention of the right of any person to arrest someone without a warrant or even probable cause. The standard is that a person can arrest someone reasonably suspected of committing a felony, even if the felony did

not occur in the presence of the individual making the arrest. The person making the arrest could become civilly and criminally liable for results of that arrest.

47. Article 6, Section 2.

48. Blawis, *Tijerina and the Land Grants,* pp. 49–50.

49. Each state has a statute on citizen's arrest powers and sometime duty, as in helping a police officer, but federal law controls. See California Penal Code, Section 837, for an example. North Carolina does not permit citizen's arrest but does permit "detention." This is termed the "Shopkeepers' Privilege" for a store owner/manager to detain someone suspected of theft on store property. Laypersons can educate themselves on citizen's arrest on the internet. One useful site is www.FindLaw.com.

50. Nabokov, *Tijerina and the Courthouse Raid,* p. 35.

51. Nabokov, *Tijerina and the Courthouse Raid,* p. 55.

52. The Communist Party USA was formed in 1919 and harassed by AG Bonaparte Palmer in the 1920s and more so with passage of the Smith Act in 1940 outlawing the Party. But SCOTUS in *Yates v. U.S.,* 354 US 298 (1957) held that membership in and of itself was not a violation of the Smith Act. Even teaching Marxist ideology was not illegal; it is a concept. Illegal activity is to engage in action leading to the overthrow of the U.S. government. The Communist Party USA during Tijerina's time regularly ran candidates for president of the United States and had ballot status in New Mexico.

53. See Tijerina, *They Called Me King Tiger,* pp. 64–74, for Tijerina's account of what happened at Echo Amphitheater and the days that followed. Nabokov details aspects of both the Echo Amphitheater takeover and the meeting with the governor on pages 16–21 of *Tijerina and the Courthouse Raid.* Gardner discusses this on pages 127–132 of *Grito!*

54. Nabokov, *Tijerina and the Courthouse Raid,* pp. 53–54.

55. Tijerina, *They Called Me King Tiger,* pp. 67–71.

56. 357 U.S. 449 (1958).

57. Nabokov, *Tijerina and the Courthouse Raid,* p. 54.

58. Nabokov, *Tijerina and the Courthouse Raid,* pp. 54–59.

59. Nabokov, *Tijerina and the Courthouse Raid,* p. 63.

60. Memorandum from SAC, Albuquerque to Director, FBI, dated February 16, 1968, states, "There is forwarded herewith Xeroxed copies of the membership cards of captioned organization. They are being forwarded herewith to the Bureau

for indexing purposes. The only identifying data concerning individual's names therein is shown. The source of these membership cards is as follows: [redacted approximately four to five lines.]." The last paragraph reads: "On 6/9/67 EDUARDO CHAVEZ, Treasurer, AFDM, executed an affidavit in the USDC at Albuquerque, New Mexico, stating that the cards in these filing cabinets were the membership cards of the AFDM." The pages that are accompanying this memorandum number 260, and some pages, such as p. 1, contain only one card, whereas p. 23 has three cards copied. The card with the name "Cargo J.A, Adelaida 14089 2857 2020 Murriel N.E. Albuq. N.M. Marzo 29, 66" is on p. 88.

61. Nabokov, *Tijerina and the Courthouse Raid,* pp. 76–79.

Chapter 3. Citizen's Arrest

1. Rudy V. Busto, *King Tiger: The Religious Vision of Reies Lopez Tijerina* (Albuquerque: University of New Mexico Press, 2005), p. 51.

2. Busto, *King Tiger,* p. 56.

3. Patricia Bell Blawis, *Tijerina and the Land Grants: Mexican Americans in Struggle for Their Heritage* (New York: International Publishers, 1971), p. 38 n. 7. She gives full credit to Tijerina as the author on p. 185.

4. Busto, *King Tiger,* pp. 56–57; Peter Nabokov, *Tijerina and the Courthouse Raid* (Berkeley, CA: Ramparts, 1970), p. 16; Blawis, *Tijerina and the Land Grants,* pp. 52, 54; Richard Gardner, *Grito! Reies Tijerina and the New Mexico Land Grant War of 1967* (New York: Bobbs-Merrill, 1971), p. 122.

5. Reies López Tijerina, *They Called Me "King Tiger": My Struggle for the Land and Our Rights,* ed. and trans. José Angel Gutiérrez (Houston: Arte Público Press, 2000), p. 64.

6. Gardner, *Grito!,* p. 123.

7. Busto, *King Tiger,* p. 71.

8. *The Spanish Land Grant Question Examined* (Albuquerque: Alianza Federal, 1966).

9. *Spanish Land Grant Question,* p. 1.

10. *Spanish Land Grant Question,* p. 2.

11. *Spanish Land Grant Question,* p. 3.

12. *Spanish Land Grant Question,* pp. 4–5.

13. See Gardner, *Grito!* for a short biographical account of Jerry Noll on pp. 124–127; for mentions with some description Nabokov, *Tijerina and the Courthouse Raid,* pp. 53–54; and Michael Jenkinson, *Tijerina* (Albuquerque: Paisano Press, 1968),

pp. 13-14.

14. Gardner, *Grito!*, pp. 16-17.

15. Tijerina, *They Called Me King Tiger*, pp. 66-67.

16. Busto, *King Tiger*, p. 57.

17. Tijerina, *They Called Me King Tiger*, pp. 64-66.

18. Gardner, *Grito!*, p. 128.

19. Tijerina, *They Called Me King Tiger*, p. 66.

20. Mike Scarborough, *Trespassers on Our Own Land* (Indianapolis: Dog Ear Publishing, 2011), pp. 111-112.

21. Gardner, *Grito!*, p. 129.

22. Busto, *King Tiger*, p. 57.

23. Blawis, *Tijerina and the Land Grants*, p. 57.

24. Gardner, *Grito!*, p. 129. On pages 128-132, Gardner has an engaging narrative of what happened that day and ensuing days, including the trial and Tijerina's victory speech, before the arrests were made by federal officers.

25. These letter codes refer to Assault on Federal Officer, AFO, and Theft of Government Property, TGP.

26. Gardner, *Grito!*, p. 129.

27. Tijerina, *They Called Me King Tiger*, p. 67.

28. Blawis, *Tijerina and the Land Grants*, p. 59.

29. Busto, *King Tiger*, p. 57.

30. Tijerina, *They Called Me King Tiger*, p. 69.

31. Gardner, *Grito!*, p. 132.

32. Blawis, *Tijerina and the Land Grants*, pp. 60-61.

33. Tijerina, *They Called Me King Tiger*, p. 69.

34. See *United States of America v. Reies Lopez Tijerina*, cause no. 23,112 Criminal, filed on December 15, 1967. I have placed copies of court cases I reviewed in the folder marked "Court Cases," including this order of sentencing by Judge Howard Bratton.

35. Blawis, *Tijerina and the Land Grants*, pp. 62-65.

36. Blawis, *Tijerina and the Land Grants*, p. 65.

37. See Scarborough, *Trespassers on Our Own Land*, pp. 128-145, for this and subsequent quotations from Valdez on events at the courthouse. Nabokov,

Tijerina and the Courthouse Raid, has the narrative on pp. 81-103; Gardner, *Grito!,* on pp. 1-18; Blawis, *Tijerina and the Land Grants,* on pp. 81-89; Jenkinson, *Tijerina,* on pp. 72-85; and Busto, *King Tiger,* on pp. 60-62. Tijerina's account is on pp. 79-87 of *They Called Me King Tiger.*

38. Gardner, *Grito!,* p. 80.
39. Tijerina, *They Called Me King Tiger,* p. 81. See Tijerina's account of how the shooting of Eulogio on June 5 and subsequent murder on the eve of the trial were all linked by the media, police, and prosecution to Tijerina (pp. 99-101, 218-219, 226-227).
40. Blawis, *Tijerina and the Land Grants,* p. 89.
41. Blawis, *Tijerina and the Land Grants,* p. 90.
42. Tijerina, *They Called Me King Tiger,* pp. 88, 91.
43. Blawis, *Tijerina and the Land Grants,* p. 90. See also Nabokov, *Tijerina and the Courthouse Raid,* pp. 104-106.
44. Nabokov, *Tijerina and the Courthouse Raid,* p. 111.
45. Nabokov, *Tijerina and the Courthouse Raid,* pp. 108-110, 123.
46. Nabokov, *Tijerina and the Courthouse Raid,* p. 112.
47. Nabokov, *Tijerina and the Courthouse Raid,* p. 169.
48. Nabokov, *Tijerina and the Courthouse Raid,* p. 169.
49. Tijerina, *They Called Me King Tiger,* p. 85.
50. Memo from SAC, Albuquerque to Director Hoover. David Correia, "'Rousers of the Rabble' in the New Mexico Land Grant War: *La Alianza Federal de Mercedes* and the Violence of the State," *Antipode* 40, no. 4 (2008), p. 581 n. 38, has a citation for this same memo, which he found at the Center for Southwest Research, University of New Mexico, in Box 3, Folder 17.
51. Correia, "Rousers of the Rabble," p. 581.
52. Blawis, *Tijerina and the Land Grants,* pp. 91-92. See also Tijerina, *They Called Me King Tiger,* p. 84, for that encounter; and Gardner, *Grito!,* pp. 168-170.
53. Tijerina, *They Called Me King Tiger,* p. 87.
54. Gardner, *Grito!,* pp. 170-171.
55. Gardner, *Grito!,* pp. 162-163.
56. Tijerina, *They Called Me King Tiger,* pp. 71-72.
57. Interview with Maria Escobar, July 17, 2000, p. 18. Maria had trouble recalling the year, but thought it was 1960. She had help from daughter Rosa, who

pegged her age to the divorce year, 1962. Nabokov places the year at 1963, but he does say, "By 1963, Tijerina was no longer living with his wife, Maria" (p. 213), not necessarily the divorce year.

58. See the photo section of Gardner, *Grito!,* between p. 150 and p. 151; the pages containing photos are not numbered. Nabokov, *Tijerina and the Courthouse Raid,* has photos between p. 144 and p. 145. The photos speak for themselves and corroborate their narrative and contradict these official declarations by state police officers and Adjutant General Jolly.

59. See U.S. Code, Section 1503, Title 18.

60. Interview with Rosa Tijerina Duran by author, July 3, 2000, Albuquerque, pp. 16–26.

61. Tijerina, *They Called Me King Tiger,* pp. 87–88.

62. SCOTUS in the case *In Re Medley,* 134 U.S. 160, 168 (1890), saw solitary confinement as inhumane and cruel. In *Madrid v. Gomez,* 889 F. Supp. 1146 (N.D. Cal. 1995), the federal court viewed it as having no place in civilized society.

63. Tijerina, *They Called Me King Tiger,* pp. 90–91.

64. Tijerina, *They Called Me King Tiger,* pp. 135–136.

65. See "Solitary Confinement for Pregnant Women, Children and the Mentally Ill in the Land of Enchantment," *New Mexico Injury Attorney Blog,* Collins & Collins, n.d., www.collinsattorneys.com/injuryblawg/civil-rights/solitary-confinement-pregnant-women-children-mentally-ill/. In New Mexico last April 2017, and in New Jersey in December 2016, Governors Susana Martinez and Chris Christi, respectively, vetoed legislation that would have outlawed the practice of placing pregnant women and the mentally ill in solitary confinement. See Morgan Lee, "New Mexico Governor Vetoes Solitary Confinement Restrictions," *Washington Times,* April 6, 2017. www.washington times.com/news/2017/apr/6/new-mexcio-governor-acts-on-wide-variety-bills.

66. LHM dated June 23, 1967, by airtel to Director, FBI from SAC, Albuquerque.

67. The letter is an undated form letter and checked on item 1, which pertains to threatening or attempting to threaten a government official.

68. See my works *Albert A. Pena, Jr. Dean of Chicano Politics* (East Lansing: Michigan State University Press, 2017), pp. 148–151, for a brief review of that event from a participant view, and *The Making of a Chicano Militant: Lessons from Cristal* (Madison: University of Wisconsin Press, 1998), pp. 111–113, for my role in and views on this event.

69. All five pages have this penciled in a correction of number at bottom right and

are in sequence from p. 235–241; p. 243 is the handwritten report mentioned in the text on this subject.

70. No precise citation can be provided because the FBI document with this information is just a copy of a newspaper clipping of an article titled "Tijerina Travels to Chicago Meet" sent out by the Associated Press and has no date, no source, other than a "2" at bottom indicating it is part of some report. The pages before and after this one page are notices of "FOIPA Deleted Page Information Sheet," the first withholding two pages entirely under exemptions "B7C, D" and the other withholding one page entirely under exemptions "B1, B2, B7C, D."

71. Tijerina, *They Called Me King Tiger,* p. 97.

72. Tijerina, *They Called Me King Tiger,* p. 98.

73. Tijerina, *They Called Me King Tiger,* p. 97.

74. Tijerina, *They Called Me King Tiger,* pp. 46, 48–49.

75. Tijerina, *They Called Me King Tiger,* pp. 48–49.

76. Tijerina, *They Called Me King Tiger,* p. 47.

Chapter 4. The War against Tijerina

1. Peter Nabokov, *Tijerina and the Courthouse Raid* (Berkeley, CA: *Ramparts,* 1970), p. 121.

2. See my work *The Eagle Has Eyes: The FBI Surveillance of César Estrada Chávez of the United Farm Workers Union of America, 1965–1975* (East Lansing: Michigan State University Press, 2019), for the narrative and bibliography of secondary sources that support this comment.

3. Richard Gardner, *Grito! Reies Tijerina and the New Mexico Land Grant War of 1967* (New York: Bobbs-Merrill, 1971), p. 217.

4. Reies López Tijerina, *They Called Me "King Tiger": My Struggle for the Land and Our Rights,* ed. and trans. José Angel Gutiérrez (Houston: Arte Público Press, 2000), pp. 27–28

5. Tijerina, *They Called Me King Tiger,* pp. 80–81.

6. Gardner, *Grito!,* p. 124.

7. Gardner, *Grito!,* p. 124.

8. Tijerina, *They Called Me King Tiger,* p. 82.

9. Nabokov, *Tijerina and the Courthouse Raid,* pp. 231–232.

10. Gardner, *Grito!,* p. 241.

11. Gardner, *Grito!*, p. 241.
12. Patricia Bell Blawis, *Tijerina and the Land Grants: Mexican Americans in Struggle for Their Heritage* (New York: International Publishers, 1971), p. 103.
13. Nabokov, *Tijerina and the Courthouse Raid*, p. 232.
14. Blawis, *Tijerina and the Land Grants*, p. 103.
15. Blawis, *Tijerina and the Land Grants*, p. 232.
16. Gardner, *Grito!*, p. 241.
17. Gardner, *Grito!*, p. 251.
18. Nabokov, *Tijerina and the Courthouse Raid*, p. 233.
19. Tijerina, *They Called Me King Tiger*, p. 143.
20. Tijerina, *They Called Me King Tiger*, p. 203.
21. Tijerina, *They Called Me King Tiger*, p. 204.
22. Tijerina, *They Called Me King Tiger*, p. 204.
23. Tijerina, *They Called Me King Tiger*, p. 207.
24. Tijerina, *They Called Me King Tiger*, p. 208.
25. Tijerina, *They Called Me King Tiger*, p. 210.
26. Tijerina, *They Called Me King Tiger*, p. 213.
27. Tijerina, *They Called Me King Tiger*, p. 214.
28. Tijerina, *They Called Me King Tiger*, p. 219.
29. Tijerina, *They Called Me King Tiger*, p. 222.
30. Tijerina, *They Called Me King Tiger*, p. 227.
31. Tijerina, *They Called Me King Tiger*, p. 227.
32. Tijerina, *They Called Me King Tiger*, p. 195.

Chapter 5. Poor People's Campaign

1. Interview with Maria Escobar, July 17, 2000.
2. Reies López Tijerina, *They Called Me "King Tiger": My Struggle for the Land and Our Rights*, ed. and trans. José Angel Gutiérrez (Houston: Arte Público Press, 2000), pp. 11–12.
3. Tijerina, *They Called Me King Tiger*, p. 13.
4. Tijerina, *They Called Me King Tiger*, p. 47. See also interview with Maria Escobar.
5. There is a literature written by Native American scholars that can and should be consulted on these conditions; and there are biographies of Native

American leaders to learn of their personal struggles with both Spanish/ Mexican colonization and ultimately Anglo occupation of their lands, homeland, and reservation. One such biography is on Cochise, a Chiricahua Apache of the Chokonen people, born sometime between 1800 and 1810 in what is now southeastern Arizona. See Peter Aleshire, *Cochise: The Life and Times of the Great Apache Chief* (New York: John Wiley & Sons, 2001).

6. See Roxanne Dunbar-Ortiz, *Roots of Resistance: A History of Land Tenure in New Mexico* (Norman: University of Oklahoma Press, 2007) for an analysis of the role land has played in the histories of Native Americans, the colonizers, and current conditions in New Mexico over land, minerals, and water.

7. Tijerina, *They Called Me King Tiger,* p. 119.

8. Tijerina, *They Called Me King Tiger,* p. 119.

9. Tijerina, *They Called Me King Tiger,* p. 101.

10. The FBI developed an interest in Elijah Muhammed perhaps as early as 1932. The FBI has open access to twenty sections of declassified files beginning in 1942, with section 1 under file number 105-24822.

11. Tijerina, *They Called Me King Tiger,* p. 17.

12. The conference was held at the Palmer House in Chicago from August 29 to September 4, 1967.

13. Ernesto B. Vigil, *The Crusade for Justice: Chicano Militancy and the Government's War on Dissent* (Madison: University of Wisconsin Press, 1999), pp. 54–55.

14. Vigil, *Crusade for Justice,* p. 101.

15. K. Gordon Mantler, *Power to the Poor: Black-Brown Coalition and the Fight for Economic Justice* (Chapel Hill: University of North Carolina Press, 2015), p. 109.

16. See Amy Nathan Wright, "Civil Rights 'Unfinished Business': Poverty, Race, and the 1968 Poor People's Campaign," doctoral dissertation, University of Texas at Austin, 2007, p. 151.

17. See Samuel I. Rosenman, ed., *The Public Papers and Addresses of Franklin Delano Roosevelt* (New York: Harper and Bros., 1950), 13:40–42.

18. Tijerina, *They Called Me King Tiger,* pp. 101, 103.

19. Tijerina, *They Called Me King Tiger,* p. 103.

20. *Albuquerque Journal,* April 26, 1968, p. A-6. Tijerina responded, and the newspaper printed his rebuttal on May 1.

21. Tijerina, *They Called Me King Tiger,* p. 105.

22. Mantler, *Power to the Poor,* p. 147.

23. Juan Haro, a hard-core Crusade for Justice cofounder and head of security, uses "Rudolfo" as Corky's first name. Corky's namesake son, "Rudy," also signed his own name as "Rudolfo." See Haro's revised edition of *The Ultimate Betrayal: An Autobiography* (n.p.: Dorrance Publishing, 1998), pp. vi-viii, 2, and 15. Vigil, *Crusade for Justice*, uses only "Rodolfo" (p. 3, for example). Mantler, *Power to the Poor*, uses "Rodolfo."

24. U.S. Senate, Select Committee to Study Governmental Operations with Respect to Intelligence Activities ("Church Committee"), *Final Report—Book III: Supplementary Detailed Staff Reports on Intelligence Activities and the Rights of Americans* (Washington, DC: U.S. GPO, 1976), pp. 225-270. See FindLaw's *Writ*, August 5, 2002, for Senator Leahy's report on the Bush administration's TIPS program.

25. Mantler, *Power to the Poor*, p. 145.

26. Mantler, *Power to the Poor*, pp. 145-146.

27. Mantler, *Power to the Poor*, p. 146.

28. Mantler, *Power to the Poor*, p. 147.

29. Mantler, *Power to the Poor*, p. 148.

30. Mantler, *Power to the Poor*, p. 149.

31. Mantler, *Power to the Poor*, pp. 149-150.

32. Mantler, *Power to the Poor*, pp. 150-151.

33. Tijerina, *They Called Me King Tiger.*, p. 106.

34. Mantler, *Power to the Poor*, p. 158.

35. See Mantler, *Power to the Poor*, p. 138, for an aerial photo of Resurrection City on West Potomac Park, next to the Lincoln Memorial to the southwest. He disputes as unfounded rumors reports the sexual abuse and harassment of women (p. 175).

36. Mantler, *Power to the Poor*, p. 152.

37. Vigil, *Crusade for Justice*, pp. 32-33.

38. Vigil, *Crusade for Justice*, pp. 35-36.

39. Vigil, *Crusade for Justice*, p. 40.

40. Vigil, *Crusade for Justice*, pp. 163-164.

41. Vigil, *Crusade for Justice*, pp. 60-61; and author's personal knowledge.

42. Tijerina, *They Called Me King Tiger*, p. 113.

43. Tijerina, *They Called Me King Tiger*, p. 114.

44. Tijerina, *They Called Me King Tiger*, pp. 114-115.

45. Mantler, *Power to the Poor*, p. 155. A photo of Ernie Vigil getting up from the ground with police standing over him is on p. 155.

46. Tijerina, *They Called Me King Tiger*, pp. 107-112.

47. William Clayson, *Freedom Is Not Enough: The War on Poverty and the Civil Rights Movement in Texas* (Austin: University of Texas Press, 2010), pp. 136-137.

48. This information is gleaned from a twelve-page report sent by SAC, WFO to the Director, FBI, on June 11. Page 5 was withheld in its entirety under exemptions B1 and B7D.

49. Gerald D. McKnight, *The Last Crusade: Martin Luther King, Jr., the FBI and the Poor People's Campaign* (Boulder, CO: Westview Press, 1998). McKnight reveals evidence that the FBI initiated POCAM to disrupt and destroy the Poor People's Campaign.

50. Tijerina, *They Called Me King Tiger*, p. 114.

51. Tijerina, *They Called Me King Tiger*, p. 116.

52. Mantler, *Power to the Poor*, pp. 182-183.

53. Mantler, *Power to the Poor*, pp. 183-184; and author's personal knowledge and experience. My first wife, Luz Maria Bazan, and I ran a rural Head Start program under the Texas Migrant Council in Crystal City, Texas, not being able to be hired in San Antonio upon college graduation.

54. By airtel of January 2, 1969, to the Director, FBI, with copies to New York and Washington Field Office of the FBI, the SAC, Albuquerque sent copies in the LHM accompanying the airtel of the petition sent by Tijerina via radiogram message.

Chapter 6. Local Police and Hoover's Hand

1. Claire A. Culleton, *Joyce and the G-Men* (New York: Palgrave Macmillan, 2004); and for writers of every sort see Natalie Robins, *Alien Ink: The FBI's War on Freedom of Expression* (New York: William Morrow and Company, 1992).

2. The book by Richard Gid Powers, *Secrecy and Power: The Life of J. Edgar Hoover* (New York: Free Press, 1987) is a good example of a work covering Hoover's penchant for monitoring politicians, especially those with presidential ambitions, and closely utilizing the drama of interrogations of Hollywood's best by the House Un-American Activities Committee. For his interest in ferreting out gays and lesbians working for the federal government, see David K. Johnson, *The Lavender Scare: The Cold War Persecution of Gays and Lesbians in the*

Federal Government (Chicago: University of Chicago Press, 2004).

3. William Maxwell, *F. B. Eyes: How J. Edgar Hoover's Ghostreaders Framed African American Literature* (Princeton, NJ: Princeton University Press, 2015); and his edited book with notes from FOIA-obtained files, *James Baldwin: The FBI File* (New York: Arcade Publishing, 2017). Dr. Maxwell also is the curator and creator of an archival file he created with these documents at Washington University, St. Louis, MO. See the F.B. Eyes Digital Archive at http://lithub.com/a-look-inside-james-baldwins-1884-page-file/.

4. See Subcommittee on Constitutional Rights report, *Army Surveillance of Civilians: A Documentary Analysis* (Washington, DC: U.S. GPO, 1972), p. v.

5. Subcommittee on Constitutional Rights, *Army Surveillance of Civilians*, p. v.

6. Alfred W. McCoy, *In the Shadows of the American Century: The Rise and Decline of US Global Power* (Chicago: Haymarket Books, 2017), p. 124.

7. McCoy, *In the Shadows*, p. 125.

8. Nathan Theoharis, *The FBI and American Democracy: A Brief Critical History* (Lawrence: University Press of Kansas, 2004), pp. 117-118.

9. Theoharis, *FBI and American Democracy*, pp. 122-123.

10. Theoharis, *FBI and American Democracy*, p. 125.

11. Theoharis, *FBI and American Democracy*, pp. 126-127.

12. Center for Southwest Research (CSWR), Zimmerman Library, University of New Mexico, MSS 93 BC, Box 2, Folder 17, Item 16.

13. Interview with Maria Escobar, p. 35.

14. Interview with Maria Escobar, p. 35.

15. Interview with Maria Escobar, p. 35-36.

16. Vincent Sellers, *Eyes Pried Open: Rookie FBI Agent* (n.p.: Black Rose Writing, 2014), p. 65. See www.blackrosewriting.com/.

17. Sellers, *Eyes Pried Open*, p. 67.

18. Sellers, *Eyes Pried Open*, pp. 227-228.

19. See William Sullivan, *The Bureau: My Thirty Years in Hoover's FBI* (New York: Norton, 1979), p. 218.

20. Sellers, *Eyes Pried Open*, p. 225.

21. Howard Bryan, "Grant Leader Says Attorneys 'Obsolete,'" *Albuquerque Tribune*, November 20, 1968, p. A-1.

22. See *Albuquerque Tribune*, November 20, 21, 22, 25, and 26, 1968, and *Albuquerque*

Journal, November 21, 22, 23, 26, and 27, 1968 for front-page stories clipped and made part of the FBI reports from SAC, Albuquerque to Director, FBI.

23. See *Albuquerque Journal,* December 4, 1968, p. A-1.

24. I did the interview with Tim Chapa in Albuquerque, New Mexico, on June 7, 2000, in the presence of Reies López Tijerina and Eloy Garcia, now an attorney in El Paso. The original videotape and transcription are with the Center for Regional Studies, Zimmerman Library, University of New Mexico. The transcription is ninety pages. Page citations will be entered as (p. x) so the reader can find the source. Copies of this interview are also available at the Michigan State University Library under my name and at the Lillia Benson Latin American Collection at the University of Texas, Austin, under my name.

25. Interview with Hugh David Tijerina, Albuquerque, New Mexico, June 28, 2000, p. 1.

26. "-C*- Cover Page," p. 2. The SAC, Albuquerque submitted a huge LHM to Hoover on December 13, 1968. The memorandum was twenty-nine pages long, perhaps more but not included in the disclosure, and it covered a long period from September 23 to the end of the Tierra Amarilla trial. It was a review of Tijerina's history before the trial. Copies of this large document were sent to the U.S. Secret Service, FBI HQ (nine copies), OSI, 17th District, 112th MI Group, NISO, US Attorney in Albuquerque, and three copies kept at the Albuquerque FBI office. The second page, marked at bottom "-B- Cover Page" is almost completely redacted, but the manner in which it was done suggests it contains a list of informants and where they can be found. The top of the page, other than the "AQ" file number of "100-2567," has two headings "Identity of Source" and "Location." The redactions begin just below and there are eight, possibly nine, such blotted-out entries. At the bottom, a redacted couple of lines hide who was to "follow and report prosecutive action in federal and state courts" (p. 2). Every page that follows has redactions except three: 7, 9, and 11. Pages that are copies of newspaper clippings are also not redacted: 8, 10, 16, and 17. Two pages, 4 and 5, are completely redacted, but for the "AQ 100-2567" file number at top left of each page.

27. Short biography and campaign material on Cargo are found in the CSWR, MSS 93 BC, Box 2, Folder 36, Item 8, and in Folder 14.

28. Interview with Rosa Tijerina Duran, pp. 32–34.

29. Interview with Hugh David Tijerina, pp. 38–40.

30. Interview with Hugh David Tijerina, pp. 40–41.

31. Reies López Tijerina, *They Called Me "King Tiger": My Struggle for the Land and Our*

Rights, ed. and trans. José Angel Gutiérrez (Houston: Arte Público Press, 2000), p. 186.

32. Chuck Anthony, "Splinter Alianza Unit Loses Catholic Funds," *Albuquerque Journal,* July 12, 1972, p. A-1.

33. James Saggus, "Attorney Higgs Is 'Guilty,'" *Clarion-Ledger* (Jackson, Mississippi), February 15, 1963, pp. A-1, 4.

34. Curt Gentry, *J. Edgar Hoover: The Man and His Secrets* (New York: Plume, 1992), p. 575. See also Richard Hack, *Puppetmaster: The Secret Life of J. Edgar Hoover* (Beverly Hills, CA: New Millennium Press, 2004), p. 324, and Darwin Porter, *J. Edgar Hoover and Clyde Tolson* (n.p.: Blood Moon Productions, 2012), pp. 460–461.

35. "Trial Postponed for Dynamite Blast Victim," *Albuquerque Journal,* July 5, 1968, page not legible.

36. Patrick Lamb, "Man Loses Right Hand in Explosion," *Albuquerque Journal,* April 17, 1968, p. A-1.

37. Jack Brown, "Police Investigating Dynamite Explosion," *Albuquerque Tribune,* April 17, 1968, p. D-4.

38. Layne Vickers, "Term Stayed in Dynamite Case Here, "*Albuquerque Journal,* June 11, 1968, p. A-1.

39. See "Alianza Obtains New Insurance for Building," in CSWR, MSS 93 BC, Box 1, Folder 31, Item 93.

40. "The Alianza Bombings," *New Mexico Review,* September 1969, p. 1.

41. This federal statute was repealed in 1970 and changed to different section and number.

42. Ann Mari Buitrago and Leon Andrew Immerman, *Are You Now or Have You Ever Been in the FBI Files: How to Secure and Interpret Your FBI Files* (New York: Grove Press, 1981), p. 164.

43. *Albuquerque Tribune,* March 17, 1969, p. C-3.

44. Tijerina, *They Called Me King Tiger,* p. 153.

45. Tijerina, *They Called Me King Tiger,* pp. 120, 140.

46. Tijerina, *They Called Me King Tiger,* p. 154.

47. Tijerina, *They Called Me King Tiger,* p. 136.

48. See David Duran, "Hearing Held Up an Hour." *Albuquerque Tribune,* June 17, 1969, p. A-1.

49. See Howard Bryan, "Poses Threat to Others, Judge Says," *Albuquerque Tribune,* June 17, 1969, p. A-1.

50. Report of SA [name redacted] to U.S. Attorney and Director, DFBI, dated September 1, 1969, p. "-P-" and penciled number 636, bottom left.

51. Tijerina, *They Called Me King Tiger,* p. 167.

Chapter 7. Tim Chapa: The Informant

1. Alexandra Natapoff, *Snitching: Criminal Informants and the Erosion of American Justice* (New York: New York University Press, 2009). For a view into the military history of spying and informants and adaptations in the internet age see Yasha Levine, *Surveillance Valley: The Secret Military History of the Internet* (New York: Public Affairs, 2018).

2. Wikipedia, s.v. "Ghetto Informant Program," last modified March 4, 2019, 20:55, https://en.wikipedia.org/wiki/Ghetto_Informant_Program.

3. Gerald McKnight, *The Last Crusade: Martin Luther King, Jr., the FBI, and the Poor People's Campaign* (Boulder, CO: Westview Press, 1998).

4. Frank del Olmo, "Provoked Trouble for Lawman, Chicano 'Informer' Claims," *Los Angeles Times,* February 1, 1972, p. A3.

5. Ron Einstoss, "Hotel Fire Indictments Reveal Heroism of Rookie Policeman," *Los Angeles Times,* June 7, 1969, p. 1A; and Ruben Salazar, "Brown Berets Hail 'La Raza' and Scorn the Establishment," *Los Angeles Times,* June 16, 1969, p. 3A.

6. Associated Press, "Proposal to Kill Reddin Told by Trial Witness," *Los Angeles Times,* August 6, 1971, p. B3.

7. See Richard Valdemar, "Chicano Power and the Brown Berets," *Gangs* (blog), *Police,* October 11, 2011, https://www.policemag.com/373939/chicano-power-and-the-brown-berets.

8. Rodolfo F. Acuña, *Occupied America: The Chicano Struggle toward Liberation,* 5th ed. (New York: Longman Press, 2003), pp. 265–268. This book is now in its eighth edition under the title *Occupied America: A History of Chicanos* (Upper Saddle River, NJ: Pearson Publishing, 2014).

9. Dennis G. Fitzgerald, "Inside the Informant File," *The Champion,* May 3, 1998, https://www.nacdl.org/CHAMPION/ARTICLES/98may03.htm.

10. Trevor Aaronson, in "The Informants," *Mother Jones,* September–October 2011, describes the FBI's post-9/11 use of informants to counter terrorism. The author's research reveals that for every official informant, there are three unofficial ones. The growth in the use of counterterrorism informants has spiraled their cost up to $3.3 billion, as compared to $2.6 billion for informants to fight organized crime. In 1975, the FBI had 2,800 informants in a network

called Domain Management.

11. Interview with Tim Chapa, Albuquerque, New Mexico, June 7, 2000. A transcription of the interview is on file at the Center for Regional Studies, Zimmerman Library, University of New Mexico. The transcription is ninety pages. The material in this chapter is largely taken from that interview; page numbers cited refer to the transcription.

12. See Natapoff, *Snitching*, for a history of the use of informants by the government and analysis of the methods employed for their use. An important resource on the subject of informants and their role in the administration of justice process is http://www.snitching.org, which has as its purpose the monitoring of criminal informant law; review of policies; and research state by state on this practice of utilizing informants or snitches in police and intelligence work. A much earlier work is Gary T. Marx, *Under Cover: Police Surveillance in America* (Berkeley: University of California Press, 1988), which traced the use of undercover policing by the federal, state, and local governments in the United States. He noted that regulations on the use of informants and covert agents was very limited among the federal agencies, nonexistent in most local and state governments. It remains a dark secret of the "deep state," term used to denote the work of government the public does not see and is unaware of, to this day.

13. This agency was made part of the U.S. Treasury Department in 1930 until it was merged with the Bureau of Drug Abuse Control in 1968, an agency of the Food and Drug Administration, to create the new Bureau of Narcotics and Dangerous Drugs within the Department of Justice. This new bureau became the predecessor of the Drug Enforcement Administration (DEA) established in 1973 under the Reorganization Plan No. 2 implemented by President Richard Nixon on July 28, 1973. Like the FBI director, the DEA administrator is a political appointee. The DEA headquarters are located across from the Pentagon in Arlington, Virginia. The DEA trains its agents at the U.S. Marine Base at Quantico, Virginia, next to the FBI Training Academy. DEA has an annual budget that exceeds $2 billion (2014) to maintain over 10,800 people (1979 figures) working in headquarters, 221 field offices, and 92 foreign offices in 70 countries. Of these, 4,600 are special agents and 800 intelligence analysts. The DEA field office with jurisdiction over New Mexico is located in El Paso, Texas. See "History," United States Drug Enforcement Administration, https://www.dea.gov/history, for this information on the DEA.

14. When New Mexico became a U.S. Territory after the U.S. war on Mexico in 1846, it became necessary to establish a territorial police force. In 1905, the

territorial legislature established the New Mexico Mounted Police. In 1933, the state police force became known as the New Mexico Motor Patrol, and in 1935 the name was changed to the New Mexico State Police. The mounted police remain an auxiliary force to the state police. "A Brief History of the New Mexico State Police," New Mexico Department of Public Safety, https://www. dps.nm.gov/index.php/public-information/history.

15. The New Mexico State Police noted in its annual reports dating to 2011 that they have a "Covert Unit" and a "Training and Recruitment" component within the agency. In 2015, they reported having "full-time covert personnel assigned to the areas of Santa Fe, Albuquerque, Roswell, and Las Cruces," with no mention of the number of personnel doing the work, much less information on informants. I could not find annual reports dating to 1967-1974, the crucial time of Chapa's role as a snitch and undercover police officer. See New Mexico Department of Public Safety, State Police Recruiting and Selection, issued on May 21, 2007, https://www.dps.nm.gov/images/ DPSPolicies/TRG.-05-R-6-State-Police-Recruiting-and-Selection-043018.pdf. I assume both state patrol officers and informants undergo some training, but there are no figures on how many such persons or officers were doing this type of police work. Only the County of Bernalillo (Albuquerque) has an operation manual for its sheriff's office with a section that deals with "Undercover License/Identification/Covert Operations" by its police force. See Section 325-1 for identification, 325-2 for covert operations, 325-6 for use of decoys, and 325-8 for surveillance operations. For a copy of the entire regulation see Bernalillo County Sheriff's Department, Rules and Procedures, effective March 1, 2012, http://www.bernalillocountysheriff.com/bernalillo-county-sheriff/bcso_sop.pdf.

16. Reies López Tijerina, *They Called Me "King Tiger": My Struggle for the Land and Our Rights,* ed. and trans. José Angel Gutiérrez (Houston: Arte Público Press, 2000), p. 74.

17. Marx, *Under Cover,* p. 4.

18. The FBI had a "Manual of Investigative Operations and Guidelines" (MIOG) in use during the 1960s. Section 137 of that manual dealt with "Criminal Informants" in Part II, 137-1, "Responsibility for the Development and Operation of Informants." See 137-1 (1) to learn that each SAC in every field office was made personally responsible for the "establishment of informant coverage concerning criminal activity of interest to the FBI. . . . Informants are an integral part of the office's overall criminal informant and cooperative witness intelligence base." Item (2) of that same section reads: "Each

Supervisor must ensure that Agents under his/her supervision make every effort to develop quality informants." It is a mandate to find informants to carry out the business of the FBI field office.

19. See Elizabeth (Betita) Martinez, "A View from New Mexico," *Monthly Review* 54, no. 3 (July–August 2002), p. 4, http://monthlyreview.org/2002/07/01/a-view-from-new-mexico/. See also Elizabeth Martinez, "Social Justice Salutes Beverly Axelrod," *Social Justice,* Spring–Summer 2002, pp. 17–19.

20. The archived papers of "Martinez (Elizabeth "Betita" Sutherland)" are at Stanford University, Stanford, California under Collection Number M1854. The quotation comes from the SNCC Digital Gateway at Duke University found at https://snccdigital.org/people/elizabeth-betita-martinez-sutherland/. More biographical material on her is available at www.latinopia.org at the link to biographies; and, an oral history interview of March 3, 2006, done by Loretta Ross with Betita is at Smith College, North Hampton, Massachusetts under the Voices of Feminism Oral History Project.

21. SNCC Digital Gateway, profile of Elizabeth (Betita Martinez) Sutherland.

22. Loretta Ross interview of Elizabeth (Betita Martinez) Sutherland, Voices of Feminism Oral History Project, Smith College, March 3, 2006.

23. "A View from New Mexico" contains Betita's views on the Alianza, Tijerina, and the land recovery movement, which were the basis for her move away from them as their voice. See pp. 3–4.

24. Larry Calloway, "The Courthouse Raid Recalled," p. 8, at http://calloway.com/courthouse-raid/. Larry Calloway was the reporter hiding in the telephone booth during the citizen's arrest attempt at the Tierra Amarilla Courthouse.

25. SNCC Digital Gateway, profile of Maria Varela.

26. See Kate Coleman, "Souled Out," *New West,* May 19, 1980, p. 27. Axelrod negotiated the book deal with Ramparts Press to have all royalties go to his legal defense fund; she was entitled to a percentage that he never paid. This breach-of-contract claim was the basis for her civil suit.

27. Ramparts Press in 1968 was first to publish *Soul on Ice; Three Letters* was published in *Theory into Practice* 8, no. 2 (April 1969), pp. 111–113, as a co-authored piece with Axelrod.

28. Tijerina, *They Called Me King Tiger,* p. 116.

29. See Kathleen Sullivan, "Beverly Alexrod—attorney to the Black Panthers," *SFGate,* June 21, 2002, https://www.sfgate.com/bayarea/article/Beverly-Axelrod-attorney-to-Black-Panthers-28.

30. See Martinez, "Social Justice Salutes Beverly Axelrod," for Betita's written eulogy for Axelrod.

31. See David Correia, "Las Gorras Blancas of San Miguel County," New Mexico History.org, www.newmexicohistory.org/people/las-gorras-blancas-of-san-miguel-county.

32. See Kent Paterson, "The Black Berets Live On," *Frontera NorteSur* (blog), New Mexico State University, October 10, 2012, https://fnsnews.nmsu.edu/the-black-berets-live-on/.

33. In "A View from New Mexico," p. 5, Betita wrote: "The Berets and El Grito were partners, sharing news, analysis and sometimes members like reporter Antonio Cordova, who along with Beret Rito Canales, was assassinated by police in 1972."

34. See also the appellate opinion at 86 N.M. 697, 526 P 2d. 1290 (Ct. App. 1974) denying relief to the families of Canales and Cordova in *Cordova v. City of Albuquerque,* the civil suit filed and denied on January 29, 1972.

35. Tijerina, *They Called Me King Tiger,* p. 129.

36. Peter Nabokov, *Tijerina and the Courthouse Raid* (Berkeley, CA: Ramparts, 1970), p. 79.

37. Tijerina, *They Called Me King Tiger,* p. 187.

38. Tijerina, *They Called Me King Tiger,* p. 220.

39. David Correia, "'Rousers of the Rabble' in the New Mexico Land Grant War: *La Alianza Federal de Mercedes* and the Violence of the State," *Antipode* 40, no. 4 (2008), p. 577, citing records in Tijerina's collection with the Center for Southwest Research (CSWR), Zimmerman Library, University of New Mexico, MSS 93 BC, Box 2, Folder 5.

40. Tijerina, *They Called Me King Tiger,* p. 192.

41. Correia, "'Rousers of the Rabble,'" p. 577, citing material in CSWR, MSS 93 BC, Box 2, Folder 5.

42. Tijerina, *They Called Me King Tiger,* pp. 171–172.

43. Interview with Rosa Tijerina, Albuquerque, New Mexico, July 3, 2000, pp. 31–33.

44. Calloway, "The Courthouse Raid Recalled," p. 8.

45. See the obituary of Ethel Mundy, New Mexico Obituary and Death Notice Archive, dated February 18, 2005, p. 231, http://www.genlookups.com/nm/webbbs_config.pl/noframes/read/231. A son, James Walter Mundy, passed away on April 22, 2015. He was a veterinarian in Chama, New Mexico, and when he

retired he dedicated himself to converting the Mundy Ranch into a recreational area for hunting. He also subdivided parcels of the ranch for real estate sales. His obituary with this information is also on the website previously cited. Another of Bill and Ethel Mundy's children remains alive, Emitt Mundy.

46. Calloway, "The Courthouse Raid Recalled," p. 8.

47. Calloway, "The Courthouse Raid Recalled," p. 8.

48. See Correia, "Rousers of the Rabble," pp. 576-577, citing material in CSWR, MSS 93 BC, Box 35, Folder 11; Nabokov, *Tijerina and the Courthouse Raid,* p. 243; and Tijerina, *They Called Me King Tiger,* p. 128.

49. Correia, "Rousers of the Rabble," p. 577.

50. See Samuel Taylor's "Rime of the Ancient Mariner."

51. Tijerina, *They Called Me King Tiger,* p. 191.

52. Tijerina, *They Called Me King Tiger,* p. 194.

53. Tijerina, *They Called Me King Tiger,* p. 195.

54. Tijerina, *They Called Me King Tiger,* p. 194.

55. Tijerina, *They Called Me King Tiger,* p. 200.

56. Tijerina, *They Called Me King Tiger,* p. 207.

57. Tijerina, *They Called Me King Tiger,* p. 210.

58. Tijerina, *They Called Me King Tiger,* p. 219.

59. Tijerina, *They Called Me King Tiger,* p. 226.

60. John Robertson, "Anaya to Release Part of Salazar Murder Probe," *New Mexican,* August 16, 1977, p. 1A; and, see the Associated Press story, "AG to Release Salazar Report," August 16, 1977, no page cited.

61. John Robertson, "AG: Tijerina Followers Killed Salazar," *New Mexican,* August 17, 1977, p. 1A; and see also John Ware, "Land Grant Boss Unaware of Any Killing," *Albuquerque Journal,* August 17, 1977, p. A-1. This last article states that Sevedeo Martinez, an Alianza member accused of being the driver of Salazar's car to the dump site where it was found, was cleared of any suspicion as well. Lee R. Wood, who Tijerina suspected had been involved in the murder, was cleared by AG Anaya. Wood had a peg leg and that type of footprint was found at the murder scene. Wood's ranch was adjacent to where the body was found.

Chapter 8. Prison Years

1. Reies López Tijerina, *They Called Me "King Tiger": My Struggle for the Land and Our Rights,* ed. and trans. José Angel Gutiérrez (Houston: Arte Público Press, 2000),

pp. 135, 169, 201, 205.

2. Sofia Espinoza Alvarez, "Latinos and the U.S. Criminal Justice System: The Road to Prison," in Martin Guevara Urbina and Sofia Espinoza Alvarez, eds., *Ethnicity and Criminal Justice in the Ear of Mass Incarceration: A Critical Reader on the Latino Experience* (Springfield, IL: Charles C. Thomas Publisher, 2017), pp. 130–131.

3. Patrick A. Lanan, John V. Fundis, Lawrence A. Greenfield, and Victoria W. Schneider, "Historic Statistics on Prisoners in State and Federal Institutions Yearend 1925–1986," Bureau of Justice Statistics, Washington, DC, May 1988. The 1972 statistics for state and federal prisoners are on page 11 and those for 1986 on page 13, and at the bottom of each of these pages is the breakdown by individual state.

4. A. J. Beck, J. C. Karberg, and P. M. Harrison, "Prison and Jail Inmates at Midyear 2001," Bureau of Justice Statistics, Washington, DC, April 2002.

5. Brian Kincade, "The Economics of the American Prison System," May 21, 2018, https://smartasset.com/mortgage/the-economics-of-the-american-prison-system.

6. Mark Hugo Lopez, "A Rising Share: Hispanics and Federal Crime," February 18, 2009, Pew Hispanic Center, Washington, DC, at http://pewhispanic.org/author/mlight/.

7. Urbina and Alvarez, *Ethnicity and Criminal Justice,* pp. 4–5.

8. Urbina and Alvarez, *Ethnicity and Criminal Justice,* p. 12.

9. See E.O 13767.

10. See E.O. 13768.

11. Chris Isidore and Jeanne Sahadi, CNN Business, January 26, 2017, www.money.cnn.com/2017/01/25/news-money-trump-mexico-border-wall-cost/index.html/.

12. The White House, Memorandum for the Secretary of Defense, The Attorney General, The Secretary of Homeland Security, April 4, 2018, Subject: Securing the Southern Border of the United States, Washington, DC, www.whitehouse.gov/presidential-actions-presidential-memorandum-secretary-of-defense-attorney general-secretary-homeland-security/.

13. 50 U.S.C. 1541–1548.

14. See White House, Memorandum, April 4, 2018.

15. Bush was authorized under Public Law 109-47, made part of the Secure Fence Act, and Obama just added to those troops already authorized.

16. Tijerina, *They Called Me King Tiger*, p. 15.
17. Tijerina, *They Called Me King Tiger*, p. 53.
18. Tijerina, *They Called Me King Tiger*, p. 92.
19. Tijerina, *They Called Me King Tiger*, p. 100.
20. Tijerina, *They Called Me King Tiger*, pp. 105, 136.
21. Tijerina, *They Called Me King Tiger*, p. 112.
22. Tijerina, *They Called Me King Tiger*, p. 135.
23. Tijerina, *They Called Me King Tiger*, p. 136.
24. Tijerina, *They Called Me King Tiger*, p. 141.
25. Tijerina, *They Called Me King Tiger*, p. 142.
26. Tijerina, *They Called Me King Tiger*, p. 143.
27. Tijerina, *They Called Me King Tiger*, p. 142.
28. See B. A. Nelson, "The Coming Triumph of Mexican Irredentism," American Immigration Control Foundation, Monterrey VA, 1984.
29. Tijerina, *They Called Me King Tiger*, p. 138.
30. See Reies López Tijerina, "From Prison: Reies Lopez Tijerina," in Ed Ludwig and James Santibañez, eds., *The Chicanos: Mexican American Voices* (Baltimore: Penguin, 1971), pp. 215–222.
31. Tijerina, *They Called Me King Tiger*, pp. 140–141.
32. Tijerina, "From Prison," p. 215.
33. Tijerina, "From Prison," p. 221.
34. Tijerina, "From Prison," p. 219.
35. The Bureau of Prisons was established in 1930, pursuant to Pub. L. No. 71-218, 46 Stat. 325.
36. See https://www.bop.gov/locations/institutions/lat/index.jsp and find the link for FCI La Tuna and then Inmates.
37. Jill Filipovic, "Is the US the Only Country Where More Men Are Raped than Women?," *Feministe* (blog), *Guardian Comment Network*, February 21, 2012, https://www.theguardian.com/commentisfree/cifamerica/2012/feb/21/us-more-men-raped-than-women.
38. David Kaish and Louisa Stannow, "Prison Rape and the Government," *New York Review of Books*, March 11 and March 25, 2010, and March 24, 2011. They took data from the government source: www.bjs.ojp.usdoj.gov/.

39. Christine Peek, "Breaking Out the Prison Hierarchy: Transgendered Prisoners, Rape, and the Eighth Amendment," *Santa Clara University School of Law Review* 44 (2003), pp. 1211-1248.

40. See Maurice Dammah, "Rape in the American Prison," February 25, 2015. See theatlantic.com/politics/archive/2015/dz/rape-in-the-american-prison/385550.

41. The PREA Audits can be downloaded from the Bureau of Prisons website at bop.gov and link to audits.

42. PREA Audits, p. 16. See entry for 115.73—Reporting to Inmate and 115.76—Disciplinary sanctions for staff.

43. See http://www.bop.gov/inmateloc/# for Register No. 38974086 for his prison records.

44. Anthony Curcio with Dana Batty, *Heist and High* (Portland, OR: Nish Publishing, 2013); and his website, www.acurcio.com, has many more details of his life.

45. His website, www.georgejung.com, has the details of his new career post-drug dealing. The book by Bruce Porter is *Blow: How a Small Town Boy Made $100 Million with the Medellín Cocaine Cartel and Lost It All* (New York: St. Martin's Griffin, 1993).

46. See his website for these details and http://bop.gov/inmateloc/# for Register No. 19225-004 for his prison records.

47. Peter Maas, *The Valachi Papers* (New York: Perennial, 1968), p. 16.

48. Maas, *The Valachi Papers,* pp. 11-12.

49. Maas, *The Valachi Papers.* The first movie made based on his character was made in 1972 with the same title as the Maas book. Many of the scenes in *The Godfather Part II* of 1974 were based on Valachi's testimony during his federal hearings by the U.S. Senate Committee on Government Operations, Subcommittee on Investigations, chaired by Senator John. L. McClellan in the early 1960s. The Maas book in the pages following the last numbered one, 263, contains his entire criminal record, which fills two pages.

50. Maas, *The Valachi Papers,* p. 25.

51. Maas, *The Valachi Papers,* p. 3.

52. Maas, *The Valachi Papers,* p. 1.

53. Maas, *The Valachi Papers,* p. 8.

54. Maas, *The Valachi Papers,* pp. 253-256.

55. Maas, *The Valachi Papers,* p. 32n.

56. Tijerina, *They Called Me King Tiger*, pp. 160–161.

57. See Wilcox Collection of Contemporary Political Movements at the Spencer Research Library, University of Kansas Libraries.

58. John Drabble, "From White Supremacy to White Power: The FBI COINTELPRO—White Hate and the Nazification of the Ku Klux Klan in the 1970s," *American Studies* 48, no. 3 (Fall 2007), p. 52.

59. J. Harry Jones Jr., *The Minutemen* (New York: Doubleday, 1968). They are not to be confused with Chris Simcox and James Gilchrist's group called the Minutemen Project from the 1990s based in Arizona.

60. *United States v. DePugh*, 266 F. Supp. 435 (1967) is the case filed by DePugh and Peyson asking for a new trial and denied.

61. 401 F.2d 346 (8th Cir. 1968),

62. *United States v. Edwards*, 443 F.2d. 1286 (1971).

63. Harry Jones Jr., "Minuteman Says Mud to Fly," *Kansas City Times*, April 2, 1970, p. 9A, and Harry Jones Jr. and Joe Henderson, "DePugh Stays Firm on Principles," *Kansas City Times*, April 18, 1970, p. 3A.

64. Eric C. Beckmeier *Can You Survive? Guidelines for Resistance to Tyranny for You and Your Family* (n.p.: Desert Pub, 1973). The DePugh book on being imprisoned could not be found. The Beckmeier book, *Traitors Beware! A History of Robert Depugh's Minutemen*, is criticized for not being substantive. He published the book himself out of Hardin, Missouri in 2007.

65. For the poster go to http://fbimostwanted.us/zc/images/poster864.jpg/. For the 1967 photograph of him and DePugh go to https://outlet.historicimages.com/productds/dfpz99557, put out by The Historic Images Outlet.

66. Tijerina, *They Called Me King Tiger*, p. 160.

67. Tijerina, *They Called Me King Tiger*, p. 163.

68. See David McCullough, *Truman* (New York: Simon and Shuster, 1992); Gary A. Donaldson, *Truman Defeats Dewey* (Lexington: University Press of Kentucky, 1999); and Zachary Karabell, *The Last Campaign: How Harry Truman Won the 1948 Election* (New York: Alfred A. Knopf, 2000) for these views that Barkley as running mate made the victory possible.

69. John Ghaelian, "Alben W. Barkley: Harry Truman's Unexpected Political Asset," *Kaleidoscope* 7, Article 15 (2008), pp. 75–91.

70. Tijerina, *They Called Me King Tiger*, pp. 143–144.

71. Tijerina, *They Called Me King Tiger*, p. 160.

72. The medical records were obtained with a FOIA request and are grouped in a folder titled "Bureau of Prisons." I was unable to obtain state prison or state police records.

73. This document is undated and unsigned, with a heading of "CLASSIFICATION STUDY (continued)" under Tijerina's name and register number of "A-2-45707-T." At bottom left is typed "USPO: District of New Mexico." The "(continued)" subtitle suggests more documents precede this one, but they are not to be found among those in the medical records received.

74. Tijerina, *They Called Me King Tiger*, pp. 161–162.

75. Tijerina, *They Called Me King Tiger*, p. 156.

76. Tijerina, *They Called Me King Tiger*, p. 157.

77. Tijerina, *They Called Me King Tiger*, p. 157.

78. Tijerina, *They Called Me King Tiger*, p. 154.

79. Tijerina, *They Called Me King Tiger*, pp. 166–167.

80. There are eleven pages titled "Clinical Record" and "Nursing Notes." These are most helpful in reading the nearly day-by-day life of Tijerina while in Springfield. These handwritten entries begin with the date of "1-22-70 Rec from U.S. Marshalls" on the top line. The last entry on the eleventh page, bottom two lines, is "7/26/71 Released to R & D for parole to State of New Mexico."

81. Tijerina, *They Called Me King Tiger*, p. 135.

82. Tijerina, *They Called Me King Tiger*, p. 141.

83. Tijerina, *They Called Me King Tiger*, p. 142.

84. Tijerina, *They Called Me King Tiger*, p. 154.

85. Tijerina, *They Called Me King Tiger*, p. 136.

86. Tijerina, *They Called Me King Tiger*, p. 162.

87. Tijerina, *They Called Me King Tiger*, p. 170.

88. Tijerina, *They Called Me King Tiger*, pp. 174–175.

89. Tijerina, *They Called Me King Tiger*, p. 166.

90. Tijerina, *They Called Me King Tiger*, p. 143.

91. Tijerina, *They Called Me King Tiger*, p. 144.

92. Tijerina, *They Called Me King Tiger*, p. 142.

93. Tijerina, *They Called Me King Tiger*, p. 143.

94. See letter date November 30, 1970, from Pasquale Ciccone to Phillip A. Martinez in the medical records file.

95. Tijerina, *They Called Me King Tiger*, p. 155.
96. Memo in the medical records dated January 15, 1971, regarding "Reies Tijerina-45707-146" from someone named "Lemons" and initialed above that name "ML" to a "Mr. Tappana."
97. Tijerina, *They Called Me King Tiger*, pp. 168–169.
98. Tijerina, *They Called Me King Tiger*, p. 143.
99. See the three pages titled "Sentence Computation Record" found among the medical records under Bureau of Prisons file, prepared on January 27, 1970.
100. In 2017 the Sentence Computation statute is 18 U.S.C. 3585. As of 1992, SCOTUS in *United States v. Wilson*, 503 U.S. 329, 112 S. Ct. 1351, sentence computation would be under the U.S. attorney general, but that person could delegate the responsibility to the BOP.
101. See the single page titled "Sentence Data Summary" found among the medical records under Bureau of Prisons file, prepared at Springfield, Missouri.
102. Mark Colvin, "The 1980 New Mexico Prison Riot," paper presented at the Southwestern Social Science Association Annual Conference, Dallas, Texas, March 1981, and his introduction, "Descent into Madness," in Mike Rolland, *Descent into Madness: An Inmate's Experience of the New Mexico State Prison Riot* (Colorado Springs, CO: Lexis/Nexis Group, Matthew Bender & Company, 1997).
103. Notice of action signed by parole executive James R. Pace.
104. Actual date stamp bottom left of letterhead "Parole Form H-7" is "May 25, 1971," signed by the parole executive James R. Pace.
105. October 8, 1970, p. 1.
106. Rudy Busto, *King Tiger: The Religious Vision of Reies Lopez Tijerina* (Albuquerque: University of New Mexico Press, 2005), pp. 68–69.
107. Colvin, "Prison Riot," p. 23.
108. Colvin, "Prison Riot," p. 25.

Chapter 9. Mexico: Love It and Leave It

1. Reies López Tijerina, *They Called Me "King Tiger": My Struggle for the Land and Our Rights*, ed. and trans. José Angel Gutiérrez (Houston: Arte Público Press, 2000), p. 1.
2. Tijerina, *They Called Me King Tiger*, p. 13. Moreover, what Tijerina refers to as "sexual education" is a questionable conclusion on his part because from the late 1950s through the 1970s most public schools only taught "health,"

in which only one unit of many was dedicated to reproduction; and that consisted of diagrams of the reproductive system and their functions. Biology in high schools also included a lecture on the reproductive system of mammals and the function of body parts related to that process, among many other topics. I do not recall any discussion of sex much less sexual practices and activity in my public schooling in the late 1950s through my years as school board president in the early 1970s.

3. Tijerina, *They Called Me King Tiger*, p. 22.

4. Reies "David" Hugh Tijerina, interview, Albuquerque, New Mexico, June 28, 2000, p. 7.

5. Maria Escobar, interview, Albuquerque, New Mexico, July 17, 2000, p. 61.

6. Tijerina, *They Called Me King Tiger*, pp. 15-16.

7. Tijerina, *They Called Me King Tiger*, p. 231.

8. Tijerina, *They Called Me King Tiger*, p. 8

9. Tijerina, *They Called Me King Tiger*, p. 25.

10. Tijerina, *They Called Me King Tiger*, p. 25.

11. Tijerina, *They Called Me King Tiger*, p. 61.

12. Tijerina, *They Called Me King Tiger*, pp. 32-33.

13. Tijerina, *They Called Me King Tiger*, p. 42.

14. See Judith Adler Hellman, *Mexican Lives* (New York: New Press, 1994), pp. 115-119, for a brief statement of what the Cárdenas agrarian reform era did for the creation of community-owned lands, *ejidos*, and their subsequent demise.

15. Tijerina, *They Called Me King Tiger*, pp. 213-214.

16. Tijerina, *They Called Me King Tiger*, p. 214.

17. Tijerina, *They Called Me King Tiger*, p. 215.

18. Tijerina, *They Called Me King Tiger*, p. 218.

19. Tijerina, *They Called Me King Tiger*, pp. 218-219.

20. Tijerina, *They Called Me King Tiger*, p. 219.

21. Tijerina, *They Called Me King Tiger*, p. 220.

22. Tijerina, *They Called Me King Tiger*, p. 231.

23. Tijerina, *They Called Me King Tiger*, p. 220.

24. Tijerina, *They Called Me King Tiger*, p. 212.

25. Jefferson Morley, *The Ghost: The Secret Life of CIA Spymaster James Jesus Singleton*

(Brunswick, Victoria: Scribe Publications, 2017), pp. 184–185.

26. Morton H. Halperin, Jerry J. Berman, Robert L. Borosage, and Christine M. Marwick, *The Lawless State: The Crimes of the U.S. Intelligence Agencies* (New York: Penguin, 1976), p. 135.

27. Halperin et al., *The Lawless State,* p. 148.

28. See United States Senate Select Committee to Study Governmental Operations with Respect to Intelligence Activities, "CIA Intelligence Collection about Americans: Chaos and the Office of Security," *Supplementary Detailed Staff Reports on Intelligence Activities and the Rights of Americans,* S. Rep. No. 94-755, bk. 3 (Washington, DC: Government Printing Office, 1976), p. 679.

29. Frank J. Rafalko, *MH/CHAOS: The CIA's Campaign against the Radical New Left and the Black Panthers* (Annapolis: Naval Institute Press, 2011). The "MH" in the title is never explained. The CIA website, under the Glossary link, does not contain an entry for MH/CHAOS, nor does the U.S. Department of State, Glossary of Terms. According to John S. *Friedman, The Secret Histories: Hidden Truths That Challenged the Past and Changed the World (New York: Macmillan, 2005), p. 278,* "'MH' was a CIA code indicating [a] worldwide area of operations."

30. Rafalko, *MH/CHAOS,* p. 21.

31. Rafalko, *MH/CHAOS,* p. 13.

32. Rafalko, *MH/CHAOS,* pp. 23–24.

33. Rafalko, *MH/CHAOS,* p. 34.

34. Morley, *The Ghost,* p. 186.

35. Rafalko, *MH/CHAOS,* p. 29.

36. Rafalko, *MH/CHAOS,* pp. 38–39. Interestingly, in Rafalko's index, pp. 317-328, there is not one listing for a Chicano group, organization, leader, or event; the focus is, as his title suggests, only on the radical Left and Black Panthers.

37. I wish to acknowledge the assistance of Jack D. Novik, National Staff Counsel, American Civil Liberties Union in New York, who helped with correspondence to file appeals from the denial of records on both Tijerina and myself in April 1977 by the CIA. I had begun the request for CIA files on Tijerina in 1981. The CIA informed me by letter dated April 7, 1983, that the fee for the original search quoted in February 1983 was incorrect; it would only cost me $2,550 and that payment for half of that amount, $1,275.00, would initiate the search for records associated with my request, F81-0561. With the help from Jack Novik I was eventually able to get a few pages released without payment.

38. Tijerina, *They Called Me King Tiger,* p. 220.

39. Tijerina, *They Called Me King Tiger*, pp. 221-222.

40. Tijerina, *They Called Me King Tiger*, p. 224-225.

41. Tijerina, *They Called Me King Tiger*, p. 225.

42. Tijerina, *They Called Me King Tiger*, p. 227.

43. Tijerina, *They Called Me King Tiger*, p. 229.

44. José Angel Gutiérrez, *The Making of a Chicano Militant: Lessons from Cristal* (Madison: University of Wisconsin, 1998), p. 235, has a photo of that occasion.

45. Tijerina, *They Called Me King Tiger*, pp. 233-234.

46. Rodolfo F. Acuña, in *The Making of Chicana/o Studies: In the Trenches of Academe* (New Brunswick, NJ: Rutgers University Press, 2011), p. 45, briefly discusses the role of Guzman with the Ford Foundation-funded Mexican American Study Project. He expands this discussion in the forthcoming second edition.

47. Several sources can be consulted for more details on the Raza Unida Party. Richard Santillan, *La Raza Unida* (Los Angeles: Tlaquilo Press, 1973); John Shockley, *Chicano Revolt in a Texas Town* (Notre Dame, IN: University of Notre Dame Press, 1974); Ignacio Garcia, *United We Win: The Rise and Fall of the Raza Unida Party* (Tucson: University of Arizona, 1989); Armando Navarro's *The Cristal Experiment: The Struggle for Chicano Community Control* (Madison: University of Wisconsin Press, 1998) and *La Raza Unida Party: A Chicano Challenge to the U.S. Two-Party Dictatorship* (Philadelphia: Temple University Press, 2000); and my own work, *The Making of a Chicano Militant*.

48. Nicholas C. Chriss, "Mexico Says It Won't Pay Land Claims of 1800s," *Los Angeles Times,* February 18, 1978, p. A-1.

49. Rudy V. Busto, *King Tiger: The Religious Vision of Reies Lopez Tijerina* (Albuquerque: University of New Mexico Press, 2005), p. 71.

50. "Presidential Statement: Carter Details FBI Charter," *CQ Almanac 1979,* 35th ed. (Washington, DC: Congressional Quarterly, 1980), pp. 48-E-49-E. See also https://library.cqpress.com/cqalmanac/document.php?id=c qal79-861-26160-1182934.

51. Navarro, *La Raza Unida Party,* pp. 254-260, details his analysis of the Chicano-Mexicano connection during these years. I have my own narrative in *The Making of a Chicano Militant,* pp. 234-241, and a chapter on that topic, "The Chicano in Mexicano Norte Americano Foreign Relations," in Tatcho Mindiola and Max Martinez, eds., *Chicano-Mexicano Relations,* Mexican American Studies Program, Monograph No. 4 (Houston: Mexican American Studies Program, University of Houston, 1986). Dr. Bustamante also has an article in

this monograph detailing the Mexican perspective.

52. Tijerina, *They Called Me King Tiger,* p. 214, and Busto, *King Tiger,* p. 165.

53. None of the other two documents have underscoring of lines or paragraphs as does this first one. Perhaps it is another person, other than the original author, who is underscoring for another purpose, such as checking for confidentiality, secrecies, classified material, or something of that order. See also Maria Rosa Garcia-Acevedo, "Return to Aztlan: Mexico's Policies toward Chicanas/os," in David R. Maciel and Isidro D. Ortiz, eds., *Chicanas/Chicanos at the Crossroads: Social, Economic, and Political Change* (Tucson: University of Arizona Press, 1999), pp. 130–155.

54. The Hannigan case was a horrible instance of gross injustice. A father and two sons, the Hannigans, stopped three undocumented persons in Arizona who were searching for work. The father, George, and sons, Patrick and Thomas, proceeded to kidnap them, beat them, and rob them before leaving them for dead. The Hannigans were tried three times for this crime over a five-year period, once in a Tucson state court and twice in federal court in Phoenix. The father escaped conviction because he died before the trial. The first trial, with an all-white jury in Tucson, acquitted the brothers. In federal court they were again acquitted. In the second trial on civil rights violations, Patrick was convicted and Thomas acquitted. Patrick was given a three-year sentence, and Thomas a month later was caught and convicted of possession of marijuana. The case enraged many people across the country and was a rallying cry for immigration reform.

55. See Leo Grebler, Joan Moore, and Ralph Guzman, *The Mexican American People: The Nation's Second Largest Minority* (New York: Free Press, 1970).

56. See obituary in *Los Angeles Times,* October 13, 1985.

57. The law dates to 1799 and most recently was in the news during the Michael Flynn controversy as national security advisor to President D. Trump while continuing to receive money from foreign governments. See 1 Stat. 613 USC 953 (1799). The law prohibits private U.S. citizens from interfering with diplomatic relations between the United States and foreign governments; it is felony punishable with up to three years imprisonment and or fine.

Bibliography

Books

Acuña, Rodolfo F. *Anything but Mexican: Chicanos in Contemporary Los Angeles*. New York: Haymarket, 1996.

———. *The Making of Chicana/o Studies: In the Trenches of Academe*. New Brunswick, NJ: Rutgers University Press, 2011.

———. *Occupied America: The Chicano Struggle toward Liberation*. 5th ed. New York: Longman Press, 2003.

Aleshire, Peter. *Cochise: The Life and Times of the Great Apache Chief*. New York: John Wiley and Sons, 2001.

Allen, Gary. *The Rockefeller File*. Seal Beach, CA: '76 Press, 1976.

Balko, Radley. *Rise of the Warrior Cop: The Militarization of America's Police Force*. New York: Public Affairs, 2014.

Becker, Marc. *The FBI in Latin America: The Ecuador Files*. Durham: Duke University Press, 2017.

Bedolla, Lisa Garcia. *Latino Politics*. 2nd ed. Malden, MA: Polity Press, 2014.

Blawis, Patricia Bell. *Tijerina and the Land Grants: Mexican Americans in Struggle for Their Heritage*. New York: International Publishers, 1971.

Boykoff, Jules. *Beyond Bullets: The Suppression of Dissent in the United States.* Oakland, CA: AK Press, 2007.

Buitrago, Ann Mari, and Leon Andrew Immerman. *Are You Now or Have You Ever Been in the FBI Files" How to Secure and Interpret Your FBI Files.* New York: Grove Press, 1981.

Burnham, David. 1989. *A Law unto Itself: Power, Politics, and the IRS.* New York: Random House.

Busto, Rudy V. *King Tiger: The Religious Vision of Reies Lopez Tijerina.* Albuquerque: University of New Mexico Press, 2005.

Caffey, David L. *Chasing the Santa Fe Ring: Power and Privilege in Territorial New Mexico.* Albuquerque: University of New Mexico Press, 2014.

Chalkley, John F. *Zach Lamar Cobb: El Paso Collector of Customs and Intelligence during the Mexican Revolution, 1913–1918.* Southwestern Studies No. 103. El Paso: Texas Western Press, 1998.

Chavez, John R. *The Lost Land: The Chicano Image of the Southwest.* Albuquerque: University of New Mexico Press, 1984.

Clayson, William S. *Freedom Is Not Enough: The War on Poverty and the Civil Rights Movement in Texas.* Austin: University of Texas Press, 2010.

Coronado, Juan David. *"I'm Not Gonna Die in This Damn Place": Manliness, Identity, and Survival of the Mexican American Vietnam Prisoners of War.* East Lansing: Michigan State University Press, 2018.

Correia, David. *Properties of Violence: Law and Land Grant Struggle in Northern New Mexico.* Athens: University of Georgia Press, 2013.

Davenport, B. T. *Soldiering at Marfa, Texas 1911–1945.* Kearney, NE: Morris Publishing, 1997.

De Burton, Maria Amparo Ruiz, 1885, 2004. *The Squatter and the Don.* New York: Modern Library Publishers.

del Castillo, Richard Griswold. *The Treaty of Guadalupe Hidalgo: A Legacy of Conflict.* Norman: University of Oklahoma Press, 1990.

De Leon, Arnold. *They Called Them Greasers: Anglo Attitudes toward Mexicans in Texas, 1821–1900.* Austin: University of Texas Press, 1983.

Dunbar-Ortiz, Roxanne. *Roots of Resistance: A History of Land Tenure in New Mexico.* Norman: University of Oklahoma Press, 2007.

Ellsberg, Daniel. *Secrets: A Memoir of Vietnam and the Pentagon Papers.* New York: Penguin, 2002.

Fernandez-Armesto, Felipe. *Our America: The Hispanic History of the United States.* New York: Norton, 2014.

Garcia, F. Chris, Paul L. Hain, and Harold V. Rhodes, *State and Local Government in New Mexico.* Albuquerque: University of New Mexico Press, 1979.

Garcia, John A. *Latino Politics in America: Community, Culture, and Interests.* 2nd ed. Lanham, MD: Rowman & Littlefield, 2012.

Gardner, Richard. *Grito! Reies Tijerina and the New Mexico Land Grant War of 1967.* New York: Harper Colophon Books, 1970.

Gentry, Kurt. *J. Edgar Hoover: The Man and His Secrets.* New York: Norton, 1991.

Glynne-Jones, Tim. *The Book of Numbers.* London: Arcturus, 2007.

Gonzalez, Nancie L. *The Spanish-Americans of New Mexico: A Heritage of Pride.* 2nd ed. Albuquerque: University of New Mexico Press, 1969.

Guzman, Ralph. *Mexican American Causalities in Vietnam.* Santa Cruz: University of California Santa Cruz, 1970.

Hellman, Judith Adler. *Mexican Lives.* New York: New Press, 1994.

Hersh, Seymour M. *The Samson Option: Israel's Nuclear Arsenal and American Foreign Policy.* New York: Random House, 1991.

Horgan, Paul. *Lamy of Santa Fe: His Life and Times.* New York: Noonday Press, 1975.

Ibarra, Lee. *Vietnam Veteranos: Chicanos Recall the War.* Austin: University of Texas Press, 2004.

Johnson, Benjamin Heber. *Revolution in Texas: How a Forgotten Rebellion and Its Bloody Suppression Turned Mexicans into Americans.* New Haven: Yale University Press, 2005.

Kells, Michelle Hall. *Vicente Ximenes, LBJ's Great Society, and Mexican American Civil Rights Rhetoric.* Carbondale: Southern Illinois University Press, 2018.

Levine, Yasha. *Surveillance Valley: The Secret Military History of the Internet.* New York: Public Affairs, 2018.

MacLachlan, Colin M. *Anarchism and the Mexican Revolution: The Political Trials of Ricardo Flores Magon in the United States.* Berkeley: University of California Press, 1991.

Mantler, K. Gordon. *Power to the Poor: Black-Brown Coalition and the Fight for Economic Justice.* Chapel Hill: University of North Carolina Press, 2015.

McKnight, Gerald D. *The Last Crusade: Martin Luther King, Jr., the FBI, and the Poor People's Campaign.* Boulder, CO: Westview Press, 1998.

Mearsheimer, John J. and Stephen M. Walt. *The Israel Lobby and U.S. Foreign Policy.*

New York: Farrar, Straus and Giroux, 2007.

McWilliams, Carey. *North from Mexico: The Spanish Speaking People of the United States.* 1948. New ed., updated by Matt S. Meier, n.p.: Greenwood Press, 1990. 3rd ed., updated by Alma M. Garcia, Santa Barbara, CA: Praeger, 2016.

Miles, Elton. *More Tales of the Big Bend.* College Station: Texas A & M University Press, 1988.

Morley, Jefferson. *The Ghost: The Secret Life of CIA Spymaster James Jesus Angleton.* New York: St. Martin's Press, 2017.

Nabokov, Peter. *Tijerina and the Courthouse Raid.* Berkeley, CA: Ramparts Press, 1970.

Natapoff, Alexandra. *Snitching: Criminal Informants and the Erosion of American Justice.* New York: New York University Press, 2009.

Navarro, Armando. *Mexican American Youth Organization: Avant-Garde of the Chicano Movement in Texas.* Austin: University of Texas Press, 1995.

Nelli, Humbert S. *The Business of Crime: Italians and Syndicate Crime in the United States.* New York: Oxford University Press, 1976.

Nolan, Frederick. *The Lincoln County War: A Documentary History.* Norman: University of Oklahoma Press, 1992.

O'Reilly, Kenneth, with David Gallen, eds. *Black Americans: The FBI Files.* New York: Carroll & Graf, 1994.

Pitt, Leonard. *Decline of the Californios: Social History of the Spanish-Speaking Californias, 1846–1890.* Berkeley: University of California Press, 1966.

Porter, Darwin. *J. Edgar Hoover & Clyde Tolson: Investigating the Sexual Secrets of America's Most Famous Men and Women.* New York: Blue Moon Productions, 2012.

Rafalko, Frank J. *MH/CHAOS: The CIA's Campaign against the Radical New Left and the Black Panthers.* Annapolis: Naval Institute Press, 2011.

Rocco, Raymond A. *Transforming Citizenship: Democracy, Membership, and Belonging in Latino Communities.* East Lansing: Michigan State University Press, 2014.

Rosenbaum, Robert J. *Mexicano Resistance in the Southwest.* Dallas: Southern Methodist University Press, 1998.

Rosenus, Alan. *General M.G. Vallejo and the Advent of the Americans.* Albuquerque: University of New Mexico Press, 1995.

Scarborough, Mike. *Trespassers on Our Own Land,* Indianapolis: Dog Ear Publishing, 2011.

Scott, James M. *The Attack on the Liberty: The Untold Story of Israel's Deadly 1967 Assault on a U.S. Spy Ship.* New York: Simon and Schuster, 2009.

Sellers, Vincent. *Eyes Pried Open: Rookie FBI Agent*. N.p.: Black Rose Writing, 2014.

Sepulveda, Juan. *The Life and Times of Willie Velasquez: Su Voto es Su Voz*. Houston: Arte Público Press, 2005.

Shahak, Israel. *Jewish History, Jewish Religion*. London: Pluto Press, 2008.

Thomas, Evan. *Robert Kennedy: His Life*. New York: Simon & Schuster, 2000.

Tijerina, Daniel E. "Daniel E. Tijerina." In Alan Rinzler, ed., *Manifesto Addressed to the President of the United States from the Youth of America*. New York: Macmillan, 1970.

Tijerina, Reies López. *Mi lucha por la tierra*. Mexico City: Fondo de Cultura Económica, 1978. Ed. and trans. José Angel Gutiérrez as *They Called Me "King Tiger": My Struggle for the Land and Our Rights* (Houston: Arte Público Press, 2000).

Torrez, Robert J., and Robert Trapp, eds., *Rio Arriba: A New Mexico County*. Los Ranchos, NM: Rio Grande Books, 2010.

Trejo, John C. *Carnales: A History of Chicano Vietnam Veterans*. New York: Leeds and York, 2013.

Trujillo, Charley. *Soldados: Chicanos in Viet Nam*. San Jose, CA: Chusma House Publication, 1993.

Valentine, Douglas. *The CIA as Organized Crime: How Illegal Operations Corrupt America and the World*. Atlanta: Clarity Press, 2017.

Vasquez, Carlos, ed. *La vida del Rio Grande: Our River–Our Life*. Albuquerque: National Hispanic Cultural Center, 2004.

Wilson, Vincent, Jr. *The Book of Presidents*. Maps by Peter Guilday. Brookeville, MA: American History Research Associates, 1993.

Wise, David. *The Politics of Lying: Government Deception, Secrecy, and Power*. New York: Random House, 1973.

Documentaries and Commercial Movie

Casillas, Jaime, dir. *Chicano*. commercial movie in Spanish (Mexico D.F., Mexico), 1975.

Galan, Hector. "Willie: Your Vote Is Your Voice." Latino Public Broadcasting (Austin, Texas) and PBS Broadcasting (New York), 2016.

Trevino, Jesus. "Yo Soy Chicano." KCET Television (Los Angeles), 1972.

Wallace, Mike. "The Most Hated Man in New Mexico" and "The Hate that Hate Produced." Two of three-part series produced by WNTA Television (New York) that first aired July 13-17, 1959.

Monographs, Articles, and Professional Papers

Alianza de Pueblos Libres with Kathelyn Koffman. *San Joaquin del Rio de Chama.* Trans. Carlos E. Chavez. Santa Fe: Synergetic Press, 1983. The inside cover has a different title: *The Legend of the Town of San Joaquin del Rio de Chama.*

Chicano Coordinating Council. *Chicano Plan for Higher Education: Analyses and Position by the Chicano Coordinating Council on Higher Education.* Santa Barbara: La Causa Publications, 1971.

Correia, David. "'Rousers of the Rabble' in the New Mexico Land Grant War: *La Alianza Federal De Mercedes* and the Violence of the State." *Antipode* 40. no. 4 (2008), pp. 561–583.

Garcia-Acevedo, Maria Rosa. "Return to Aztlan: Mexico's Policies toward Chicanas/ os." In David R. Maciel and Isidro D. Ortiz, eds., *Chicanas/Chicanos at the Crossroads: Social, Economic, and Political Change,* pp. 130–155. Tucson: University of Arizona Press, 1999.

Gutiérrez, Jose Angel. "Monitoring Mexicans: FBI Files on Diego Rivera, Carlos Fuentes, Cesar E. Chavez, and Reies Lopez Tijerina; the Why, When, What Happened." Paper presented at the Western Political Science Association Annual Conference, Seattle, WA, April 16–19, 2014.

———. "Reies and Malcolm: A Comparative Research Note on Their *Persona* and Leadership Styles." Paper presented at the National Association of Chicano Latino Studies Annual Conference, Houston, Texas, April 3–5, 2001.

———. "Tracking King Tiger: The Political Surveillance of Reies Lopez Tijerina by the Federal Bureau of Investigation." Paper presented at the Twenty-Third National Association of Chicana and Chicano Studies Annual Conference, Chicago, Illinois, March 20–23, 1996.

Klein, Christine L. "Treaties of Conquest: Property Rights, Indian Treaties and the Treaty of Guadalupe Hidalgo." *New Mexico Law Review* 26 (Spring 1996), pp. 201–265.

Knowlton, Clark L. "The New Mexico Land War." *The Nation* 206, no. 25 (June 17, 1968).

———. "Reies L. Tijerina and the Alianza Federal de Mercedes: Seekers after Justice." *Wisconsin Sociologist* 22, no. 4 (Fall 1985), pp. 49–67.

———. "Reies Lopez Tijerina and the Alianza: Some Considerations." Paper presented at Rural Sociological Society Annual Meeting, College Station, Texas, August 24, 1984.

———. "Tijerina: Hero of the Militants." *Texas Observer* 61, no. 6 (March 28, 1969).

Lundholm, Nicholas B. "Cutting Class: Why Arizona's Ethnic Studies Ban Won't Ban Ethnic Studies." *Arizona Law Review* 53 (October 17, 2011), p. 1041.

Nelson, B. A. "The Coming Triumph of Mexican Irredentism." American Immigration Control Foundation, Monterrey, VA, 1984.

Nichols, John. "Reies Lopez Tijerina: A Man Like the Northern Weather." *New Mexico Review and Legislative Journal* 3, no. 11 (November 1972), pp. 12-13.

Ross, Caroline, and Ken Lawrence. *J. Edgar Hoover's Detention Plan: The Politics of Repression in the United States, 1939–1976.* Jackson, MS: American Friends Service Committee, 1978.

Schock, Kurt. "Nonviolent Action and Its Misconceptions: Insights for Social Scientists." *PS Online*, October 2003, pp. 705-712. www.apsanet.org.

Swadesh, Frances L. "The Alianza Movement of New Mexico," pp. 52-68, in H. J. Tobias and C. E. Woodhouse, eds., *Minorities and Politics.* Albuquerque: University of New Mexico Press, 1969.

———. "The Alianza Movement of New Mexico: Catalyst for Social Change in New Mexico." In June Helm, ed., *Spanish-Speaking People in the United States: Proceedings of the 1968 Annual Spring Meeting of the American Ethnological Society,* pp. 162-177. Seattle: American Ethnological Society, 1968.

United Nations. *Reports of International Arbitral Awards, Convention of November 19, 1941, United Mexican States, United States of America.* Vol. 4, pp. 765-769. New York: United Nations, 2006.

United States Commission on Civil Rights. *Mexican Americans and the Administration of Justice in the Southwest: Summary of a Report of the United States Commission on Civil Rights, 1970.* Washington, DC: U.S. Government Printing Office, 1970.

United States, Department of Interior, Surveyor General of New Mexico, United States Congress, House Committee on Private Land Claims. 1923. "Private Land-Claims in New Mexico: Letter from the Secretary of the Interior, Transmitting, in Compliance with Act of July, 1854, Three Reports of the Surveyor-General of the Territory of New Mexico on Private Lands in Said Territory." Printed in the United States. Nabu Public Domain Reprints.

Wilson, Vincent, Jr. *The Book of Presidents.* Maps by Peter Guilday. Brookeville, MA: American History Research Associates, 1993.

Wolfe, Patrick. "Settler Colonialism and the Elimination of the Native." *Journal of Genocide Research* 8, no. 4, (December 2006), pp. 387-409.

Interviews

Tim Chapa. Albuquerque, New Mexico, June 7, 2000.

Rosa Tijerina Duran, Albuquerque, New Mexico, July 3, 2000.

Maria Escobar, Albuquerque, New Mexico, July 17, 2000.

Valentina Valdez Martinez, Tierra Amarilla, New Mexico, August 6, 2000.

Abran Tapia, Rowe, New Mexico, August 6, 2000.

Reies "David" Hugh Tijerina, Albuquerque, New Mexico, June 28, 2000.

Noe Tijerina, Albuquerque, New Mexico, August 5, 2000.

Vicente Ximenes, Albuquerque, New Mexico, June 25, 2004.

Index